Some South Carolina
County Records

Vol. I

Abstracted By:

Brent Holcomb, C.R.S.

Published By:

Southern Historical Press, Inc.

Please direct all correspondence and orders to:

www.southernhistoricalpress.com
or
SOUTHERN HISTORICAL PRESS, Inc.
PO BOX 1267
375 West Broad Street
Greenville, SC   29601
southernhistoricalpress@gmail.com

ISBN #0-89308-014-4

Printed in the United States of America

Preface By The Publisher

It is indeed a pleasure to bring to you the reader this brand new book of South Carolina County records. As anyone who has done research in South Carolina only too well knows, there has been little published on the records of this state in years past. This book is the first in a series of proposed books of South Carolina source material - in fact this book has been in process for some two years.

It has been my great pleasure to be associated with Mr. Brent Holcomb who was commissioned by me to abstract the material contained in these pages. I believe you will find his work thorough and exacting. Together, Mr. Holcomb and I wish to express our gratitude to Mr. Elmer Parker of Columbia, South Carolina, former Archivist of the United States, for his generosity in preparing the new map used in this volume of the Equity Court Districts of S.C. in 1808.

The Rev.Silas Emmett Lucas,Jr.+
Publisher

INTRODUCTION

This volume is a compilation of several types of records from various counties of South Carolina. A few words of introduction are necessary concerning each section.

The Spartanburg District Will Book A is the first extant will book for that county. (The term district properly applies from 1800-1868). However, there are wills and estates extant from the formation of the county in 1785. The records prior to 1900 were transferred to South Carolina Archives in 1972.

Marlboro County Deed Book A is the first deed book for that county, beginning in 1786. Prior to 1785 or 1786, all deeds recorded in S. C. were done so in Charleston. However, quite often deeds were not recorded until years after their execution. A number of deeds in this volume date from the 1770's and are extremely valuable. This book is in the Court House in Bennettsville.

Cheraws Equity District was the last of the equity districts to be divided, and an equity court established for each county. It was created by an act of 1808 and included the district of Darlington, Marlboro, and Chesterfield. It is quite important as all Chesterfield records were destroyed by fire in 1865. This abstract is only the equity decree book. For a complete picture of the case, the original papers—complain, answer, exhibits (if any) and decree—should be examined. These papers were apparently divided between the Marlboro and Darlington Court Houses. They can be seen on microfilm at South Carolina Archives. A map showing the Equity Districts of 1808 is found in the Appendix.

Lexington Deed Book M is the first extant one from that county after the fire of 1839. Fortunately, this and the following books survived a subsequent fire in 1865 in which the probate records were destroyed. This book contains some deed which date before 1839, and the long chians of title give information on deeds no longer extant. The dower renunciations are quite valuable in naming the wives of the grantors. The delivery information found at the end of the deed is somewhat unusual, and occasionally states a relationship.

The Trustee and Guardina Bond Book for Columbia and Lexington Equity Districts is found among the records of Lexington County, rather than Richland where it would be expected. At least some of the Lexington County Equity records have survived, and are found in the office of the Probate Judge in Lexington. The Columbia District Equity papers to which these bonds belong are filed within the Richland County Equity records and are housed at South Carolina Archives. Columbia District was another of the Equity Districts formed by an act of 1808. It included the districts of Richland, Lexington, and Fairfield. (See map in Appendix.) These records are important to Lexington because of the Court House fires mentioned above, and the Richland Court House fire of 1865 in which the deeds were destroyed.

Fairfield County Will Book 2 contains wills, inventories, appraisements, and appointments of guardians. The first Fairfield Will Book has been abstracted and published in The South Carolina Magazine of Ancestral Research, Kingstree, S. C.

Maps are included from Mills Atlas of Spartanburg, Lexington, Marlboro, Chesterfield, Darlington, and Fairfield Districts.

Brent Holcomb, G. R. S.
Clinton, S. C. 29325
April 6, 1976

TABLE OF CONTENTS

MAPS

Pp. 1-2: Will of JOEL TRAYLOR of Spartanburgh Dist...rec. 1 Nov 1810...to wife CATHARINE
        1/3 of estate...to son RICHARD, $10...son WILLIAM, $31.50...son THOMAS J.
TRAYLOR $13...daughter MARY TRAYLOR, $33...son JOEL $33...children JESSE TRAYLOR, REBEKAH
WOOD, RICHARD TRAYLOR, BETSEY FOSTER, WM TRAYLOR, POLLY TRAYLOR, & JOEL TRAYLOR, THOMAS
J. TRAYLOR...friend ISAM FOSTER and JOHN FOSTER, Exrs...10 Oct 1809...JOEL TRAYLOR (X),
Wit: ISM FOSTER, JOHN FOSTER (X).
        Proven by Col. ISHAM FOSTER and JOHN FOSTER before CHRISTOPHER GOLIGHTLY, ordy.
JESSE TRAYLOR & ROBERT FOSTER qualified as admrs. with the will annexed. 8 Jan 1810.

Pp. 3-5: Will of JOHN GOWEN...rec. 8 Nov 1810...excepting property already bestowed to
        my children...to son WINN B. GOWEN, land in Greenville Dist on both sides
Middle Tygar River and two Negroes (named)...to my daughter LILLY, a plantation known
by ANNE EARLEYS (EASLEYS?) place & 3 Negroe girls (named)...unto my daughter MINERVA
a tract on the S side Saluda, where my son JAMES GOWEN attended two Negroes (named),
and $100 to purchase a home tract... to my daughter ELIZABETH WOODSON, a tract on
Saluda known as Sulsids (?) place... to son JAMES GOWEN, 800 A beginning at the foard
of the So Pacolate where he now lives to include the school house spring where DAVIS
teached (sic) adj. JOHN RODDY, so as to include the JAMESON fields...to my grandson
JOHN GOWEN, son of WILLIAM decd, all the lands between what I have given WINN & LILLY
(LETTY?) & one girl named Hannah...unto my granddaughter MAHULDA, a Negro Burk...unto
LETTY my granddaughter...son WINN & JAMES BLANSINGAME& STREET THIRSTON, my son in laws,
Exrs...deeds of gift to ATLANTIC & DORENDAS, daughter of POLLY SAUNDERS...wife LETTY
decd...20 Aug 1809...JNO GOWEN, Wit: THERON EARLE, W. McVAY, WILLUS F. BROWN.
        Proven by all 3 witnesses and 3 exrs. qualified 8 June 1810. CHRISTOPHER
GOLIGHTLY, O. S. D.

Pp. 5-6: Will of CHRISTOPHER JOHNSON of Spartanburgh Dist...rec. 8 Nov 1810...I am
        about to set out for Charleston and many there is who die on the road & never
return to their Family...to my beloved wife, all my Estate...any of the children we
now have...to school my son THOMAS & support him until he learns the Latin & Greek
language...wife (not named), sole Extx....22 May 1804...CHRISTOPEHR JOHNSON (SEAL), Wit:
ELIJAH SMITH, WM SMITH.
        Proven by ELIJAH SMITH before CHRISTOPHER GOLIGHTLY & qualified ELIZABETH JOHN-
SON, Extx.19 Jan 1810.

Pp. 6-9: Will of SAMUEL LANCASTER of Spartanburg County...rec. 8 Nov 1810...to my eldest
        sons LARKIN & LEVI LANCASTER, 200 A in Union County on both sides of Woffords
Road...to son LEMUEL LANCASTER, 162 A in Union County on both sides Boggans Branch...
to my four daughters POLLY, SELAH, NAZARETH, & CLERYMOND, each one feather bed & furniture & saddle...my tract known as WHITEs tract be sold to purchase a negro wench &
children...to my four sons MOSES, AARON, WILLIAM, & SAMUEL LANCASTER each one good
horse & saddle...all lands not disposed of to be divided amongst sd. four sons...to
wife AGNESS, use & labour of all Negroes...sons LARKIN, LEVI & LEMUEL, Exrs....29 Aug
1797...SAML LANCASTER (SEAL), Wit: WILLIS WILLIFORD, JOSEPH SMITH.
        Proven by both witnesses 9 Feb 1810. CHRIST. GOLIGHTLY, O. D. S.

Pp. 9-11: Will of PENNUEL WOOD of Spartanburgh Dist...rec. 9 Nov 1810...my plantation,
        200 A where I now live to remain the property of my wife CONNEY WOOD, and
at her death to go to SOLOMON POWERS WOOD...my land adj. to JOHN JONES & JOHN WOOD,
THOMAS CAVE & JOSHUA BENSON, 200 A being invested in the hands of CONNEY WOOD, daughter
of PENNUEL WOOD, JUNR & the same land to her, as she now lives with me....friends
HENRY WOOD & JOSHUA BENSON, Exrs...3 June 1809...PENNUEL WOOD (SEAL), Wit: JOHN WOOD,
JOHN JONES, REUBEN MAYFIELD (X).
        Proven by JOHN JONES & REUBIN MAYFIELD 10 Apr 1810, CHRISTOPHER GOLIGHTLY, Ordy.

Pp. 11-14: Will of WILLIAM LIPSCOMB of Spartanburg Dist...rec. 9 Nov 1810...made 17
        July 1808...unto ELIZABETH LIPSCOMB, the land where I now live on the E
side of main Thicketty, adj. THOMAS LITTLEJOHN...horse ford on McBees branch...BURCH-
FIELDs...STEENs & AUSTILLs corner...six choice negroes...to son WILLIAM LIPSCOMB decd
children, four Negroes (named)... to my grandson DAVID LIPSCOMB, $300 & he is to receive
$300 from his father WILLIAM's estate...educating him at the Latin school...to my son
DAVID LIPSCOMB, 8 negroes (named)...my son JOHN LIPSCOMB, 6 Negroes (named)...to my
daughter NANCY WOOD, 6 Negroes (named) & 2 tracts, one purchased of WM WOOD, the other
of JOSEPH CHAMPION where the sd. NANCY WOOD now lives...to my daughter MARY LITTLEJOHN,
8 Negroes (named) & tract whereon THOMAS LITTLEJOHN lives on main Thicketty on the path
from WILLIAM THOMPSONs old place to my house, adj. THOMAS COLLINS, ROSS, BURCHFIELD...
to son NATHAN LIPSCOMB, 7 Negroes (named) & 400 A on Muddy Creek Kentucky whereon sd.
NATHAN now lives...to son SMITH LIPSCOMB, 4 Negroes (named)...land laid off for my wife
...I have 3 tracts in partnership with WILLIAM THOMSON known as the lime kiln tracts,
one conveyed by WILLIAM BRATTON, one by CAPT JAMES MARTAIN, the other we have JAMES

MARTIN's bond for...son JOHN to receive equal part of Negroes...wife to live with son SMITH LIPSCOMB...sons DAVID, JOHN, NATHAN, & SMITH,Exrs....WM LIPSCOMB (SEAL), Wit: WILLIAM BOSTICK, JOSHUA RICHARDS, JOHN HERREN.

    Proven by WILLIAM BOSTICK & JOSHUA RICHARDS 11 Apr 1810. JOHN & SMITH LIPSCOMB qualified as Exrs. 12 Apr 1810. NATHAN LIPSCOMB qualified 26 Oct 1810.

Pp. 15-16: Will of WILLIAM COOPER of Dist. of Spartanburgh...rec. 19 Nov 1810...made 8 Aug 1808...wife FRANCES COOPER one feather bed & furniture & plantation during her widowhood only...to my eldest son MYCAJAH, one mare & saddle...to son MATHEW one mare & saddle & $8...to son WILLIAM, one colt & work steer...to son JAMES, one mare & saddle...to son SILAS, 160 A which I now live on...to my daughters MARY & PHEBE, 100 A...remainder divided equally among my children...JOSHUA RICHARDS & DANIEL AMOS, Exrs.... WILLIAM COOPER (SEAL), Wit: CHARLES AMOS, CION COOPER, BENJAMIN STANLEY.

    Proven by CION COOPER & CHARLES AMOS 26 May 1810. JOSHUA RICHARDS qualified as Exr...DANIEL AMOS qualified 17 June 1810. CHRISTOPHER GOLIGHTLY, O. S. D.

Pp. 17-18: Will of THOMAS HOUSE of Spartan Dist., planter...Rec. 30 Sept 1811...unto WILLIAM, 120 A where he now lives including the Bentfield up the River... to MOSES, 100 A where he now lives...to JOHN 100 A at the lower line of WILLIAM, adj. DAVID MOOREs land...balance of land to AMELIA, my wife...as REBEKAH has had a horse & cow & calf, the other 3 girls should have an equal part with her...JOHN HOUSE, SENR. & THOMAS THORNTON, Exrs...9 Aug 1811...THOMAS HOUSE (T) Wit: MARTIN COLE, WILLIAM HOUSE.

    Proven before WILLIAM LANCASTER, Esq., Ordinary of Spartanburgh Dist., 30 Sept 1811, by MARTIN COLE & WILLIAM HOUSE.

Pp. 18-20: L. W. & T. of ANDREW BARRY of Dist. of Spartanburgh...rec. 10 Sept 1811... son JOHN, my daughter POLLEY, & my son CHARLES, I have given a full part... daughters CALEY & PEGGY & VIOLET each to have $100 paid in property...sons ANDREW, RICHARD, & HUGH, my land to be equally divided...ANDREW to have the upper part of my plantation, HUGH the middle part including the house I now live in, and RICHARD the lower part...unto my wife PEGGY...Negro woman Mimey...unto my daughter ALLEY(?)... wf PEGGY, Extx, & CHARLES & ANDREW, RICHARD BARRY & GENL. THOMAS MOORE, to assist... ANDREW BARRY (SEAL), Wit: CHAS MOORE, SAML MILLER, C. W. HANNA. Will dated 5 May 1809.

    Proven by CHARLES MOORE & SAMUEL MILLER 7 Oct 1811. W. LANCASTER, Ordinary of Spartan Dist.

Pp. 20-21: L. W. & T. of RICHARD PRINCE...rec. 29 Nov 1811...of Spartanburgh Dist.... to son JOSIAH, $5...to daughter MARTHA PRINCE, loom & implements...to son WILLIAM PRINCE & JOHN PRINCE, tract I now live on & mill tract to WILLIAM PRINCE.... tract I bought of PRICE to JOHN PRINCE...JOHN to take immediate possession of his land & WILLIAM to take possession of his also with the charge of my wife & MARTHA and not to dismiss them...RICHARD PRINCE (R) Attest: JOHN RED, VELINTINE SMITH. Dated 28 Mar 1811.

    Proven by JOHN RED & VELINTINE SMITH 4 Oct 1811, before W. LANCASTER, Ord. of Spartan. Dist.

Pp. 21-22: L. W. & T. of JESS DAVIS...rec. 2 Apr 1812...of Spartanburgh Dist...LOOKEY, the woman of colour that now lives with me and has for many years, shall be the legal heir...EDWARD BALLINGER, Ear...11 Feb 1812. JESS DAVID (T) (SEAL), Wit: ALEXR. RODDY, CYRUS SEAY, MARY LEWIS.

    Proven by CYRUS SEAY 23 Mar 1812, W. LANCASTER, Ordinary of Spartanburgh Dist.

Pp. 22-23: L. W. & T. of JOHN HEWATT of Spartanburgh Dist...rec. 7 June 1812...to wife ELENDER, all my estate real & personal...after her death, to be divided between my sons ROBERT & ALEXANDER HEWATT...son RICHARD, Exr....3 Nov 1811...JOHN HEWATT (SEAL), Wit: JOHN GRIST, WILLIAM PRINCE, HARDY WILLIFORD.

    Proven by all three wit...7 June 1812...W. LANCASTER, O. S. D.

Pp. 24-25: L. W. & T. of WILLIAM UNDERWOOD of Dist. of Spartanburgh...rec. 6 Sept 1812... to my wife KEZIAH, negro boy JIM...if she marries, to the two boys WILLIAM D. & JOHN UNDERWOOD...to WILLIAM D. & JOHN, my tracts of land...to daughter AGNES, $20... to be paid when my two sons comes (sic) of age...wife & JAMES YOUNG, Esqr. Exrs...11 Feb 1812...WILLIAM UNDERWOOD (T) (LS), Wit: JOHN McCLURE SENR., HENRY MONROE, JOHN McCLURE.

    Proven by HENRY MONROE & JOHN McCLURE JUNR, 8 Aug 1812...W. LANCASTER, Ord. of Spartanburgh Dist.

Pp. 25-27: L. W. & T. of DANIEL WALLING of Dist. of Spartanburgh, farmer...rec. 9 Nov 1812...to wife SUSANNAH WALLING, all my estate real & personal except for a bay mare to my son MICHAEL WALLING...son DANIEL, s5...son RICHARD, s5...son JAMES, s5...

to daughter MARY, s5...to daughter SUSANNA, s5...if MICHAEL stays and takes care of his mother during her life, he is to have my estate...30 June 1812...DANIEL WALLING (X) (SEAL) Wit: JOHN VAUGHAN, THAD OWEN, RICHARD WALLING.
 Proven by JOHN VAUGHAN and THADEUS OWEN 9 Nov 1812. W. LANCASTER, O. S. D.

Pp. 27-28: L. W. & T. of CHRISTOPHER RHODES SENR of Spartanburgh Dist...rec. 8 July 1813 ...tract where I now live after the death of my wife to my son THOMAS RHODES on the S side of the road running from ISAAC CROWS to HEADS ford...son CHRISTOPHER RHODES, BENJAMIN, WILLIAM, & THOMAS RHODES, my daughter ELIZABETH GRIZEL, NANCY HENDRIX, JUDITH BARKER, HANNAH STROUD, RACHEL WALDROPE, to have an equal potion...sons CHRISTOPHER, BENJAMIN, and WILLIAM RHODES to divide the property...15 Mar 1806...CHRISTOPHER RHODES (LS), Wit:. WILLIAM STEWART, A. CASEY, MARTIN NEWMAN.
 Proven by AARON CASEY (no date). W. LANCASTER O. S. D.

Pp. 28-30: L. W. & T. of THOMAS WILLIAMSON, of Spartanburgh Dist...rec. 12 July 1813... to wf ANN WILLIAMSON, one third of land & negroes...to son WILLIAM WILLIAMSON & son in law JOHN MEANS, remainder of negroes...remaining 2/3 of property to be sold & money divided between WILLIAM WILLIAMSON, JOHN MEANS, & my daughter ELIZABETH ALEXANDER, decd, my daughter ELIZABETH part ot be equally divided between her three children, viz., JAMES, THOMAS & ANN ALEXANDER...son WILLIAM & son in law JOHN MEANS, Exrs...THOMAS WILLIAMSON (SEAL), Wit: DANL McKIE, JAMES OTTS, THOMAS DRUMMOND. Dated 2 Apr 1813.
 Proven by JAMES OTTS & THOMAS DRUMMOND 14 July 1813. W. LANCASTER, O. S. D.

Pp. 30-31: L. W. & T. of EDWARD HERRING of Dist. of Spartanburgh...rec. 14 July 1813... made 26 July 1811...wife MARIAN HERRIN have all property and at her death to divide amongst my children(not named)...EDWARD HERRING Wit: JESSE MATHIS, WILLIAM CANTRELL, MANNING BARNES (X).
 Proven by JESSE MATHIS 5 July 1813. W. LANCASTER O. S. D.

Pp. 31-33: L. W. & T. of PETER FRIE of Dist. of Spartanburgh...rec. 2 Sept 1813...allow my wife MARY FRIE her bed & furniture, cow & calf I bought from VINSENT BOMAR also pewter dish & plates...my four children WILLIAM,BARBARA,GILBERT & TARLETON... to son GILBERT, upper part of plantation I now live on...conditional line betwixt MR. ABRAHAMS & myself...to son TARLETON, lower part of plantation...friends JOHN RIDINGS & WILLIAM KELSO, Esqr. & HUGH EWING, Exrs...11 Jan 1813...PETER FRIE (X) (SEAL), Wit: GEO. WELCH, DANIEL MORROW, WILLIAM JACKSON.
 Proven by GEORGE WELCH & WILLIAM JACKSON 2 Aug 1812. W. LANCASTER O. S. D.

Pp. 34-35: L. W. & T. of JAMES BALLENGER SENR of Dist. of Spartanburgh...rec. 3 Sep 1813 ...plantation on which I now live, Negores, cattle to my wife DORCAS BALLENGER during her life...to my daughter FRANCES BALLENGER, $300...unto my daughter PEGGY LEWIS a mare...to RICHARD FOSTER, $1...to my sons JOHN BALLENGER, EDWARD BALLENGER, JAMES BALLENGER, WILLIAM BALLENGER, ELIJAH BALLENGER, PEGGY LEWIS, FRANCES BALLENGER, & TABITHA FOSTER, an equal share of my estate...sons EDWARD & JAMES, Exrs...19 July 1813...JAMES BALLENGER (SEAL), Wit: W. PERRIN, EDWARD BALLENGER SENR., JAMES BALLENGER, son of JOHN.
 Proven by JAMES BALLENGER & WILLIAM PERRIN 2 Aug 1813. W. LANCASTER, O. S. D.

Pp. 35-38: L. W. & T. OF ROBERT BENSON, Esqr. of Spartanburgh Dist...rec. 8 Sept 1813... to my sister NANCY WALKER a negro woman Rose...to my brother ELIAS BENSON, one negro boy OSBURN...to my brother NIMROD BENSON, negro Stephen...to brother JAMES BEN- SON, tract on the glassy mountain which was allotted to me as part of my Fathers estate ...to my brother ABNER BENSON, land purchased by him & myself of EDMOND BISHOP, 300 A... on Lawsons Fork, also my part of land purchased of GEORGE HUGHE adj. the sd. tract, also tract purchased from JAMES TEMPLETON, ...also land purchased from the heirs of ROLLEY FAUCET by him & myself...also sd. ABNER, a tract lying near to the widow SEAYs, which was allotted to me as part of my Fathers estate...ABNER, ELIAS, NIMROD BENSON, Exrs... 15 May 1813...ROBERT BENSON (LS), Wit: E. RODDY, E. B. BENSON, ELIJAH FOSTER.
 Proven by EPHRAIM RODDY, & ELIAS B. BENSON...6 Sept 1813...W. LANCASTER OSD.

Pp. 38-40: L. W. & T. of JOHN ARNOLD of Spartanburgh Dist...rec. 23 Nov 1813...to wife NANCY, my house and land on E side of the spring branch...each child not married one horse & saddle, viz., JAMES, WILLIS, NANCY, SALLY, POLLEY ,GEORE M. as they become of age WM & FANNEY & JAMES have got 120 A each, and now to my son WILLIS 120 A on N side spring branch...to son GEORGE M. 100 A adj. Enoree River, to be laid off in good form for a plantation, the remainder he may have for $3 an acre...my daughter LUCY has had all of her part until the death of her mother...wf NANCY & WILLIAM ARNOLD, Exrs... 19 July 1813. JOHN ARNOLD (SEAL), Wit: JOHN ALLEN SR., SIMON STONE, RICHARD SHACKLEFORD, JR.
 Proven by RICHARD SHACKLEFORE & SIMON STONE 23 Nov 1813. W. LANCASTER O. S. D.

4

Pp. 40-41: L. W. & T. of JOHN WOFFORD SENR of Dist. of Spartanburgh...rec. 25 Nov 1813...
to son ISAAC WOFFORD, one Negor man Cyrus...to son WILLIAM WOFFORD, 2 tracts of
land, one of 26 A taken up by myself, the other 240 A purchased from JOSEPH LANNOM; a
Negro woman Tempey...for the rest of my children, I have given them what I designed them
to have...son WILLIAM WOFFORD & friend WILIE WILLIFORD, Exrs...3 May 1808...JOHN
WOFFORD (J) (SEAL), Wit: WILIE WILLIFORD, MARK BENNET, JAMES BENNET.
Proven by all 3 wit. 25 Nov 1813. W. LANCASTER, Ord. of Sp. Dist.

Pp. 41-43: L. W. & T. of THOMAS WEAVER of Spartanburgh Dist...rec. 15 Dec 1813...to wife
MARY all real & personal estate during her widowhood untill our youngest
daughter SARAH becomes of age...children REBEKAH, ELIZABETH, GEORGE, WINNEY & AMEY KELAH
& SARAH...wife MARY Extx, friends DA D BRAY JUNR, & ISAAC WOOTEN, Exrs...13 Apr 1813...
THOMAS WEAVER (X) (LS), Wit: GEORGE THOMASON, JOHN THOMASON.
Proven by GEORGE THOMASON 15 Dec 1813...W. LANCASTER O. S. D.

Pp. 43-45: L. W. & T. of MOSES FOSTER of Dist. of Spartanburgh, planter...rec. 18 Dec
1813...to wife ELIZABETH during her widowhood, plantation whereon I now live
...to son in law JOHN KELSO, s5...to my granddaughter ELIZABETH FOSTER KELSO, for the
purpose of her or her mother MARGARET, taking good care of my helpless daughter CATHERINE
...sons JOHN & ANDREW guardian for sd. helpless daughter...to my son in law THOMAS KELSO
s5...to my son in law JOSEPH KELSO, s5...to my son JOHN FOSTER, part of tract whereon I
now live, 25 A...also land adj. to that he lives on, adj. corner of JAMES RIELEIGHS(?),
and 200 A, ½ of 400 A tract, also 105 A on NW of my old tract & W of where he now lives...
to son ANDREW FOSTER, all the rest of my lands...sons JOHN & ANDREW Exrs...15 Nov 1809...
MOSES FOSTER (LS), Wit: JULIET LANCASTER, CLARY LANCASTER, W. LANCASTER.
Proven by JULIET LANCASTER & CLARY LANCASTER 18 Dec 1813. W. LANCASTER, Ord.
of Spar. Dist.

Pp. 45-47: L. W. & T. of JOHN WALKER of Dist. of Spartanburgh...rec. 17 Jan 1814...to
wife MARGARET WALKER her maintenance on the plantation whereon I now live
which land I give to my two sons JOHN WALKER & ABSALOM WALKER all the West part of my
land as far down Tyger River to the mouth of Distilles branch...two neighbors MR. JOHN
MULLINAX & MR. JOHN HINDMAN, trustees of sd. land, until sd. sons arrive at age of 21...
to my sons WILLIAM WALKER & DAVID WALKER, negro woman Sally & her child Jack to be sold...
to my four daughters SABRA, MARGET, MARY & REBEKAH WALKER, one feather bed & furniture...
untill daughters arrive at full age or marry...my sons & daughters WILLIAM, SAMUEL,
DAVID, JOHN, ABSALOM, , ELISABETH VISE, SABRA WALKER, MARGARET WALKER, NANCY WALKER, &
REBEKAH WALKER...16 Dec 1813...JOHN WALKER (LS), Wit: GIDEON HARELSON, JOHN MULLINAX,
JOHN HINDMAN.
Proven by JOHN MULLINAX & JOHN HINDMAN 15 Jan 1814. W. LANCASTER Ord. Spartan.
Dist.

Pp. 47-48: L. W. & T. of JOHN LEWIS of Dist. of Spartanburgh...rec. 4 May 1814...to son
JOEL, tract I now live on, should he die without heirs, land is to be equally
divided amongst my brothers & sisters except PRUDY HAWKINS to have $50 worth over &
above an equal share...unto my wife my Negro Molly...divided between my wife & son...
brother in law JOHN CLARKE & son JOEL Exrs...2 Dec 1813...JOHN LEWIS (SEAL), Wit: ALEXR.
RODDY, JOEL LEWIS, MARY LEWIS.
Proven by MAJ. ALEXANDER RODDY 4 May 1814. W. LANCASTER, Ord. Spar. District.

Pp. 48-50: L. W. & T. of OSBORN WEST of Spartanburgh Dist., farmer, rec. 27 Aug 1814...
to wife DORCAS WEST all my personal estate,all land, Negroes, etc....at her
marriage or decease to be divided among my nine children CASEY, CATY, PEGGY, DAVID, MASSEY,
ANNY, CILEY, WILLIAM, JENNY...wf DORCAS Extx...31 Aug 1804...OSBORN WEST (LS), Wit:
GEORGE T. SLOAN,W M. WOFFORD, THOMAS MEADOWS.
Proven by GEORGE T. SLOAN & WILLIAM WOFFORD 9 July 1814. W. LANCASTER, Ord. SD.

Pp. 50-53: L. W. & T. of ZACHARIAH LEATHERWOOD of Spartanburgh Dist...rec. 29 Aug 1814...
to grandson HOLLAND LEATHERWOOD, 75 A on two branches of Jamies Creek, which
I purchased of JOHN WOODRUFF 28 June 1814...to my granddaughter POLLY HOBBY a bay mare...
to my daughter PEGGY LEATHERWOOD, one negor woman...JENNY LENGFORD to take sd. PEGGY &
negro woman & take care of them...the remaining part of my estate to be sold for £90s14
Va. money & money to be equally divided between ELIZABETH HOBBY, WILLIAM LEATHERWOOD,
decd his heirs, NANCY COLBERT, FRANEY (FRANCES?) EDWARDS, FANNEY JOHNSTON, LYDIA LANG-
FORD, JOHN LEATHERWOOD & THOMAS LEATHERWOOD...my children viz. GEORGE LEATHERWOOD, JENNY
LANGFORD, POLLY LANGFORD, RUTHY LANGFORD, & PEGGY LEATHERWOOD...DANIEL McKIE, JOHN
LEATHERWOOD & JAMES LEATHERWOOD, Exrs...28 June 1814...ZACHARIAH LEATHERWOOD (X) (SEAL),
Wit: SAMUEL WOODRUFF SENR., JESSE LEATHERWOOD, JOHN LANGFORD (S).
Proven by JESSE LEATHERWOOD & JOHN LANGFORD...1 Aug 1813. W. LANCASTER. Ord.
S. D.

Pp. 53-55: L. W. & T. of WILLIAM STONE of Spartanburgh Dist...rec. 30 Aug 1814...all
estate to wife FRANCES...at her death or marriage to be divided amongst the
whole of my children to wit NANCY, JOHN,WILLIAM,JAMES, TILMAN, SEABORN, COBERN, & MAYBORN
...two negroes FELIX & DICK to be set free when $200 is paid...wife FRANCES & THOMAS
MURRY, Exrs...WM STONE (LS), Wit: STEPHEN CRUCE, RICHARD KERBY, SAMUEL STONE. Dated 2
July 1814.
Proven by STEPHEN CRUCE & SAMUEL STONE9 Aug 1814, W. LANCASTER, Ord S. D.

Pp. 55-56: L. W. & T. of BENJAMINE BONNER of Spartanburgh Dist....rec. 19 Jan 1815...
to wife FRANCIS BONNER Negro Dick, and dwelling, etc., with her son BRIANT if
she ehooses...to son DEMPSEY BONNER, waggon and hind gears...to daughter DELITHA MORRISON
a pice of land on right hand side of the path leading from NATHAN BYARS to the Furnace...
land adj. to NATHAN P RS, SILAS YARBOROUGH and WILSON NESBITT, 100A...to son BRIANT
BONNER, land and plantation where I now live to take care of his mother...BENJAMINE
BONNER ((|)) (SEAL), Wit: THOMAS WHITAKER,SILAS YARBROUGH (X), JAMES MATTHEWS (X). Dated
9 July 1814.
Proven by SILAS YARBOROUGH 19 Jan 1815.

Pp. 56-58: L. W. & T. of ABNER WINGO of Dist. of Spartanburgh...rec. 19 Jan 1815....to
son JOHN and daughter REBEKAH, one shilling each, as they already received
the rest of their portions...to my two daughters HARRAH (HANNAH?) and POLLY sufficient
schooling and feather bed & furniture....to sons WILLIS and ABNER, the land on which I
live...to wife ELIZABETH all my goods and chattels during her lifetime...4 Feb 1812...
ABNER WINGO, Wit: ELISHA BOMAR, JAMES HUNT, JOHN WINGO.
Proven by JOHN WINGO & ELISHA BOMAR 19 Jan 1815. ELIZABETH WINGO and JAMES
NESBITT qualified as Exrs... W. LANCASTER O. S. D.

Pp. 58-59: L. W. & T. of AMEY GOLIGHTLY of Spartanburgh Dist...rec. 19 Jan 1815...to
my son DAVID all my land being granted to me since I became a widow...to my
daughter CLAREMONT LANCASTER my corner walnut cupboard...to my daughter MARY McDANIEL my
weaving loom and gears...my five children CHRISTOPHER, WILLIAM SHANDS, CLAREMONT, DAVID
& MARY...my two sons CHRISTOPHER & WILLIAM SHANDS Exrs...____ 1812. Wit: PHEBE SMITH
(SP), JULIET LANCASTER, W. LANCASTER. AMEY GOLIGHTLY (LS),
Proven by PHEBE SMITH & JULIET LANCASTER 19 Jan 1815. W. LANCASTER O. S. D.

Pp. 59-62: L. W. & T. of HENRY O NEILL of Dist. of Spartanburgh, planter...rec. 11 Feb
1815...to wife HANNAH during her life or widowhood, tract whereon we now live
my negro man George, negro woman Courtney, household & kitchen furniture, etc...to son
JOHN O NEILL, after death of my sife, the tract where I now live and negroes (named) and
watch...to my daughter NANCY LOVE negroes (named)...to grandson HENRY O NEILL LOVE, $50...
to my daughter MARY WINGO negroes (named),...to daughter HANNAH WILSON negroes (named)...
griends ZACHARIAH McDANIEL & JOHN McDOWELL, Exrs...11 Jan 1815...HENRY O NEILL (H) (SEAL),
Wit: THERON LANCASTER, ELIJAH BALLENGER, W. LANCASTER.
Proven by THERON LANCASTER and ELIJAH BALLENGER 31 Jan 1815. W. LANCASTER Ord.
Spartan Dist.

Pp. 62-64: L. W. & T. of MICHAEL MILLER of Spartanburgh Dist...rec. 2 Aug 1815...to wife
AGNESS my dwelling House, 400 A including the mill and negroes (named)...
my son JOHN has sufficiently been assisted with land in Greenville Dist, he shall have
one small negro valued at $300...other three sons HENRY, JAMES & ALEXANDER....JONES and
BROOKES tracts, the forge & land belonging to it (the oar bank tract excepted)...all
children to live with their mother, make what they can, and as they marry or fo off get
their own earning...sons in law JOHN MONTGOMERY, DAVID DANTZLER, THERON EARLE & JAMES
ANDERSON be notified to keep schedule of what property they have receive from me....
son JOHN MILLER, JOHN MONTGOMERY & THERON EARLE Exrs...8 Feb 1815...MICHAEL MILLER
(LS), Wit: ALEXR RODDY, ALEXR THOMSON, JOHN CRAWFORD.
Proven by ALEXANDER THOMSON & JOHN CRAWFORD 1 July 1815. W. LANCASTER Ord.
Sptg. Dist.

Pp. 64-66: L. W. & T. of JOEL LEWIS of Spartanburgh Dist, planter,...rec. 15 Aug 1815...
to wife POLLEY LEWIS, tract whereon I now live...six Negroes (named)...my
two children FRANCES and JOHN LEWIS...to daughter FRANCES, tract I purchased from DAVID
LEWIS also 30 A, part of the tract I purchased from MR. DRURY HUTCHISON, also ten negroes
(named)...to son JOHN LEWIS, plantation I purchased from JAMES LEWIS, and 60 A that lies
between the mill and WILLIAM WEATHERFORD on the S side of the Creek, also 200 A that I
purchased from JOHN COUCH, also ten engroes (named)...to each child $50 per year until
they come of age...JOHN CHAPMAN Esqr and POLLEY LEWIS Exrs...14 Jan 1815...JOEL LEWIS
(SEAL), Wit: JOHN MACHEN, REBEKAH HAWKINS, PETER HAWKINS.
Proven by JOHN MACHAN 7 Aug 1815. W. LANCASTER Ord. Sptg. Dist.

Pp. 66-68: L. W. & T. of EDWARD SMITH of Dist. of Spartanburg...rec. 15 Aug 1814...to wife
SALLEY during her widowhood, all my real & personal property...at her decease
to be divided among my seven children CHARLES SMITH, HOLMAN SMITH, my son in law JOHN
LIPSCOMB, DAVID LIPSCOMB, RICHARD SIMMONS, REUBEN SMITH and JOHN WILLIS...requesting
my two sons to be liberal to my three daughters BETSEY, FRANCES & PATSEY...to son in
law WILLIAM BURTON, s5...to my son in law THOMAS SMITH s5...to the heirs of my son WILL-
IAM SMITH s5...sons CHARLES & HOLMAN SMITH, Exrs...17 Apr 1815...EDWARD SMITH (SEAL),
Wit: WILLIAM SMITH, MOSES WATERS, BETSEY WATERS.
        Proven by WILLIAM SMITH (not dated) The executors requested one month of
deliberation on quallification which was granted them W. LANCASTER O. S. D.

Pp. 68-69: L. W. & T. of THOS WRIGHT of Newberry Dist...rec. 11 Oct 1815...property to
be divided between his Brothers JOHN WRIGHT, ABSALOM WRIGHT and WILLIAM
WRIGHT...25 Aug 1815...THOMAS WRIGHT, Wit: JOHN A. RUFF, SOLOMON SUBER(?).
        Proven in Spartanburg Dist. by JOHN A. RUFF 11 Oct 1815. W. LANCASTER, Ord. of
Sptg Dist.

Pp. 69-73: L. W. & T. of GEORGE BREWTON of Spartanburgh Dist....rec. 26 Oct 1815...to wf
CATHERINE BREWTON, house and plantation whereon I now live & my riding chair
with negroes (named)...which I bid off at the sale of the estate of DANIEL BRAGG decd....
my eldest daughter ELIZABETH BRAGG has received of my estate two Negroes (named)...my
second daughter POLLEY GRACE has received a negro woman (named)...to my eldest son JOHN
BREWTON a negro boy Bob and tract whereon he now lives 242 A...to my third daughter
ABIGAIL BRAGG, 2 negroes (named) and tract whereon PETER BRAGG now lives 119 A....to my
fourth daughter CATHERINE GAMBRILL a negro Salley and other negroes (named)...to my fifth
daughter DELILAH OTTS tract whereon WILLIAM OTTS now lives and negroes (named)...to my
sixth daughter NAOMI ACKER negroes (named)...to my second son GEORGE BREWTON, tract of
land where he settled 273 A, 45 of which lies on the S side fo the Georgia Road also negro
Prince...to my seventh daughter CASANDER BREWTON, one feather bed, a negro (named) and a
walnut chest...to my third son JOEL BREWTON tract whereon I now live part of seven tracts
including my still with all the utensils, 486 A and 2 negroes when he comes of age...
ELIZABETH BRAGGS part to be enjoyed by her during her life time and then be equally divided among her children except POLLEY CLAYTON...JOHN BREWTON, GEORGE GRACE, GEORGE BREWTON
and JOEL BREWTON , Exrs...6 July 1815...GEORGE BREWTON (LS), Wit: PHILIP BREWTON, JOHN
BRAGG, ENOCH BREWTON CASANDER BREWTON.
        Proven by PHILIP BREWTON 23 Oct 1815. W. LANCASTER Ord Sptg Dist.

Pp. 73-75: L. W. & T. of JAMES WOFFORD of Spartanburgh Dist...rec. 2 Nov 1815...to wife
CATEY WOFFORD all my household & kitchen furniture with plantation & tools,
three negroes (named)...my four sons NATHANIEL, JOHN, JESSE, & ISAAC WOFFORD, Negroes
(named)...to my daughter DIDAMEA JOHNSON, 300 A on waters of Broad River, in Spartanburgh
Dist adj. ARTHUR CROCKER and the N. C. line, originally granted to THOMAS SABS(?) and
conveyed to ROBERT LEE...to my daughter PEGGY MOORE, $2, she having already received her
part...to my daughter REBEKAH RHODES (?), $2, she already having received her part...to
my daughter CATY MOORE, $2, already having received her part... my son NATHANIEL WOFFORD
and WILLIAM RHODES Exrs...22 June 1815...JAMES WOFFORD (LS), Wit: JOHN CROCKER, WM
HENDRIX, EPHRAIM DRUMMON.
        Proven by EPHRAIM DRUMMON 27 Oct 1815. W. LANCASTER Ord. Sptg Dist.

Pp. 75-78: L. W. & T. of GEORGE McCARTER of Dist. of Spartanburgh, planter...rec. 2 Nov
1815...to wife ANN 1/3 of plantation where I now dwell during her widowhood or
life & also my dwelling house and Negro (named)...amongst my sons JAMES & WILLIAM, MARY
FINLEY & HANNAH McCARTER...to sons JAMES and WILLIAM all my lands at my wifes death, still
and vessels...all my cash, bonds notes , etc. between JAMES & WILLIAM, ROSANNA THOMPSON,
ELIZABETH CUNNINGHAM, MARY FINELY & HANNAH McCARTER...friend JOHN McDOWELL & son JAMES,
Exrs...11 Oct 1815...GEORGE McCARTER (LS), Wit: SETH POOL, STEPHEN CRUCE, WM WHITE.
        Proven by all 3 wit. 30 Oct 1815. W. LANCASTER Ord. S. D.

Pp. 78-79: L. W. & T. of ABSALOM LANCASTER of Dist. of Spartanburgh...rec. 9 Dec 1815...
the whole of my land to my wife SALLEY LANCASTER during her widowhood, then
to my son ALLEN...to my daughters NANCY, CYNTHIA, & LOVE one bed & furniture...to my dau.
LO , a Heifer & young cow & calf...as to the rest of my children WILLIAM, JOHN & son in
law ALEXANDER GRAY as much of my living as I have given the rest...son ALLEN, Exr....
3 May 1814...A. LANCASTER (LS), Wit: A. BENSON, GEO. THOMASON, THOS POOL.
        Proven by GEORGE THOMASON & ABNER BENSON 4 Dec 1815. W. LANCASTER, Ord. Sptg.
Dist.

Pp. 79-81: L. W. & T. of SALLEY BOBO of Spartanburgh Dist...rec. 26 Dev 1816...to son
BURREL, $100...to son ABSALOM my colt... to son CHANEY, one Negro girl Marsy...
to son JEREMIAH, one Negro Lynda... to son SIMPSON's five children, viz. POLLEY, JOHN,

NANCY, BETSEY, & SALLEY, $500....my son WILLIAM WILDER, my son SPENCER BOBO, my son BARAM
...my son ABSALOM, my son CHANEY, my son HIRAM, my son JEREMIAH, my son WILLIS, my dau.
LOVINA, my dau. POLLEY, my dau BETSEY, my daughter NANCIES children SALLEY RACHELL and
SAMUEL SIMPSON...sons CHANEY & HIRAM, Exrs...20 Jan 1813...SALLEY BOBO (SEAL), Wit: A.
CASEY, M. CASEY.
     Proven by AARON CASEY 26 Feb 1816 W LANCANSTER Ord. Spt. Dist.

Pp. 81-82: L. W. & T. of THOMAS MEADOWS of Spartanburgh Dist... rec. 6 Mar 1816...to wife
     ELENDER MEADOWS all my estate real & personal and all my lands...at her death
to be divided among my eight children GEORGE, WILLIAM, CASANDER, BENJAMINE, MATTY, LAWSON,
JENNY, ESTHER...wife ELENDER & son GEORGE, Exrs...THOMAS MEADOWS (X) (SEAL), Wit: GEORGE
T. SLOAN, DAVID BURTON, THOMAS THORNTON.
     Proven by GEORGE T. SLOAN 6 Mar 1816. W. LANCASTER Ord. S. D.

Pp. 82-83: L. W. & T. of DAVID BREWTON SENR of Spartanburgh Dist...rec. 26 Feb 1816....
     wife SUSANNAH to have part of plantation whereon I now live...to son GEORGE
BREWTON one feather bed which was his mothers in her lifetime...50 A, the title made
by DANIEL BRAGG...son in law JOHN WILLIAMS to have one shilling stelring if he applies
for any part of my estate, he has received what I conceive to be his part...my six sons
GEORGE, JONAS, ENOCH, DAVID, ISAAC, and PHILIP...JONAS BREWTON, ISAAC BREWTON and ISAAC
TIPPINS Exrs....17 Mar 1815...DAVID BREWTON (LS), Wit: G. BREWTON, JOHN BREWTON, NANCY
BREWTON, JOEL BREWTON.
     Proven by JOHN BREWTON, Esqr 27 Feb 1816 W. LANCASTER Ord. Sptg. Dist.

Pp. 83-84: L. W. & T. of SARAH PENNY...rec. 29 Apr 1816...to my daughter MARY PERSON, one
     shilling...to my son JOHN PENNY one shilling...to my son in law ROBERT McCRORY
one shilling...to my grandson ROBERT McCRORY one horse and tract whereon I now live...JOHN
COLLINS and SAMUEL BRICE, Etxs...16 May 1810...SARAH PENNY (C), Wit: JAMES NESBITT,
SAMUEL BRICE, JOHN COLLINS.
     Proven by JAMES NESBITT 19 Apr 1816. W. LANCASTER O. S. D.

Pp. 85-86: L. W. & T. of SAMUEL OTTS...rec. 19 Apr 1816...my wife to keep and raise my
     children and to school them as long as she remains a widow...wife SARAH and
JOHN OTTS, Exrs...10 July 1813...SAMUEL OTTS, Wit: WILLIAM ROGERS, JASON MOORE, ROBERT
LIGON.
     Codicil, I appoint my brother WILLIAM OTTS one of the exrs...27 Feb 1816...
Wit: ANDREW B. MOORE, NANCY POSEY, MARTIN OTTS.
     Proven by ANDREW B. MOORE and ROBERT LIGON 19 Apr 1816. W. LANCASTER Ord. S.D.

Pp. 86-88: L. W. & T. of THOMAS COLE of Spartanburgh Dist...rec. 19 Apr 1816...to son
     OBADIAH COLE, all my land & plantation where I now live, to take care of his
father and mother ...my daughter PATSEY has recd as follows which is to be reduced from
her part...the rest of my heirs is as follows: MARY ARENDALE, SARAH FONDREN, GROVE COLE,
SUSANNAH COOPER, NANCY GASTON, ELIZABETH DEWBERRY, JOHN COLE, PATSEY KENADY, THOMAS COLE
...WILLIAM DEWBERRY and THOMAS COLE, Exrs...20 Feb 1816...THOMAS COLE (*) (SEAL), Wit:
THOMAS ARENDALE, SILAS COOPER, JAMES COOPER (X).
     Proven by SILAS COOPER and JAMES COOPER 16 Apr 1816 and qualified Exrs...
W. LANCASTER Ord. S. D.

Pp. 88-89: L. W. & T. of JOHH SMITH of Spartanburgh Dist...rec. 5 July 1816...to wife
     ELIZABETH SMITH, all my movable property, for support of her, her daughter
MARY SMITH, and her son MICAJAH SMITH...8 Nov 1812...JOHN SMITH (LS), Wit: HUGH WHITE.
     10 Dec 1812, I acknowledge the within to be my will....JOHN SMITH, Test:
DAVID COOK.
     17 Nov 1814. I acknoweldge the within to be my will, JOHN SMITH, Wit: JOHN
RAKESTRAW.
     Proven by HUGH WHITE and JOHN RAKESTRAW, there being no Exr. shall grant
letters of admn. with the will annexed. W. LANCASTER Ord Sptg Dist (no date).

Pp. 89-90: L. W. & T. of SPENCER BOBO of Spartanburgh Dist...rec. 5 July 1816...to wife
     JANE BOBO my land where I now live & negroes (named)...all the remainder of
my real and personal estate to the Baptist Church of Jesus Christ by the name of Newhope
Church and head of Cedar Shoal Church of sd. Dist...also the Baptist church near me
by the name of Bethel Church...Brother BARRAM BOBO, Exr...I also appoint as managers to
the different churches, that is to Newhope, LANDR MILES, to upper Cedar Shoal, JOSEPH
BARNETT and MILES RAINWATER...to Bethel PETER BRAGG and WILLIAM RODES...to wife JANE, $
520...19 Feb 1816...S. BOBO (LS), Wit: WM FARROW, WM HENDRIX, JONAS BREWTON.
     Proven by JONAS BREWTON 30 May 1816. W. LANCASTER, O. S. D.

Pp. 91-93: L. W. & T. of JOHN GRIST of Spartanburg County...rec. 10 July 1816...to son JOHN GRIST tract on Dutchmans Creek, purchased of BENNETT DAFFRON...to son WILLIAM GRIST, tract on Cain Creek, purchased of JAMES GRANT...to son THOMAS GRIST and BENJAMIN GRIST tract on Dutchmans Creek, purchased of WM BRATCHER...if my mother should not make enough to support JOHN GRIST and WM is find her support...to wife RACHEL that tract whereon I now live...sons THOMAS and BENJAMIN GRIST, when they come of age....to LUSA (SUSA?) GRIST and FANNY GRIST, my daughters, the tract where I now live...to dau. FRANNA GRIST...my three true and lawful sons JOHN GRIST, DANIEL McHAM and WILLIAM GRIST, Exrs...19 Jan 1816...JOHN GRIST (LS), Wit: WM POOL, WM VARNER, DRURY PARHAM.
Proven by DRURY PARHAM & HENRY VARNER 5 July 1816. W. LANCASTER Ord. Sptg. Dist.

Pp. 93-94: L. W. & T. of JOHN CASEY of Dist. of Spartanburg...rec. 14 Aug 1816...to my wife ISABELA all my lands, during her widowhood...if my wife dies before my grandson JOHN F. CASEY arrives at the age of 21, my land shall remain for use of my children and grandchildren who now live with me...my eight children JOSEPH, MOSE, JESSE, ALLISON, JENNY, SUSANNAH, MARY & CASANDER and my two grandson ALFRED and JOHN whom I have raised....son JOSEPH, Exr...5 Dec 1815...JOHN CASEY (SEAL), Wit: M. CASEY, CHARLES L. STEWART, JAMES STEWART.

Proven by JAMES STEWART 13 July 1816. JOSEPH CASEY Qualifies as Exr., ISABELLA CASEY reufsing to qualify. W. LANCASTER Ord.Sptg. Dist.

Pp. 94-97: L. W. & T. of RICHARD BARRY of Dist. of Spartanburg...rec. 15 Aug 1816... wife ROSE BARRY, half of land I now live on including my dwelling house, at her death to my son RICHARD BARRY, the other half of my land...GENL THOMAS MOORE & ANDREW B. MOORE, to superintend the above division...to wife, Negroes (named)...to POLLEY SMITH, my daughter...to my grandsons JOHN SLOAN, ADAM SLOAN, & ANDREW SLOAN tract whereon my daughter now resides, on the S fork of Tyger River... their mother CATHERINE SLOAN...to son in law ADAM SLOAN, $25 which I loaned to him & all debts which I have paid for him to different persons...wife, son in law ISAAC SMITH, & son RICHARD BARRY, Exrs...16 May 1816...RICHARD BARRY (LS), Wit: THOS MOORE, ANDREW B. MOORE, CHAS MOORE.
Proven by CAPT CHARLES MOORE & GENL THOMAS MOORE 15 Aug 1816. W. LANCASTER, Ord. Sptg. Dist.

Pp. 98-100: L. W. & T. of DAVID LIPSCOMB of Spartanburgh Dist, farmer...rec. 22 Aug 1816. ...my property remain together to school & raise my children until the youngest attains to the age of 14 years...the HEADEN tract, the AUSTELL tract, and that part of the STEEN tract lying on the N side of the Charleston Road, to wife during her widowhood...two negroes lent to my daughters SARAH PETERSON and ELIZABETH PETERSON.... children that is to have my property SARAH PETERSON, ELIZABETH PETERSON, MINOR LIPSCOMB, UNITY LIPSCOMB, PATSEY LIPSCOMB, MARCENICE LIPSCOMB, HOPSON LIPSCOMB, CATEY LIPSCOMB, DOOLEY LIPSCOMB, IRENA LIPSCOMB...friend WILLIAM LIPSCOMB & SMITH LIPSCOMB, Exrs... 3 June 1816...DAVID LIPSCOMB (LS), Wit: JOHN LIPSCOMB, ELIZABETH LITTLEJOHN (X), THOMAS HANCOCK.
Proven by JOHN LIPSCOMB, Esqr. and ELIZABETH LITTLEJOHN 16 Aug 1816...W. LANCASTER, Ord. Sptg. Dist.

Pp. 100-101: L. W. & T. of RICHARD CHESNEY of Dist. of Spartanburg...rec. 22 Aug 1816... to wife ESTHER, $400 in silver...to son THOMAS CHESNEY, 125 A adj. JOHN CHESNEY, which formerly belong to LONGSHORE LAMB...to son NATHANIEL RICHARD CHESNEY, 125 A, the balance of the tract I gave to his brother THOMAS...each of my daughters $500, MARGARET SMITH, ALICE ALEXANDER, JANE CHESNEY, SALLEY CHESNEY....wife ESTHER and friend WILLIAM YOUNG, Exrs...18 July 1816...RICHD CHESNEY (+) (LS), Wit: RICHARD YOUNG, JAMES ALEXANDER.
Proven by JAMES ALEXANDER 22 July 1816. W. LANCASTER, Ord. Sptg.Dist.

Pp. 102-103: L. W. & T. of WILLIAM WILBANKS of Spartanburgh Dist...rec. 19 Feb 1817... to wife PHEBE WILBANKS all of my Real estate during her life and at her death to my two sons WARREN & ELIJAH...to my daughter MARIAH negro girl (named)...to my daughter TERESY negro George...to daughter SUSANNA, $10 worth of property...to wife Negroes (named)...friend JAMES NEWMAN, Exr...2 Geb 1816...W. WILLBANKS (SEAL), Wit: S. FARROW, CARLETON GREER.
Proven by SAMUEL FARROW (no date). W. LANCASTER O. S. D.

Pp. 103-104: L. W. & T. of BENJAMIN COUCH of Dist. of Spartanburgh...rec. 20 Feb 1817... tract on Lishes(?) Creek to my sons LEVI COUCH & ELI COUCH...my younger children to be schooled equal to my elder children...estate real and person to wife while she remains my widow...JESSE BRIGGS & CHANEY STONE, Exrs...24 Apr 1816. BENJAMIN COUCH (C) (SEAL), Wit: JAMES BURK, WILLIAM CAMPBEL (X), JOSEPH VINES(?).

Proven by WILLIAM CAMPBELL 11 Nov 1816. W. LANCASTER, O. S. D.

Pp. 104-107: L. W. & T. of BENJAMIN HIGH of Spartanburgh Dist...to my daughter ELIZABETH
BOMAR a negro girl Daphne...my three daughters PATSEY GRAMBLING, CHARITY
HIGH, and NANCY HIGH have one small negro...my daughter REBEKAH RUSSEL $200...remainder
of estate to wife SARAH HIGH during her widowhood...after her death each of my sons Viz.
RICH HIGH, BURREL HIGH, BENJAMIN HIGH, PASCHAL HIGH, SWEPSTON HIGH & DAVID HIGH have $200
...two grandsons THOMAS MARTIN & JOHN MARTIN, $100 each...son RICHARD R. HIGH have power
of attorney to bring suit against the estate of MOSES OVERTON late of State of Virginia,
decd for money due me from that state...son in law THOMAS BOMAR & son BURNALL HIGH, Exrs.
4 May 1816. BENJAMIN HIGH (LS), Wit: EDWARD BOMAR, JOHN BOMAR.
Proven by JOHN BOMAR 3 Feb 1817. Proven by EDWARD BOMAR on 3 Mar 1817.
THOMAS BOMAR qualified 7 Apr 1817. W. LANCASTER Ord. Sptg. Dist.

Pp. 107-109: L. W. & T. of JAMES CAMP of Spartanburgh Dist...rec. 15 May 1817...to my
son ALFRED, a negro Carter when he arrives at 21...to daughter NARCISSEE, a
negro girl Riah on her marriage day...to my son JOSEPH a negro Patsum...to my son GEORGE
when he arrives at 21...to my son LANGLEY when he arrives at 21...to my daughter HARIET
on her marriage day...to my two youngest sons JAMES & WILLIAM, $500 and one negro boy
each...to wife SARAH CAMP, balance of estate and negroes (named)...house and plantation
where I now live adj. to it over the river...wife to sell my land in Virginia & also
my land on Buck Creek, known by the name of WEST HARRISSes place...wife & JAMES YOUNG,
Exrs...28 Jan 1817...JAMES CAMP (SEAL), Wit: ALEXANDER COPELAND, GEORGE McWILLIAMS,
WILLIAM COPELAND.
Proven by ALEXANDER COPELAND and GEORGE McWILLIAMS. 9 Apr 1817. SARAH
CAMP Qualified as Extx. JAMES YOUNG refusing to qualify. W. LANCASTER O. S. D.

Pp. 109-111: L. W. & T. of SAMUEL NESBITT of Dist. of Spartanburgh...rec. 19 May 1817...
to my son in law THE REVD. JAMES GILLELAND, all that plantation I purchased
of BULOW in possession of sd. GILLELAND and negroes (named)...to my grandson SAMUEL NES-
BITT GILLELAND one negro Bob...to my granddaughter NANCY GILLELAND, $250...to my son in
law JOSHUA BENSON, plantation on South Tygar River, about 600 A, which I purchased from
DYSON & SMITH, also negroes (named)...to grandson SAMUEL NESBITT BENSON, $250...to wife
NANCY NESBETT, $300 annually...to son WILSON NESBITT, residue of my money, lands, chattels
...son WILSON & REV. JAMES GILLELAND, Exrs...3 Sept 1816...SAMUEL NISBITT (LS), Wit:
JAMES SWANZY, HUGH BALEY, JOHN BRASON(?).
Proven by HUGH BALEY and COL. WILSON NESBITT and JAMES GILLELAND qualified
5 May 1817. W. LANCASTER O. S. D.

Pp. 111-112: L. W. & T. of SAMUEL SNODDY...rec. 9 June 1817...my son JOHN to hold negro
in his possession...to son ISAAC when he comes of age, a negro George and
148 A on Jamies Creek...my three youngest sons ANDREW, SAMUEL and ALEXANDER, tract where
I now live...my wife and JAMES CROOK, Exrs....6 Apr 1817...SAMUEL SNODDY (X) (SEAL),
Wit: SAML JAMISON, JAS CHAMBLIN, JOSEPH CROOK.
Proven by SAMUEL JAMESON & JAMES CHAMBLIN and JAMES CROOK and ELIZABETH
SNODDY qualified Exrs...2 June 1817. W. LANCASTER Ord. Sptg. Dist.

Pp. 112-114: L. W. & T. of SAMUEL DUNNAWAY of Spartanburgh Dist...rec. 21 Oct 1817...
to wife MARY the third part of my estate excepting two colts which I have
given to my two Grandsons JOHN & WILLIAM DUNNAWAY...to my daughter SARAH DUNNAWAY, s5
sterling...rest of my estate to be equally divided between ROBERT DUNNAWAY, SAMUEL DUN-
NAWAY, & ELIZABETH PROCTOR...ROBERT & SAMUEL DUNAWAY, Exrs...9 May 1810...SAMUEL
DUNNAWAY (LS), Wit: REUBIN WARREN, JOHN BESS, JONATHAN GUTRY.
Proven by JONATHAN GUTRY 21 Oct 1817. W. LANCASTER O. S. D.

Pp. 114-117: L. W. & T. of ISAAC CROW of Spartanburgh Dist...rec. 22 Oct 1817...unto my
wife, half of tract I ___?___ and negroes (named)...to my daughter HANNAH
land on Tyger River, tract I bought of EDWARD HARKER(?), 132 A...to my daughter HANNAHs
son JOHN, land on Jamies Creek bought of WILLIAM CHUMBLES and THOMSON CLUMBLES & ISAAC
CROW the son of JAMES...to my son SAMUEL CROW and REBEKAH CROW his wife one negro Jack.
...to ISAAC CROW, son of SAMUEL CROW one negro girl Marah...to SAMUEL CROWS daughter
SARAH one negro CHARLOT...to JAMES CROW son of SAMUEL CROW one negro John...to ELIZABETH
CROW daughter of SAMUEL CROW one negro Allen...to SAMUEL CROW, JR. son of SAMUEL CROW
Senr, one negro Lewis...one other tract on Tyger River....tract on Cedar Shoal Creek,
waters of Enoree to ISAAC and JAMES CROW...to BENJAMIN CROW son of SAMUEL CROW, 100 A
on waters of Jamies Creek a tract bought of MICAJAH LINDSEY and the rest of the heirs
of the Widow McCLURKEN...I want the hundred acres taken off of the upper end of sd.
tract adj. CHESNEY & WM POSEY...to SAMUEL CROW son of ISAAC CROW JUNR, all the balance
of the tract given to BENJAMIN CROW, son of SAMUEL CROW...to SARAH CROW one set of cur-
tains...rest of my estate to be divided amon wife, my daughter HANNAH LANGSTON, SAMUEL

CROW & ISAAC CROW...JOSEPH BARNETT and SAMUEL WOODRUFF, Esqr. Exrs...ISAAC CROW (/) .
Wit: JOSEPH BARNETT, SAMUEL WOODRUFF SENR., ESTHER SHURLY (/).
        Proven by JOSEPH BARNETT, SAMUEL WOODRUFF & HESTER SHURLY 22 Oct 1817. W. LANCASTER
Ord. Sptg. Dist.

Pp. 117-119: L. W. & T. of HANNAH TIMMONS...rec. 23 Oct 1817...to my neice MARY ANN WINGO
            boy George...(later names her as MARIUM)...to my nephew JESSE TIMMONS my
mare...to my nephew SPARTAN ALLEN...½ dozen chairs and flax wheel be sold...money divided
between MARIUM WINGO and CATY WINGO...if MARIUM or CATY should die before coming of age,
should go to surviving one...my sister DOLLY ALLENs children...my sister ELIZABETH TIM-
MONS, Extx...9 May 1817. HANNAH TIMMONS (+) (SEAL), Wit: THOS. BOMAR, EDWARD BOMAR,
JOHN TIMMONS.
        Proven by THOMAS BOMAR and JOHN TIMMONS. 23 Oct 1817. W. LANCASTER, O. S. D.

Pp. 119-121: L. W. & T. of MATTHEW McBEE of Dist. of Spartanburgh...rec. 23 Oct 1817...
            to my son MATTHEW McBEE, land I now live on lying on Packolet River...the
other part of sd. tract to my son JEREMIAH McBEE...to my daughter RACHEL McBEE, tract on
head of Horse Creek...divided between my daughters RACHEL and ANNA at my wifes death....
to my granddaughter BETSY DODD, one cow & calf...to my sons JOHN, ELIJAH & WILLIAM McBEE
and JAMES DODD, five shillings...wife FANNY and sons JOHN, JEREMIAH to be Exrs...9 Jan
1817...MATTHEW McBEE (LS), Wit:WILLIAM GORE, JEREMIAH McBEE, MATTHEW McBEE.
            Proven by WILLIAM GORE 6 Sept 1817. Exrs. qualified 23 Oct 1817.

Pp. 121-122: L. W. & T. of JOHN FOSTER of Dist. of Spartanburgh...rec. 24 Oct 1817...
            to wife MARY FOSTER, negroes (named)...plantation and household furniture
to wife...to be divided between sons JOHN & WILLIAM FOSTER...to MAHALA FOSTER, dau. of
my son JOHN FOSTER, negroes (named)...to my daughter JANE HART, negro Molly...son JOHN
FOSTER and grand son in law ANDREW CRAMBLING, Exrs...14 Feb 1817...JOHN FOSTER (+) (LS)
Wit: ROBERT WOOD, E. CLEMENT.
            Proven by ROBERT WOOD and EDWARD CLEMENT 24 Oct 1817. W. LANCASTER O. S. D.

Pp. 122-124: L. W. & T. of THOMAS COMPTON of Dist. of Spartanburgh...rec. 24 Oct 1817...
            to wife RACHEL COMPTON all my land with the husband utensils...my sons
THOMAS COMPTON & MATTHEW COMPTON, land and house to be equally divided upon paying
JAMES COMPTON and WILLIAM COMPTON my sons, $50 each...to my daughter DELILAH COMPTON...
children WM & JAMES & DELILAH COMPTON & MARY HOUSE...wife & son THOMAS COMPTON, Exrs....
8 Mar 1817...THOS COMPTON, Wit: WM BEARDAN, JAMES HAM SENR., JOHN BEARDAN SENR.
            Proven by WILLIAM and JOHN BEARDAN 24 Oct 1817. W. LANCASTER O. S. D.

Pp. 124-125: L. W. & T. of JOSEPH WOODRUFF of Dist. of Spartanburgh...rec. 18 Dec 1817...
            to wife ANNA WOODRUFF, one negro LUCY...to sons SAMUEL & THOMAS & CALEB
WOODRUFF and daughters POLLEY ALLEN, EUNICE SPARKS, SALLY HENDRY, & ELIZABETH ALLEN,
$100 each...to daughter ANNA WOODRUFF, $150...sons JOSEPH WOODRUFFs heirs...to my son
JOSEPH $2....JOHN CROCKER, NATHANIEL WOODRUFF, son of THOMAS WOODRUFF, Exrs....22 Sept
1817...JOSEPH WOODRUFF (/) (SEAL), Wit: WM. L ALLEN, JOHN B. HENDRIX, WILLIAM JONES (X).
            Proven by JOHN B. HENDRIX...24 Nov 1817. W. LANCASTER, Ord. Sptg. Dist.

Pp. 125-127: L. W. & T. of COL. ISHAM FOSTER of Dist. of Spartanburgh, planter,...rec. 4
            Mar 1818...to wife HOLLEY, one negro man Abram and negro woman and plantation
I live on ...after her death to be divided among my children, except for the land which
is for DAVID FOSTER...to son DAVID, negro John...to daughter DELILAH, negro Reuben...to
grandson ABRAHAM (ABSALOM?) FOSTER, $100...when he comes of age....to daughter ANNE HAWK-
INS, negro Betsey...sons ROBERT FOSTER, PATSEY BROWN, NANCY FOSTER, POLLEY TRAYLOR, each
five shillings...sons ROBERT & DAVID FOSTER, Exrs....5 Aug 1816...ISHAM FOSTER (LS),
Wit: ALEXANDER RODDY, JAMES VERNON, BYRD LEATHERWOOD (LINTHERON??).
            Proven by all three wit. 15 Oct 1817.

Pp. 127-128: L. W. & T. of WILLIAM OWEN of Dist. of Spartanburgh...rec. 10 Mar 1818...
            to URIAH WALLING two cows and calves...all the rest to wife SUSANNAH OWEN
and at her decease to my youngest daughter MARTHA OWEN....daughter MARTHA, Extx...7
June 1817...WILLIAM OWEN (X) (LS), Wit: THOMAS POOLE, WILLIAM TURNER, JISTON CHILDS.
            Proven by THOMAS POOL 1 Dec 1817. W. LANCASTER Ord. Sp. Dist.

Pp. 128-129: L. W. & T. of THOMAS SARRATT of Spartanburgh Dist...rec. 10 Mar 1818...
            to wife SARAH SARRATT all that I possess, except for when my daughters
marry they are to have one bed & furniture a piece...to son JOHN SARRATT, one feather
bed at his marriage...wife SARAH & son JOHN Exrs...12 Aug 1817...THOMAS SARRATT (T)
(SEAL), Wit: WILLIAM GRIST, JOHN GRIST, JAMES WATKINS.
            Proven by JOHN GRIST & WILLIAM GRIST 17 Jan 1817 (sic). W. LANCASTER, O. S.
D.

Pp. 130-131: L. W. & T. of JOHN JONES of Spartanburgh Dist...rec. 11 Mar 1818...made 22 Mar 1812...son SAMUEL JONES have land on S side of the branch that runs through my land...called Reedy fork of Abners Creek...son MATTHEW JONES have all land on N side of sd. branch....my wife may live on same during her widowhood....to my daughter PATTY THOMAS JONES, one cow & calf...the rest of my children ANNE HARRISS, ELENOR JONES, WILLIAM JONES, MARJORY JONES, JANE MAYFIELD, one half dollar in trade...sons SAMUEL & MATTHEW Exrs...JOHN JONES (LS), Wit: BENJAMIN WOOD, JOHN WOOD, ALCY WOOD (=).
    Proven by JOHN WOOD and WILLIAM WOOD 2 Feb 1818. W. LANCASTER Ord. Sptg. Dist.

Pp. 131-133: L. W. & T. of WILLIAM FOSTER of Spartanburgh Dist...rec. 20 June 1818...to my daughter ANNA YOUNG, one negro Sarah...to son JONES FOSTER, one negro Abram...to son JAMES one negro Ben...to son MOSES, negro Jack...to daughter MARION(?) SMITH, one negro Beck...to my son ELIJAH FOSTER, negro woman Chany...to daughter SALLY CHAPMAN, negro Nancy...to son GARLAND FOSTER, negro Jude...to son CALVIN FOSTER, negro CAto...to wife MARYAN remainder of estate....son JAMES & JAMES YOUNG Esqr, Lxrs...1 Mar 1817...WM FOSTER (LS), Wit: ARMIN HAWKINS, JANE JONES, HERBERT HAWKINS.
    Proven by all 3 wit 9 Apr 1818. W. LANCASTER Ord. S. D.

Pp. 133-135: L. W. & T. of SAMUEL STEWART of Spartanburgh Dist...rec. 2. Sept 1818...to my son and daughter ROBERT and ANN WHITE, one third part of plantation which has already been surveyed and on which the sd. ROBERT WHITE already has made improvement...to wife MARY STEWART the 2/3 of my plantation, 130 A...to son and daughter SAMUEL & BETSY PEARSON, one half of land and property bequeathed to their mother....to son and daughter WILLIAM & POLLY FRAZER, other half of sd. land...to PATRICK COLWELL, son of WILLIAM and PEGGY COLWELL, my saddle...MR. JOHN CRAWFORD, JOHN PATTON and THOMAS GASTON, Exrs....13 Sept 1814...SAMUEL STEWART (X), Wit: JAMES GILLELAND, WILSON NESBITT.
    Proven by COL. WILSON NESBITT 3 Aug 1818. W. LANCASTER ORD. Sptg Dist.

Pp. 135-137: L. W. & T. of MATTHIAS TURNER of Dist. of Spartanburgh...rec. 2 Sept 1818...to son WILLIAM TURNER, $350...to wife MOLLY TURNER, remainder of my estate...at her death or marriage, estate to be divided among children who may be living....wife MOLLY & COL. WILSON NESBITT, Exrs....29 May 1818...MATTHIAS TURNER (T) (LS), Wit: A. BENSON, WILLIAM COLLINS, THOMAS COLLINS.
    Proven by ABNER BENSON 3 Aug 1818...W. LANCASTER Ord. Sptg Dist.

Pp. 137-138: L. W. & T. of JOHN TURNER of Spartanburgh Dist...rec. 2 Sept 1818...to son NATHAN TURNER, negro Job, as I believe he is an insane person, my executor to take charge of his property...to daughter SALLY TURNER, negro Sarah...wife REBEKAH TURNER...after her death, to be divided among my children or their lawful heirs...JOSEPH PRICE and JOSHUA RICHARDS, Exrs....9 May 1813...JON. TURNER (SEAL), Wit: JESSE TURNER (X), RACHEL PRICE (X), ROBERT PRICE (X).
    Proven by JOSHUA RICHARDS and JOSEPH CAMP Esqr says "he could not prove the hand writing of the decd tho had seen his hand writing, was often with him & never discovered but what he was in his right mind" 17 Aug 1818..JOSEPH PRICE was quallified as Exr 21 Aug 1818. W. LANCASTER O. S. D.

Pp. 138-140: L. W. & T. of GEORGE LEWIS of Spartanburgh Dist...rec. 3 Sept 1818...to my brother EPHRAIM LEWIS, 1000 A on the S side of Tenessee (sic) River granted to me by N. C... to wife MARY LEWIS, the whole of my lands which I now live on and negroes (named)...brother EPHRAIM, Exr....21 Mar 1818...GEORGE LEWIS (LS), Wit: ELIAS BENSON, A. LANCASTER, MAHALA BISHOP.
    Proven by DR. ELIAS BENSON and MAHALA BISHOP 3 Aug 1813 (sic) W. LANCASTER. Ord. Sptg. Dist.

Pp. 140-141: L. W. & T. of BENJAMIN HOWARD of Dist. of Spartanburgh...rec. 3 Sept 1818...to my granddaughter MARTHA CROCKER negro Hester at mine and my wifes death...to my daughter ELIZABETH BATES, remainder of estate...son in law ANTHONY BATES and JAMES POOL, Exrs...20 Feb 1817...BENJAMIN HOWARD (LS), Wit: JAMES POOL, NANCY BATES, MATTHIAS BATES.
    Proven by JAMES POOL 20 Aug 1818. W. LANCASTER, Ord. Sptg Dist.

Pp. 141-142: L. W. & T. of ANN GOODLETT of Dist. of Spartanburgh...rec. 22 Jan 1818....to my grandson ROBERT GOODLETT, son of JAMES & POLLEY GOODLETT, my third of the land which my husband ROBERT GOODLETT possessed at his death whereon I now live...son JAMES GOODLETT, Exr...14 Mar 1818...ANN GOODLETT ( ) (LS), Wit: SPARTAN GOODLETT, PETER GRAY, MARY JONES (X).
    Proven by PETER GRAY and MARY JONES 2 Nov 1818. W. LANCASTER Ord. Sptg. Dist.

Pp. 142-144: L. W. & T. of GEORGE ROWLAND of Dist. of Spartanburgh...rec. 23 Mar 1819...unto my daughter HANNAH WALKER, during her lifetime negroes...to wife NANCY

ROWLAND three negros (named)...also my plantation, if she marries to return to my son
HENRY J. ROWLAND...rest of my children ELIZABETH ROWLAND, ROLLY M. ROWLAND, FABYAN ROW-
LAND, PEGGY ROWLAND, RAMOTH ROWLAND, HENRY ROWLAND...land on Richland Creek, I purchased
of ISHAM FOSTER, which was the property of TINSLEY...the other tract purchased of JOHN
ANDREWS, another tract purchased of JAMES PARK, which JOHN N. CRUSE made the right to,
also tract in N. C. which is in WHITESIDES Settlement...to RAMOTH ROWLAND, my daughter
land on Lawsons Fork, purchased at Sheriffs sale, which was the property of JAMES BARRETT
...daughter MERIA(?) ROWLAND, $20...   wife N. NANCY ROWLAND, JOHN DODD, Exrs...23 Apr
1817...GEORGE ROWLAND (LS), Wit: NICHOLAS WOODY (X), WILLIAM WOODY, _____.
         Proven by NICHOLAS WOODY 1 Mar 1819. W. LANCASTER Ord. Sptg. Dist.

Pp. 144-145: L. W. & T. of EDWARD BARNETT of Spartanburgh Dist....rec. 23 Mar 1819...
         estate to be divided between my wife and my grandson JOHN BARNETT...WILLIAM
W. HARRISS and JAMES FOSTER, Exrs...4 Feb 1819...(+); Wit: DAVID GOLIGHTLY, PHILIP OTTS,
THOMAS VAUGHN.
         Proven by all 3 wit. DAVID GOLIGHTLY saith: The will was read to him & he
made this mark as his signature to the will and was of a sound disopsing mind,Memory,
& understanding The reason why he did not sign the will was not the fault of the decd
but the fault of this witness...1 Mar 1819. W. LANCASTER Ord. Spt. Dist.

Pp. 145-147: L. W. & T. of THOMAS MAYES of Dist. of Spartanburgh...rec. 2 Dec 1819...
         my father and mother JAMES MAYS & JEAN MAYS and my sister JEAN MAYES, to
have negro Toby...brothers MATTHEW MAYS & EDWARD MAYES...stock to fall back into my
fathers estate...19 Apr 1814...THOS MAYES (LS), Wit: SAML ARCHEBALD, J. P. MEANS.
         Proven by ARCHEBALD 15 Sept 1819 and quallified MATTHEW MAYES, Admr. with
the will annexed. W. LANCASTER O. S. D.

Pp. 147-149: L. W. & T. of THOMAS HARRISON of Spartanburgh Dist...rec. 2 Dec. 1819...
         wife JEMIMAH HARRISON to have all my lands, negroes, etc....after her
death son THOMAS HARRISON JUNR, shall have negro Violet...children ANNY BONNER, SARAH
MILLER, MARY PHILIPS, BAYLIS HARRISON, REBEKAH JAMES, WILLIAM HARRISON, MARTIN HARRISON
& THOMAS HARRISON, each an equal share...sons BAYLIS & THOMAS, Exrs...23 Apr 1819...
THOMAS HARRISON (X) (LS), Wit: THOMAS CLARY (X), BRIANT BONNER, JOSEPH CAMP.
         Proven by THOMAS CLARY and JOSEPH CAMP 4 Oct 1819. W. LANCASTER Ord. S. D.

Pp. 149-150: L. W. & T. of JANE THOMSON of Spartanburgh Dist...rec. 2 Dec 1819...to son
LAWSON THOMSON, plantation on which I live, 400 A...to daughter ESTHER
BURTON, $100...to MARY WRIGHT, $100...to SARAH TRAIL, $100...son LAWSON, Exr...17 Feb
1816...JEAN THOMSON (SEAL), Wit: JAMES COMPTON, THOMAS MILLER, JAMES CALVERT.
         Proven by all 3 wit. 2 Aug 1819. W. LANCASTER Ord. S. D.

Pp. 150-151: L. W. & T. of JOHN D. PALMER of Dist. of Spartanburgh...rec. 2 Dec 1819...
         to Brother ELIAS PALMER, all my estate real and personal...brother ELIAS
Exr...J. D. PALMER (LS), Wit: JOHN R. EARLE, W. HUNT, SIMPSON FOSTER.
         Proven by all 3 wit. 9 Nov 1819. W. LANCASTER Ord. S. D.

Pp. 151-153: L. W. & T. of JAMES HAM of Spartanburgh Dist...rec. 22 Dec 1819...to wife
AVADILLA HAM, all my land...at her marriage or death to be divided among
my seven children JEAN HAM, DIANNA HAM, WILLIAM HAM, JAMES HAM, MOSES & JACOB JAM, SAMUEL
HAM...friend ANDREW THOMSON, son JAMES HAM, Exrs...5 Feb 1804...JAMES HAM (SEAL), Wit:
THOMAS WILLIAMS, GEORGE THORNTON, MARK THORNTON.
         Proven by GEORGE THORNTON 10 Dec 1819. W. LANCASTER O. S. D.

Pp. 153-155: L. W. & T. of JOHN WOOD of Dist. of Spartanburgh...rec. 22 Dec 1819...
         to my wife MADEN WOOD, plantation I now live on, at her death to be divided
among the children...to son JAMES WOOD, tract where he now lives, quantity unknown
running from Lawrence line (sic) to the Creek, GRAYS line, JOSEPH LAWRENCE line...son
JOHN WOOD & son COLEMAN WOOD...my daughters to have one bed and furniture at their
marriage...sons JAMES & JOHN WOOD, Exrs...27 Dec 1802 N. B. the part of the mill
that is in Co. my self & Brannon, I leave to my wife...28 Dec 1802. JOHN WOOD (+)
Wit: ISM FOSTER, JOHN CHAPMAN, JOHN WINGO.
         Proven by JOHN WINGO 22 Dec 1819. W. LANCASTER O. S. D.

Pp. 155-156: L. W. & T. of THOMAS PRICE...rec. 25 June 1820...all to be in hands of my
wife....
         Proven by ROBERT LIGON, Esqr., ANN THOMAS & DAVID P. WILMOTT say that
sd. PRICE was in his proper senses, they saw sd. decd on 25 Apr last at night, and he
said that he would sign it in the morning...letters of admn. granted with will annexed
17 May 1820. W. LANCASTER O. S. D.

Pp. 156-157: L. W. & T. of ASA CALLICOT of Spartanburgh Dist...rec. 12 Dec 1820...made 21 Aug 1820...the whole of my estate to my wife MARGET CALLICOT to raise and support my three children WILLIAM, JAMES, and ASA...ALEXANDER PREWITT SENR, Exrs... ASA CALLICOT (LS), Wit: SML. HAMM, JOSEPH RED, JOHN HINDMAN.
Proven by JOSEPH RED & SAMUEL HAMM 28 Oct 1820. W. LANCASTER Ord. S. D.

Pp. 157-159: L. W. & T. of JOHN LEATHERWOOD of Dist. of Spartanburgh...rec. 13 Dec 1820... to wife PRISCILLA, 4 negroes (named)...350 A of land...150 A I give to my son JAMES LEATHERWOOD ...90 A to son ISAAC, half of tract purchased of my fathers estate on Jamies Creek...to daughter ELIZABETH LEATHERWOOD, bed & furniture...to daughter JANE LEATHERWOOD bed & furniture...to daughter NANCY...to sons and daughters JOHN B. LEATHER-WOOD, SPENCER LEATHERWOOD, WILLIAM LEATHERWOOD, MILES LEATHERWOOD, ELIZABETH LEATHERWOOD, ISAAC LEATHERWOOD, JANE LEATHERWOOD, NANCY LEATHERWOOD, JAMES LEATHERWOOD, ZACHARIAH LEATHERWOOD, grandson NATHANIEL son of JESSE LEATHERWOOD, gets and equal portion...son JOHN B. LEATHERWOOD and WM YOUNG, Exrs....14 June 1820...JOHN LEATHERWOOD (LS), Wit: WM YOUNG, JOSEPH BARNETT, JAMES HOBBY.
Proven by WILLIAM YOUNG and JOSEPH BARNETT 24 Aug 1820. W. LANCASTER, O. S.D.

Pp. 160-161: L. W. & T. of SAMUEL CATHCART of Dist. of Spartanburgh...rec. 15 Dec 1820... to son JAMES ½ of all my lands, adj. JOHN REDs fence, across the fence between JOHN & JAMES already agreed upon...to son JOHN other ½ ....to daughter MARTHA CLARK, SALLY HINDMAN, NANCY FOSTER, ANNA GRICE they have had as much as I intend... son JAMES, Exr...29 May 1820...SAMUEL CATHCART (LS), Wit: ASA COLLICOT, JOHN HINDMAN, W. LANCASTER.
Proven by ASA CALLICOT & JOHN HINDMAN...19 Aug 1820. W. LANCASTER, O. S. D.

Pp. 161-164: L. W. & T. of JOHN VOINSET of Spartanburgh Dist...rec. 15 Dec 1820... to wife MARY VOINSET, all my lands etc. during her widowhood; my daughters LUCY, PATSEY, & MARY VOINSET each a feather bed & furniture when they marry or arrive at age...to daughter RHODA MORNINGSTAR...sons JOHN & JOHSNON VOINSET...wife and friend THOMAS FARMER, Exrs...16 Apr 1820...JOHN VOINSET (X) (LS), Wit: FENDAL W. ROBERTSON, EDWARD GREEN (X), ELIZABETH ROBERTSON (X)...to THOMAS FARMER the house and plantation where he now lives...23 Apr 1820. JOHN VOINSET (X) (LS),
Proven by EDWARD GREEN & ELIZABETH ROBERTSON 14 Sept 1820. W. LANCASTER, Ord. S. D.

Pp. 164-168: L. W. & T. of JOHN HINDMAN of Dist. of Spartanburgh...rec. 16 Dec 1820... to wife MARTHA HINDMAN, part of land I now live one adj. THOMAS PREWITS line, Colliers Branch, Tyger River, adj. JOHN WALKERS line and WILKINS line...100A.... to son DANIEL HINDMAN, the sd. land and improvements thereon...to son SAMUEL HINDMAN, part of sd. 400 A tract adj. JOHN VINES, THOMAS WRIGHT, Boswells Spring branch, JOHN WILLIAMS line, 100 A...to son ALEXANDER HINDMAN, part of sd. 400 A...to daughters MARTHA & JINNY HINDMAN, each bed & cotton wheel...at my wifes death to DANIEL, PATSEY, & JENNY HINDMAN...to DANIEL my Bible...son WILLIAM one of Westleys Notes...to son JOHN...to son JAMES, the death of Abel...to son ALEXANDER, my testament...to son SAMUEL Moores book on Baptism...to daughter JENNY my song book...divided between WILLIAM HINDMAN, ROBERT HINDMAN and JAMES HINDMAN...wife and son JOHN, Exrs...10 Apr 1819... JOHN HINDMAN.
Proven by ELI VICE, JOHN WILLIAMS, who testified to his handwriting. 17 Nov 1820. JOHN HINDMAN quallified as Exr. 20 Oct 1820. W. LANCASTER O. S. D.

END OF WILL BOOK A

Page 1: 27 Nov 1784, WILLIAM THOMAS of Cheraw Dist., to MORGAN BROWN of same, for ₺14s10
SC money...land in St. David's Parish, on NE side Pee Dee, beginning at the divid-
ing line between sd. THOMAS and BROWN, head of small branch of Hicks's Creek, adj. to
tract granted to BEDINGFIELD, 79 A...WM THOMAS, Wit: DAVID LARGE, EDWARD BROWN.
Rec. 28 Mar 1786. Proven 7 Mar 1786 by WILLIAM THOMAS, JNO WILSON, Clk C.

Page 2: 27 Nov 1784, WILLIAM THOMAS of St. Davids Parish to MORGAN BROWN of same, for
₺28s10...land on NE side Peedee River, adj. BEDINGFIELD, Hicks Creek, including
a new improvement made by sd. BROWN...WILLIAM THOMAS (LS), Wit: DAVID LARGE, EDWARD BROWN.
Rec. 26 Mar 1786. Proven by WILLIAM THOMAS 7 Mar 1786. JNO WILSON Clk. C.

Page 3: PHILIP PLEDGER of Marlborough County, for divers good causes gives to the regular
Baptist Church at the Cheraws, 2 acres, part of 100 A granted to WILLIAM ANCRUM
10 Jan 1771 and conveyed from sd. ANCRUM to JOSEPH PLEDGER by L. & R. 2 & 3 Sept 1771,
conveyed from JOSEPH PLEDGER to PHILIP PLEDGER by deed 2 Sept 1784...in Marlborough Co.,
on the NE side Peedee River on naked Creek and the end of sd. PHILIP PLEDGERS saw-mill...
30 Oct 1785. PHILIP PLEDGER (LS), Wit: THOMAS COCHRAN, WELCOM HODGES, BENJN DAVID.
Rec. 22 Mar 1786.

Page 4: 24 Nov 1785, WILLIAM GORDEN of Marlborough Co., to MORGAN BROWN of same, for ₺200
...200 A on NE side Peedee River, in the swamp of Hicks's Creek, reedy marsh of
the beaverdam Creek, adj. WILLIAM BEDINGFIELDs line, granted to ANTHONY HUTCHINS 24 Apr
1762, conveyed by him to JOHN WRIGHT by deed, and by sd. WRIGHT to ALEXANDER GORDON, by
deed 11 Jan 1773, and by the sd. ALEXANDER GORDON to WILLIAM GORDON in the L. W. & T. of
sd. ALEXANDER 1 April 1785 and by deed of partition from MARY GORDON 23 Nov 1785...WILLIAM
GORDON (LS), Wit: CARNEY WRIGHT, GEORGE STROTHER. Rec. 29 Mar 1786.

Page 5: WILL REED by and with the consent of WM PEGUES and CLAUDIUS PEGUES Esqrs, Exrs.
of ESTATE of JAMES REED decd, for ₺20 s11 d5 sterling, paid by HUBERT STEPHENS
...50 A granted 25 Apr 1763... 4 July 1785,...WILL REED (X) (LS), Wit: CLAUDIUS PEGUES, JR.,
ROBERT BEJGERT(?). Rec. 4 Apr 1786.

Pp. 6-7: 8 July 1785, HUBBARD STEVENS of Dist. of Charraws, planter, to JAMES GILLESPIE
of same, for ₺50 sterling...50 A on NE side Peede River adj. JOHN McBRIDES, near
GORDONS land called Davis folly...granted to JOHN CRAWFORD 20 Apr 1763, conveyed to JAMES
REED 15 Nov 1763, conveyed from JAMES REED to WILLIAM REED by L. W. & T. , then to sd.
HUBBARD STEVENS...HUBBART STEVENS (H) (LS), Wit: WM GORDON, JAMES DEU(?), JAMES McCARTHY
(X). Rec. 4 Apr 1786.

Pp. 7-8: 25 Nov 1783, JOHN BROWN of Anson Co., N. C. planter, to JOHN HUSBANDS of St.
David's Parish, S. C., for 700 Spanish milled dollars...90 A part of 200 A
granted to JOHN BURY 6 Oct 1748, then conveyed to EDWARD IBRY, then to WILLIAM HAMAR, adj.
to property of heirs of WILLIAM LITTLE, heirs of FRANCIS GILISPIE, adj. JOHN WILSON...
JOHN BROWN (LS), Wit: MORGAN BROWN, THO POWE Q. J., JOHN SPEED.
Proven December term by MORGAN BROWN & JOHN SPEED. JNO WILSON Clerk Ct.
Rec. 6 Apr 1786.

Pp. 9-10: 23 Nov 1785, MARY GORDON, widow of ALEXANDER GORDON, late deceased of Marlborough Co., to WILLIAM GORDON of same,..whereas sd. ALEXANDER GORDON decd did by
his L. W. & T. dated 1 Apr 1785, did devise unto sd. MARY one third part of tract of 300
A and to WILLIAM GORDON his son two thirds of 300; for s 10, sd. MARY sells to WILLIAM
her land on Hicks Creek, adj. WILLIAM BEDINGFIELDs line, 200 A granted to ANTHONY
HUTCHINS 24 Apr 1762, conveyed to JOHN WRIGHT, and then to ALEXANDER GORDON 11 Jan 1773...
MARY GORDON (+) (LS), Wit: MORGAN BROWN, JOHN HUSBANDS, JAMES GILESPIE.
Proven Dec term. JNO WILSON Clerk. Rec. 7 Apr 1786.

Pp. 11-12: 23 Nov 1785, WILLIAM GORDON of Marlborough Co., son of ALEXANDER GORDON decd.,
to MARY GORDON, widow of sd. ALEXANDER, for s 10...100 A granted to ANTHONY
HUTCKINS 24 Apr 1762, conveyed to JOHN WRIGHT, then to sd. ALEXANDER GORDON, on N side
Pee Dee...WILLIAM GORDON (LS), Wit: MORGAN BROWN, JOHN HUSBANDS, JAMES GILESPIE.
Proven December term. Rec. 10 Apr 1786.

Pp. 13-14: 8 Nov 1777, JOHN DARBY to BURJESS WILLIAMS, for ₺ 500...100 A, the NW part of
200 A granted to sd. JOHN DARBY 15 May 1771, on NE side Pee Dee adj. BURJESS
WILLIAMS, SAMUEL WISE, and vacant land...JOHN DARBY , Wit: EDWARD GEAGIN, FUSTRAM THOMAS,
JAMES HICKS.
Rec. 18 Apr 1786.

Pp. 14-15: 7 June 1784, BURJESS WILLIAMS of Cheraw Dist., to THOMAS HARRINGDINE of same,

for £ 100...100 A granted to sd. WILLIAMS, 10 Apr 1771 in Cheraw Dist., on N side Pee Dee
bounded on all sides by vacant land...BURJESS WILLIAMS (+) (LS), Wit: JOHN PLEDGER, E.
JONES, GULLY MOORE.
    So Carolina, Cheraw District: Proven by JOHN PLEDGER before TRESHAM THOMAS, J. P.
15 Apr 1785.   (No rec. date.)

Pp. 16-21: 25 Nov 1778, SAMUEL WISE of St. Davids Parish, SC, Esqr., to WILLIAM THOMAS of
           same, for (lease s5, release £ 10,000 Va. money)...several tracts (1)350 A
on N side Pee Dee adj. CLAUDIUS PEGUES, CLARK, part of a tract granted to JOHN CLARK in
N. C., 500 A 2 Oct 1751 and by sd. JOHN conveyed   unto THOMAS WADE 26 June 1770, and
by sd. THOMAS to sd. SAMUEL 14 July 1774;(2) 400 A in Craven County, on N side Pee Dee
granted to THOMAS WADE, dated in Charlestown 17 May 1776 by sd. THOMAS conveyed to sd.
SAMUEL 14 July 1774 (3) 150 A granted to PHILIP PLEDGER on __Nov 1770, conveyed by sd.
PLEDGER to BETTY WISE 18 May 1774 (4) 150 A granted to PHILIP PLEDGER 31 Aug 1774, and
conveyed unto sd. SAMUEL (5) 250 A granted to sd. SAMUEL ___ (6) 300 A granted to sd.
SAMUEL 31 Aug 1774 (7) 250 A granted to sd. SAMUEL 4 May 1776, except that part sold by
sd. SAMUEL to JOHN HEARD for 50 A on lower side Hicks's Creek (8) 500 A granted to sd.
SAMUEL 31 Aug 1774, where CLAUDIUS PEGUES SENR now liveth, on Hardick's branch...land where
WILLIAM HARDICK now liveth (9) part of 1000 A granted to sd. SAMUEL 9 June 1775, 700 A...
adj. to NC-SC line, adj. to gr.ARCHABALD GRAHAM ...total 2450 A...SAMUEL WISE (LS), Wit:
TRISTRAM THOMAS, JAMES DUE, JOHN GOODING (+). Rec. 6 June 1786. Proven 8 Oct 1779 before
CLAUDIUS PEGUES, SENR Esqr.

Pp. 22-23: 24 May 1786, THOMAS LIDE of Marlborough Co., to JOHN WILSON of same, for £800
           sterling...246 A on NE side Pee Dee adj. to river, and estate of FRANCIS
GILESPIE decd, Estate of JAMES REID, decd...THOMAS LIDE (LS), Wit: JAMES FAULCONER,
NATHAN LEAVENWORTH.
    Proven by THOMAS LIDE June term 1786, JNO WILSON Clk. Rec. 8 June 1786.

Pp. 23-24: 8 May 1786, DICKSON PEARCE of Marlborough Co., to DANIEL SPARKS of same, for
           £ 14 sterling...300 A granted to DIXON PEARCE by WILLIAM BULL 2 Apr 1773,
150 A bounded by sd. PEARCE's old survey, BURJESS WILLIAMS, GULLY MOORE...DICKSON
PEARCE (LS), Wit: JAMES MOORE, JAMES COOK, ALEXR. BEVERLY.
    Proven June term 1786. Rec. 8(?) Aug 1786.

Pp. 25-26: 21 Jan 1784, BURJESS WILLIAMS, NEOMAH WILLIAMS & ELIZABETH HARRINGDINE of St.
           Davids Parish, S.C. to JOHN HODGES of same, planter, for £450...250 A granted
to SILAS HARRINGDINE 17 May 1767 on NE side Great Pee Dee, on E side Crooked Creek,
vacant on all sides...BURJESS WILLIAMSON (+) (LS), NEOMAH WILLIAMS ( ) (LS), ELIZABETH
HARRINGDINE (+) (LS), Wit: WILLIS HODGES ( ), JOHN HARRINGTON.
    S. C. Cheraw Dist.: Proven by JOHN HARRINGTON before TRISTRAM THOMAS, 7 Jan
1784.
    Rec. 4 Aug 1786.

Pp. 26-28: 19 Feb 1784, JOHN HODGES _& JAMES COOK, both of St. David's parish, SC, to
           JAMES COOK of same, for one horse...150 A granted unto SILAS HARRINGDINE 7
May 1767, on NE side great Pee Dee, E side Crooked Creek...JOHN HODGES (J) (LS), SARY
HODGES (+) (LS), Wit: GULLEY MOORE, JAMES MOORE.
    Proven by GULLEY MOORE before TRISTRAM THOMAS, J. P. for Cheraw Dist, 1 Feb
1785. Rec. 4 Aug 1786.

Pp. 28-29: 1 Aug 1786, THOMAS HARRINGDINE of Cheraw Dist., to JAMES COOK of same, for
           £ 100 sterling...250 A on Crooked Creek, granted to SILAS HARRINGDINE 17
May 1767...THOMAS HARRINGDINE (LS), Wit: JAMES HODGES, JOSHUA DAVID, GULLEY MOORE.
    Rec. 2 Nov 1786.

Pp. 30-31: 22 Jan 1784, JOSHUA DAVID of Cheraw Dist., to TRISTRAM THOMAS of same, for
           £ 1000...50 A granted to OWEN 1 Feb 1758, and descended from OWEN DAVID to
JOSHUA DAVID by heirship, on NE side Pee Dee, Craven County adj. to OWEN DAVID, WILLIAM
SCRIVEN, and vacant land...and a tract granted to WILLIAM SCRIVEN 29 Nov 1750, 100 A...
conveyed by sd. SCRIVEN to OWEN DAVID by L. & R. 18 & 19 May 1756, in the Welsh tract in
Craven County adj. JOHN EVANS, WILM. JAMES's, WILM. SMITHs...JOSHUA DAVID (LS), Wit:
WELCOM HODGES, BENJ. DAVID. Rec. 9 Dec 1786.

Pp. 31-33: 15 June 1786, GEORGE HICKS of Marlborough Co., planter, to DRURY ROBERTSON of
           same, for (lease & release s 10)...55 A granted 7 June 1774 by WILLIAM BULL...
GEORGE HICKS (LS), SARAH HICKS (LS), Wit: D. HICKS, JOEL WINFIELD, THO. GODFREY.
    Rec. 15 Dec 1786.

Pp. 34-36: 15 & 16 June 1786, GEORGE HICKS of Marlborough Co., planter, to DRURY ROBERTSON
of same, gent., for (lease s20, release Ł 140)...100 A on NE side Pee Dee,
adj. GEORGE HICKS's land, originally property of SAMUEL WILLIAMS, and on all other sides
vacant...surveyed for JACOB LAMPLEY 28 Sept 1770, conveyed by sd. LAMPLEY to REUBEN
TAYLOR by L. & R., 13 & 14 Mar 1772, then to sd. HICKS 15 Oct 1773...GEO HICKS (LS),
SARAH HICKS (LS), Wit: D. HICKS, JOEL WINFIELD, THO. GODFREY.
Rec. 18 Dec 1786.

Pp. 36-37: 22 Apr 1786, PHILLEMON THOMAS of Marlborough Co., planter, to AARON KNIGHT of
same, Hatter, for Ł 29 sterling...land on Welch's Branch, on NC-SC line, at
head of Mountain Branch, part of 1000 A granted to SAMUEL WISE 1775, conveyed by sd.
WISE to WM. THOMAS, then conveyed to PHILLEMON THOMAS...PHILLEMON THOMAS (LS), Wit: J__
SPEED, JOHN WRIGHT JUNR.
Plat recorded in deed book showing: NC line and lands granted to SAMUEL WISE
on all other sides. Rec. 4 Sept 1786.

Pp. 37-38: 2 Aug 1786, BURJESS WILLIAMS of Marlborough Co., to THOMAS HARRINGDINE of same,
for Ł 50 sterling...75 A on NE side Pee Dee, the NW part of 150 A conveyed
from JOHN DARBY to BURJESS WILLIAMS 8 Nov 1777, adj. to sd. BURJESS WILLIAMS...BURJESS
WILLIAMS (X) (LS), Wit: JOSHUA DAVID, WELCOM HODGES. Rec. 4 Sept 1786.

Pp. 38-39: 4 Sept 1786, PHILLEMON THOMAS of Marlborough Co., to WILLIAM THOMAS, son of
sd. PHILLEMON, of same, for Ł5 s16 sterling...300 A granted to SAMUEL WISE
31 Aug 1774, sold unto WILLIAM 25 Nov 1778, and part was conveyed to sd. PHILLEMON 1 June
1779, 150 A...PHILEMON THOMAS (LS), No wit. Rec. 4 Sept 1786.

Pp. 39-40: 19 Aug 1786, DANIEL SPARKS of Marlborough Co., planter, to ALEXANDER BEVERLY
of same, planter, for Ł 30 SC money...50 A on S side Crooked Cr., part of 300
A granted to DIXON PEARCE by WILLIAM BULL, 2 Apr 1773, conveyed to SPARKS by PEARCE 18
May last...DANIEL SPARKS (LS), No Wit: Rec. Sept term 1786 JNO WILSON Clk.

Page 41 : 4 Sept 1786, GEORGE TRAYWEAK of Marlborough Co., planter, to WILLIAM TOWNSHEND
son of JOHN TOWNSHEND of same, planter, for Ł 5 sterling...150 A, part of 640
A, granted to sd. TRAYWEAK 5 June 1786, by WILLIAM MOULTRIE...GEORG TRAWEAK (LS), Wit:
WM WHITFIELD, JOHN HILLSON, JESSE JOHN. Rec. 4 Sept 1786.

Page 42 : GEORGE TRAYWEEK, planter, to BENJAMIN TOWNSHEN of same, planter, for Ł 5 sterling...150 A, part of 640 A granted to sd. TRAYWEEK 5 June 1786...GEORG
TRAWEAK (LS), Wit: JOHN HILLSON, JESSE JOHN, WILLIAM WHITFIELD. Rec. 4 Sept 1786.

Page 43: 10 Oct 1780, JOSEPH GAINS of St. Davids Parish, Craven Co., SC, to JAMES STUBS
of same, for Ł 1000...250 A on Crooked Creek, adj. ENOCH THOMSON...JOSEPH
GAINS (LS), Wit: WELCOM HODGES, JOSIAH DAVID. Łroven by both wit. 4 Sept 1786.

Pp. 43-44: 11 Nov 1773, THOMAS BINGHAM of Craven Co., SC to PHILIP PLEDGER of same, for
Ł 1000... 100 A granted to sd. BINGHAM 3 June 1765, on the three Creeks, at
the mouth of Carters Creek...THOS BINGHAM (LS), Wit: JOSEPH PLEDGER, JESSE COUNSELL.
Proven 3 Nov 1774 by JOSEPH PLEDGER before CLAUDIUS PEDGUES, ESQR, produced
in Court Septr. term, 4th day, 1786. JNO WILSON Clk. Ct.

Pp. 44-45: 31 Oct 1785, PHILIP PLEDGER of Marlborough Co., S. C., to JESSE VINING of same,
for Ł 100 sterling...100 A granted to THOMAS BINGHAM 3 June 1765, on Carters
Cr....PHIL PLEDGER (LS), Wit: JOSEPH PLEDGER, WILLIAM PLEDGER. Rec. 5 Sept 1786.

Pp. 45-45: 25 July 1778, MATTHEW WHITFIELD of Cheraws Dist., SC to EDWARD FEAGIN of same,
for Ł300...land on NE side Pee Dee, on causeway branch, granted to JOHN CHAM-
LESS 2 Apr 1773, sold to WHITFIELD by L & R 11 & 12 July 1773...MATTHEW WHITFIELD
(LS), Wit: AARON DANIEL, ELISABETH DANIEL.
S. C. Cheraw Dist.: Proven before ABEL KOLB, J. P. by AARON DANIEL 25 July
1778. Rec. 5 Sept 1786.
(N. B. There are two pages numbered 45).

Pp. 45-46: 22 Jan 1780, TRISTRAM THOMAS of Craven Co., Cheraw Dist., to ISHAM HODGES of
same, for Ł 1300...5½ A (excepting a lease to JOSEPH PLEDGER), the Se part of
a tract granted to JOSEPH PLEDGER 15 May 1771...on NE side Pee Dee & also another tract
of 100 A granted to THOMAS JAMES, and conveyed to ISHAM HODGES by L & R 24 Oct 1777,
then to sd. THOMAS 17 Jan 1779...TRISTRAM THOMAS (LS), Wit: DANIEL WALSH, EDWARD FEAGIN.
Rec. 5 Sept 1786.

Pp. 46-49: 15 May 1773, FRANCIS WHITTINGTON of Craven Co., planter, to GULLY MOORE of
same, planter, for ₺25...150 A on N side Pee Dee in Welch tract, granted by
WILLIAM BULL, 10 Jan 1771, adj. SILAS HERINGTON...FRANCIS WHITTINGTON (LS), Wit: DAVID
GLENDINING, THOMAS BRYANT (+).
Cheraw Dist.: Proven by THOMAS BRYANT before PHILIP PLEDGER, J. P., 28 July
1773. Rec. 5 Sept 1786.

Pp. 49-52: 27 Jan 1778, WILLIAM ALLSTON of Georgetown to MACKEY McNATT of Craven Co.,
Cheraw Dist., for ₺5000,250 A grant 6 May 1771 on NE side Pee Dee, granted to
JOHN WAETHERS and sold to WILLIAM ALLSTON...on each side of the broad road including
McNATTs race path...WILLIAM ALLSTON (LS), Wit: WILLIAM BEASELY, JOEL McNATT.
Proven before ABEL KOLB 9 May 1778 by JOEL McNATT. Rec. 5 Sept 1786.
Plat included in deed showing road and "Land supposed to be granted to DANIEL SPARKS."

Pp. 52-53: 5 Sept 1786, NICHOLAS DARBY late of Marlbrough Co., planter, to JOHN EDENS of
same, planter, for ₺ 30 sterling...land where JOHN DARBY formerly lived & fell
to NICHOLAS by heirship, 100 A granted to THOS BRIGMAN 22 Oct 1768 by WILLIAM BULL...on
NE side Pee Dee...NICS. DARBY (LS), No wit. Proved by NICHOLAS DARBY 5 Sept 1786 &
recorded. JOHN WILSON Clk. Ct.

Pp. 53-55: 16 Aug 1785, PHILIP PLEDGER of Cheraws Dist., to TRISTRAM THOMAS and JOSEPH &
JOHN PLEDGER of same, for ₺ 1000 sterling...250 A granted to JOHN STUBBS on the
23 Dec 1771 & conveyed to PHILIP PLEDGER 24 May 1774 on Crooked Creek in Craven Co.,
on NE side Pee Dee...also 400 A granted to JOSEPH HARPER 9 Sept 1774, and conveyed
to sd. PHILIP 2 May 1775 in the Welch tract, adj. to JOHN STUBBS, HARDE FLOWERS,
SAMUEL CORD, WILLIAM BAKER...also 200 A granted 26 Aug 1774 to HARDY FLOWERS, and
conveyed by him to sd. PHILIP 25 Nov 1775 in Welch tract adj. ANDREW JOHNSTON's,
JOHN WEATHERS, JOSEPH HARPER, JOHN STUBBS,...and 50 A granted to JOHN STUBBS 23
June 1774, and conveyed to sd. PHILIP 16 June 1775 adj. JOHN STUBBS, WILLIAM ALLSTON
...300 A granted to JOHN ODHAM (sic) 31 Aug 1774 and conveyed to sd. PHILIP 20 Apr
1775 on Crooked Creek, adj. WILLIAM FIELDS, THOMAS BINGHAM, BURJESS WILLIAMS, ENOCH
THOMSON, JOHN STUBBS, FRANCES WHITTINGTON, WILLIAM COTTONHAM & unknown persons...
that part of tract, 100 A...300 A granted to SAMUEL WISE and 200 A granted to JOHN
CARBY....PHIL PLEDGER (LS), Wit: PETER HUBARD, EDWARD JACKSON (X).
Cheraw Dist.: Proven by PETER HUBARD before GEORGE HICKS, J. P. 16 Sept 1785. Rec. 5
Sept 1786.

Pp. 55-57: 17 June 1786, JOHN PLEDGER & JOSEPH PLEDGER to TRISTRAM THOMAS, for ₺ 500...
(tracts in preceding deed)...JOHN PLEDGER (LS), JOSEPH PLEDGER (LS), Wit: WM
BARTLET, EDWARD JACKSON (𝔏) , Rec. 5 Sept 1786.

Pp. 57-59: 20 June 1786, TRISTRAM THOMAS to JOSEPH PLEDGER, for ₺ 250...tracts in preceding deeds...TRISTRAM THOMAS (LS), Wit: WILM. BARTLET, EDWARD JACKSON (X).
Rec. 5 Sept 1786.

Pp. 59-60: 9 Nov 1778, MAJ. SAMUEL WISE to EDWARD CROSLAND, both of S. C., for ₺ 1000...
land in Craven Co., at the SE of QUILOH QUICKs land, JOSEPH JOHNSTON, over
Crooked Creek, adj. NC-SC line, 300 A part of 1000 A granted to sd. SAMUEL WISE, by WILL-
IAM BULL, 9 June 1775...SAMUEL WISE (LS), Wit: JOHN HAMER, MORGAN BROWN JUNR., JOHN HUS-
BAND. Proven by JOHN HUSBAND before THOMAS LIDE. 23 Nov 1778. Rec. 4 Oct 1786.

Pp. 61-62: 26 Nov 1776, JAMES HICKS of SC, planter, to THOMAS QUICK of same, plnater, for
₺ 200...125 A part of 400 A granted to JOSEPH JOHNSTON 8 Dec 1774, and sold
to sd. HICKS 17 Nov 1775 on Naked Creek...JAMES HICKS (LS), Wit: ROBERT HICKS, JESSE
BAGGETT. Proven by ROBERT HICKS before GEORGE HICKS J.P. 28 Nov 1776. Rec. 4 Dec
1786.

Page 62: 27 June 1786, JARROTT WHITTINGTON of Marlbrough Co., to EPHRAIM WHITTINGTON of
same, for ₺ 5 sterling...133 A in Kraggtonn (?) neck adj. WM ALLSTON, THOMAS
AYERS, STALLION, SLAWN...JARROTT WHITTINGTON (LS), Wit: R. WHITTINGTON, BARNET WHITTING-
TON, JOHN COX (+).

Page 63: 16 Sept 1786, JOHN STUBBS SENR & wf EDITH of Marlborough Co., to DANIEL SPARKS
of same, for ₺ 28...150 A, part of 500 A granted to sd. STUBBS by WILLIAM BULL
10 Apr 1771...JOHN STUBBS (+) (LS), EDITH STUBBS (+) (LS), Wit: SILAS PEARCE, THOMAS
STUBBS (+), LEWIS STUBBS (B). (No rec. date.)

Pp. 64-66: 9 & 10 June 1775, JOHN MIKELL of Cheraws Dist., Craven Co., SC, planter, to
AARON DANIEL of same, planter.... (lease sl0, release ₺ 20)...200 A in Welch
tract, on Muddy Creek adj. DANIEL JAMES, PETER SMITH, & vacant land...granted 13 Sept <u>1775</u>

to JOHN MIKELL...JOHN MIKELL (LS), Wit: EDWARD JONES, EDWARD FEAGIN.
    Proven before PHILIP PLEDGER, J. P. by EDWARD JONES. 10 June (year not given).
No rec. date.

Page 67: 30 Dec 1786, GEORGE TRAWECK of Cheraw Dist., Malburg (sic) Co., to JACOB GREEN
        of same, for Ł 5 sterling...150 A on E side of three creeks, adj. RUSSELs line,
including the plantation where sd. JACBO GREEN now lives...GEORGE TRAWECK (LS), Wit:
JAMES SPEERS, HENRY TRAWEEK, MASHACK GEN (+). (No rec. date.)

Pp. 68-69: 11 Dec 1767, PETER SMITH of Craven Co., SC, planter, to MATHEW WHITFIELD of
        same, planter, for Ł 100...300 A where sd. PETER SMITH now lives...PETER
SMITH (LS), ANN SMITH (+) (SEAL), Wit: ALEXD. OUTLAW, EDWARD OUTLAW. ABSALOM DAVIS (+).
        Cheraws Dist.: Proven before CLAUDIUS PEGUES, J. P. by EDWARD OUTLAW, 14 Apr
1778. Rec. 4 Dec 1786.

Page 69: 21 Jan 1778, THOMAS HARMON of Craven Co., Cheraw Dist., SC, to JOHN DANIEL, son
        of AARON of same, for Ł1030...100 A granted to sd. THOMAS HARMON, 22 Oct 1768...
in Welch Tract on Causey Branch, vacant on all sides...THOMAS HARMON (T) (LS), Wit:
MATTHEW WHITEFIELD, ALEXANDER WALDEN, SARAH WALDEN (X). Rec. 4 Dec 1786.

Page 70: 23 Sept 1786, AARON DANIEL of Marlborough Co., planter, to JESSE WILDS of same,
        planter, for s 10 sterling...200 A on Muddy Creek, NE side Great Pee Dee, adj.
DANIEL JAMES, PETER SMITH, ABEL WILDS, granted to JOHN MIKELL 13 Sept 1775, conveyed to
sd. DANIEL by L & R 9 & 10 June 1775...AARON DANIEL (LS), Wit: EDWARD FEAGIN, JOHN ROANE,
GEORGE WILDS. Rec. 5 Dec 1786.

Page 71: 4 Oct 1786, MATTHEW WHITEFIELD & wf ANN of Cheraw Dist., Marlborough Co., to
        JESSE WILDS of same, for Ł 300...300 A on Muddy Creek, granted to sd. WHITEFIELD
4 July 1785...MATTHEW WHITEFIELD (LS), ANN WHITEFIELD (ᑌ) (LS), Wit: EDWARD FEAGIN, JOHN
ROANE, GEORGE WILDS. Rec. 5 Dec 1786.

Page 72: 10 Nov 1786, MATTHEW WHITEFIELD & wife ANN to JESSE WILDS, for Ł 200...200 A
        adj. JOHN LUKEs line, part of 300 A including a mill seat, surveyed for PETER
SMITH 18 Oct 1763, on muddy Creek, granted by WILLIAM BULL, conveyed from SMITH to
WHITEFIELD 11 Dec 1767...MATTHEW WHITEFIELD (LS), ANN WHITFIELD (0) (LS), Wit:SAMUEL
SPARKS, EDWARD FEAGIN, JOHN LANIEL(?). (No rec. date).

Page 73: 10 Aug 1786, JAMES COOK of Cheraw Dist., to DICKSON PEARCE of same, for Ł 43...
        100 A, the NE part of 250 A granted to SILAS HERRINGDINE & may 1767, sold by
THOMAS HARRINGDINE to sd. COOK 3 Aug 1786...JAMES COOK (LS), Wit: JAMES MOORE, GULLEY
MOORE, WILLIAM BRANHAM. (No rec. date).

Pp. 74-75: 3 July 1784, ROBERT REED of St. Davids Parish, planter, to DAVID COLE of same,
        for Ł 100 sterling...191 A granted to JOHN McBRIDE of Anson County, which was
at the time in the Province of N. C., by ARTHUR DOBBS 26 May 1757, land above McBRIDEs
house...conveyed from JOHN McBRIDE to WILLIAM McBRIDE by deed of gift, 13 Jan 1759, and
by the death of sd. WILLIAM fell to HUGH McBRIDE, thence conveyed to DANIEL E. QUINN by
deed 31 Aug 1771, conveyed from him to JAMES REED, and by the Will of JAMES REED, fell to
his son ROBERT REED...ROBERT REED (+) (LS), Wit: JOHN EDENS, HARMON CLARK (+), CHRISTOPHER
MULCASTER.
        Proven by CHRISTR. MULCASTER, before GEO. HICKS, 24 July 1784. (No rec. date).

Page 75: 6 Jan 1787, ABRAHAM ODOM SNR. of Marlborough Co., planter, to JOHN ODOM of same,
        planter, for Ł 60 sterling...50 A including where JOHN ODOM now liveth...part of
300 A granted to sd. ABRAHAM ODOM by WILLIAM BULL 1 Dec 1769, adj. HICKS...ABRAHAM ODOM
(A) (LS), JEN ODOM (J) (LS), Wit: JACOB COCKRAN, WM SMITH (+), JACOB ODOM (+). Rec. 5
Mar 1787.

Page 76: 2 Feb 1787, EDWARD CROSSLAND of Marlborough Co., to LEVI QUICK of same, for Ł20
        ...300 A adj. QUILLAH QUICKS, JOSEPH JOHNSONS, granted to SAMUEL WISE 9 June
1775, conveyed to sd. CROSSLAND 19 Nov 1778...EDWARD CROSSLAND (LS), Wit: N. LEAVERNWORTH,
MORGAN BROWN. Rec. 5 Mar 1787.

Pp. 76-77: 20 Feb 1787, JOHN FRAZER, son of JOHN FRAZER decd. & ANN FRAZER his mother, of
        Dist. of Cheraws, Marlborough Co., to AARON DANIEL of same, for Ł 70 sterling
        ...200 A on Muddy Creek, granted to JOHN FRAZER by WILLIAM BULL, 13 July 1771
rec. in Secretary's Office in Book JJJ, page 119...JOHN FRAZIER (LS), ANN FRAZER (+) (LS)
Wit: MATTHEW WHITEFIELD, ALEXANDER BODIFORD (A), JOHN DANIEL. Rec. 5 Mar 1787.

Page 78: 17 Feb 1787, JOHN FRAZIER, Eldest son & heir of JOHN FRAZIER Decd, to JOHN CARRA-
    WAY HUBBARD of same, for ₤ 20 sterling...100 A, the upper part of 150 A granted
to JOHN FRAZIER decd, 19 June 1772, on SE side Muddy Creek...JOHN FRAZIER (LS), Wit: JOHN
BEATY, DAVID LUKE, WILLIAM BUSLY. Rec. 5 Mar 1787.

Pp. 79-80: Marlborough Co.:, THOMAS STEVENS, planter, bound to GEORGE CHERRY, for ₤ 40...
    interest in three Negroes Milley, Jack, and Hanner, and a black mare, three
feather beds, and household goods...to be paid by 1 Jan 1788...THOS STEVENS (LS), Wit:
WM. BRANHAM, ISAAC PERKINS. Rec. 5 Mar 1787.

Page 80: 3 Mar 1787, GEORGE TRAWOK of Cheraws Dist, Malbury Co., to MASHACK GIN of same,
    for ₤ 60...50 A on E sd three creeks adj. JACOB GREEN, WILLIAM TOWNSEN, ROBERT
BLEAR, part of 640 A granted to sd. TRAWEEK by WILLIAM MULTRY 5 June 1785...GEORG TRAWEK
(LS), Wit: LIGHT TOWNSNED (+), JOHN TOWNSEND (𝒸⌇), BENJAMIN TOWNSEND (𝒸⌇). Rec. 5 Mar
1787.

Page 81: 16 Jan 1787, GEORGE TRAWECK of Marlborough Co., to LUCY BLAIR, for ₤ 30 sterling
    ...200 A on E side Three Creeks, part of 1000 A granted to WILLIAM GOUNEY(?),
17 Dec 1772...GEORGE TRAWEEK (LS), Wit: ROBERT BLAIR, SAMUEL SPARKS, JESSE JOHN. Rec.
5 Mar 1787.

Page 82: 3 Mar 1787, JOHN DANNEL of Marlborough Co., to ISAAC PERKINS of same, for ₤ 10
    sterling...50 A, part of 250 A surveyed for sd. DANNEL adj. ROFERT HUMES...JOHN
DANNEL (J) (LS), Wit: ISAAC NEAVEL, JOHN LEE (+). Rec. 5 Mar 1787.

Pp. 82-83: 30 Sept 1786, JOHN BROWN of Marlborough Co., to SAMUEL BROWN of same, for ₤ 10
    ...125 A, the S part of 150 A conveyed by FRANCIS WHITTONTON & wf ELIZABETH to
JOHN BROWN 30 May 1766...JOHN BROWN (LS), Wit: THOM ALISON, SUSANNA NUNNY(+), SARAH NUNNY
(+), MOSES MURPHEY, ISOM STROUD(?). Rec. 5 Mar 1787.

Pp. 83-84: 30 Sept 1786, JOHN BROWN of Marlborough Co., to SAMUEL BROWN of same, for ₤ 7...
    50 A in Welch tract, granted 20 June 1754 by JAMES GLEN...JOHN BROWN (LS), Wit:
THOM ALISON, SUSANNA NUNRY (+), SARAH HUNRY (+), MOSES MURPHEY, ISOM STROUD.
Rec. 5 Mar 1787.

Pp. 84-85: 17 Feb 1787, JOHN FRAZIER, Eldest son and heir of JOHN FRAZIER SENR decd, in
    Marlborough Co., Cheraws Dist, SC, planter, to ALEXANDER BODIFORD, for ₤10
sterling...100 A on NE side Pee Dee, adj. sd. FRAZIER, Burton head, Boswell, granted by
WILLIAM BULL to sd. FRAZIER 8 July 1774...JOHN FRAZIER (LS), Wit: JOHN BUSELY, DAVID LUKE,
WILLIAM BUSELY. Rec. 5 Mar 1787.

Pp. 85-86: 6 Mar 1780, HEDER KEETON of Richmond Co., NC, to WILLIAM TERREL of St. Davids
    Parish, SC, Craven Co., for ₤ 10,000...250 A, part of 300 A granted to ABRAHAM
ODOM 1 Dec 1769, conveyed by ODOM to KEETON 28 Sept 1778, on beaverdam branch of Crooked
Creek...HEADER KEATE (LS), Wit: JEAN ODOM (+), JOS PLEDGER. Rec. 5 Mar 1787.

Pp. 86-87: 27 Dec 1780, KEDER KEATON of St. Davids Parish, Craven Co., SC, to JOHN TERREL
    of same, for ₤ 10,000...200 A, on a branch of Crooked Creek, part of 250 A
granted to ENOCH THOMSON 12 Jan 1773, conveyed from THOMSON to PHILIP PLEDGER, then to
JAMES HICKS, then to KEDER KETON, adj. HENRY COUNSEL.......KEDER KEATON (LS), Wit: JOHN
ODOM, JOS. PLEDGER. Rec. 5 Mar 1787.

Pp. 87-88: 26 Feb 1787, THOMAS BROWN of Georgetown Dist., to ABNER BROACH of Marlborough
    Co., for ₤ 25 sterling...100 A including the plantation whereon sd. ABNER
BROACH now lives, part of 400 A granted to sd. THOMAS BROWN 1 Jan 1785 bu BENJ. GUERARD...
THOMAS BROWN (T) (LS), MARY BROWN (M) (LS), Wit: THOMAS PEARCE, SAMUEL SPARKS, WILLIAM
NICKELS (𝒻), Rec. 5 Mar 1787.

Pp. 88-89: 2 Jan 1787, JOSIAH DAVID & wf SARAH of Marlborough Co., to TRUSTRAM THOMAS of
    same, for ₤ 600...50 A granted to JENKIN DAVID 5 Mar 177 , sold by him to sd.
JOSIAH 23 Aug 1779 in Welch tract adj. WILLIAM SCRIVEN...also part of a tract of 100 A
granted to WILLIAM SCRIVEN 29 Nov 1750 & conveyed to OWEN DAVID by L & R 18 & 19 May 1756,
descended from OWEN DAVID to JOSHUA DAVID, being his son and lawful heir, and conveyed
from JOSHUA to JOSIAH by deed 23 Aug 1779...adj. WM SMITH, WILLIAM JAMES...JOSIAH DAVID
(LS), SARAH DAVIS (LS), Wit: BENJM. THOMAS, ISAM HODGES. Rec. 6 Mar 1787.

Pp. 89-91: 2 Jan 1787, TRISTRAM THOMAS & wf MARY of Marlborough Co., to JOSIAH DAVID of
    same, for ₤ 700...land granted to HARDY FLOWERS 26 Apr 1774, conveyed to PHILIP
PLEDGER 25 Nov 1775, to TRISTRAM THOMAS and JOHN PLEDGER and JOSEPH PLEDGER 16 Aug 1785,
and from JOHN & JOSEPH PLEDGER to sd. THOMAS 17 June 1786...100 A on Grimes meadow, adj.

WILLIAM ALLSTON...TRISTRAM THOMAS (LS), MARY THOMAS (LS), Wit: BENJM. THOMAS, ISAM HOD-
GES. Plat included in deed. Rec. 6 Mar 1787.

Pp. 91-93: 12 Dec 1786, MORGAN BROWN & wf ELIZABETH of Marlborough Co., to NATHAN LAVING-
          SWORTH, physitian (sic), of same for ₤ 2000 sterling...tract on Great Pee Dee
granted to ANTHONY HUTCHINGS & now the property of sd. BROWN, 440 A on Hickses Creek...
a tract granted to WILLIAM TURNER & part of a tract granted to HENRY BEDINGFIELD, all
of which was the property of WILLIAM LITTLE and descended to his daughter ELIZABETH...
that part of 990 A to MORGAN BROWN & ELIZABETH by a writ of partition, adj. to property
of WILLIAM COWARD, STEPHEN PARKER & MRS. KNIGHT, SARAH BONE, ...part of land granted to
JAMES COWARD and conveyed to ARCHABALD GREYHAM, then sold to WILLIAM LITTLE...MORGAN
BROWN (LS), ELIZABETH BROWN (LS), Wit: TRESM THOMAS, THOMAS EVANS. Rec. 6 Mar 1787.

Page 93: Marlborough Co.: To TRISTRAM THOMAS & THOMAS EVANS, Esqrs, I have commissioned
         you to examine ELIZABETH BROWN wife of MORGAN BROWN concerning a deed of the
Real Estate inherited from her father WILLIAM LITTLE...4 Sept 1786 JOHN WILSON, Clk.
Rec. 6 Mar 1787.

Pp. 93-95: ELIZABETH BROWN was examined & relinquished dower, etc. TRISM THOMAS (LS)
           THOS EVANS (LS), Rec. 6 Mar 1787.

Pp. 95-97: 13 Dec 1786, NATHAN LAVINGSWORTH of Marlborough Co., to MORGAN BROWN of same,
           for ₤ 2000....(same property in preceding deed)...NATHAN LEAVENWORTH Wit:
TRISM THOMAS, THOS EVANS. Rec. 6 Mar 1787.

Pp. 97-98: 10 Jan 1787, JOHN HUSBANDS of Marlborough Co., to MORGAN BROWN of same, for
           ₤200...land on Husband's or Beaverdam Creek adj. to MORGAN BROWN, JAMES
GILLESPIE, and Estate of FRANCIS GILLESPIE, 100 A granted 6 Oct 1748 to JOHN BERRY,
sold to EDWARD IRBY, then to WILLIAM HAMER, then descended to JOHN BROWN as heir at law
and sold by BROWN to JOHN HUSBANDS 25 Nov 1783...JOHN HUSBANDS (LS), Wit: THOS POWE,
NATHAN LEAVENWORTH, WILLIAM POWE. Rec. 6 Mar 1787.

Pp. 98-99:29 Jan 1787, JOHN WILSON of Marlborough to MORGAN BROWN of same, for ₤ 10...
          20 A on S side Husbands or Beaverdam Creek...JNO WILSON (LS), Wit: MORGAN
BROWN, SILAS PEARCE. Rec. 6 Mar 1787.

Pp. 99-101: Cheraw Dist.: 22 June 1784, ANTHONY POWNEY of Dist. aforesd, planter, to
            BURREL HUGANS of same, planter, for ₤ 37 s3 sterling...100 A, part of 350 A
granted to ISOM ELLIS 31 Aug 1774, conveyed by L & R to sd. POWNEY 22 & 23 June 1775...
on NE side Pee Dee near WESTFIELDS bluff on three Bays known as DARBYS sandhill & SCOTTS
bays adj. ANTHONY POWNEY & RICHARD WHITTINGTON, AARON PEARSON, MATTHEW WHITFIELD, ABEL
WILDS, THOMAS VINING, WILLIAM EVANS, NATHL BURT, rec. in Secretarys Office in Book SSS,
p. 377...ANTHY POWNEY (LS), Wit: JOHN McIVER JUNR., MOS. PEARSON, JAMES STEERS. Rec.
6 Mar 1787.

Pp. 101-102: 6 Mar 1787, ANTHONY POWNEY of Charleston Dist., to JESSE JOHN of Cheraw
             Dist., Marlborough Co., for ₤ 200 sterling... 100 A, the SW part of tract
of 200 A on NE side Pee Dee, granted to ANDREW SLANN 7 June 1751 by JAMES GLEN...
ANTHONY POWNEY the Elder (Father of the within named ANTHONY POWNEY); sd. ANTHONY POWNEY
the younger is Exr., at Court held at Long Bluff 15 Apr 1777...ANTHY POWNEY (LS), Wit:
EDWD FEAGIN, BENJ. DAVID, WM. BRANHAM. Plat included in deed shwoing adj. to JOSEPH
BROWN, ROGER POWNEY, and P. D. River. Rec. 6 Mar 1787.

Pp. 103-104: Cheraw Dist.: 6 Mar 1787, ANTHONY POWNEY of Dist. aforesaid, planter, to
             THOS VINING of same, planter, for ₤ 10 sterling...125 A, part of a tract of
350 A granted to ISUM ELLIS in Welch Tract, on NE side great Peedee, near Westfields
Bluff and on three bays, known as DARBYS, SANHILL, & SCOTTS bay, adj. to ANTHONY POWNEY,
RICHARD WHITTINGTON, AARON PEARSON, MATTHEW WHITFIELD, ABEL WILDS, WM EVANS, NATHANIEL
BURTS, conveyed by ISUM ELLIS by L & R 22 & 23 June 1775...ANTHONY POWNEY (LS), Wit:
EDWD FEAGIN, BENJN DAVID, WM BRANHAM. Rec. 6 Mar 1787.

Pp. 104-105: 29 Dec 1786, LUKE PRYOR of Marlborough Co., to JOHN WALLER PRYOR of same,
             for ₤ 45 s17 d2...½ of tract surveyed for LUKE 4 Oct 1784 by ALEXD.
CRAIG, granted 1 May 1786...150, half of 300 A...LUKE PRYOR (LS), Wit: JAMES HARRIS,
BARTH. WHITTINGTON, JOHN SPIGHTS. Rec. 7 Mar 1787.

Pp. 105-107: 14 Nov 1771, JOHN BROWN of Craven Co., SC to MARTIN KOLB of same,(lease ₤5,
             release ₤ 500)...150 A adj. HENRY KOLB, granted to sd. BROWN 31 Mar 1761
by WILLIAM BULL...JOHN BROWN (LS), Wit: ARTHUR HART, PETER KOLB, ROBERT LIDE.
Proven by ARTHUR HART before ALEXR. MACKINTOSH, 6 Dec 1771. Rec. 7 Mar 1787.

Pp. 108-110: South Carolina, Craven Co.: 30 & 31 Oct 1783, PETER KOLB of St. Davids Parish
Craven Co., to ISAM ELLIS of same, (lease s 10, release ₺ 42 s 17 sterling)
...150 A adj. HENRY KOLB, granted to JOHN BROWN 31 Mar 1761, conveyed by BROWN to MARTIN
KOLB 14 Nov 1771, transferred by MARTIN to his son PETER by will...PETER KOLB (LS), Wit:
ALLEN CHAPMAN, THOMAS LAMPLEY (X), WILLIAM POWE.
Cheraw Dist.: Proven by THOMAS LAMPLEY before THO POWE, Q. J. 4 Nov 1783.
Rec. 7 Mar 1787.

Pp. 110-111: 25 Dec 1786, WILLIAM STUBBS of Marlborough Co., planter, to PETER HUBBARD of
same, planter, for ₺ 20....100 A, the upper part of 200 A granted to JOHN
SUTTON 4 July 1785 on NE side Peedee River on Muddy Creek adj. PHILIP PLEDGER, WILLIAM
ALLEN, FRANCIS BRIDGS,...sold by SUTTON to STUBBS 30 Oct 1786...WILLIAM STUBBS (+) (LS),
Wit: JAMES MOORE, LEWIS STUBBS (B). Rec. 7 Mar 1787.

Pp. 112-113: 20 Dec 1785, JOHN PLEDGER of Marlborough Co., to WILLIAM PLEDGER of same, for
₺ 300 sterling...100 A granted to JOHN PLEDGER 30 Oct 1772 in the Welch tract
on NE side Peedee River on Naked Creek, adj. PHILIP PLEDGER, THOMAS BINGHAM, & vacant
land...also 300 A granted to SAMUEL WISE 10 Jan 1771, conveyed to JOPSEH PLEDGER by L & R
22 & 23 June 1771, conveyed to JOHN PLEDGER 11 Nov 1773 on Naked adj. PHILIP PLEDGER,
RICHARD GREENWOOD, BURGESS WILLIAMS, CHARLES BARLIN, to sd. WILLIAM PLEDGER, 25 A of this
300...JOHN PLEDGER (LS), Wit: JOS. PLEDGER, ALEX. CRAIG. Rec. 8 Mar 1787.

Pp. 113-114: PHILIP PLEDGER of Cheraw Dist, for goodwill & affection to my grandson JESSE
COUNSEL of sd. Dist, a plantation of 286 A on NE side Pee Dee adj. DAVID
ROACH...first 21 A granted to sd. PHILIP PLEDGER 10 Nov 1761, secondly 112 A, part of 200
A granted to WALTER DOWNS 2 Mar 1743, conveyed to sd. PHILIP PLEDGER, thirdly 37 A, the
NW part of grant to SAMUEL DESAWRENCY 10 Mar 1743, conveyed by sd. SAMUEL to JACOB
DESAWRENCY, then to sd. PHILIP PLEDGER, fourthly 116 A, part of 300 A granted to JOHN
PLEDGER, 15 May 1771...PHIL PLEDGER (LS), Wit: DANIEL WALSH, JOHN PLEDGER, TRIS. THOMAS.
Plat included in deed shows creek and river. (No rec. date.)

Page 115: 20 Nov 1786, MARY GORDON of Marlborough Co., Cheraws Dist., to JAMES DEW of same,
for ₺ 150 sterling...75 A, part of 300 A on NE side Peedee, granted to SAMUEL
GREENWOOD 13 Apr 1748, by JAMES GLEN, conveyed to THOMAS ROGERS by L & R 10 Sept 1765...
to ALEXANDER GORDON 9 Mar 1766, sd. 75 A is the middle Division of sd. 350 A...MARY
GORDON (LS), Wit: JESSE PERKINS (+), WM GORDON, JOSEPH RED. Rec. 8 Mar 1787.

Pp. 116-118: 17 & 18 Sept 1775, MATTHEW WHITEFIELD of Welch tract in Craven Co., SC,
planter, to BARNABAS HENNAGAN of same, planter, for ₺ 16 SC money...250 A
granted to WHITEFIELD by CHAS. GREVE. MONTAGUE 22 Nov 1771 on Crooked Creek...MATTHEW
WHITEFIELD (LS), Wit: THOMAS CONNER JUR., DAVID STEWART (+), JAMES BUSELY. Proven by
DAVID STUART before PHILIP PLEDGER, J. P. for Craven Co. 16 Mar 1773. Rec. 8 Mar 1787.

Pp. 118-119: 8 Mar 1787, JOB BROUGHTON of Marlborough Co., planter, to THOMAS HUCKABIB of
same, planter, for ₺ 30 sterling...200 A on NE side Pee Dee granted 4 Sept
1786 to sd. BROUGHTON. JOB BROUGHTON (+) (LS), Wit: THOS GODFREY, JAS. MOORE, MO. SUTTON
(O), Rec. 8 Mar 1787.

Pp. 119-120: 6 June 1777, BARNABAS HENAGAN of St. Davids Parish, Craven Co., SC, planter,
to DAVID STUART of same, for ₺ 65 SC money...83 A, part of 250 A granted to
MATTHEW WHITEFIELD 22 Nov 1771...BARNABAS HENAGAN (LS), Wit: THOMAS CONNER, LEWIS CONNER,
WILLIS CONNOR. Proven by WILLIS CONNOR before GEO. HICKS, 2 Jan 1787. Rec. 8 Mar 1787.

Pp. 120-122: 12 July 1773, JOHN CHAMBLESS of Craven Co., planter, to MATTHEW WHITEFIELD
of same, planter, for ₺ 80...250 A granted by WILLIAM BULL 1773 on NE side
Peedee in Welch tract...JOHN CHAMBLESS (LS), Wit: JACOB TEMPLE, PETER CHAMLESS, ANNE
BLAIR (A). Proven by ANN BLAIR before PHILIP PLEDGER 20 July 1773. Rec. 8 Mar 1787.

Pp. 122-123: 21 Sept 1765, WILLIAM LITTLE of Craven Co., to JOHN HICKS of same, for ₺ 300
...50 A adj. JOHN HICKS, TURNERs survey, Hicks Creek...WM. LITTLE (LS), Wit:
JAS. STEWART, CARNEY WRIGHT. Recd. 22 Nov 1769, of JOHN HICKS s5...CATHERINE LITTLE.
Proven by JAMES STEWART before CLAUDIUS PEGUES. 29 Jan 1766. Rec. 29 May 1787.

Pp. 124-126: 6 Apr 1778, THOMAS BINGHAM of Cravin Co., planter, & wf SUSANNAH to THOMAS
LIDE of same, planter...335 A in Cravin Co., on Pee Dee, adj. JOHN BROWN,
ABRAHAM COLSON, granted to THOMAS ELLERBEE 5 Sept 1749, sold unto JOHN CROWFORD SENR.,
conveyed by deed of gift to JOHN CRAWFORD JUNR his son, all that tract on lower side of
Phills Creek, and sold by sd. CRAWFORD JUNR 20 Nov 1759 to THOMAS BINGHAM, rec. in Nook
Ŧ, No3. p. 193...for ₺ 500...adj. land formerly sold by BINGHAM to CHARLES BEDINGFIELD,
ABRAHAM COLSON, JOHN BROWN...127½ A...THOMAS BINGHAM (LS), SUSANNAH (X) BINGHAM, Wit:

JOSEPH PLEDGER, JAMES HICKS. Proven by JOSEPH PLEDGER before WM THOMAS 30 Apr 1780.
Rec. 29 May 1787.

Page 127: 4 June 1787, AARON PEARSON of Cheraw Dist, Marlborough Co., to JOHN HALKIM for
        Ŀ 9sterling...100 A on a bay of great Reedy Creek, granted to sd. PEARSON by
WILLIAM MOULTRIE 1 jan 1787...AARON PEARSON (LS) of great Peedee., Wit: JAS. BOLTON,EDWD.
FEAGIN, THOS COCHRAN. Rec. 4 June 1787.

Page 128: 1 Feb 1777, JOHN HATHHORN of Anson Co., N. C. to MOSES PARKER of Craven Co.,
        S. C., for Ŀ 100...land where sd. PARKER now lives, 400 A granted to RICHARD
ODAM by WILL BULL 30 May 1773...JOHN HATHHORN (LS), SARAH HATHHORN (X) (LS), Wit: THOMAS
BROWN (+), HENRY GOODMAN (+), SAMUEL PATE. Proven before GEO. HICKS by THOMAS BROWN 13
Aug 1785. Rec. 4 June 1787.

Pp. 129-130: 6 & 7 Apr 1786, WILLIAM POWE of St. David's Parish, Chesterfield Co., to
        WILLIAM WHITFIELD of same parish, Marlborough Co., (lease s10, release Ŀ 86
sterling)...land granted to sd. POWE by WILLIAM MOULTRIE, 6 Mar 1786, 300 A on NE side
Peedee, adj. WILLIAM ALLSTON & JAMES TOWNSING (sic)...WILLIAM POWE (LS), Wit: ALEXANDER
CRAIG, GEORGE BULLARD, ALLEN CHAPMAN. Rec. 4 June 1787.

Pp. 131-132: 13 Jan 1787, MATTHEW WHITFIELD & wf ANN of Marlborough Co., Cheraw Dist.,
        to BURGESS FEAGIN of same, for Ŀ 29 sterling...100 A on NE side great Pee
dee, granted to JOHN CHAMBLESS 2 Apr 1773, adj. EDWARD FEAGIN...MATTHEW WHITFIELD (LS),
ANN WHITIFELD (A) (LS), Wit: EDWARD FEAGIN, JOSIAH BEESELY, GEORGE BEESELY. Rec. 4
June 1787. Plat included in deed.

Page 132: 8 Feb 1787, ANTHONY POUNCEY of Charlestown Dist., planter, to JOHN BEESELY of
        Cheraw Dist., Marlborough Co., planter, for Ŀ 21...100 A, the N corner of
350 A in Welch tract on NE side great pee dee near Westfields Bluff and on three bays,
adj. MATTHEW WHITFIELDS, THOMAS VININGS, WILLIAM EVANS, NATHANIEL BURK, & ANTHONY
POUNCEY, granted to ISHAM ELLIS 31 Aug 1774, sold to sd. POUNCEY by L & R 22 & 23 June
1775...ANTHY. POUNCEY (LS), Wit: MATTHEW WHITEFIELD, AARON DENIEL, JOHN DANIEL. Rec.
5 June 1787.

Page 133: 3 Mar 1787, AARON PEARSON of Marlborough Co., to JESSE JOHN of same, for s20
        sterling...100 A, part of 405 A adjacent JOHN WARING, JOHN HODGES, ANTHONY
POUNCEY, JOHN WESTFIELD, ISHAM ELLISS, WILLIAM POUNCEY and vacant land granted to
WILLIAM HENRY MILLS and conveyed to AARON PEARSON by L & R 17 & 18 Nov 1775...AARON
PEARSON (LS) of great pee dee, Wit: EDWD FEAGIN, AARON PEARSON, JONATHAN MEEKINS (X).
Rec. 4 June 1787.

Page 134: 1 June 1787, JOHN PLEDGER of Dist. of Cheraws, Marlborough Co., to PETER HUBBARD
        of same, for Ŀ 36...200 A granted to JOSEPH JOHNSON 4 May 1775, sold to sd.
PLEDGER 30 & 31 Mar 1787, in Craven County, on muddy Creek adj. WM BAKER, PHILIP PLEDGER,
JOSEPH HARPER, WILLIAM CORD...JOHN PLEDGER (LS), Wit: JAMES HODGES, WILLIS WILLIAMSON,
EDWD. FEAGIN. Rec. 5 June 1787.

Page 135 missing.

Page 136: 10 Jan 1787, JOHN BROWN of Marlborough Co., to MORGAN BROWN of same, for Ŀ 200
        ...land on Husbands Creek adj. JAMES GILLESPIE, estate of FRANCES GILLISPIE, 100
A, part of a grant to JOHN BERRY 6 Oct 1748, conveyed to EDWARD IRBY, then to WILLIAM
HAMER, then descended to MARY BROWN, wife of STEPHEN BROWN , then to JOHN BROWN, heir at
law...JOHN BROWN (LS), Wit: NATHAN LEAVENWORTH, JAMES BROWN. Rec. 5 June 1787.

Page 137: 27 Nov 1777, JOHN DARBY of Cheraws Dist., planter, to JOHN PLEDGER of same,
        planter, for Ŀ 100...100 A, the SE part of 200 A granted to sd. DARBY 15 May
1771 adj. BURGESS WILLIAMS, SAMUEL WISE, & vacant land....JOHN DARBY (LS), Wit: JOSEPH
PLEDGER, TRISTRAM THOMAS, PHIL: PLEDGER. Rec. 7 June 1787.

Pp. 138-140: 23 & 24 June 1771, SAMUEL WISE of St. David's Parish, SC to JOSEPH PLEDGER
        of same, for (lease 10, release Ŀ 500)...300 A on Naked Creek...adj. PHILIP
PLEDGER, BURGESS WILLIAMS, THOS. BINGHAM...SAMUEL WISE (LS), Wit: THOMAS JONES, THOS.
ELERBE, JESSE COUNCELL. Proven before WILLIAM PEGUES 11 Nov 1775 by THOMAS ELERBY.
Rec. 7 June 1787.

Page 141: 11 Nov 1773, THOMAS BINGHAM of Craven Co., SC to JOHN PLEDGER of same, for Ŀ
        2000...150 A (Excluding what lies on an older Survey if any), granted to sd.
BINGHAM 15 May 1771 adj. SAMUEL WISE, JOSEPH PLEDGER...THOMAS BINGHAM (LS), Wit: JOSEPH
PLEDGER. JESSE COUNCELL. Proven before CLAUDIUS PEGUES by JOSEPH PLEDGER 3 Nov 1774.

Preceding deed rec. 7 June 1787.

Page 142: 11 Nov 1773, JOSEPH PLEDGER of Craven Co., to JOHN PLEDGER of same, for ₤ 1000
     50 A granted to sd. JOSEPH 27 Nov 1770 in Craven Co., on NB side Pee dee,vacant
on all sides...JOSEPH PLEDGER (LS), Wit: JESSE COUNCELL, THOS. BINGHAM. Proven by
THOMAS BINGHAM before CLAUDIUS PEGUES 3 Nov 1774. Rec. 7 June 1787.

Page 143: 16 Jan 1787, JOHN HUSBAND of Marlborough Co., to JOHN WILSON of same, planter,
     for ₤ 200 sterling...200 A on N side Pee Dee on Beaverdam alias Husbands Creek,
part of tract granted to JOHN BURRY 6 Oct 1748, conveyed to EDWARD IRBY, then to WILLIAM
HAMER, the sd. HAMER having no issue fell to his sister the then wife of sd. HUSBANDs...
110 A...JOHN HUSBAND (LS), Wit: MORGAN BROWN, JAMES GILLESPIE. Rec. 7 June 1787.

Pp. 144-146: 5 & 6 May 1767, OWEN DAVID of Craven Co., SC, planter, to JOSEPH FULLER of
     same, (lease s5, release ₤ 200 SC money)...250 A granted to sd. DAVID 30
May 1756...OWEN DAVID (LS), Wit: JOHN BEESELY, DANILE JAMES.
     Draven Co.: Proven by JNO BEESELY before ALEXR. MACKINTOSH 4 Mar 1769.
Rec. 3 Aug 1787.

Pp. 146-147: 2 May 1775, JOSEPH HARPER of Craven Co., SC to PHILIP PLEDGER of same, for
     ₤ 3000...400 A granted to sd. HARPER 9 Sept 1774 in Welch tract adj. SAMUEL
CORD, WILLIAM BAKER, FRANCIS WHITTINGTON, JOHN STUBBS, on Crooked Creek...JOSEPH HARPER
Wit: ALICE HARPER, JOSEPH PLEDGER. Proven before SAML WISE by JOSEPH PLEDGER 6 May 1775.
Rec. 4 Aug 1787.

Pp. 147-148: 25 Sept 1773, JOSEPH FULLER of Craven Co., SC, St. Davids Parish, to PHILIP
     PLEDGER of same, for ₤ 2000...250 A granted to OWEN DAVID 13 May 1756...
to sd. FULLER by L & R,5 & 6 May 1767...adj. THOMAS PAGETT, and vacant land...JOSEPH
FULLER (LS), Wit: JOS. FULLER JUNR (+), PHILIP SNEAD, JOS. PLEDGER. Proven before CLAUDIUS
PEGUES by JOSEPH PLEDGER 3 Nov 1774. Rec. 4 Aug 1787.

Page 149: 24 May 1774, JOHN STUBBS SENR of Craven Co., SC, to PHILIP PLEDGER of same, for
     ₤ 2000...200 A granted to sd. STUBBS 23 Dec 1771 on N side Pee dee, vacant on
all sides...JOHN STUBBS (X) (LS), Wit: DANIEL SPARKS, ABEL KOLB, JOSEPH PLEDGER.
Proven by JOSEPH PLEDGER before CLAUDIUS PEGUES. Rec. 15 Aug 1787.

Page 150: 12 July 1775, JOHN HAWTHORN of Craven Co., SC to JOSEPH PLEDGER of same, for
     ₤ 1000...50 A granted to sd. HAWTHORN 19 Aug 1774 adj. to Great Pee Dee on a
lake called Gardners, adj. JOHN HUDGES, JOHN WESTFIELD, OWEN DAVID, HOWELL JAMES, SAMUEL
GREENWOOD...JOHN HAWTHORN (LS), Wit: WILLIAM THOMAS (W), ISAM GARDNER. Proven by GARDNER
before SAMUEL WISE. 10 Aug 1775.   Rec. 16 Aug 1787.

Page 151: 20 Dec 1786, WINDSOR PEARSE of Randolph Co., N. C. to WILLIAM BENNETT of Marl-
     borough Co., SC, Cheraw Dist., for ₤ 50 sterling...200 A on Crooked Creek...
WINDSOR PEARSE (LS), Wit: ABNEAR BROACH, GRIEF CARREL, JAMES BENNETT.
Rec. 3 Sept 1787.

Page 152: 11 Aug 1787, JAMES BLANTON of State of S. C., planter, to JAMES GILISPIE of same
     planter, for ₤ 50 sterling...land in Marlborough Co., on NE side Pee Dee between
Hicks and Husbands Creek, part of 200 A granted to JAMES BLANTON 3 Apr 1786, 50 A...JAMES
BLANTON (I) (LS), Wit: JNO WILSON, JOHN HUSBAND. Rec. 3 Sept 1787.

Page 153: 11 Aug 1787, JAMES GILISPIE of Cheraws Dist., Marlborough Co., planter, to JAMES
     BLANTON of same, planter, for ₤ 50...50 A adj. JOHN McBRIDE, near GORDENS land
called Davids folly...granted to JOHN CRAWFORD 20 Apr 1763, conveyed from CRAWFORD to
JAMES REED 15 Nov 1763, then conveyed from JAMES REED by his L. W. & T. to WILLIAM REED
a free Molattoe [sic] , from sd. WILLIAM to HUBBARD STEVENS, then to sd. JAMES GILISPIE...
JAMES GILISPIE (LS), Wit: JNO WILSON, JOHN HUSBAND. Rec. 3 Sept 1787.

Page 154: 29 June 1787, WELCOME HODGES of Marlborough Co., to JAMES HODGES, for ₤ 71...
     the SE part of 100 A on NE side Pee Dee, conveyed from JOHN DARBY to BURGESS
WILLIAMS by deed 8 Nov 1777, from WILLIAMS to sd. WELCOME HODGES by deed 16 Dec 1777...
WELCOME HODGES (LS), Wit: BENJN. DAVID, SARAH DAVID, SAMEL [sic] UNDERWOOD. Rec. 3 Sept
1787.

Page 155: 6 June 1787, THOMAS BINGHAM of Georgetown Dist., SC to GEORGE STROTHER of Marl-
     borough Co., for ₤ 100 sterling...200 A granted to ALEXANDER GORDON 25 May 1757
on NE side Pee dee on N side Phills Creek, place known as Davids folly...THO. BINGHAM
(LS), Wit: JOHN HUSBAND, ELISABETH FIELDS. Rec. 3 Sept 1787.

Page 156: 17 Apr 1787, THOMAS CONNER of Cheraws Dist., to DANIEL McINTYRE [no residence
            stated], for ₺ 25 sterling...100 A on NE side Great Pee Dee near Little Pee Dee
...granted by GOV. MOULTRIE to THOMAS CONNER 17 Aug 1786...THOMAS CONNER (LS), Wit: JOHN
McREA, JOHN McTIMER [?]. Rec. 4 Sept 1787.

Page 157: 3 Apr 1787, JOEL BULLARD of Marlborough Co., to AQUILLA QUICK of same, for ₺ 50
            ...200 A, part of a tract of 400 A granted to sd. BULLARD on Croocked [sic] Cr.
....JOEL BULLARD (LS), Wit: SAMUEL TAYLOR, ALLEN CHAPMAN, Plat included in deed.
Rec. 4 Sept 1787.

Page 158: 10 Nov 1783, SARAH KOLB of St. Davids Parish, to EDMUND BAFFORD [?], ABEL
            EDWARDS, MAGNIS CARGILL, & JOHN DAVID, Deacons of the Baptist Church holding
Calvinistic Doctrines agreeable to the baptist confession of faith at the Welsh neck on
Pee dee...land originally granted to DAVID JAMES...SARAH KOLB (LS), Wit: GEO. HICKS,
JAMES SMART. Rec. 4 Sept 1787.

Pp. 159-160: 30 & 31 Mar 1787, JOSEPH JOHNSON of Prince Georges parish, S. C., to JOHN
            PLEDGER of State Afresd., planter, in Cranven County, Great Pee Dee, (lease
s10, release ₺ 5 sterling)...200 A in Craven Co., on muddy creek , adj. WILLIAM BAKER,
PHILIP PLEDGER, JOSEPH HARPER, WILLIAM CORD...JOSEPH JOHNSON (LS), Wit: HARDY STEWARD (X)
BENJN. OUTLAW (+), JOS. PLEDGER. Rec. 4 Sept 1787.

Page 161: 18 Oct 1775, PHILIP PLEDGER of Craven Co., to JOSEPH PLEDGER of same, for ₺ 2000
            ...part of 250 A granted to OWEN DAVID 13 May 1756, conveyed to JOSEPH FULLER
SENR. by L & R, 5 & 6 May 1767, conveyed to sd. PHILIP PLEDGER 25 Sept 1773...145 A adj.
THOMAS PAGETT...PHIL: PLEDGER (LS), Wit: THOS BINGHAM, TRISTRAM THOMAS, MATTHEW WHITEFIELD.
Rec. 6 Sept 1787.

Page 162: 19 Apr 1787, PHILEMON THOMAS Of Marlborough Co., planter, to WILLIAM COWARD of
            same, for ₺ 23 s6 d8...land on NW side Whites Creek, part of grant to MAJOR
SAML. WISE 9 June 1775 containing 1000 A, 164 A conveyed to PHILEMON THOMAS...PHILEMON
THOMAS (LS), Wit: WILLIAM HARDICK, SAMUEL THOMAS. Rec. 6 Sept 1787.

Page 163: 22 Apr 1784, JOHN DAVID of Cheraw Dist., planter, to AZARIAH DAVID of same,
            planter, for ₺ 300 sterling...150 A, the NW part of 300 A granted to JENKIN
DAVID 5 Dec 176], conveyed unto sd. JOHN DAVID, his lawful heir...JOHN DAVID (LS), Wit:
DYER [?], JOEL McNATT. Proven by JOHN DYER before TRISTRAM THOMAS, J. P. 23 Oct 1784.
Rec. 6 Sept 1787.

Page 164: 22 Apr 1784, JOHN DAVID to AZARIAH DAVID, for ₺ 200 sterling...50 A, the NW ·
            part of 100 A, granted to EDWARD BOYKIN 20 Nov 1750, conveyed to JENKIN DAVID
by L & R, 5 Nov 1751, and conveyed to JOHN DAVID his lawful heir...JOHN DAVID (LS), Wit:
JNO DYER, JOEL McNATT. Proven by JOHN DYER before TRISTRAM THOMAS, 23 Oct 1784.

Page 165: 8 Nov 1787, WILLIAM GORDON of Marlborough Co., to JAMES FILLESPIE of same, for
            ₺ 150...land on Great Pee Dee about half a mile above Guardners Bluff, adj.
WILLIAM & JOHN PLEDGER, JOHN PLEDGER, JAMES DUE, 200 A, granted to SAMUEL GREENWOOD
30 Apr 1748, conveyed to THOMAS ROGERS by L & R, 10 Spet 1765, transfered to ALEXANDER
GORDON by Deed of Bargain & sale 9 Mar 1766, to WILLIAM GORDEN by Gift and devise in his
L. W. & T....WM GORDON (LS), Wit: MORGAN BROWN, JOSEPH BROWN, JAMES McCARTY (+). Rec.
3 Dec 1787.

Pp. 166-167: Grant to WILLIAM THOMAS, for s13 d1, 29 A on NE side Great Pee Dee on Hicks
            Creek...WILLIAM MOULTRIE, 4 Sept 1786. Plat included dated 4 Mar 1786,
showing Hicks Creek, land of Morgan Brown and SAML WISE. ALEXR. CRAIG, Dep. Survr.
Recorded in Grant Book RRRR, p. 617. Rec. 3 Dec 1787.

Pp. 167-168: 14 Aug 1787, DANIEL SPARKS of Marlborough Co., to STEPHEN MacCLENDEL of
            same, planter, for ₺ 30 sterling...125 A on Crooked Creek including the
plantation STEPHEN MacCLENDOL now lives on,1/2of tract granted to sd. SPARKS 3 July
1786...DANIEL SPARKS (LS), Wit: JAMES HODGES, WELCOM HODGES, WILLIS WILLIAMSON. Rec. 4
Dec 1787.

Pp. 168-169: 24 Jan 1787, JOHN PONE of Marlborough Co., to ISAM HODGES of same, for ₺ 50
            ...land granted to JOHN ASHBURY 22 Nov 1771, conveyed to MATTHEW WHITEFIELD
by L & R, 5 Aug 1773, then to sd. JOHN PONE by L&R, 30 June 1774...JOHN PONE (I) (LS),
Wit: JOSIAH DAVID, JOSIAH EVANS. Rec. 4 Dec 1787.

Pp. 169-170: 27 Oct 1787, ISAM HODGES of Marlborough Co., to JOHN STUBBS of same, for ₺50
            ...80 A granted to JONATHAN ASHBURY 22 Nov 1721, conveyed to MATTHEW WHITE-

FIELD, 5 Aug 1773, then to JOHN PONE 20 June 1774, then to sd. ISAM HODGES 4 Jan 1787...
ISAM HODGES (LS), MARY HODGES (LS), Wit: DUNKEN McFORSHEN (X), JOHN WISE (X), Rec. 4
Dec 1787.

Pp. 170-171: 4 Dec 1787, JONATHAN JOHN of Marlborough Co., , planter, to JOHN WILSON of
same, planter, for ₺ 200...150 A granted to sd. JOHN 17 Dec 1770...JONATHAN
JOHN (LS), Wit: MOT PEARSON, JAMES EASTERLING. Plat included in deed. Rec. 4 Dec 1787.

Pp. 171-172: 4 Dec 1787, THOMAS CONNER of Marlborough Co., to DANIEL SPARKS of same, for
s 10 sterling...250 A adj. NATHL. NOTS & vacant land...granted to ROBERT
CLARY by GOV. LITTLETON, conveyed to THOMAS CONNER by L & R, 8 & 9 Dec 1757...THOMAS
CONNER (LS), Wit: D. ROBERTSON, LEWIS CONNER, SILAS PEARSE. Rec. 4 Dec. 1787.

Pp. 172-173: 30 Nov 1787, DANIEL SPARKS of Marlborough Co., planter, to WILLIAM SMITH of
same, planter, for ₺ 30...125 A including the plantation where HARDY CLARK
now lives, part of 250 A granted to sd. SPARKS by WILLIAM MOULTRIE 3 July 1786, the other
half transferred to STEPHEN McCLENDOL...DANIEL SPARK (LS), MARTHA SPARKS(LS), Wit: THOMAS
STEVENS, THOMAS PEARSE, HARMON HOLLEYMAN. Rec. 4 Dec 1787.

Page 173: 23 Oct 1787, THOMAS CONNER SENR of Marlborough Co., to ISAAC WEATHERLY of same,
planter, for ₺ 50 sterling...100 A adj. WM ALSTON, CHARLES COTTONGIMS, JOHN WOOD
...including the plantation where THOMAS CONNER JUNR now liveth, granted to CHARLES PATE
by GOV. MONTAGUE 21 May 1772...THOMAS CONNER (LS), Wit: LEWIS CONNER, WILLIAM CONNER,
THOS(?) CONNER. Rec. 4 Dec 1787.

Page 174: 11 Oct 1787, DANIEL SPARKS of Marlborough Co., to PEARSE STEVENS of same for
₺ 50 sterling...100 A, part of 300 A granted to DICKSON PEARSE 2 April 1773
and conveyed unto DANIEL SPARKS 18 May 1786...adj. BURGESS WILLIAMS, GULLEY MOOR, ALEXAN-
DER BEVERLY, 50 A from the sd. 100 A....DANIEL SPARKS (LS), Wit: DAVID DUDLEY JUNER,
SAMUEL SPARKS, BENJAMIN ARRANDELL. Rec. 5 Dec 1787.

Page 175: 11 Nov 1785, THOMAS BINGHAM of Georgetown Dist., to PHILIP PLEDGER of Charraws
Dist., for ₺ 100 sterling...200 A granted to sd. BINGHAM 27 Nov 1770 in Craven
Co., adj. sd. PLEDGERS land, WILLIAM GARDNERs...THOS. BINGHAM (LS), Wit: JOS. PLEDGER.
JOHN PLEDGER. (No rec. date.).

Pp. 175-176: 1 Aug 1787, TRISTRAM THOMAS of.Marlborough Co., to CLAUDIUS PEGUES, GEORGE
HICKS, MORGAN BROWN, TRISTRAM THOMAS, CLAUDIUS PEGUES JUNR., MOSES PEARSON,
& THOMAS EVANS Esquires, Justices of the County Court of Marlborough...an act to lay
off counties and erect the Publick Buildings passed 12 Mar 1785...for regard and good
will to the publick welfare of sd. county, doth give to Marlborough County land on N side
Crooked Creek near the main road leading up & down Pedee river, about one Quarter of a
mile above the dwelling house of the sd. TRISTRAM THOMAS, 2 acres...TRISM. THOMAS (LS),
Wit: JOHN PLEDGER, JOS. PLEDGER, NAT. LEAVENWORTH. Rec. 5 Dec 1787.

Pp. 176-177: 15 May 1788, JAMES GILLISPEE of Marlborough Co., planter, to EDWARD CROSSLAND
of same, planter, for ₺ 150... land about half a mile above Gardner's Bluff,
adj. WILLIAM & JOHN PLEDGER, JOHN PLEDGER, JAMES DUE...200 A part of a grant to SAMUEL
GREENWOOD 13 Apr 1748, conveyed to THOMAS ROGERS, then to ALEXANDER GORDON, then to WILLIAM
GORDON, then to sd. GILLISPIE...JAMES GILLISPEE (LS), Wit: JN. WILLSON, JOSEPH BROWN.
Rec. 20 Nov 1788.

Pp. 177-178: 15 Nov 1787, JOHN HATHORN of Robison County, N. C. to CHRISTOPHER McRAW of
Richmond County, N. C. for ₺ 60 specie...land in Cheraws Dist., S. C. on
the head of Three Creeks, adj. lands surveyed DARBY HANNIGAN, 100 A, part of 300 A granted
to sd. JOHN HAWTHORN by Gov. MONTAGUE, 3 Apr 1772...JOHN HAWTHORN (LS), Wit: JNO.
McALUTA(?), DARBY HENAGAN. Proven in Marlborough County by DARBY HENAGAN before MOS.
PEARSON J. P. 4 June 1788. Rec. 3 Mar 1788.

Pp. 178-179: __ Mar 1788, ISOM HODGES and wf MARY of Marlborough Co., to WILLIAM STUBBS of
same, for ₺ 50 sterling...400 A on E side Pee Dee on Beaver Dam branch,
which said branch makes out of Crooked Creek...granted to ENOCH THOMPSON 4 Nov 1772 by
Gov. MONTAGUE, conveyed to sd. HODGES by SAMUEL THOMPSON, heir of ENOCH THOMPSON, decd....
ISOM HODGES (LS), MARY HODGES (X) (LS), Wit: JAMES BUSLY, JOHN STUBBS. Rec. 4 Mar 1788.

Page 179: 22 Feb 1786, LUKE PRYOR of Marlborough Co., to GEO. CHERRY of same, for ₺ 39 s5
d8... 100 A, conveyed from ABEL LEWIS to sd. PRYOR 2 Sept 1785 in Craven Co.,
on NE side Pee Dee...LUKE PRYOR (LS), Wit: MOS. PEARSON, MOSES MURPHEY, JOHN PRYOR.
Rec. 4 Mar 1788.

Page 180: 3 June 1788, DANIEL SPARKS of Marlborough Co., to SILAS PEARSE of same, for ₤100
...108 A on NE side greate Pee Dee on Crooked Creek , granted 4 Sept 1786 adj.
DICKSON PEARSE, THOMAS DEAN...DANIEL SPARKS (LS), Wit: W. WHITEFIELD, LUKE PRYOR, SAMUEL
TERRAL. Proven by SAMUEL TERRAL before WM. EASTERLING. 3 June 1788. Rec. 20 Nov 1788.

Page 181: 16 May 1788, WILLIBY BROUGHTON of Marlborough Co., planter, to THOMAS HUCKABE,
of same, planter, for ₤ 2 sterling...land granted to sd. BROUGHTON by Gov.
MOULTRIE, on NE side Pee Dee, granted 5 June 1786...WILLIBY BROUGHTON (X) (LS), Wit:
BENJA. HERNDON, YOUNGER NEWTON, CHARLES HUCKABE (X). Proven by YOUNGER NEWTON before
WM EASTERLING. Rec. 20 Nov 1788.

Page 182: 19 Mar 1788, ROBERT THOMAS & wf MARY of Geo. Town Dist., planters to WILLIAM
EASTERLING of Marlborough Co., planter, for ₤ 50 sterling...100 A including the
plantation where sd. EASTERLING now liveth, part of 300 A granted to JOHN SMITH 19 June
1772, conveyed to sd. THOMAS 24 Nov 1782, near the Beaverdam Creek...ROBERT THOMAS (LS),
MARY THOMAS (X) (LS), Wit: JESSE BATHEA, DAVID BEATHEA. Proven by DAVID BATHEA before
TRISTRAM THOMAS. 2 June 1788. Rec. 20 Nov 1788.

Page 183: 5 Dec 1787, GILES NEWTON of Charlotte Co., Va., planter, to YOUNGER NEWTON of
Marlborough Co., SC, for ₤ 100...640 A granted to sd. GILES NEWTON by WILLIAM
MOULTRIE 7 Aug 1786...GILES NEWTON (LS), Wit: BENJAMIN HERNDON, JAMES NEWTON, NANCY
HERNDON (X). Proven by BENJAMIN HERNDON before WILLIAM EASTERLING 10 May 1788. Rec.
20 Nov 1788.

Page 184: 24 Dec 1787, JOHN STUBBS of Marlborough Co., to JACOB DARBY of same, for ₤ 30
sterling...land conveyed to sd. STUBBS by grant....[details of land absent]
...JOHN STUBBS (LS), Wit: JOSEPH BROWN, MARY BROWN, MARY GORDON (X). Rec. 6 Mar 1788.

Page 185: 1 Mar 1788, JAMES NEAL of Darlington Co., SC to BURREL WHITTINGTON of Marlborough
Co., for sl0 sterling...200 A adj. CHARLES KERBY, GREEF WHITTINGTON, GEORGE
CHEARRY...JAMES NIEL (X) (LS), Wit: LUKE PRYOR, JNO. LEE (J). Rec. 20 Nov 1788. Proven
before TRISTAM THOMAS by LUKE PRYOR 4 Mar 1788.

Pp. 186-187: 5 Oct 1782, WELCOM HODGES of Cheraw Dist., planter, to THOMAS COCHRAN of same,
planter, for ₤ 5000...150 A, the SW part of 200 A adj. GREENWOOD, JOSEPH
PLEDGER, TRUSM THOMAS, granted to HOWEL JAMES by Gov. LITTLETON 1758, conveyed to JOSEPH
FULLER, then to WELCOM HODGES 1781...WELCOM HODGES (LS), Wit:GEORGE HARRIS (X), JAMES
HODGES. Proven by GEORGE HARRIS before GEORGE HICKS J. P. 5 Oct 1782. Rec. 20 Nov 1788.

Pp. 187-188: 3 & 4 June 1788, WILLIAM POWE of SC, to FRANCIS BRIDGES of same, for (lease
sl0, release ₤ 15 sterling)...150 A on NE side Pee Dee, granted 5 Nov 1787...
WILLIAM POWE (LS), Wit: JAMES BEESELY, MOSES FORT. Rec. 20 Nov 1787.

Page 189: 13 June 1788, JAMES CONNER of Marlborough Co., planter, to DANIEL HERRING of
same, for ₤ 30 sterling...100 A where sd. HERRING now liveth, granted to
JAMES CONNER by Gov. BULL 3 Apr 1786...JAMES CONNER (SEAL), SARAH CONNER (X) (SEAL), Wit:
LEWIS CONNER, DAVID STEWART, WILLIAM FLOWERS. Rec. 18 Feb 1789. Proven by LEWIS CONNER
before WM EASTERLING 1 Sept 1788.

Pp. 190-191: 18 Oct 1788, ALEXANDER CRAIG of Chesterfield Co., SC,Surveyor, to JOHN STUBBS
of Marlborough Co., planter, for ₤ 25 sterling...250 A in Marlborough Co.
on muddy creek, adj. JOHN FRAIZERS, WILLIAM BEATLEYS, AARON PEARSONS, & vacant land...
ALEXR CRAIG (LS), Wit: MARTHA ALLCON, NATHANIEL CRUTHARDS. Proven by MARTHA ALLEN before
THOS EVANS, Justice of Marlborough Co., 7 Nov 1788. Rec. 25 Feb 1789.

Pp. 191-192: 6 Dec 1786, WILLIAM STUBBS of Marlborough Co., planter, to JOHN McNATT of
same, for ₤ 20 sterling...1/2 of 200 A granted to JOHN SUTTON 4 July 1785...
on NE side Pee Dee near Muddy Creek adj. PHILIP PLEDGER, WILLIAM ALLEN, FRANCIS BRIDGES,
& vacant land...WILLIAM STUBBS (X) (LS), Wit: JNO DYER, JAMES HODGES. Proven by JOHN
DYER before THOS EVANS J. P. 22 Aug 1788. Rec. 25 Feb 1789.

Pp. 192-193: 12 Apr 1788, AARON PEARSON of Marlborough Co., Cheraw Dist., planter, to
WILLIAM CONNER of same, planter, for ₤ 7 sterling...land on Hgans [sic]
prong of the three Creek, 100 A, part of 640 A granted to sd. PEARSON by Gov. PINCKNEY
7 May 1787...AARON PEARSON (LS), Wit: CILRON[?] CONNER, ALEXANDER BEVERLY, TABITHA
DARBY (+), Proven before WM. EASTERLING 1 Sept 1788 by ALEXANDER BEVERLY. Rec. 25 Feb
1789.

Pp. 193-194: 7 Nov 1788, JOHN STUBBS of Marlborough Co., to JAMES BUNLY[?] of same, for
₤ 15 sterling... 100 A, the NE part of 250 A on Muddy Creek...granted to

ALEXANDER CRAIG by Gov. MOULTRIE 5 Dec 1784...JOHN STUBBS (LS), Wit: WM BUSELY, SAMUEL SPARKS. Proven by WILLIAM BUSELY before THOS EVANS 7 Nov 1788. Rec. 25 Feb 1789.

Pp. 194-195: 18 July 1788, JOHN ODAM of Marlborough Co., to CHARLES BARRUNTINE of same, for Ł 5.s12...70 A, part of a grant to sd. ODAM 7 Jan 1788...adj. DRURY ROBERTSON, ENOCH TOMPSON...JOHN ODOM (SEAL), Wit: ELISHA FARLESS, JAMES STUBBS (X), JACO BEARRENTEN (2). Proven before TRISM. THOMAS by JAMES STUBBS 24 Nov 1788. Rec. 25 Feb 1789.

Pp. 195-196: 24 Aug 1788, WILLIAM FIELDS of Marlborough Co., to JOHN TEAGUE of same, for s5...275 A, part of 350 A granted to JAMES GRIFFITH 10 Apr 1771, transferred to SAMUEL GRIFFITH as his lawful Heir, then to PHILLIP PLEDGER 12 Feb 1773, then to THOMAS BINGHAM 2 Sept 1774, then the above 275 A to sd. WILLIAM FIELDS 29 Dec 1787... WILLIAM FIELDS (LS), Wit: BENJ. HICKS, BENJ. OUTLAW (X). Proven by BENJAMIN HICKS before WILLIAM EASTERLING, 22 Mar 1789. Rec. 28 Apr 1789.

Pp. 197-198: 26 Mar 1789, JOHN TEAGUE of Marlborough Co., to BENJAMIN HICKS of same, for Ł 3 sterling...20 A, part of 350 A granted to JAMES GRIFFITH [same chain of title as in preceding deed]... adj. a tract of 300 A belonging to the estate of NICHOLAS BEDGEGOOD, formerly granted to DAVID ROACH....JOHN TEAGUE (|—) (LS), Wit: EDMUND HINDMAN (E), NANCY BEDGEGOOD. Proven by NANCY BEDEGOOD before WM EASTERLING 28 Mar 1789. Rec. 28 Apr 1789.

Pp. 199-202: 22 Mar 1774, GEORGE SWEETING of Craven County, S. C. to WILLIAM ALLSTON SENR. of same, for Ł 300...granted to JOHN PLOWMAN by WILLIAM BULL 18 Jan 1765, and 150 A granted by Gov. LYTTLETON 18 Oct 1757 in the fork of the three Creeks...GEORGE SWEETING (X) (LS), Wit: WM McTYER, MANUEL COX. Proven by WILLIAM McTYER before JOSEPH GOURLY 2 Apr 1774. Rec. 28 Apr 1789.

Pp. 2C3-205: 7 & 8 Feb 1765, MORRICE of Craven Co., SC to ROBERT WEAVER. marchant, (lease s10, release Ł 300)...50 A granted to THOMAS WALLEY by Gov. MES GLEN, 8 Jan 1743, conveyed to MORRIS MURFEE 5 & 6 Mar 1760...MORRIS MURPHEY (LS), Wit: SAML. BUXTON, WM WISEMAN. Proven before JAMES ALVAN J. P. by SAMUEL BUXTON 26 Nov 1766, Rec. 1 May 1789.

Pp. 206-208: 6 & 7 Jan 1773, JOHN WOODBERY of Charlestown, Merchant, to WILLIAM ALLSTON of George Town, Planter, for (lease 10, release Ł200)...200 A in Craven Co., on NE side Great Pee Dee adj. CAPTAIN CHARLES AUGUSTUS STEWARD, Esqr. & vacant land...granted to sd. WOODBERY by Gov. BULL 14 Sept 1771...JOHN WOODBERY (LS), Wit: PHILLIP HENRY, DAVID NICHOS. CONSTANCE. Proven by DAVID NICHOLAS CONSTANCE before GEORGE GABRIEL POWEL, Esqr., J. P. for Berkley County, 13 Jan 1773. Rec. 2 May 1789.

Pp. 209-212: 5 & 6 Mar 1760, THOMAS WALLEY of Craven Co., planter, to MORRIS MURPHY of same, for (lease s20, release Ł 300)...50 A adj. to land laid out by MR. GILLASPIE...THOMAS WALLEY (T) (LS), Wit: JOHN ALVAN, FRANCIS WHITTINGTON. Rec. 4 May 1789.

Pp. 213-214: 6 Oct 1786, ROGER LOUNCEY of Marlborough Co., to WILLIAM THORNWELL of same, for Ł 100 sterling...ROGER LOUNCEY & wf ELIZABETH...100 A granted to ANDREW SLANN 20 June 1750 on NE side Pee Dee on the NW side of the three creeks in the Welch Tract, conveyed to ANTHONY POUNCEY [LOUNCEY?]...ROGER POUNCEY [LOUNCEY?] (LS), ELIZABETH POUNCEY (X) (LS), Wit: ELIJAH HUGHS, REUBEN WINDHAM, JOHN GEORGE (X). Rec. 4 May 1789. Proven by REUBIN WINDHAM before MOSES PEARSON JP.

Pp. 214-218: 11 & 12 Mar 1772, CHARLES AUGUSTUS STEWARD of St. Davids Parish, Craven Co., to WILLIAM ALLSTON of same (lease s10, release Ł 130)...1000 A granted to sd. STEWARD by WILLIAM BULL Ma: 1771 on a creek called the Three Creeks near a place called the Roundabout, vacant on all sides...S. STEWARD (LS), CHARLES AUGS. STEWARD (LS), Wit: ELIZH: WARING (+), HUMPY. HOPKINS.. Proven by JOSEPH DUBOURDIEU, J. P. of Craven County, by HUMPHREY HOPKINS 7 July 1772. Rec. 6 May 1789.

Pp. 218-221:26 & 27 Nov 1785, ELISHA SCREVEN of Prince Fredricks Parish, Craven Co., to ISAAC NEAVEL of same, for Ł 100...two tracts, 150 A and 37 A in St. Davids Parish in Alvan Neck on big Pee Dee adj. GEORGE CHERRY, CURNEALUS DUPREE, THOMAS CONN, JOHN ALVAN...ELISHA SCREVEN (LS), Wit: JOHN McCANTS, JAS. MONTGOMERTY. Proven by JAS. MONTGOMERTY before ANTHY. WHITE, J. P. 17 July 1787. Rec. 8 May 1789.

Pp. 221-222: [deed very dim]...84 A to BENJAMIN BEVERLY...MATTHEW WHITEFIELD (LS), Wit: DAVID BETHEA, PETER SMITH, AZARIAH DAVID. Rec. 9 May 1789.

Pp. 222-224: 1 Dec 1787, ABNER BROACH of Cheraw Dist., to WILLIAM BENNET of same, planter, for Ł 50...100 A...granted by Gov. BENJ. GUERARD, 21 Jan 1784[?]...ABNER

BROACH (X) (LS), PEANALIPY BROACH (X) (LS), Wit: HARMAN HOLLEYMAN, THOMAS HUCABY (T), WILLIAM LUSTRY (S), THOS. PEARCE. Proven before WM. EASTELRING by THOS. PEARSE 28 June 1788. Rec. 13 May 1789.

Pp. 224-227: 12 & 13 Mar 1778, PAUL TRAPIER, ESQR. of Georgetown, S. C. to ISAAC NEAVEL of Prince George Parish, Craven Co., SC, for (lease s10, release Ł 800)... 50 A granted to THOMAS WALLEY 18 Jan 1743 in Welch Tract, also 150 A granted to MALICHI MURPHY 7 May 1767 adj. ISAAC NEAVEL, MAURICE MURPHY...PAUL TRAPIER (LS), Wit: JAMES GREGG, JOHN BIDGGOOD.
                    Proven in Georgetown Dist., Craven County before JOB ROTHMAHLER ESQR., J.P. by JAMES GREGG 14 Mar 1778. Rec. 13 May 1789.

Pp. 228-229: 4 Mar 1788, WILLIAM ALLSTON of George Town, S. C. to WILLIAM THOMAS of Marl- borough Co., for Ł 210...several tracts (1) 150 A granted to GEORGE SWEETING 18 Oct 1757, conveyed to sd. ALLSTON 22 Mar 1774...(2) 200 A granted to JOHN WOODBERY 14 Sept 1771, conveyed to ALLSTON 7 Jan 1773...(3) 1000 A granted to CHARLES AUGUSTUS STEWARD and conveyed to sd. ALLSTON 12 Mar 1772...(4)650 A granted to sd. ALLSTON 14 Sept 1771... 2000 A total...W. ALSTON (LS), Wit: ISAAC DELEISSELINE, NICHOLAS ROGERS. Proven before MORGAN BROWN by NICHOLAS ROGERS 10 Apr 1788. Rec. 14 May 1789.

Pp. 230-231: 7 Dec 1776, CHARLES PATE of Craven Co., SC planter, to THOMAS CONNER SENR of same, planter, for Ł 500...200 A on three Creeks adj. WM. AULSTONS [sic], PHILLIP PLEDGER, JOHN WARD, & vacant land...granted 21 May 1772, Memorial entered in Book L, N 11, page 345 13 Aug 1772...CHARLES PATE (LS), SARAH PATE (X) (LS), Wit: JAMES CONNER, LEWIS CONNER, BARBANAS HANAGAN.   Proven by JAMES CONNER before GEORGE HICKS 7 June 1777. Rec. 14 May 1789.

Pp. 231-233: 1 Sept 1788, MATTHEW WHITEFIELD of Marlborough Co., to DAVID STEWARD of same, for Ł 5 sterling...83 A on a prong of Crooked called Beverlys Mill prong, including the plantation whereon WILLIAM BEVERLY did live, part of 250 A granted to sd. WHITEFIELD by Gov. MONTAGUE 22 Nov 1771...MATTHEW WHITEFIELD (LS), Wit: JAMES BEESLY, JNO. CYER. Proven by JOHN DYER before MORGAN BROWN, 1 Sept 1788. Rec. 15 May 1789.

Pp. 233-234: 13 Jan 1789, DANIEL HERRING Of Marlborough Co., planter, to DAVID McCALL of same, planter, for Ł 50 sterling ...land granted to sd. HERRING on Reedy Creek including where sd. McCALL now lives, granted 6 Nov 1786...DANIEL HERRING (H) (LS), S. CHUSANA HERRING (LS), Wit: BARNABAS HENAGAN, DARBY HENAGAN, SOLOMON McCALL. Proven by BARNABAS HENAGAN before TRISM. THOMAS, 2 Mar 1789, who said he saw DANIEL HERRING & wf. SUSANNAH sign.

Pp. 234-235: 18 Feb 1789, WILLIAM MIXSON of Marlborough Co., to LAMUEL BURKETT of same, for Ł 25 sterling...100 A on Muddy Creek, part of a grant of 250 A to sd. MIXSON 5 June 1786...WILLIAM MIXSON (W) (LS), Wit: BARTHO. WHITTINGTON, BURREL WHITTINGTON (GB), JESSE STEVENS. Rec. 20 May 1789.

Pp. 235-236: 17 Jan 1789, JOHN DYER, Schoolmaster of Marlborough Co., to AZARIAH DAVID of same, for Ł 100 sterling...220 A, part of Ł 500 A granted to THOMAS EVANS, 5 June 1786 near Crooked Creek in the Welch Tract, transferred from sd. EVANS to sd. DYER 20 Nov 1786, adj. JENKIN DAVID...JNO. DYER (LS), Wit: WELCOM HODGES, DANJ. DAVID. Proven by BENJAMIN DAVID before TRISTRAM THOMAS 17 Jan. 1789. Rec. 22 May 1789.

Pp. 237-238: 1 Sept 1788, WILLIAM THOMAS of Marlborough Co., to MORGAN BROWN of same, for Ł 50...land adj. STEPHEN PARKER, Estate of WILLIAM HARDWICK, the other part of this tract conveyed to JACOB ABBOTT by sd. MORGAN BROWN, 190 A, part of 2 tracts granted to JAMES COWARD, conveyed to ARCHIBALD GREYHAM, then to WILLIAM LITTLE, and from him descended to sd. WILLIAM THOMAS, WILLIAM THOMAS & wf SARAH decd. as Heirs at law, from them to ISAAC BARTLETT then to WILLIAM THOMAS...WM. THOMAS (LS), Wit: JACOB ABBOTT, JOHN LIDE. Proven by JACOB ABBOTT before THOMAS EVANS 2 Dec 1788. Rec. 25 May 1789.

Pp. 238-239: 29 Aug 1788, JOHN STUBS of Marlborough Co., planter, to THOMAS COOK of Gilford [sic] Co., North Carolina, for Ł 50...50 A, including the plantation where ELIZABETH HITCHCOCK now lives on Beaverdam Branch, part of 250 A granted to sd. STUBS 21 Apr 1774...JOHN STUBS (X) (LS), Wit: WILLIAM LISTER (O), THOMAS STUBS (X). Proven before WILLIAM EASTERLING by WILLIAM LISTER 1 Mar 1789. Rec. 26 May 1789.

Pp. 239-240: 1 Sept 1788, MORGAN BROWN of Marlborough Co., to JACOB ABBOTT of same, for Ł 50...land adj. MRS. KNIGHT, STEPHEN PARKER, late the property of WILLIAM COWARD, 150 A, part of a grant to JAMES COWARD, conveyed to ARCHIBALD GREYHAM, then to WILLIAM LITTLE, then to MORGAN BROWN & wf ELIZABETH, then to NATHAN LEAVENWORTH then to MORGAN BROWN...MORGAN BROWN (LS), Wit: WM THOMAS, JOHN LIDE. Rec. 26 May 1789.

Pp. 240-241: 3 Nov 1788, JOHN HALCOME of Marlborough Co., planter, to YOUNGER NEWTON of
for ₺ 40 Va. money...200 A granted by Gov. MOULTRIE to sd. JOHN HALCOME 7
Jan 1788...JOHN HALCOME (X) (LS), CATHERINE HALCOME (X) (LS), Wit: BENJAMIN HERNDON,
DANIEL COTTINGHAM, DILL COTTINGHAM. Proven before WILLIAM EASTERLING by BENJAMIN HERNDON
16 Nov 1788, Rec. 27 May 1789.

Pp. 241-242: 12 Feb 1789, THOMAS CONNER JUNR of Georgetown Dist., planter, to PETER WAY
of same, planter, for ₺ 50 sterling...100 A in Georgetown Dist., part of 200
A granted to sd. CONNER by Gov. THOMAS PINCKNEY, part in Cheraw Dist., Marlborough Co....
granted 17 May 1787, on a marsh of little Pee Dee called the line marsh...THOMAS CONNER
JUNR. (LS), Wit: JESSE BROWN, BENJAMIN MORRIS, JESSE BETHEA. Proven by JESSE BATHEA JR.
12 Feb 1789. Rec. 27 May 1789.

Pp. 242-243: 10 Feb 1789, THOMAS SUMRAL of Marlborough Co., to ISAAC SUMRAL of same, planter, for ₺ 40 sterling...150 A including the plantation whereon sd. ISAAC now
liveth, granted to sd. THOMAS 20 May 1772 also plantation where WM HATHCOCK now liveth &
part of the wheat field, part of 300 A... THOMAS SUMRAL (LS), ANN SUMRAL (||) (LS), Wit:
BENJAMIN HERNDON, JAMES EASTERLING, THOMAS SUMRAL JUNR. Proven by JAMES EASTERLING before
WILLIAM EASTERLING, 25 Feb 1789. Rec. 27 May 1789.

Pp. 243-244: 3 June 1788, SAMUEL SPARKS of Marlborough Co., to WILLIS WILLIAMSON of same,
for ₺ 20...45 A on Muddy Creek granted to one BOUTWELLS and JOHN FASHURE SENR
, part of 445 A granted by WILLIAM MOULTRY [sic]...SAMUEL SPARKS (LS), LUCY SPARKS (X)
(LS), Wit: AARON SNOWDEN, REBEKAH DARBY, BENY. WILLIAMSON. Rec. 27 May 1789.

Pp. 244-245: 3 Sept 1788, DICKSON PEARCE of Marlborough Co., to SILAS PEARCE of same, for
₺ 50...100 A about two miles from the beauty spot near Carter branch...
granted to sd. DICKSON by Gov. MONTAGUE 3 Apr 1772...DICKSON PEARCE (LS), Wit: SAMUEL
COUNCIL, JOSHUA AMMONS, SHADRACH EASTERLING. Proven before WILLIAM EASTERLING by SHADRACH
EASTERLING 16 Sept 1788. Rec. 28 May 1789.

Pp. 245-246: 3 Sept 1789, DICKSON PEARCE to SILAS PEARCE, for ₺50...150 A on Crooked Cr...
half of grant to DICKSON PEARCE 2 Apr 1773...DICKSON PEARCE (LS), Wit:
SAMUEL COUNSELL, JOSHUA AMMONS, SHADRACH EASTERLING. Rec. 28 May 1789.

Pp. 246-247: 4 Mar 1788, WILLIAM COUNCELL of Marlborough Co., planter, to DANIEL SPARKS
of same, for ₺ 30 sterling...100 A on Crooked Creek about a mile from the
Beauty Spot adj. JOHN STUBBS, JOHN FRASER, ENOCH THOMSON, granted to Gov. BULL to HENRY
COUNCEL 3 Feb 1773, conveyed to sd. WILLIAM COUNSEL, the lawful heir of sd. HENRY...WILLM
COUNCELL (LS), Wit: W. FALCONER, J. WINFIELD. Rec. 4 Mar 1789.

Pp. 247-248: 29 Dec 1788, JAMES HARRISS of Marlborough Co., to JAMES MEGEE of same, for
₺ 10...100 A, part of 300 A granted to sd. HARRIS 6 Nov 1786...JAMES HARRISS
(LS), Wit: LUKE PRYOR, JOHN MOORE, ZACCHEUS AYER. Proven by JOHN MOORE before SAML BROWN
12 Feb 1789. Rec. 2 Sept 1789.

Pp. 248-249: 10 July 1788, LUKE PRYOR to JAMES MeGEE, both of Marlborough Co., for ₺3 s14
...330 A in Marlborough Co., on head of Muddy Creek granted to sd. PRYOR
2 Oct 1786......LUKE PRYOR (LS), Wit: JOHN PRYOR, JOHN SMITH (I), Proven by JOHN SMITH
before SAML BROWN. 25 Feb 1789. Rec. 2 Sept 1789.

Pp. 249-250: 28 Aug 1786, RICHARD JAMES of Georgetown Dist., Silver Smith of Maden Down,
to MR. JOHN HODGES of same, for s5 sterling, 246 A, part of 1000 A granted
to ANTONEY ALKISON, sold by ROBERT ALKISON being the lawful heir to JOSEPH SILLIVAN...
RICHARD JAMES (LS), Wit: JAMES SINETH, JOSEPH JONES.

Page 251: Blank.

Pp. 252-253: 16 Apr 1768, DANIEL DWONALD of Prince George Parish, Craven Co., SC planter,
to ABEL WYLDS, THOMAS EVANS, THOMAS JAMES, JOHN SUTTON & ABEL EDWARDS of
same, planter, for the Love & affection to the church or congregation of Christeans [sic]
now and for many years past meeting for divine services at or upon the premises hereafter
given commonly called Baptists Distringuished by the name of particular Baptists holding
Believers Baptism with the Calvinistic Doctrins of particular Redemption, Special Vocation,
Justification by faith & the final perseveratnce of the Saints...2 acres in the Welch tract
where the sd. DANIEL DWONALD now resides & which he Inherits from his Father DANIEL DEBON-
ALD decd, granted 2 Mar 1743 by Gov. GLEN, part of 200 A...DANIEL DWONALD (LS), Wit:
ELIZABETH JAMES, MAGNESS CARGILL. Proven by both wit. before ALEXR. MACKINTOSH 25 Apr
1768. Rec. 9 Sept 1789.

Pp. 253-254: 15 & 16 Jan 1790, WILLIAM POWE of Chesterfield Co., to THOMAS STEVANS of
Marlborough Co., for ₺ 10 sterling...400 A on Donahus Bay, granted 6 Nov
1786...WM POWE (LS), Wit: F. JOHNSTON, JN. PUNCH, THOS POWE. Rec. 15 June 1790.

Page 254: 5 Dec 1789, THOMAS PEARCE of Marlborough Co., planter, for Goodwill and
affection to ANTHONY BRIGGS my loving son-in-law of same, Negro known as
Cater and woman Hanner boy Pompey, girl Jude, girl Milly...THOMAS PEARCE (LS), Wit:
JESSE BAGGETT, DICKSON PEARCE. Prov n by DICKSON PEARCE before THOMAS EVANS 1 Mar 1792.

Page 255: ISAM HODGES & ANN THOMPSON, for ₺ 50 sterling to JOSHUA DAVID, negro Stan...
ISAM HODGES (LS), ANN THOMSON (LS), Wit: B. DAVID, PRISCILLA OLIPHANT. Proven by
PRISCILLA OLIPHANT 16 August 1794.   Rec. 16 Aug 1794.

Page 255: Marlborough Co., SC.: DUNCAN McPHERSON, planter, for ₺ 25 to JOHN MURDOCK,
merchant...a Featherbed, a mans saddle, an Iron Teakettle, two Iron Pots, one
Pewter dish, one Earthen Dish, one Earthen Tea pot, four pewter plates, one Iron frying
pan, six Earthen plates, one Earthen Dish, one Earthen Tea pot, One Earthen Bowl two
Glass Tumblers, one handsaw, one claw hammer, one timber chest, one case with Bottles, a
Birght Sorrel horse about 14 and 1/2 hands high,... DUNCAN McPHERSON (X) (LS), Wit:
SOLOMON McCOLL, Proven by McCOLL 2 Sept 1794, Rec. 8 Sept 1794.

                           END OF DEED BOOK A

Pp. 1-2: ROBERTSON CARLOSS & CO. vs. JESSE W. PLEDGER et alii:
The State of South Carolina: Darlington, Marlborough & Chesterfield Districts, In Equity, February Term 1806.
Whereas ROBERT CARLASS and ANDREW SMITH exhibited their Bill of Complaint before the Judges of the Court of Equity and shew that JOHN PLEDGER JUNIOR and JESSE W. PLEDGER being indebted to them gave their joint bond in the penal some of Ł 144 s19 d11 on or before the 1st day of Sept 1804 and in order to secure the payment of the same, the sd. PLEDGERS by a deed of Demise and assignment by way of mortage [sic] 17 Feb 1804...two tracts containing 400 A originally granted to HENRY COUNCIL 30 Oct 1772, sold by sd. HENRY COUNCIL to PHILIP PLEDGER, and by PHILIP PLEDGER bequeathed to his son WILLIAM PLEDGER, and by WILLIAM PLEDGER conveyed to sd. JOHN PLEDGER JUNIOR and JESSE W. PLEDGER, 14 Apr 1803...to sd. sum of Ł 72 s9 d11 was not paid to them, the same remains due...the sd. JOHN PLEDGER JUNIOR one of the said Mortgagors departed this life intestate leaving MARY PLEDGER his widow and JESSE COUNCIL PLEDGER an infant son surviving him...pray that the sd. JESSE W. PLEDGER, MARY PLEDGER, and JESSE COUNCIL PLEDGER might be decreed to come to a just and fair account...the Judges WILLIAM JAMES and WADDY THOMPSON, decreed that the sd. JESSE W. PLEDGER, MARY PLEDGER be garred and foreclosed of and from all benefit of claim on sd. mortgaged premises...and this is to be binding on sd. JESSE COUNCIL PLEDGER, unless he attain the age of 21 within six months.

Pp. 3-10: JOHN ROGERS vs. NATHANIEL THOMPSON.
The Decree Hereunto annexed and do certif [sic] that the Same agrees with the Bill answer and decretal order made at and entered in the minutes of The late Court of Equity holden at Greenville on the second Monday in February in 1806 for the United Districts of Darlington, Marlborough, and Chesterfield. 4 Mar 1806, JNO WINFIELD, Comr.
JOHN ROGERS vs. NATHANIEL THOMPSON) In this case a verdict at Law in action of Trover[?] has been obtained by Deft against Complt. for $1950 or to return negroes in Bill mentioned, the Prayer of the Bill is to obtain against Deft, a perpetual injunction to restrain him from carrying the Judgmt. at Law into Effect upon the Equity stated...the Bill has relied much upon the illegal conduct of the Complt. in obtaining possession of sd. negroes...the Complt. in right of MARY & SARAH SUTTON an equitable claim to recover said negroes? ...power of attorney by STEPHEN TERRY & MARY his wife(formerly MARY SUTTON) & SARAH SUTTON...negroes were bequeathed by JOHN CLARY decd to sd. SARAH & MARY, his neices ...his wife ANN now wife of Deft. should have "the use of his negro Bet till Cate comes of age ["]...Deft "after taking away & Keeping the negroes in North Carolina brought back to this State Cate & Toby, Ben & Lucy, children of the sd. wench Bet named in said Will &C ["]...that "JOHN CLARY the son has died an infant of ten years of age without heirs" &c...therefore the sd. MARY & SARAH SUTTON claim the said negroes...court is of opinion that sd. MARY & SARAH SUTTON have a right under the Will of JOHN CLARY the elder to recover sd. negroes... W. JAMES.
South Carolina, Cheraw District, In Equity, JOHN ROGERS vs. NAT. THOMSPON
Bill for an Injunction
This cause coming on to be heard on the second monday in June 1810 before the hon. WILLIAM JAMES, Esquire, one of the Judges of the sd. Court in the presence of Counsel on both sides...JOHN CLARY, late of The District of Chesterfield, S. C. on 20 Jan 1789, duly made his will & shortly afterwards died without altering or revoking the same and sd. Will appointed WILLIAM ELLERBE JUNIOR and ROBERT ALLISON Executors that sd. JOHN left wife ANN CLARY and an only son JOHN CLARY surviving him...the sd. WILLIAM ELLERBE JUNIOR and ROBERT ALLISON refusing to qualify on the sd. will, ANN CLARY the widow proved the said will in County Court of Chesterfield 8 June 1789 and had letters of administration with the will annexed, said JOHN CLARY son of the testator was at the complainant about four or five years of age and that the said son died under ten years of age...MARY SUTTON & SARAH SUTTON became entitled to said negroes..."I bequeath to my beloved son JOHN CLARY all my negroes viz. old Tom, Chloe, Young Tom, Bet, Cate and their increase forever ...as soon as he comes of age, and in case he dies under that age or without heirs for them to go to my beloved neices Mary and Sarah Sutton..." that ANN CLARY shortly after she had possessed herself of the negroes of the Testator as aforesaid married one NATHANIEL THOMPSON, and he removed the negroes into North Carolina and upon various pretences [sic] disposed of some of the negroes...the said STEPHEN TERRY and SARAH SUTTON residing in the District of Fairfield at a distance from the defendant persuaded the complainnat to act as their attorney...the said SARAH SUTTON having arrived at the age of 21 years on the 9 June 1806...sd. JOHN ROGERS entered into an agreement with his brother NICHOLAS ROGERS who was the Sheriff of Chesterfield District that the said NICHOLAS should arrest & carry away from home the defendant, while the complainant should carry away the negroes....had the said son JOHN CLARY lived he would have arrived to the age of 21 on the 21 Dec 1808...testimoney of ROBERT TEMPLE... the defendant to recover his damages for illegal conduct and the costs at law from the complainant...WILLIAM JAMES.   Certified 16 Sept 1810 by JAMES R. ERVIN, Comr. in Equity.

Pp. 11-12: In Equity for Cheraw District
        Between DUNCAN McRA and JOHN CHESNUT, survivors of DUNCAN McRA & COMPANY, com-
plainants and MALACHAI NICHOLAS BADGEGOOD and WILLIAM VERNON son and heir at Law of
CHRISTOPHER VERNON, deceased, Defendants. Tuesday the 14 Feb 1809.
        Heard before THEODORE GAILLARD, Esquire one of the Judges of the Court of Equity
in presence of counsel on both sides...the complainants sometime in the year 1791 in the
Court of Common Pleas for Cheraw District recovered a Judgment against one BENJAMIN HICKS
for ₺ 46 s5 d11 and that certain other judgements having been obtained against the sd.
BENJAMIN prior to the Judgment of the Complainants and execution thereon issued, the lands
of sd. BENJAMIN were levied on, advertised and offered for sale under the said executions
on 2 July 1795, the said CHRISTOPHER VERNON at that sale attended and to prevent the persons present from bidding for and giving the value of the land declared that he would pay
all the Just debts of sd. BENJAMIN HICKS and that he was making the purchase of the said
land for the beneift of his children...the property was purchased at a small price, much
below its real value and not sufficient to discharge the demands which had a preference to
the claim of the complainants and the said lands were the only visible property which the
said BENJAMIN HICKS possessed and that he has since removed from this State without leaving any property in it and without satisfying the Judgment of the Complainants, the Bill
charges that the money paid by the said CHRISTOPHER VERNON was furnished by the said BEN-
JAMIN HICKS...the defendant WILLIAM VERNON, who is an infant, by WILLIAM LITTLE THOMAS,
his guardian, for that purpose, that he was young at the time of his father's death and
has no knowledge of the matters and Things in the Bill of complainant.

Pp. 13-17: Administrator of MEHITIBLE LIDE Complainant vs. DUNCAN McRA Admr. & JOHN LIDE
           & others devisees of THOS. LIDE decd
Heard on the second Monday in Feb 1811 at Cheraw Court House before the Hon. THEODORE
GAILLARD one of the Judge of the Court of Equity...admr. of MEHITIBLE LIDE, the widow &
relict of THOMAS LIDE & mother of the Complainant that THOMAS LIDE on 7 Nov 1787 made
his L. W. & T. whereby he bequeathed unto his said wife MEHITIBLE LIDE, ₺ 50 sterling per
annum...having so made his will, he departed this life on the same day and sd. MEHITIBLE
LIDE survived her said husband until the [   ] day of Feb 1804 without having received
more than the two first years annuity which had been paid her by DUNCAN McRA, the admr.
cum testaments annexo, and the balance of the annuity was still due amounting to ₺ 712
s10 with the interest, and that the defendants JOHN LIDE, THOMAS LIDE, ROBERT LIDE, CHARLES
M. LIDE, JAMES W. LIDE, & ANN LIDE now wife of ABSALOM BURN had taken possession of the
real Estate devised to them by their Father & refused to pay the said annuity which was
attached thereto...there was a marriage contract entered into by THOMAS LIDE and MEHITIBLE
LIDE that neither should acquire any right to estate real or personal of the other...the
complainant CHARLES IRBY has frequently told him sicne the death of the said MEHITIBLE
that it was not the intention of his intestate to compel this defendant to pay any part of
the said legacy...reuled the complainant recover $5080...JOSIAH J. EVANS, Comr in Equity,
at Cheraw Court House 15 May 1811.

Pp. 17-22: South Carolina, Cheraw District. In Court of Equity. Enrollment of Decree.
        14 June 1810 JOHN MURDOCH Complainant & JAMES FEAGIN defendant.
Heard before WILLIAM JAMES, a Judge of the Court of Equity, the complainant and defendant
on or about the month of May or June 1803 executed a certain Deed containing articles of
partnership to establish a store at the Defendants plantation for the purpose of carrying
on trade merchandise for and furing the term of three years conducted under the name of
JAMES FEAGIN & Company...that the complainant should furnish the said store with reasonable
supplies of West Indies & dry Goods and should have all owed him 5% on the amount of the
first cost of said Goods for a satisfaction for his part in purchasing of them except
salt which he was to be allowed only the customary freight...defendant should keep a set
of books in which he should enter a faithful account of all the transactions of the said
Store...that he defendant should be furnished with a reasonable supply of provisions for
himself & family out of the partnership Funds during the said term of three years...
the clear profits arising from the business of the said partnership to be equally divided
between the complainant and defendant...it further appeared that on or about 7 June 1803
the complainant furnished several parcels of goods to commence business in the said store
and furnished other parcels in the month of February following and continued...partnership
was dissolved in 8 Oct 1809...the complainant furnished goods for the amount of ₺ 6000...
defendant had been of being Frequently intoxicated, wasting and destroying the effects of
the partnership....receiver to pay to MURDOCH the money owed...20 Apr 1811 JOSIAH J.
EVANS.

Pp. 22-23: CHARLES IRBY, admr. of MEHITIBLE LIDE vs. DUNCAN McRAE admr. et al. In Equity
        Cheraw Dist., application for a rehearing in the nature of a Bill of Review.
W. THOMPSON, Cheraw, June Term 1814.

Pp. 23-25: DALILAH FREEMAN vs ROBERT COCHRAN Decree
    The Bill states that Compt is the daughter of ROGER POUNCEY, who died intestate
leaving considerable real & personal Estate & six children with whom she was entitled to a
distribution share. That at the time of her fathers death she was married to MATTHEW
FREEMAN, but lived separate from him, before the Estate was divided Complt. made an absolute conveyeance by bill of sale, of her right to it, to ANTHONY POUNCY her brother & one
of the Admrs. to hold the property in turst for her, in order to defeat the claim of
FREEMAN that FREEMAN afterwards sold his right to WM NEVILL; & POUNCEY purchased the claim
of NEVILLE for a horse . That Complt. part of the estate was two negro boys & a tract of
land. That FREEMAN died in 1806 & POUNCEY is dead & defts are his representatives. It
appears from the evidence for Complt. that POUNCEY acknowledge the trust before three witnesses & did npt claim the property as his own until after the end of eleven years, in
1806 when FREEMAN was dead...purchased the property, 1/2 of 175 A for $215 & the hire of
the negro boys was worth $50 each per year. Complts.'s mental capacity was proved to ap-
proach near to idiocy...POUNCEY took his sister home and supported her in a plain manner
for eleven years...advantage was taken of her idiocy...neither complt. nor witnesses could
write and made their marks on a blank piece of paper which POUNCEY later filled up...
Complt. to be paid out of the estate of POUNCEY. WM. D. JAMES.

Pp. 26-27: 1812 June. PHILIP PLEDGER & SARAH his wife vs. Admrs. of BENJAMIN DAVID &
    others.
The Bill is brought to have a partition of the estate of BENJAMIN DAVID and an account of
the rents & profits received by the defendants JAMES POUNCEY & JOSIAH DAVID; obtain an
allowance for the maintenance of the defendants JAMES, BENJAMIN, SARAH & ELIZABETH DAVID.
...profits claimed by Complainant SARAH in her own right,..Complainant SARAH was before
her marriage to MR. PLEDGER the widow of BENJAMIN DAVID & entitled as such to one third
of the real & personal estate; also to a real estate in her own right. Before her marriage
to PLEDGER, she conveyed by deed to the Defendants JAMES,BENJAMIN, SARAH & ELIZABETH, her
children by her first husband, the whole of her interest reserving only one third...this
deed is not valid, because it grants an Estate in futuro & puts a freehold in abeyance,
also that the habendum is repugnant to the premises, the estate in one being fee simple...
the children of the second marriage will be unprovided for and the mother herself will be
left without a competent supprot. But the Court cannot for these reasons set aside the
deed. It is not indeed as formal as it ought to have been but the intention is too mani-
fest to be mistaken & this will cure any informality.   THOS. WATIES[?].

Pp. 27-28: JOHN KEITH vs. ROBERT CAMPBELL Decree Filed 10th June 1818 GEO. BRUCE, Com.
    Complt. alledges in his Bill that he entered into a written contract with the
deft. on 13 Sept 1797 for the delivery of 900 bushels of corn at 2/6 per bushel...before
the 20th of Dec next...after that a renewal of same was made for winter of 1798...Compt.
made various payments, but the account not being closed, complt. in the year 1808 invited
deft. to make a settlement & he shortly afterwards presented an account for ₤ 70 s. 5
against complt. Complt. expressed surprise at the sum & said he owed nothing or if anything a trifling sum...Complt. being unable to find his receipt liquidated the account
by his note on 4 Apr 1803 which he has paid. He lately found a letter from deft. to compt.
dated 8 Oct 1798 enclosing a receipt from ISAAC COURSE dated 29th of same month for ₤50
on account of ROBERT CAMPBELL....compt. in summer of 98 being about to go to No. Island
for his health left in the hands of JOSIAS ALLSTON then a student of law in his office
₤ 50 for the purpose of making the above payment...Deft has overpaid said monies & on the
footing of a trust, pray it may be reapid with interest...in examining the letter of 8
Oct 1798, it appears that he does say "that he would take an opportunity of calling upon
Mr. ALLSTON for the money by Mr. COURSE who goes to Town in a few days....ordered that
deft. repay ₤ 50 with interest from 29 Oct 1798. WM. D. JAMES

Page 29: P. THOMAS vs. the Admr. of T. THOMAS Decree Darlington Court
    On application for partition the following question arose, whether the Complain-
ant is entitled to the preoceeds of a plantation sold by him for $7500, or only to so much
as will make his share of his fathers estate equal to that of the other children, the
father died intestate, the compl. claimed the lands he sold under a parol[?] gift from
his father, If I were to admit the evidence I should still think that the gift has not
been ?   but I reject it....It must be referred to the Comr. to report the sum due by
the Complainant & it is decreed that he do pay the same to the Admr. of his fathers estate.
Darlington Court Ho. 13 Feb 1822.

Page 29: JAS. POUNCEY & others agt. D [E?] MAUDEVILLE, Darlington Court.
    The Complainants have obtained the discovery they sought, but it avails them no-
thing, the defendant is in possession of the land the partition of which is prayed....ord-
ered that the Bill be dismissed with costs. THEODORE GAILLARD. Darlington Court Ho.
Feby 13th 1822.

Page 29: ANN MILLER, Admx. of THOS MILLER vs. JAMES STUBLES[??] & wife
       SARAH arrived at the age of 18 & died, I am of opinion that THOMAS under the will
takes the share or proportion of the Estate left to her by her father the testator.
THEODORE GAILLARD Darlington Court Ho, Feby 13th 1822.

Page 30: S. ROGERS & others vs. R. CARLOSS
       STEPHEN ROGERS & others vs. R. CARLOSS adm BRITTON. In this case it being repre-
sented that STEPHEN ROGERS and JOHN JACKSON are both insolvent. It is therefore ordered
that the said ROGERS and JACKSON do respectively convey to some trustee, to be named by
the Commissioner of this Court, the share of their respective wives in Estate prayed to
be divided to the separate use of the Wife. W. THOMPSON

Page 30: JONATHAN PENNYWELL & others vs. BEN DAVID & ROBERTSON CARLOSS, Exrs. of the
       Executor of MASON LEE, decd and ROBERT B. CAMPBELL) Bill for account and for
review on the estate of MASON LEE, decd.
On hearing the bill and answer of ROBERT B. CAMPBELL and with consent of the Complainants
and of CHARLES C. MASON, Solicitor and attorney in part of the State of Tennessee, It is
ordered and decreed that the Contract made between the defendants BENJAMIN and ROBERT B.
CAMPBELL for hiring the slaves of the estate of sd. MASON LEE...ROBERT B. CAMPBELL is
discharged from any liability to account for the hire of sd. slaves, bond given to said
BENJAMIN DAVID is discharged. HENRY W. DESAUSSURE 14 Feby 1832.

Pp. 30-31: South Carolina, Cheraw District In the Court of Equity Feby Term 1834.
       Exrs. of WILLIAM F. ELLERBE deceased vs. WILLIAM T. ELLERBE, THOMAS R. ELLERBE
& others Bill.
       The case has been submitted...the only question is whether the pecuniary legacy
of $30,000 to THOMAS R. ELLERBE, the infant son of the testator must be charged on the
plantation devised to his other two sons...WILLIAM T. ELLERBE the devisee is of age and
has survived ALEXANDER the other devisee, and by his answer consents to divide the said
real estate with his brother THOMAS R. ELLERBE. I have no hesitation in adopting the
recommendation of the Commissioner that the said real estate should be sold, and the proceeds equally divided between the defendants, THOMAS R. ELLERBE.and WILLIAM T. ELLERBE.
HENRY M. DESAUSSURE.

Page 31: PARISH MILLER & CO. vs. JOHN BROWN, GEO. B. WHITFIELD & W. S. WHITFIELD Bill for
       Relief
In this case it appeared that GEORG B. WHITFIELD was the legal owner of the land mentioned
when the complainants obtained their judgements & lodged their execution...the sd. WHIT-
FIELD in order to defraud the creditors, induced BROWN to cancel the deed(which had never
been recorded) and to make a new deed to WILLIAM S. WHITFIELD, the son of sd. G. B. WHIT-
FIELD...ordered that sd. JOHN BROWN execute a deed to Complainant. W. THOMPSON.

Pp. 32-35: Ex. & Receivers of MASON LEE vs. JAMES ERVIN In the Court of Equity, Cheraw
       District, Winter Term 1835
Ap 9, 1835 The demurer admits all the facts stated in the bill...the case made by the
bill is twofold: the plaintiff states that the defendant threatens to set up payment and
discount when his notes shall fall due & be sued on which payments and discounts they believe it would be unjust to allow, and that now they would be able to prove them unjust,
but may be unable to do so hereafter from the death of witnesses or the decay of their
recollection.
       This makes no case for a discovery....LEE sold and conveyed a tract of land to
ERVIN in 1815 for $25,000 on account of which LEE held at his death two notes one dated
25 Sept 1815 for $12,500 due 1 Jan 1836 signed by ERVIN the purchaser and GAVIN WITHERSPOON
the security, the 2nd for $3000 dated Nov 10 and payable 1 Jan 1836 signed by ERVIN alone,
both notes state expressly that the consideration is the land sold by LEE to ERVIN....
J. JOHNSTON
       In the matter of Estate of MASON LEE Brief.
The authorized agent of the State of Tennessee assigned one moiety of two notes due by
JAMES ERVIN to MASON LEE, to ROBERT B. CAMPBELL. CAMPBELL assigned sd. moiety to LAWRENCE
PRINCE and ISAIAH DUBOSE jointly, ISAIAH DUBOSE assigned the same to ELIAS D. LAW, who
render the assignment has already received one half...the other half the commissioner
refuses to pay...ROBBINS McIVER move for an order ...10 Jan 1838 ROBBINS & McIVER.
A. D. SIMS.
       In the matter of Estate of MASON LEE. Darlington Jany Term 1838.
[No new information] DAVID JOHNSON

R. B. CAMPBELL, WM POUNCEY et all vs. R. B. WIGGINS Darlington Jany Term 1838
       By an Act of the Legislature passes in Decr 1829, it is enacted that MASON
LEE late of Marlborough District, had by his L. W. & T. devised one moiety of his estate to
the State of South Carolina...and after providing for the costs incurred by BAKER, WIGGINS,

late of North Carolina, Decd, to be divided amongst them in the following manner...to
JONATHAN PENNYWELL, 1/4 part, to WILLIAM PENNYWELL 1/4 part, to heirs at law of JOHN
TAYLOR, 1/4 part, and to BLAKE B. WIGGINS 1/4 part....

Pp. 36-39: In the Matter of the Estate of MASON LEE.
      Both JOHN TAYLOR and BLAKE B. WIGGINS had heirs in different degrees of prox-
imity to themselves, i. e., both had children living, and grandchildren, the issue of
deceased children, the question is whether their children and grandchildren take of the
portions granted them equally, pro capita, or by representation ....[they] are entitled
under a grant of the Legislature, to take per capita and not per stapins[?], as the
case of DAVENPORT & HARDING[?], LEIGH vs. NORBURY, CROPLEY vs CLAN, BUTLER vs STRATTON,
McRETHAGE vs. GALBRATH & LIGHT D. RAWLS. have been relied on...under the act of 1791,
in an intestate case , the widow is entitled to 1/3 and the remaining 2/3 to be divided
among the children and grandchildren (children of decd. children)...In England according
to common law, the lands of the tenant descends to the eldest son, who is emphatically
called the heir at law...I infer from the cases that MSSRS PENNYWELLS & JOHN TAYLOR &
BLAKE B. WIGGINS all married sisters of MASON LEE, and the intention of the legislation
is that they should all have equal parts...under the Act of 1791, the grandchildren of
TAYLOR & WIGGINS would be excluded as the fourth Section of that act limits the distribution to children of deceased brothers and sisters ...however, the decree is that the
grandchildren shall have the share that would have been their parents.. [There is a
conflicting opinion rendered by another judge, but yields no new information.]

Pp. 39-45: MARGARET A. LAMB, Admx of ALEXANDER LAMB vs. CARNEY W. LAMB, Admr. of JOSEPH
      A. LAMB and others, heirs of ALEXANDER LAMB. Cheraw, July Term 1843.
ALEXANDER LAMB, the Compt. intestate died in Nov 1836 and administration of his estate
was committed to the Compt. on 29 Dec 1836, his widow. Besides, he has left six children
by that marriage, all of whom are parties dys, and the children by a former marriage, viz.
the defts.CARNEY W. LAMB and his intestate JOSEPH A. LAMB who died a few days after his
father & JANE LYDE, wife of JOHN J. LYDE and administration of the estate of the decd.
son JOSEPH was granted to the deft. CARNEY W. LAMB on 16 Jan 1837. The estate of intestate
consisted principally of land and negroe Slaves and this bill was filed 8 Jan 1838, prays
for a writ of partition. On 17 Jan 1840, the Comr. appointed to make partition made a
return, but on motion of MR. DAVID, the Solr. of the deft CARNEY W. LAMB, the writ was
referred back to the same commissioners for further action, on what ground it does not
appear. It was later determined that one of the slaves listed in the estate was the property of sd. CARNEY W. LAMB....issue was tried at Marlborough in fall term 1844. JOSEPH
A. LAMB lived in his fathers family up to the time of the death of the latter whom he
only survived a few days & that his residence them was only interrupted by a visit to
his friends in Alabama where he remained about a year.

Pp. 45-48: JOSEPH DIXON et ux vs. JOHN R. DONALDSON et ux et al. Cheraw Feby 1846
      The Object of these proceedings was to set aside a deed executed by the wife
of the Complt. the eve of their intermarriage, the substantial charges of the bill fully
sustainedby the testimony....it was not the duty of DONALDSON to surrender the deed.
The great indebtedness of MRS. HASKEW was well known. She was the owner of property to
pay her debts. The marriage took place on 24 Dec 1844. Eleven days previously, she
executed the deed of which a copy is filed with the answer. When M. J. LEWIS was called
on by DONALDSON to go and witness the deed, LEWIS expressed some doubt whether MR. DIXON
would marry MRS. HASKEW if he knew of this deed. DONALDSON replied "DIXON was not obliged
to know anything about it." and requested the witness to keep it still.
      The deed was a fraud in the rights of the Complt. It is ordered that the deed
be set aside. BENJ. F. DUNKIN.
      In this case the court having referred it to the Commissioner to report the
proper terms of a settlement upon the Complainants wife of her share of the estate of
MOSES P. HASKEW about to be divided...her children by the former marriage....GEO. W.
DURGAN 7 Feb 1849.

Pp. 49-51: In Equity, Cheraws Dist., June 7th 1821. CLAUDIUS COCHRAN vs. WM. E. PLEDGER.
      I can see nothing in this case as stated in the bill which would give juris-
diction to a court of Equity. The complainant alleges that he claims certain negroes
under a deed from his half brother WHITWEL D. HUNTER who afterwards sold the same to
the deft. If the complainants deed is a valid one there dan be no obstacle to the Est-
ablishment of his right at law. THOS WAFIES[?].
      PLEDGER vs COCHRAN, In Equity, Darlington, Feby 1825. This case has been ar-
gued with great zeal...The complainant has established by unquestionable evidence three
demands. One a note of HUNTER with interest in Dec 1818 for $120, endorsed to PLEDGER
in Dec 1820; another of $207, a third of $37 on the 20th Sept 1820 , being moneys advanced
by PLEDGER for HUNTER of which resecued him from goal[sic]. He was drunk when he executed
a deed on 10 May 1820 to CLAUDIUS COCHRAN for slaves, interest from his mother's estate.

Pp. 52-58: W. H. De BERRY & WIFE vs. H. H. WILLIAM & others At Cheraw, Feby 1849.
          The defendant HENRY H. WILLIAMS is the Father of his co-Defendants, who are
the Infants & of the wife of the Complainant W. H. DeBERRY who intermarried with her in
the year 1846. The Defendant WILLIAMS was at a former period of his life in easy circumstances but having unfortunately become involved as surety in the pecuniary liabilites of
his friends, his Estate was swept from his possession. This misfortune left him nearly
pennyless with a family to support consisting of a wife & 4 children. His wife is Dead,
the children are still living and are parties to this will. MAJR. WM. PLEDGER, the father
of his deceased wife made some provision for his Daughter by his will. The said Testator
grave his whole estate to his wife MRS. ELIZABETH PLEDGER during her natural life & after
her death to his children in the manner declared in the will, particularly described in
the commissioners report to JOHN BERRIL, JOSIAH EVANS, JAMES FORNISS, JAMES IRBY & his
son, ELLIS PLEDGER, in trust to permit his daughter CAROLINA WILLIAMS to use possess & en-
joy the same without the control of her husband...MRS. ELIZABETH PLEDGER died in the year
1805, about which time WILLIAMS got the possession of his wifes property left to her by
her father. MRS. CAROLINE WILLIAMS, the wife of the defendant, died on the 8th of April
1838, so that the right of her to the possession to the effect on the first day of the
succeeding January among the children. The Complainant W. H. DEBERRY, who intermarried
with MARIA D., the Daughter of Deft. WILLIAMS, have filed for her part.
          Note endorsed by CAPTAIN JOHN TERREL, Exr....estate of WILLIAM PLEDGER, the
testator, paid by WILLIAMS & EMANUEL, who had also married one of the testators daughters,
and PHILIP W. PLEDGER directed him to deliver up the instruments.....GEO W. DARGAN.

Pp. 59-65: ELIZABETH DICKSON vs WM R. SMITH, FRANCIS J. MILES, Exors. JOS. DICKSON & others
          In Equity, Marlborough District, Feby Term 1855.
Before DARGAN Chancellor. JOSEPH DICKSON, late of citizen of So. Carolina, residing in the
District of Marlborough in the month of January 1852 emigrated to the State of Alabama:
where he died in August of the same year. He carried with him a considerable portion of
his personal property. The property he left in S. C. consisted in certain chores in action
due by persons living in this State, and were at the time of his death, in the possession
of his agent, one ROBERT A. McTYER, to be collected by him, also one negro named March.
          Previous to his emigration from S. C., the sd. JOSEPH DICKSON duly executed his
L. W. & T. and a codicil thereto by the provisions of which, to the entire exclusion of
his wife, he gave the whole of his estate to his collateral relations, namely his brother,
& sister, and the children of a deceased brother; he having no issue of his own The will
was executed in S. C. He left his wife behind him without any provision for her support.
She never went to Alabama.
          The statute law of Alabama on this are as follows: Sec. 3 "When any person shall
die intestate, or shall make his L. W. & T. and not therein make any express provision for
his wife...widow may signify her dissent thereto in the Circuit or County Court in the
County in which she resides within one year of the probate of such will, and she shall
be entitled to one third part of all lands..." Ordered that she is entitled to her part.

Pp. 65-68: BAKER WIGGINS et al vs ROBERTSON CARLOSS, Exor. of MASON LEE. At Chambers on
          motion for Injunction. Decree.
This Bill is to obtain injunction of restraint to the Exors. of MASON LEE from selling or
disposing of any of the property. [No new information on this case.]

Pp. 69-71: MINARD VANCAVERY, Heirs of vs. MARGT LAMB, Heirs of. Bill ofr Judgment, Relief
          Decree.
This is a bill to enjoin a suit, brought by the Defendants at Law, for the recovery of a
tract of land, alleged to have been entered into between the ancestors of the respective
parties, about 300 A, sold by the Sheriff of Marlborough on the 1st Monday in Feb 1822,
under an execution of ERVIN & WHITFIELD against MINARD VANCAVERY, the ancestors of the
plaintiff and was purchased at the sum of $54 by his cousin ALEX. LAMB, the ancestor
of the Defendants. By the testimony it appears to have been worth at the time of sale
about $15,000. VANCAVERY lived on the land at the time of sale and continued to occupy it
until his death in 1839. In 1836, LAMB died, and a suit being brought by his heirs to
recover the possession of the land. VANCAVERY filed his bill in 1839, the year of his own
death, against them alleging that LAMB had purchased the land under an agreement with him
that he would convey it to him upon being refunded the purchase money. CARNEY W. LAMB
admits his belief of the allegation of the bill. [Accounts of four witnesses, not named
are given.]. Ordered that the Bill be dismissed. J. JOHNSTON

Pp. 71-74: MARY A. E. ALLEN by her next friend vs. DAVID CROSLAND et al. Bill for Account
          &c. Decree.
The late MATTHEW ALLEN, who died in 1834, by his L. W. & T. gave to his widow one third
part of all his Estate, real and personal and the following are the terms in which he
gave the remaining two thirds to the Complainant, his only child. I give and bequeath to
my daughter MARY ANN ELIZABETH, when she marries or attains the age of twenty one years,

then and in that case, I give, devise and bequeath to my beloved wife ELIZA ANN ALLEN,
one moiety of the two thirds of my estate, and the other remaining moiety of the two thirds
I give devise and bequeath to the surviving children of my brother ROBERT ALLEN, &c."...
JOHN R. EASTERLING and THOMAS McCONNELL were executors...estate was sold 7 Jan 1835...
except a plantation on the Pee Dee River called Hasty Point, which was acquired after the
will...the testators widow intermmaried with one COOK who died shortly thereafter, and
then intermarried with the Deft, DAVID CROSLAND who at the Court of Equity, Jan. term
1839, for Georgetown Dist., was appointed Guardian in chief of the Compt.and on 4 Mar 1839
entered into bond with the Comrs. of that Court in the penalty of $16,000 for the faith-
ful discharge of his duties with the Defts. SAMUEL SPARKS & JOHN W. BOUYER, the Intestate
of the Deft. JEMIMA BOUYER, as sureties, on the 22d March of the same year, admr. with
the will annexed (McCONNELL the Exor. having died some time before) was granted to the
Deft. with HOLDEN W. LILES and P. E. CROSLAND, sureties...McCONNEL who had died appointed
by his will E. H. MILLER his Exor., who after CROSLAND had been appointed guardian, wished
to be guardian[?--unclear]...At March Court for Georgetown Dist., 1844 guardianship was
granted to Deft. CROSLAND.

Pp. 75-76: MARY A. E. ALLEN vs. D. CROSLAND & others. Bill for Account. [No new info.]

Pp. 76-81: SARAH G. EMANUEL et al vs SIMON EMANUEL & N. EMANUEL. Bill for Account.
          Decree Feby 1850.
The pleadings and the evidence present this state of facts. The Defendents are brothers.
The complainants are the wife and children of the Defendants NATHAN EMANUEL. For some
years prior to 1822 NATHAN EMANUEL had kept a store in Georgetown. His brother SIMON had
lived with him from an early age and for the last year or two had served him as a clerk in
the store. At the period last mentioned, NATHAN EMANUEL became a bankrupt but instead of
surrendering his property to his creditors, he transferred his stock of goods with fifteen
or sixteen hundred dollars to the said SIMON EMANUEL, whom he established in business at
the three Creeks in Marlborough District. SIMON EMANUEL admits in his answer that the
principal object of NATHAN EMANUEL was to secrete his property from his creditors, and
his name was not to appear in Marlborough establishment.Although, NATHAN was to receive
half of the profits. Evidence given by COL. LEVY. Instrument dated 16 Mar 1824:
State of S. C., In consideration that NATHAN EMANUEL furnished me with the funds with
which I commenced the mercantile business, I bind myself to the arrangement we entered
into, and settle in the iwfe and children of the said NATHAN EMANUEL, one half of the
stock of goods....Witnessed by C. LEVY.
        Prior to the execution of this deed NATHAN EMANUEL had removed with his family
to the state of New York. Until the year 1836 or 1837, the deft. SIMON EMANUEL remitted
annually to NATHAN the sum of $300.... A letter written from sd. NATHAN to sd. SIMON,
dated Poukeepsie, N. Y., Aug. 23, 1842 states that a letter had been written to MR. J. A.
INGLES to stop proceedings....Sometime in 1847, NATHAN EMANUEL & his family returned to
Georgetown. On 28 Oct 1848, bill was preferred by the wife & children of sd. NATHAN
against sd. SIMON. It is ruled that the ttansaction of 1824 was fraudulent. The obligation of SIMON is release by the settlement with NATHAN in 1842.

Pp. 82-86: ALEX J. McQUEEN & wife vs JOSHUA FLETCHER, JESSE BETHEA, JOEL EASTERLING.
          Feb Term 1851[1850?]. Decree
The plaintiff MRS. CAROLINE McQUEEN is one of the daughters of SHOCKLEY ADAMS, late of
Marlborough District, who died intestate the 10th of October 1824. At his death he left
as his distributees, his wife ISABELLA and eight children, of whom it is necessary to
mention only three WM. L. ADAMS, who became his admr., HANES R. ADAMS and MRS. McQUEEN.
        The intestate wasy, at his death, the owner of the tracts of land in Marlbor-
ough and which are the subjects of litigation in this case, viz. 1st, the plantation
known as the Home tract or Home place, 200 A, the tract that the widow had been in possession of from 1825, sold to the deft. BETHEA in 1836.
        2nd, The Mill tract of 602 A levied on by sheriff as the property of WM. L.
ADAMS, & sold to the deft: FLETCHER 20 Dec 1832 at price of $2000.
        3rd, The Easterling tract, 300 A, sold as the property of HANES R. ADAMS
[name appears here to be HARRIS R. ADAMS] and sold to JOEL EASTERLING, for $600 to whom
the sheriff conveyed it 4 March 1836.
        There was a writ of partition as early as 1826, but MRS. McQUEEN was no party
to it. She was married with the coplaintiff as far back as 1838 or 1841 during her minor-
ity. The following extract from proceedings of Spring Term 1826, was given in evidence.
Mr. ERVIN attorney in the proceedings is dead. Mrs. McQueen received certain negroes,
DR. MOLLAY who was her guardian. Proceeding of 1826 was upheld and the present bill was
dismissed. Feby 1851. J. JOHNSTON.

Pp. 86-92: THOMAS HAMER & others vs. SUSANNAH HAMER et al. Decree
        The complainants and defendants are the heirs at law of JOHN HAMER, late of
Marlborough District, who died intestate and the bill was filed for the partition of his

real estate. The bill describes in a particular manner, the lands that the intestate was seized of at the time of his death, and charges that some of the Defendants to wit: WM HAMER, ALFRED HAMER, ELI HAMER and the heirs of DAVID HAMER, set up a draw title to portions of land which the Complainant described as part of the real estate of the intestate. The defendants had no title, but that they were put in possession by the intestate in his life time--that possession on their part was not adverse to that of the intestate, that it was undefined in extent, that is was expressly by & with the consent of the intestate that they claimed any right and that they were mere tenants at will. The return must be set aside and a new partition made.   GEO. W. DARGAN.

Pp. 93-95: MEREDITH SWEAT vs LEVI IVEY. Bill for account &c. Decree Feby 1854
            At the sitting of Feb. 1852, this cause was referred to the Commissioner to take evidence, Etc. In June 1841, the Plaintiff resided on a tract, 100 A, as the tenant of one LAUCHLIN McCALL. He had a large family and small means. The defendant undertook at his instance, to purchase the land from McCOLL for $300 give his own notes for $100 each, payable 1st Jan 1842, 1843, 1844 with interest.   The land was sold in Feby 1849, purchaser was J. E. DAVID, Esq.....Defendant to pay $274.11 to plaintiff.... BENJ. F. DUNKIN.

Pp. 95-98: ALFRED PARISH Exor vs LEVI IVEY & wf & others. Bill for Construction of Will,
            Account &c. Decree.
The questions presented in this case arise on the will of SHADRAC FULLER, decd., the Testator died Nov. 1850, having been twice married and leaving children by each marriage. His will was executed bg the 29th April previous to his death and the disposing clauses are as follows "to my four first children I make the following donations, to my daughter SARAH ANN IVEY, I give $20...to my daughter NANCY CARMICHAEL I have given $200...to my son WYATT FULLER, $200 and to the heirs of the body of DRUSILLA STUBBS, I devise a tract of land on which they now live in Marion Dist., on Sweat Swamp purchased by me from CATHARINE McLAURIN...my wife NANCY FULLER should remain upon my plantation...at her death to my son JAMES N. FULLER, if he should die without heirs, to be sold and proceeds divided among my living children, possession of which he is to have when he attains the age of 21 years... my five children, viz. WILLIMINA, EMILY, MARTHA, MARTHA, and MACEY...my granddaughter EMMA GAUSE, $200 if she lives to attain the age of 21 years."
            JAMES N. FULLER the Devisee died 18 Jan 1851, unmarried and intestate, and not having attained the age of 21. The widow NANCY FULLER died 1 Nov 1852, and the family of the testator have removed from the place and no longer reside together. The Executor _?_ the land and has hired out the Negroes for 1853, and on 7 Nov 1853 filed the Bill praying the Auction of the Court especially in relation to the conflicting of claims of the children of the first and second marriage.
            The will seems to have been rather hastily prepared, and on looking at the original, there are no marks of punctuation and no capital appear from beginning to end. Those of the former marriage were grown, married and settled off. The family of the second marriage consisted of his wife and six children. It appears from the will that he had already made advancements to the children of the former marriage. He mentions the five daughters of his second marriage. "My intention is that my property remain amongst these my last children forever". The proceeds of negroes to be divided among the children of the second marriage....BENJ. F. DUNKIN.

Pp. 98-101: DUNCAN McRAE and others vs JOSHUA DAVID, Ordinary. Bill for Account & Relief
            Decree.
DANIEL McRAE late of Marlborough District, departed this life on the 5th Aug 1842, intestate and left a personal Estate estimated at the time as worth between Four and five thousand dollars. The Defendant who was then and is now ordinary of the Dist. granted letters of admn. to COLIN McRAE. The latter executed an administration bond to the ordinary, bearing date 29 Aug 1842 to which EPHRAIM L. HENAGAN and JOHN L. MCRAE were sureties. COLIN made only one return. He reduced the assets to possession and in the year 1845 died intestate and insolvent without having accounted for any portion of the estate of JOHN L. McRAE which had come into his possession. After his death, the ordinary administered de bonis non on the estate of DANIEL McRAE as a derelict estate. The sureties have both died intestate and insolvent, nothing could have been derived from their estates to satisfy the claims of the distributees of DANIEL McRAE. The charge is that the Ordinary is guilty of maladministration of COLIN McRAE, and liable on account of his official default and misconduct in taking in adequate and insolvent security. Much evidence has been given. The acts of 1679 and 1739 require the ordinary to take sufficient security. Ordered that the Plaintiffs have leave to prove themselves distributees of DANIEL McRAE....GEO. W. DARGAN.

Pp. 101-104: NATHAN THOMAS JR. et al vs. NATHAN THOMAS SR. Decree.
            The case involves a question whether certain negroes have been lawfully emancipated by Deft. THOMAS BINGHAM, the maternal Grandfather of Complt, father in law of Deft, by his L. W. & T. bequeathed as follows:"I lend to my daughter NANCY THOMAS for her

life one negro man Prince & one negro woman Rachel & her increase; at her death, to her
children to be equally divided amongst them; Afterwards in 1801, the defendant obtained an
absolute bill of sale of Rachel and the children she had(about whom this suit arises) from
the testator BINGHAM, and Deft. after the death of his wife in May 1813, emancipated Rachel
her children & grandchildren. Soon after his marraige to his wife, & of his having remained in possession and paid taxes for her children, until the time of emancipation. Of
the bill of sale he says, he drew it at the request of the testator, but that he did not
tell him it was to be in trust, otherwise he would have drawn it so. The evidence was all
on the side of Complt. JOHN THOMAS brother of the Deft., stated that BINGHAM was sick and
long bedridden at the time he executed the bill of sale in question & another to himself,
who had married another daughter. He first solicited BINGHAM, at the request of his brother,
to make the bills of sale & gave as a reason that BINGHAMs wife might sell his and his
brothers negroes, as she had lately done some of his own. That the whole affair was kept
as a secret from MRS. BINGHAM, who was spirited[?] & as it appeared from the witness, more
intelligent than her husband, for she claims the negroes she sold, as a separate estate,
that BINGHAM was much attached to the entailing of property, or keeping it in his own family, & his brother not se. When he married his wife, the testator only left him the negros
that went home with him. But he does not know upon what terms his brother received his.
He thinks BINGHAM did not intend to make an absolute bill of sale, especially if he had
thought it would cut off one of his grandsons, who was a great favorite, That BINGHAM was
reluctant to execute the bill of sale, but was told it was only to prevent his wife from
selling, and not to alter the will, and then he __?__ NANCY CONVINGTON examined by commission state, that deft. after the death of his wife, told her in a conversation attending a courtship, that the negroes he had in his possession did not belong to him, but were
given to his children, by their grandfather, and she understood distinctly. ANNE THOMAS,
also examined by commission, stated that the Deft. told her twice expressly that he might
set them free, if they were not willed to NANCY. Ordered that Complts. be reinstated in
possession of Negroes.

Pp. 104-105: CANNON vs WHITFIELD Decree
        This case come up on Reports of Commissioners & execution thereto, the first
exception is, because the Commisioner has allowed the sum of $500 for the Negroes delivered
upon by the Complainant, to the Defendant when it appeared that the negroes were not worth
so much so much at the time of sale, and a great price was given for the land.
        ...the amount of an order drawn by JAMES MOODY as Defendant for $268 & the
interest thereon...bill was filed 18 Feb 1823...[full names of parties involved not given.]

Pp. 106-110: JAMES J. HARLLEE Exor. DAVID S. HARLLEE decd vs. NEILL McNAIR & wife & others.
        Marlborough February 1858.
The will of the testator DAVID S. HARLLEE bears date 25 Aug 1854... At that time his family consisted of his wife, and seven children to wit: the plaintiff JAMES J. HARLLEE, ELIZA
BETH the wife of NEILL McNAIR, MARY ANN the iwfe of BENJAMIN H. COVINGTON, WILLIAM F. HARL-
LEE, and JULIA J. HARLLEE, HARRIET ELLEN HARLLEE, and THOMAS H. CARLLEE, the three last
named residing at the time with their parents.
        By the first clause, the Estate, real and personal, is devised and bequeathed
to the plaintiff in trust, nevertheless for the purposes therein after declared. By the
second clause, testator directs that after payment of his debts, the residue of his estate
shall be held by the trustee for the benefit of the testators wife during her natural life.
The fourth and fifth clauses provide for partial appropriations of the corpus of the Estate
upon particular contingencies. The sixth clause if imperfectly expressed, but the meaning
is sufficiently intelligible, that on the death of his widow, the plaintiff should cause to
be distributed the remainder among the testator's children. The testator probably died
shortly after the date of his will. The testators widow died in August 1855.
        In January 1856, a writ of partition was issued by the Commissioner, and in
Feb. the return was confirmed. On 8January, 1857, JULIA J., one of the testator's daughters
intermarried with JOHN N. McCOLL; and on the same day, HARRIET ELLEN, another daughter intermarried with ROBERT GRAHAM.[No other pertinent information.]

Pp. 111-114: JAMES C. HAMER & wife vs PHILIP M. HAMER admn. ELI THOMAS decd & other.
        Marlborough, February 1858.
On 23 July 1846, the intestate ELI THOMAS executed the deed of which a copy is filed with
the pleadings. He was at the time, in very feeble health. One of the witnesses said he
was very low, and another stated that the old man afterwards told him he did not expect to
live twenty hours when he made the deed. He was, however, entirely capable of making any
disposition of his property he thought proper. On the same day, he executed other deeds
in favor of other children.
        JOHN B. McDANIEL, the trustee had married a daughter of the intestate; and
his (intestate's) son ROBERT D. THOMAS, was in embarrassed circumstances, and as it would
seem, had already been favored by his father. The deed provides that the negroes shall be
held for the special use and behoof of the donor's son, R. D. THOMAS and family. It was

accepted in writing by the trustee on the same day; the instrument was recorded on 8 Sept following. The donor recovered from his indisposition and survived until 22 Aug 1854. The court infers from the evidence that the negroes given to the other children in July 1846 went into possession of the respective donees at the time. But for some reason, those included in the deed to MCDANIEL, intrust for ROBERT D. THOMAS still reamined in possession of the donor. At the time, ROBERT was a resident of this state, but early in the fall of that year he removed with his family to FLORIDA where he died in 1848. He left a widow & six children, and all except the plaintiff and one son continue to be residents of Florida or otherwise out of the jurisdiction of this court.. The trustee removed to Arkansas, of which state he is now a resident.
   The negroes continued in the possession of the intestate until his death in 1854. They were not appraised in the admn. of the estate, but were hired out by the admr. till called for (as the witness R. N. JOHNSTON testified, who was present at the sale of ELI THOMAS's estate). ELIJAH C. HAMER testified that he lived with the intestate in 1851, and the intestate received two or three letters from his grandchildren in Florida. LEVI IVEY also appeared as a witness. Decree is that the negroes are to be delivered up to the widow and children of ROBERT D. THOMAS. BENJ. F. DUNKIN.

Page 115: A. B. HENAGAN & wife vs B. PETERKIN Ex. et al February 1854.
   Report and Exceptions.
In reference to the first Exception the Court is of opinion that the two items viz. of cotton furnished by and Merchandize sold to each of the parties, which the Commissioner has introduced into the account of JAMES PETERKEN, survivor with JESSE PETERKIN & Co.... at the close of 1844...JAMES PETERKIN should be credited with the balance due to him of $409.20 and charged with the balance due by JESSE PETERKIN of $632-25.
   2nd Exception. The court is without any distinct evidence as to the understanding to which the Commission refers, but the evidece of MR. DAVID should have been received ....BENJ. F. DUNKIN.

Pp. 116-119: HARFORD WALKER et ux vs DAVID CROSLAND et al February 1850.
   The principal facts of this case are fully and correctly stated in ALLEN vs CROSLAND 2 Rich E R 68. The bill seeks to establish and enforce the liability of the defendants HOLDEN W. SILAS and PHILIP E. CROSLAND, as sureties on the admn. bond of DAVID CROSLAND. The defence rests on two grounds which will be separately considered. First, the defendants insist they are not liable because the bond is not in the form prescribed by law. It appears that MATTHEW ALLEN died in Georgetown District in 1834, leaving a widow and one child, now the complainant MARY ANN ELIZABETH WALKER.Some years afterward DAVID CROSLAND married the widow and in January 1839, he was appointed by the Commissioner of Equity for Georgetown District guardian of the child, giving bond with the penal sum of $16,000. Both he and his sureties were residents of Marlborough District. In the latter part of March 1839, the bond was sent up to Marlborough, dated 22 Mar 1839. THe bond is payable to E. WATERMAN, Ordinary of Georgetown Dist. The bond was proved by C. W. DUDLEY Esqr., the witness.
   The Act of 1789 prescribed two forms of bond, the 20th section prescribes that an administration with the will annexed shall enter into bond with security in a sum equal to the value of the estate at least.
   DAVID CROSLAND was appointed admr. with the will annexed of MATTHEW ALLEN, decd as far as his goods and chattels had been left unadministered by THOMAS McCONNELL, decd, the Exr. of MATTHEW ALLEN decd. The alleged default is in not paying over the the Complt. the legacies to which she was entitled under her father's will. This is not a statue of North Carolina...the L. W. & T. of HARBERT PEOPLES had been duly proved in the County Court of Guilford; admn. had been granted to SALLY PEOPLES and REUBIN FOLGER. [The reason for referring to this case is not clear.]....Ordered that the bill be dismissed.

Page 120: CORNELIUS A. WEATHERLY & wife vs LOUISA A. MASON & others. Marlborough.
   February 1860.
No parol testimony was offered in this cause. The slaves which the defendant LOUISA A. MASON holds under her father's will belong to her absolutely. ....The bill to be dismissed.
BENJ. F. DUNKIN.

Pp. 120-121: BENJ. F. PEGUES Exor. WILLIAM PEGUES decd. vs. CLAUDIUS M. PEGUES & others.
   Marlborough February 1860.
The proceedings present the question submitted to the consideration of the Court. By the ancient act of Distribution, it was provided that the surplus of the intestates estate should be distributed one third to the widow, and the residue in equal protions among the children "in case any of the children are dead, unless the child had been advanced in the same manner...the child's heirs shall have his part..." The issue of MALACHI PEGUES decd are entitled to represent their parent and to take the legacies given to him in the will.
BENJ. F. DUNKIN.

Pp. 122-125: SIMON JACOBS vs WILLIAM C. EASTERLING & DANIEL DIMORY. Marlborough.
February 1860.
To the facts of this case referrence must be had to the pleadings and the voluminous evidence submitted at the hearing.. This much is stated by the bill and formally admitted by
the answer to wit: That the plaintiff who was a poor man and residing on a tract of land
adj. the defendant WILLIAM C. EASTERLING had bargained with one AARON QUICK whose tenant
he was to purchase from him the land, 105 A for $575. The was in Jan. 1851. The money
was to be paid in cash; the deft. EASTERLING "being willing to befriend the plaintiff advanced" the money to the sd. QUICK and at the most simple and effectual and least expen-
sive method of securing the repayment of the sum took the title of the said land to himself, and on 16 Jan 1851, he entered into a written agreement with the plaintiff to convey
to him....first few notes were paid, and the sum due was about $60 or $70...the defendants
brother tendered him $140.... Note was cancelled in fall of 1855. McTILRAY was sheriff in
1851...testimony of CHARLES ENGLISH & B. F. McTILVRAY[?]...ALLEN JACOBS, the plaintiff's
brother.... Ordered the case be referred to Commr. to determined how much is owed.

Pp. 126-127: PETER ODOM & ANDERSON NEWTON Exors. vs JORDAN C. KENNEDAY & wife & others
This case came on to be heard at the present term upon the report of the Commissioners on the Executor's accounts, and an exception thereto on the part of PETER ODOM,
one of the Exors. The executors, in the exercise of power given to them in the
will, sold in several parcels at different times, the whole estate of the testator at public auction. At one of these sales, PETER ODOM bid off the House Tract of about 1000 A at
$8 per acre. In making up the accounts of the Exrs., the Commissioner charged them with
this land as sold, but whose evidence submitted on the part of others of the legatees,
estimated it at $9 per acre....The act of 1839, makes the Exrs. liable for the value of the
property....The exception of PETER ODOM is overruled. February 7th 1862. JOHN A. INGLES.

Pp. 128-133: P. W. PLEDGER & wf, JOHN W. ODOM & wf et al. February 1864 Bill original &
Bill of Review[?] & Supplement.
MARY J. GRAHAM, P. W. PLEDGER. Cross Bill.
The original bill of PHILIP W. PLEDGER & wf alleges that ANANIAS GRAHAM died seized of the
tract of land purchased from HENRY EASTERLING. In her answer the defendant CAROLINA GRA-
HAM avers that a portion of this tract containing 100 A did not belong to ANANIAS GRAHAM
at his death, but was the estate of her late husband JOHN W. GRAHAM, a predeceased son of
ANANIAS GRAHAM. JOHN GRAHAM received this tract as a gift without any deed of conveyance.
All the heirs of ANANIAS recognized this as the land of sd. JOHN W. GRAHAM.
The marriage of HENRY C. GRAHAM with MARY JANE BRIGMANis established by the
evidence. The fact is deposed to by the clergyman who perforemd the marriage ceremony,
and there is no sufficient opposing evidence.
Another question in the case arises out of certain transactions between the
plaintiff PHILIP W. PLEDGER & HENRY C. GRAHAM which occurred a few months prior to the
death of the latter. On Dec 31, 1860, HENRY C. GRAHAM confessed to PLEDGER, a judgement
for $600, founded upon a promissory note made at the same time but ante-dated. On the
same day, HENRY C. GRAHAM executed for the expressed consideration of $1300 a deed purport-
ing in consideration of $4000 to convey all his portion & interest in his father's estate,
both real & personal to PHILIP W. PLEDGER. ...for value received of a debt due to him by
his brother THOMAS P. GRAHAM, for $337.50 bearing interest from 5 Mar 1859.
HENRY C. GRAHAM appears to have been of the careless kind, improvident & thrift-
less, without energy or force of character
PLEDGER in his answer sets forth that HENRY C. GRAHAM was boarding in his family, was greatly involved in debt, pressed by his Judgment & other creditors and was anxi-
ous to move to Mississippi there to pursue his profession as a Physician, but was prevented
by his debts; that he did not regard his interest in the estate of his father ANANIAS &
his brother JOHN as more than sufficient to liquidate his debts and support himself for a
time...witness NICHOLS inform us that is was adhered to [his declaration].
The brothers and sisters of JOHN W. GRAHAM except MRS. PLEDGER & MRS. ODOM have
executed a deed purporting to convey their interest in the real estate to the widow, MRS.
CAROLINE GRAHAM. JAMES McMILLAN who married ELIZA, one of the sisters has been absent from
this State and has not been heard from for some 13 years. He is presumed dead, and his
wife ELIZA is competent to make the deed. MRS JANE TERRIL, another sister, with her husband JAMES TERRIL also joined in its execution.   J. P. CARROLL.

Pp. 134-136: MARY ANN GAY, by next friend vs MARGARET A. EASTERLING & others.
The chief purpose of this cause is to procure partition among the plaintiff
and others, who are made defendants of certain real and personal property which by the
will of that late DANIEL ODOM, is limited to them in remainder, after a life estate which
is now determined. The only matter of controversy is the proportion in the distribution
now to be made. The language of the particular provision under which the title to the property is derived is "and at her death it is my will and desire that all the said property
real and personal with its increase shall be equally divided amongst MARY ANN GAY and such

of the children of EVANDER and MARGARET EASTERLING as may be living at my death and JESSE GAY and MARY ELLEN GAY children of HENRY GAY deceased." The persons thus made objects of the testators bounty are grandchildren of his wife through her three children by a former marriage. The plaintiff who is the only child of JOHN W. GAY, one of three claims that the partition is to be made per strixpes and that she is therefore entitled to one third; and this is also suggested, as the proper construction on behalf of the children of HENRY GAY, another of the three. On the other hand, it is insisted on the part of the children of EVANDER and MARGARET EASTERLING of whom there are nine living at testator's death, that the partition is to be made per capita, and there being twelve person in all to participate, that the share of the plaintiff, as of each of the others is only one twelfth. The case has been submitted for Judgment....It is the opinion of the court that partition must be made per capita....tract of land in Marlboro District devised by DANIEL ODOM to his wife WINNEY, set apart one twelfth part to MARY ANN GAY, one sixth part to HENRY ELLEN [sic] GAY, to the defendant MARGARET A. EASTERLING, the one, one hudred and eigh part in value thereof (1/108), and to JOSEPHINE MURDOCK, WILLIAM B. EASTERLING, HENRY D. EASTERLING, LAURENCE E. EASTERLING, WHITMORE J. EASTERLING, EDWARD J. EASTERLING, MARGARET E. EASTERLING, & MARTHA E. EASTERLING, each 10/108 part in value thereof....HENRY EASTERLING as admr. of estate of JESSE GAY, and to the administrator of the estate of JOSIAH R. EASTERLING, each the one twelfth part in value thereof....JOHN A. INGLES, December 10, 1864.

Pp. 137-139: ASBURY H. ODOM, LEWIS T. ODOM, HENRY K. ODOM vs ELIZABETH ODOM, JAMES W. ODOM, ALEX BEVERLY & wife, HARRIET ODOM, JOHN W. ODOM, MARY ANN ODOM, DANIEL H. ODOM, JOSIAH S. ODOM, ALEXANDER ODOM.
JAMES ODOM died intestate in August 1856, leaving a widow ELIZABETH and eleven children, and administration of his estate was duly committed to his son, JAMES W. ODOM. This Bill was filed for account and distribution of his personal Estate, and partition of the realty. It sets forth that advancements in land had been made by the Intestate to five of his children, who are defendants in the cause, namely, JAMES W. ODOM, ELIZABETH BEVERLY, wife of ALEXANDER BEVERLY, JOHN W., DANIEL J. and JOSIAH S. ODOM. Claims to the land are insisted on and d ? by the widow in her Question of title to land...and this Court at Feb. Term 1858 ordered five issues to be made up and referred to the Court of Common Please The issues were tried in October 1860....It is determined that those were valid deeds to the five children and because of the terms "give and bequeath", it appears that this was their part of the estate.

Pp. 140-141: BENJAMIN F. MOORE et al vs MARY MOORE et al. Marlborough February 1866.
This is a Bill ofr the partition and distribution of the estate of WILLIAM J. MOORE who died Intestate. The only question submitted at the hearing was, whether a tract called the House tract, forms a part of the estate. The Intestates widow claiming it as her property, i. e. MARY MOORE.
The Plaintiffs produced a title from CHARLES MANSHIP[?] to the Intestate, absolute in its terms, dated February 16, 1835. MRS. MOORE avers in her answer that "the real title was in her father JOHN ADAMS, but by his direction the conveyance was made by CHARLES MANSHIP to her husband, the true intent and meaning being that the same should be her separate estate."
JOHN PLEDGER testified that ADAMS had possession of the land eight or ten years, and it went into possession of Moore on his marriage in 1835 or 1836. That it came from ELIJAH CURTIS to ADAMS, and he thinks CHARLES MANSHIP[?] conveyed it to CURTIS. That he heard MANSHIP say he had been at MOORES to make a deed, and there was something wrong about one he had made before. In the division of ADMAS estate, the gift of this land was treated as an advancement to his daughter. Buth that does not imply that it was a gift to her separate use. Ordered that it be referred to the Commissioner.
HENRY D. LESESNE March 14, 1866.

Pp. 142-145: NANCY C. MANSHIP vs WM K. BOWDEN, Exr. et al. Marlborough February 1866.
TRAVIS MANSHIP by his will dated Feb. 26, 1864, gave and devised all his estate, real and personal, to his wife, NANCY the plaintiff, and his five children, by name in equal share, the share or one sixth part of his wife to be for her life only, and at her death to be divided among the said children. She claims her dower as well as the provision made for her by the Testator. The Bill also prays for an account from the Exr., WILLIAM K. BOWDEN. The right to dower is a clear legal right...The dower is a right that the husband cannot control.
The five children are JOHN H., ELI., ANNA[?[JANE, MARY ELLEN, & GEORGE W. JOHN H. afterwards died intestate, leaving no child, but leaving a widow LAURA, who has intermarried with the defendant ELI PEEL. GEORGE W. afterwards died intestate, having never married. The plaintiff is entitled to her dower out of 5/6 of the estate.
HENRY D. LESESNE, April 9, 1866.

Pp. 146-159: FRANKLIN MANNING vs ELI MANNING Exor. & others. Marlboro Feby Term 1866. Bill for Account, Distribution and Partition.

43

MEALY MANNING by his will dated March 26, 1862, gave to his wife MARY for life a tract of land, seven slaves and some other personal property, and directed afted her death, the same should be divided among his legal heirs. He gave the residue of his Estate, real & personal to be equally divided among his ten children ELI, THOMAS J., SARAH JANE (wife of DAVID BETHEA), WILLIAM S., JAMES R., FRANKLIN (the Plaintiff), JOHN, HOLLAND, HOUSTON, and ANGUORA[??].... The testator died soon after, leaving a considerable estate consisting of land, negroes, stock, plantation implements, etc. THOMAS J., one of the children, proved the will and was executor, until he died intestate 28th Dec 1864. ELI MANNING was then qualified as Exr, this Bill was filed, on 19 Oct 1865.
    The testators widow, MARY MANNING, died intestate in September 1863, never having received any of the property left to her. WILLIAM L. MANNING, one of the children, died intestate in August 1862, leaving a widow MARTHA J. MANNING (who intermarried with H. M. STACKHOUSE and admrd. the estate). THOMAS J. MANNING left a widow ANN M. MANNING (who administered on his estate) and four children, JAMES, ORLETTA[?[LAWRENCE, MARY JANE and MARGARET MANNING.
    The testator was the Guardian of two infants, named DELANEY J. and MARY A. KINNEY, whose estate is mingled with his, and who are not parties to this proceeding. The cause was submitted to CHANCELLOR INGLES, who on 19 Jan 1866, made an order[quoted].[Apparently problem arose because some payments were made in Confederate money, and the slaves were emancipated at the close of the War.]
                                            HENRY D. LESESNE May 4, 1866

Page 160: Ex Parte ELIZA McMILLAN in re PLEDGER vs ODOM
        On hearing the Petition and the answer of J. H. HUDSON and MARY A. McMILLAN it is adjudged that the quantity of the Petitioners estate in the premise was fixed by CHAN-CELLOR INGLES Decree of Feb. 10, 1865.
        I regret that said Decree was not brought to my notice when I signed theconsent order of Feb. 9, 1866....HENRY D. LESESNE May 14, 1866.

Pp. 160-162: B. F. MOORE et al by next friend vs T. B. MOORE Adm. et al. Marlborough
             February Term 1867.
From the report of the Commissioner and the testimony accompanying it, the inference may be drawn that the money received by WM. S. MOORE on account of his wards[?] remained un-converted until March 1863. The several sums for 1859 and 1860 were paid to him in gold. It was converted to Treasury Notes of the Confederate States. [the relationship of the plaintiff and defendant is not stated in the decree.].

Pp. 162-163: NICHOLAS ROGERS surviving Executor vs LOUISA PRINCE et al Marlborough
             February 1867.
a decretal order for foreclosure and for sale of the mortgaged premises described in the bill has been already made. In the event that the proceeds of such sale proving insuf-ficient to satisfy the mortgage debt, the bill prays that a ___?___ for the defiency may be rendered against the heir at law of ANNE E. PRINCE & LAWRENCE D. PRINCE, decd. or against the defendants JOSEPH H. SWET[?] & LOUISA A. PRINCE.... J. P. CARROLL

Pp. 164-169: S. J. TOWNSEND Guardian vs C. P. TOWNSEND Admr. et al. Marlborough,
              At Chambers, 17 Sept 1866.
In the latter part of the year 1859, J. W. HENAGAN, since deceased, was substituted as Guardian of the infant MARY F. MILES, in the place of her former Guardian, her mother AMANDA E. MILES, who afterwards became the wife of ALLEN A. MOORE. In his statement of the accounts, the Referee[?], after ascertaining what was due by MRS. MOORE, as Guardian, in 1860, charged that sum to JOHN W. HENAGAN, as if received by him of that date: and this is the first exception of the Defendants....The money received by him on the bond on A. D. CAMPBELL in 1861, was lent to Z. A. DRAKE, ...money lent to CHARLES IRBY. The note of THOMAS HASKINS was executed to receive the price of two negro slaves of the in-fant MARY F. MILES. [there were apparently problems arising because of debts paid with Confederate currency.]. [This case is not very clear.]

Pp. 170-172: JOSIAH GAY Admr. vs CHAS P. TOWNSNED Admr. Petition for account, specific
             delivery, &c.
This cause came in to be heard, by consert of parties, at Chambers, upon the report of Referee....notes payable to JOHN W. GAY and in his possession at his death.
Agreement between JOHN W. GAY and his mother MARY ODOM. MARY ODOM survived her son JOHN W. GAY.   July 13, 1867, JOHN A. INGLES.
[THis case is very difficult to read. Apparently, MARY ODOM owed her son JOHN W. GAY some debt. One MARGARET A. EASTERLING entered into the case.] JOSIAH GAY, as admr. of JOHN W. GAY, orderd to pay to CHARLES P. TOWNSEND $72.25.   JOHN A. INGLES, Aug 27, 1867.

Page 173: Blank.

Pp. 174-175: JOHN H. SMITH & NOAH GIBSON bs L. G. PATE & J. W. STUBBS. In the Court
            of Common Please at May Term 1867. Bill to cancel Judgment & Relief.
The Complainants who are Judgment Creditors of the Defendant JOHN W. STUBS, have filed
this bill for the purpose of setting aside a judgment confessed by JOHN W. STUBBS to his
co-defendant L. GARLINGTON PATE on the 18 Feb 1867 for $2000. It seems that the defendant
PATE was at the house of the Co-defendant STUBBS when GENERAL SHERMAN's Army passed
through Marlboro where STUBBS resided. His son-in-law PATE being then a citizen of Sump-
ter[sic] County, but at that time on a visit to his father-in-law, STUBBS having been
stripped of most of his personal property. STUBBS owed his friend and neighbor one
E. W. GOODWIN, $140. On 18 Feb 1867, the parties went to Bennettsville, when the confes-
sion of Judgment was rendered. The Judgement was set aside. May 28, 1869. J. M. RUTLAND.

                            END.

Pp. 1-2: State of S. C.: JOHN D. A. MURPHY of Orangeburgh Dist., for $64 pd by BENJAMIN
            JEFFCOAT JUNR of Lexington Dist., 772 A on both sides of the Waggon Road from
Charleston to Waters ferry near the head of Pond Branch, granted to ROBERT STARK 5 Aug
1793 conveyed by BENJAMIN F. TAYLOR, Exrs. of L. W. & T. of sd. ROBERT STARK, Esqr. Decd
to JOHN D. A. MURPHY...5 Aug 1836. JOHN D. A. MURPHY (SEAL), Wit: JOHN N. BARRILLON, WM.
O MARTIN. Proven by WILLIAM O. MARTIN 26 March 1839 before ELIJAH JEFFCOAT, J. P.
[Plat included in deed showing 100 A bought by JEFFCOAT from REDMOND, 172 A part of 200
A bought by JEFFCOAT from REDMOND, 500 A and deduct 50 A from SHARPS BOLAN old field tract.
Also shows MICHL SHARPS part, adj. land owners J. D. A. MURPHY, LEVI CHANEY, LEWIS FERTICK,
SOL: WALKER.] Recorded title & Plat 7 Jany 1840. JOHN N. BARRILLON, Deputy Surveyor,
5th Aug 1836.

Pp. 2-4: State of S. C., Lexington Dist.: CHARLES WILLIAMSON of Dist aforesd., for $325.50
            pd. by BENJAMIN JEFCOAT JUNR of Lexington Dist...651 A surveyed for JOHN HOOVER
4 Sept 1800 on Bull Swamp Road leading to Charleston adj. JOHN REDMON, WILLIAM JEFCOAT,
HAMPTON and BYNUM, BLANTON and MIDDLETON, JOHN HOOVER, granted to sd. HOOVER ___ Mar 1801...
also another tract of 50 A surveyed for JERUSHAH and MARY HOOVER, part of 120 A surveyed
for them 21 Sept 1801, on Bull Swamp Road on the Big Pond branch, waters of the N fork
of Edisto River adj. JOHN REDMON, JOHN HOOVER, SAMUEL MOIRS[?], granted 4 Jan 1802...
the last mentioned tract sold for $25...27 Mar 1839...CHARLES WILLIAMSON (LS), MARY WILL-
IAMSON. Wit: DAVID C. WILLIAMSON, JOHN T. WILLIAMSON, ELIJAH JEFCOAT, J.P. State of S. C.
Lexington Dist.: Proven by DAVID C. WILLIAMSON before ELIJAH JEFCOAT, J. P. 25 Mar 1839.
State of S. C., Orangeburgh Dist.: DAVID S. DANNELLY, a Justice of the Quorum for sd. Dist.
certify that MARY WILLIAMSON, wife of CHARLES WILLIAMSON, relinquished her dower, 12 Apr
1839. D. S. DANNELLY. Rec. 7 Jany 1840. R. HARMAN, R. M. C.

Pp. 4-5: State of S. C., JESSE COOGLER of Lexington Dist., for $500, pd by JACOB STACK of
            same, 110 A granted to HANNAH WEAVER, conveyed to JOHN WEED, and by him willed to
CHRISTIAN WEED, and by him conveyed to JESSE COOGLER, in the fork of Broad and Saluda Rivers
at the N side of the original tract adj. GEORGE LORICK, COOGLER & LEVERS...JESSE COOGLER
(LS), Wit: GODFREY STACK, DANIEL METZ. Lexington Dist.: Proven by DANIEL METZ, 21 Oct
1839 before SAMUEL BOUKNIGHT, Justice of the Quorum. Lexington Dist.: Before SAMUEL
BOUKNIGHT, SPARTA COOGLER, wife of JESSE, relinquished her dower...SPARTA COOGLER (S)
Rec. 8 Jan 1840. R. HARMAN, R. M. C.

Pp. 5-6: State of S. C., Lexington Dist.: JOHN KNOX of Lexington Dist., for $3500 pd. by
            JOHN K. JOHNSTON of same, 1400 A, half part of the mill tract containing 3000 A
adj. JESSE FOX, ISRAEL GAUNT, HENRY JACKSON, THOMAS QUATTLEBUM and others on Chinquepine
Creek, main Branch of North Edisto River...19 Oct 1839...JOHN KNOX (LS), Wit: EMANUEL
QUATTLEBUM, JANE JOHNSTON. Lexington Dist.: Proven by EMANUEL QUATTLEBUM before ANDERSON
STEEDMAN, J. P. 5 Nov 1839. Rec. 8 Jan 1840. R. HARMAN, R. M. C.

Pp. 6-8: State of S. C., JACOB STACK, ANNA STACK, GODFREY STACK, MARTHA WEED, and JOSEPH
            WEED of LEXINGTON Dist., for $450, pd. by GABRIEL HOYLER of Lexington Dist.,
65 A, part of an original tract granted to JOHN LAGBELT, sd. tract willed by ABRAM STACK to
JACOB STACK during his life and after his death to his heirs and if he died without body
Heirs, the sd. Land to fall back to ANNA STACK, GODFREY STACK, and MARTHA STACK, the sd.
MARTHA STACK has since intermarried with JOSEPH WEED...the land where JACOB STACK now lives,
adj. GODFREY STACK, GABRIEL HOYLERS, LEWIS RIDDLES...21 Oct 1839...JACOB STACK (+) (LS),
GODFREY STACK (LS), ANNA STACK (X) (LS), MARTHA REBECCA WEED (X) (LS), JOSEPH WEED (LS),
Wit: JESSE COOGLER, J. W. COOGLER. Lexington Dist.: Proven by JESSE COOGLER 2 Oct 1839
before SAMUEL BOUKNIGHT Q. U. Lexington Dist.: REBECCA STACK, wife of JACOB STACK, relin-
quished dower 21 Oct 1839. REBECCA STACK (X). Lexington Dist.: POLLY STACK, wife of
GODFREY STACK, relinquished dower, 21 Oct 1839. POLLY STACK (X). Lexington Dist.: MARTHA
REBECCA WEED, wife of JOSEPH WEED, relinquished dower. Rec. 8 Jan 1840. R. HARMAN, R. M. C.

Pp. 8-9: S. C. Lexington Dist.: JOSEPH MIMS of Dist.,aforesd., for $2900, pd. by SAMUEL
            WINGARD of same, land consisting of six tracts...1st, granted to JEREMIAH WEBB
40 A in the fork of Lightwood not [sic] Branch & McTeers creek; 2nd, granted to JESSE
RHODEN, 467 A; 3rd, 200 A granted to ROLAN WILLIAMS; 4th, granted to JESSE SIMKINS & IRA
SCOTT, 1000 A; 5th, granted to J. WATSON, two grants, 100 A each ; 6th, conveyance from
Sheriff WELLS, 800 A; adj. lands of GEORGE S. D. SMITH, JOHN P. CULLUM, WILLIAM E. SAWYER,
JOHN ROBERTS, BENJAMIN CATO, NANCY SCOTT, ELIAS McCARTY, THOMAS RHODEN...7 Feb 1839...
JOSEPH MIMS (LS), Wit: G. J. WILLIAMS, THOMAS JONES. Lexington Dist.: Proven by WILLIAMS
7 Feb 1839, before NATHL JONES, J. P. Rec. 9 Jan 1840. R. HARMAN, R. M. C.

Pp. 9-10: S. C. Lexington Cist.: SAMUEL WINGARD JUNR for $200 pd by GEORGE WINGARD, SENR,
            150 A surveyed for LEWIS SHEPPEARD 16 Mar 1792, on waters of Edisto River and
bounding on the N fork and Little Black Creek, plat made by WM WRIGHT, and signed by JOHN
BYNUM, Sur. Gen...18 Nov 1839. SAMUEL WINGARD (X) (LS), Wit: REUBEN HARMAN, J. H. FRANCKLON

Lexington District: Proven by J. H. FRANCKLON 14 Dec 1839 before R. HARMAN, Clk. & Q. U.

Pp. 10-11: State of S. C., JACOB SWYGERT of Lexington Dist., bind myself of JOHN SWYGERT
          SENR of Lexington Dist., for the Maintenance of him during his natural life...
to find him in good clothing, washing & mending...14 Dec 1839...JACOB SWYGERT (LS), Wit:
REUBEN HARMON, SAMUEL LOWMAN. Lexington Dist.: Proven by SAML LOWMAN, 14 Dec 1839. Rec.
9 Jan 1840. R. HARMAN R. M. C.

Page 11: State of S. C. , Lexington Dist.: I, JOHN SWYGERT SENR of Dist & State afresd.,
          for natural love & affection which I have to my son JACOB SWYGERT of same, do
give unto him all my stock of cattle, Hogs, and Sheep, I now claim in my own right. 14
Dec 1839. JOHN SWYGERT (X) (LS), Wit: REUBEN HARMAN, SAMUEL LOWMAN. Proven by SAMUEL
LOWMAN, 14 Dec 1849. Rec. 10 Jan 1840 R. HARMAN, R. M. C.

Pp. 11-12: State of S. C.:, JOHN SWYGERT SR. of Lexington Distr., for $50, paid by JACOB
          SWYGERT...150 A originally granted to HENSY[?] CREEK for 228 A in Lexington
Dist., near the Boiling Springs, Waters of Congaree Creek adj. sd JACOB SWYGERTs land,
ELISHA LEEs land, JOHN SWYGERT JR land, BATON TAYLORs land, which will also appear by
reference to a deed from JACOB BICKLEY to sd. JNO SWYGERT SENR, 27 Sept 1824...14 Dec
1839...JOHN SWYGERT (X) (LS), Wit: REUBEN HARMON, SAMUEL LOWMAN. Lexington Dist.: Proven
by SAMUEL LOWMAN 14 Dec 1839. Rec. 10 Jan 1840. R. HARMAN, R. M. C.

Pp. 12-13: S. C., Lexington Dist.: JAMES J. HALL & MARY HALL of Lexington Dist., for $250
          paid by WILLIAM HOWARD of same, sell and release all the timber suitable for
sawing for the term of ten years, with the exception of that small part lying between the
Buffalo Branch and the next branch for four years only, on E side Lightwood Creek, a
branch of N Edisto River...tract originally granted to WILLIAM BURGESS ___ 1790 for ___ A
23 Nov 1839...JAMES J. HALL (LS), MARY HALL (X) (LS), Wit: LARKIN GUNTER, WILLIAM QUATTLE-
BUM. Proven by LARKIN GUNTER 23 Nov 1839, before WILLIAM QUATTLEBUM, Q. U. Ex off. Rec.
10 Jan 1840. R. HARMAN R. M. C.

Pp. 13-14: S. C. Lexington Dist.: GARRETT TAYLOR of Dist. aforesd., for $5 paid by
          EPHRAIM EDINS of same, 100 A, part of 1000 A granted to sd. GARROTT TAYLOR on
Read Bank Creek, waters of Congaree Creek adj. lands of A.A. LITES, SARAH TAYLOR, and
others...5 Feb 1834... G. TAYLOR (LS), Wit: COLLY SOUTER, JOSHUA TAYLOR. Lexington Dist.:
Proven by COLLY SOUTER 16 Nov 1835, before DANIEL ROOF, J. P. Rec. 11 Jan 1840. R.
HARMAN, R. M. C.

Pp. 14-15: S. C., Lexington Dist.: EPHRAIM EDINS of Dist. aforesd., for $75 pd. by HENRY
          ROOF of same, 100 A, part of 1000 A granted to GARROTT TAYLOR, adj. A. A. LITES,
SARAH TAYLOR, and others...27 Nov 1835...EPHRAIM EDINS (X) (LS), Wit: JOHN W. BERRY, HENRY
MILLER (X). Proven by JOHN W. BERRY, 30 Nov 1835, before DANIEL ROOF, J. P.
          WILLIAM QUATTLEBUM, Q. U. Exofficio for Lexington Dist., certify that MARY
ANNA EDINS, wife of EPHRAIM;EDDINS, relinquished dower, 12 Nov 1838. MARY ANN EDINS (X)
Rec. 11 Jan 1840. R. HARMAN, R. M. C.

Pp. 15-16: S. C. Lexington Dist.: HIRAM GAUNTT of Dist. aforesd, for $68 pd. by ISRAEL
          GAUNTT, JUR. of same...half of tract of 906 A on Big Branch, waters of North
Edisto River...4 Jan 1840...HIRAM GAUNTT (LS), Wit: GEORGE W. McCULLOUGH, WILLIAM FRENCH.
Lexington Dist.: Proven by WILLIAM FRENCH 6 Jan 1840 before L. BOOZER, Q. U. Rec. 13
Jan 1840. R. HARMAN, R. M. C.

Pp. 16-17: S. C., Newberry Dist.: JACOB DICKERT of Dist., aforesd. for $700, pd by ANDREW
          G. DICKERT of same...66 A, part of a tract of 100 A granted to URSULA SHEALY
23 May 1774, but by resurvey contains 132 A, on head branches of Crims Creek, waters of
Broad River adj. at time or survey on lands of WM SUMMER, DAVID SHEALY, and others...
28 Sept 1836...J. J. DICKERT (LS), Wit: JOHN H. HUFF, PETER DICKERT. Newberry Dist.:
Proven by JOHN H. HUFF 5 Nov 1836 before PETER DICKERT, J. Qm.
          CHRISTIANA, wife of JACOB DICKERT, relinquished dower 5 Nov 1836, before
PETER DICKERT. CHRISTIANA DICKERT (+). Rec. 13 Jan 1840, R. HARMAN, R. M. C.

Pp. 17-18: S. C.: JOHN EPTIN JUR. of Lexington Dist., for $630, pd by ANDREW G. DICKERT
          ...70 A, part of 995 A surveyed for COL. JOHN A. SUMMER, on Drains of Crims
Creek, waters of Broad River, adj. to sd. A. G. DICKERT, the estate of BENJN KOON, WM.
MONTS, JOHN KESLER and others...28 Nov 1839...JOHN EPTIN (SL), Wit: SAMUEL SHEELY, HENRY
SHEELY. Newberry Dist.: Proven by SAMUEL SHEELY 28 Nov 1839, before PETER DICKERT.
          MARGRET EPTIN, wife of JOHN EPTIN, relinquished dower 28 Nov 1839 before PETER
DICKERT. MARGRET EPTIN. Rec. 13 Jan 1840, R. HARMAN, R. M. C.

Pp. 18-19: State of S. C.: JOHN EPTING JUR. of Lexington Dist., for $400, pd by SAMUEL

SHEALY of same...55 A granted to JOHN SWETENBERG in Lexington Dist., on the S side of the road leading from Newberry Court House to Columbia, adj. lands of DAVID SHEALY SR, ANDREW DICKERT, the sd. JOHN EPTING and others...21 Feb 1839...JOHN EPTIN (LS), Wit: A. G. DICKERT, SUMMER [sic]. PROVEN by ANDREW G. DICKERT in Newberry Dist., who swears to his and WM. SUMMERs signatures 21 Feb 1839 before PETER DICKERT, J. Qm. MARGARET, wife of JOHN EPTIN, relinquished dower 21 Feb 1839 before PETER DICKERT. Rec. 13 Jan 1840. R. HARMAN, R. M. C.

Pp. 19-20: S. C.: JOHN GABLE & REUBEN HARMON of Lexington Dist., for $10 pd. by WEST CAUGHMAN...5 1/2 A on waters of Twelve Mile Creek adj. lands held by WEST CAUGHMAN, JOHN CORLEY and JOHN DICKER [sic]...6 Jan 1840...JOHN GABLE (LS), REUBEN HARMAN (LS), Wit: J. A. ADDISON, JOHN SEAS. Lexington Dist.: Proven by COL. J. A. ADDISON, 6 Jan 1840 before R. HARMAN, Clk. & Q. U. Rec. 13 Jan 1840. R. HARMAN, R. M. C.

Pp. 20-21: S. C.: JOHN MEETZE of Lexington Dist., for $50 pd. by GEORGE MABUS of same... 50 A in Lexington Dist., on the road from Augusta to Columbia on waters of Lick Creek and Lightwood Creek adj. D. RAMBO, DRURY FORT, JOHN SHEALY, part of an original survey laid out to JOSEPH DILL for 1000 A, surveyed by THOMAS CARGILL for JOHN P. BOND, 10 July 1807...9 Jan 1840...JOHN MEETZE (LS), Wit: HENRY A. MEETZE, FRANKLIN CORLEY. Lexington Dist.: Proven by HENRY A. MEETZE 9 Jan 1840 before L. BOOZER, Q. U. NANCY MEETZE, wife of JOHN MEETZE, relinquished dower 9 Jan 1840 before LEMUEL BOOZER, Q. U. Rec. 14 Jan 1840. R. HARMAN, R. M. C.

Pp. 21-22: S. C., Lexington Dist.: SARAH POINDEXTER of Dist. aforesd., for $200 pd. by JOHN MEETZE & JACOB HENDRIX of same...80 A on Rocky Branch, waters of Saluda River adj. JOHN GARTMAN, DENNIS G. HAYES, JOHN SANDERS, FREDERICK KELLY...26 Nov 1837... SARAH POINDEXTER (LS), Wit: C. BOUKNIGHT, J. N. BOOZER. Proven by JACOB N. BOOZER 2 Aug 1839 before L. BOOZER, Q. U. Rec. 14 Jan 1840. R. HARMAN, R. M. C. Delivered to C. BOUKNIGHT.

Pp. 22-23: S. C. Lexington Dist.: ANDREW COUGHMAN JUR. of Dist. aforesd., for $220 pd. by THOMAS COUGHMAN of same...160 A, part of a tract formerly conveyed HIRAM C. KELLER to JOHN COUGHMAN, Likewise 35 A from JESSE BROWN of same, to sd. JOHN COUGHMAN, in Lexington Dist., on head of Horse Creek, waters of Saluda, adj. GREEN B. MITCHELL, JOHN COUGHMAN, ABRAHAM ANDERSON, DANIEL LOMANCK [sic]...ANDREW COUGHMAN (LS), Wit: SAMUEL LOWMAN, G. H. LAMINACK. Lexington Dist.: Proven by SAMUEL LOWMAN 6 Jan 1840. Deed dated 4 Jan 1840. ELIZABETH, wife of ANDREW CAUGHMAN, relinquished dower 10 Jan 1840, before R. HARMAN, Clk. & Q. U. Rec. 15 Jan 1840. R. HARMAN, R. M. C.

Pp. 23-24: S. C.: HENRY MEETZE of Lexington Dist., for $500 pd. by JEREMIAH HOOK of same, planter, 150 A on Beach Creek, waters of Saluda River, originally granted to JAMES SPENCE, 13 May 1768, conveyed by the widow ELIZABETH SPENCE to ARCHIBALD GLASGOW on 4 Nov 1797, and became part of the real estate of WM. P. RIDDLE decd., and being sold to effect partition among the heirs, became the property of HENRY MEETZE adj. MAHALY RIDDLE, ANDREW CAUGHMAN, JACOB RAWL & JACOB KYZER..._____ 1839...HENRY MEETZE (LS), Wit: LEWIS RIDDLE, JAMES H[?] CALK. Proven by LEWIS RIDDLE 4 Jan 1840 before R. HARMAN. ELIZABETH, wife of HENRY MEETZE, relinquished dower 4 Jan 1840 before R. HARMAN. Rec. 15 Jan 1840. R. HARMAN, R. M. C.

Pp. 24-25: S. C.: JOHN FOX, Sheriff of Lexington Dist, by a writ of Fiere Facias issued out of the Court of Common Pleas held 3 Mar 1838 at the suit of EDWIN J. SCOTT ...goods and chattels of JESSE FLOYD[?] be sold to levy the sum of $68...153 A where the Deft. now lives in Lexington Dist., on waters of Six mile creek and the road leading from Columbia to Augusta about six miles from Columbia Bridge adj. lands formerly held by JAMES H. GUIGNARD...purchased by EDWIN J. SCOTT for $106...who ordered titles made to JOHN and JESSE HOOK..22 Oct 1839...JOHN FOX (LS), Wit: WM. L. MILLER, W. H. FOX. Proven by W. H. FOX. 4 Nov 1839. Rec. 15 Jan 1840.

Pp. 25-27: S. C. Lexington Dist.: JOHN T. SEIBLES, one of the heirs and distributees of MRS. SARAH SEIBLES, filed a petition in the Court of Ordinary against HENRY SEIBLES, HENRY ARTHUR & wife, JAMES SEIBLES, and the heirs of WILLIAM SEIBLES, on 28 Jan 1839...SARAH SEIBLES died intestate leaving two tracts and sd. lands have not been partitioned... on 6 May 1839, ARTHUR H. FORT, Esqr., Ordinary for sd. Dist., did order that lands be sold on first Tuesday in June 1839...JOHN FOX, after advertising the same, sold lot of 4 A which JAMES CAYCE became the purchaser for $45...19 Dec 1839...JOHN FOX (LS), Wit: LEROY HENDRIX, CHRISTIAN RAWL. Lexington Dist.: Proven by LEROY HENDRIX 19 Dec 1839. Rec. 15 Jan 1840, R. HARMAN, R. M. C.

Pp. 27-28: RECORDING UNDER THE ACT ѲF 1839.
S. C.: JESSE HOOK of Lexington Dist., for $1, pd. by DRUCILLA HOOTEN of same...

6 A on Six mile creek, part of a tract originally granted to MICHAEL LEIGHTNER, which was
purchased by JESSE HOOK at Sheriff's sale, adj. JOHN MEETZE, JOSHUA MOORE...JESSE HOOK (L
S), Wit: JOHN HOOK, MARY HOOK (X). Lexington Dist.: Proven by JOHN HOOK 20 Jan 1840 before
R. HARMAN. Rec. 20 Jan 1840.

Pp. 28-29: J. A. ADDISON Comr. to GEORGE KAIGLER, Equity Title for Real Estate.
             S.C.: 14 Jan 1840, J. A. ADDISON, Esquire, Commissioner of the Court of Equity
for Lexington District, to GEORGE KAIGLER of ther other part....S. P. CORBIN & wife on or
about the 20 Oct 1836 exhibited their Bill of Complaint in sd. Court against MARY PARR,
S. S. SAYLOR & others stating that JOHN J. SAYLOR, late of Lexington Dist., made his will
& departed this life &c &c, the cause was heard July term 1839, real estate sold at public
auction...for $400, 1400 A granted to WALTER RUSSEL 3 Apr 1775...resurvey made by JOHN D.
A. MURPHY, Dept Sur, 1 Nov 1826...J. A. ADDISON (LS), Wit: J. A. WOLFFE, L. BOOZER.
Proven by L. BOOZER, before R. HARMAN, 20 Jan 1840. Rec. 20 Jan 1840.

Pp. 29-31: S. C.: 14 Jan 1840, J. A. ADDISON, Comr. of Equity, to JOHN KAIGLER...S. P.
             CORBIN & wife [same equity case as in preceding deed]...JOHN J. SAYLOR made
his will in August 1834 and died shortly thereafter...for $13,000...1617 A on Congaree
River adj. lands of sd. JOHN KAIGLER, HENRY SEIBLES, and others...two resurveyed plats
one executed by S. H. BOYKIN, Dep. Surveyor 12 May 1827, the other by JOHN SIGHTLER, Dep.
Sur. on 1 Jan 1839 except 150 A on W side of State Road...J. A. ADDISON (LS), Wit: J. A.
WOLFE, L. BOOZER. Proven by LEMUEL BOOZER before R. HARMAN 20 Jan 1840. Rec. 20 Jan
1840.

Pp. 31-32: S. C.: HENRY RUCKER of Lexington Dist., for $228.50, pd. by GEORGE KAIGLER of
                 same...45 3/4 A granted to JOHN MORE, and belonging to the estate of
WILLIAM TAYLOR, decd, which the sd. HENRY RUCKER obtained by intermarrying with ELIZABETH
TAYLOR, daughter of sd. WILLIAM, part of tract adj. to that conveyed to McCRACKEN, now
W. Bakers, plat No. 2 made by JOHN SIGHTLYER 6 Feb 1837...7 Jan 1839...JAMES H. RUCKER
(LS), MARY E. RUCKER (LS), Wit: HARDIWAY FARRAR, GODFREY A. CRIM. Lexington Dist.: Proven
by HARDIWAY FARRER 5 Feb 1839 before PETER A. BUYCK, P. Q.   MARY E. RUCKER relinquished
dower 5 Feb 1839 before PETER A. BUYCKE, P. Q. Rec. 22 Jan 1840, R. HARMAN, R. M. C.

Pp. 32-33: Georgia, Montgomery Co.: JEREMIAH WALKER and SARY SPIARS of State and Co. afore-
                 sd., for $50 pd. by JOHN WILLIAMS of Lexington Dist., 400 A granted to IVEN
HOWARD in 181_, on Cedar Creek at the old cross road adj.CURZEY, MERFEY...7 Nov 1839...
JEREMIAH WALKER (+) (LS), SARY SPEARS (X) (LS), Wit: EPHRAGM YOUN, HIRAM WILLIAMS.
S. C., Orangeburg Dist.:Proven by HIRAM WILLIAMS 18 Jan 1840, before JAMES GARVIN, J. Q.
Rec. 28 Jan 1840, R. HARMAN. Delivered to HENRY GRUBS.

Pp. 33-34: S. C.: NATHANIEL KLECKLEY of Lexington Dist., for $265 pd. by HENRY KLECKLEY of
                 same, sells all right to real estate (in lands which belong to my father in
his life time or interest in the lands divised [sic] by my Grand Father GODLIP KLECKLY,
decd in his L. W. & T. dated 8 Feb 1819), 320 A on S side Saluda adj. LORICK, DANIEL
KLECKLY...1 Feb 1840...NATHANIEL KLECKLEY (LS), Wit: H. J. CAUGHMAN, REUBIN HARMAN. Lexington Dist.: Proven by H. J. CAUGHMAN 1 Feb 1840, before R. HARMAN. SARAH KLECKLEY (X),
wife of NATHANIEL, relinquished dower 4 Feb 1840, before R. HARMAN. Rec. 4 Feb 1840.

Pp. 34-35: S. C., Lexington Dist.: JOHN S. ADDY, SENR., for $450 pd. by DAVID CROUT of
                 same, 140 A on Hollow Creek, waters of Saluda adj. land held by URIAH CROUT,
ISAAC VANZANT, THOMAS DERICK, JOHN S. ADDY SER, KATHARINE ADDY...27 Dec 1838...JOHN S.
ADDY SENR. (LS), Wit: URIAH CROUT, HENRY W. AUSTIN; Proven by URIAH CROUT 25 Jan 1839,
before HENRY A. SMITH, Q. U. CATHERINE (+), wife of JOHN S. ADDY SENR., relinquished dower
12 Feb 1839, before HENRY A. SMITH, Q. U. Rec. 7 Feb 1840, R. HARMAN, R. M.C.

Page 36: S. C., Lexington Dist.: JEREMIAH WINGARD of Dist. aforesd., for $2400...pd. by
              CALEB BOUKNIGHT of same, ...sale of negroes...to be pd. before 1 Jan 1841...19
Mar 1839...JEREMIAH WINGARD (LS), Wit: JOHN MEETZE. Proven by JOHN MEETZE 10 Feb 1840...
R. HARMAN. Rec. 10 Feb 1840.

Pp. 36-38:S. C. Lexington Dist.: JOSEPH TAYLOR & wf CATHERINE for $25, to DAVID TAYLOR...
              7 1/3 A, our distribution share as a Legatee of the estate of JACOB RICE, decd,
one ninth part of two thirds of 100 A on Horse Pen Creek, waters of Saluda River, adj.
JOHN S. ADDIES JR, ADAM RISH JR., GEORGE SAWYER...JOSEPH TAYLOR (+) (LS), CATHARINE TAYLOR
(X) (LS), Wit: CATHARINE SAWYER, JASPER SAWYER. Proven by JASPER SAWYER before GEORGE
SAWYER, Q. U. 21 Jan 1840. CATHARINE TAYLOR relinquished dower 4 Feb 1840. Rec. 12 Feb
1840. R HARMAN, R. M. C.

Pp. 38-39: S. C., CYRENIUS LOOMIS of Lexington Dist., for $500 pd. by JOHN DAVIDSON of same,
              1/4 A in Lexington Village adj. Main Street, EPHRAIM CORLEYs lot, JOHN MEETZE's

lot, JOHN HENDRIX's lot, originally granted to LAURENCE CHARLES alias CORLEY 4 June 1804
which descended to BARBARA CORLEY by the L. W. & T. of sd. LAURENCE CHARLES or CORLEY,
conveyed by DANIEL McGILL to sd. LOOMIS 1 June 1833...12 Feb 1840 CYRENIUS LOOMIS (LS),
Wit: REUBEN HARMAN, A. H. FORT. Proven by A. H. FORT, Esqr., 13 Feb 1840 before R. HARMAN.
MRS. LEAH LOOMIS, wife of CYRENIUS, relinquished dower 13 Feb 1840 before R. HARMAN. Rec.
13 Feb 1840.

Pp. 39-40: S. C.: JESSE DERRICK of Edgefield Dist., for $275 pd. by JESSE BOUKNIGHT of
          Lexington Dist., 93 A granted to JAMES BOYD 7 Dec 1812, for 260 A, by division
amongst JOHN DERRICK SEN., JACOB DERRICK, and JOHN DERRICK JR, the 93 A fell to JOHN
DERRICK SR., and conveyed by him to JOHN DERRICK JR on 30 Oct 1817, by him willed to the
present grantor about 1825, land in fork of Broad & Saluda, adj. THOMAS SMITH, JACOB
DERRICK & others, reference to a plat made by S. FANNIN 29 Oct 1817...16 Nov 1839...JESSE
DERRICK (LS), Wit: GEORGE DERRICK, DAVID WEED. Proven by GEORGE DERRICK, __ Nov 1839
before SAMUEL BOUKNIGHT, Q. U. Rec. 2 March 1840, R. HARMAN, R. M. C.

Pp. 40-41: S. C.: JOHN SWYGERT of Lexington Dist., for $40 pd. by SAMUEL BOUKNIGHT...8
          A granted to STROTHER, conveyed to my father CHRISTIAN SWYGERT, and by a
division of the real estate of 143 A, the 8 A fell to me adj. CHRISTIAN WEED, NANCY SWY-
GERT, SAMUEL BOUKNIGHT, in fork of Borad and Saluda, on Hollingsheads Creek, waters of
Broad River...26 Oct 1839...JOHN SWIGART (LS), Wit: JETHRO HARMON, J. U. COOGLER. Proven
by JOHN W. KOOGLER 18 Feb 1840 before G. M. FULMER, Q. U. Rec. 2 March 1840. R. HARMAN.

Pp. 41-42: S. C.: JOSHUA WINGARD of Lexington Dist., for $525 pd. by DANIEL FREY of same...
          86 A on S side Saluda , originally granted to JACOB STEEL adj. JEREMIAH HARMON,
HARMON GEIGER, the half mile branch, the sixteen mile branch, waters of Saluda...7 March
1840...JOSHUA WINGARD (LS), Wit: JACOB KELLY, D. J. HARMAN. Lexington Dist.: Proven by
D. J. HARMAN before R. HARMAN, 7 March 1840. MAGDALENA, wife of JOSHUA WINGARD, relinquished dower, 9 March 1840. Rec. 9 March 1840.

Pp. 43-44: S. C.: 7 March 1840, GEORGE MONTZE and JACOB KELLY one part, and DANIEL FREY of
          the other part...sd. FREY stands indebted to sd. KELLY & MONTZE by note for
$300 with interest from 11 Feb 1840...mortgage of 86 A on S side Saluda [land in preceding
deed]...DANIEL FREY (LS), Wit: JACOB DRAFTS, MARTIN SOX. Proven by JACOB DRAFTS, 7 March
1840...Rec. 9 March 1840, R. HARMAN, R. M. C. [note in margin of p. 43 "This mortgage
satisfied 14th Feby. 1852. The original in the possession of DANIEL FREY. JAS. E. LEE,
Regr."]

Pp. 44-45: S. C., Lexington Dist.: WALTER GAUNTT of Lexington Dist., for $2500 pd. by
          JOSEPH GANT of same, land at time or survey in Orangeburgh Dist., now Lexington
Dist., on Chinquepin Creek adj. JAMES WESTS or WINNS land, surveyed by WILLIAM WRIGHT,
15 Apr 1786, granted to WADSWORTH and TURPIN 4 Sept 1786'...half of sd. land conveyed
to WILLIAM TURPIN by deed 2 May 1791, Rec. in Conveyance Office at Charleston Book F,
No. 8, p. 104...1 Nov 1839...WALTER GANTT (LS), Wit: WILLIAM RANKIN, ISSACHAR X. GANT.
Proven by ISSACHAR X. GANTT 9 March 1840, before R. HARMON. Rec. 9 March 1840.

Pp. 45-46: S. C., Lexington Dist.: ANDREW SHEALY for $500, pd. by JONATHAN VAN PELT...
          253 A, except for one acre around the graveyard on N side Long Branch, waters
of Saluda, adj. DANIEL RAMBOES, JOHN SHEALIES, DANIEL QUATTLEBUM, GEORGE BOWERS...9 Dec
1836...ANDREW SHEALY (   ) (LS), Wit: DANIEL GUNER, SEBERN WILLIAMS. Proven by DANIEL
GUNTER 29 Feb 1804, before ISAAC VANSANT, J.P. Rec. 9 March 1840. R. HARMAN, R. M. C.

Pp. 46-47: S. C., Lexington Dist.: JOHN NELSON SUMMER of Coweta, Georgia, for $100 pd. by
          DONROD FARR of Lexington Dist., 71 A on waters of Bear Creek adj. JOHN SUMMER,
JOHN MATHIS, ANDERSON SUMMER, JOHN G. KESLERS...10 Dec 1838...JOHN N. SUMMERS (LS), Wit:
G. M. FULMER, JOHN G. KESLER. Proven by JOHN G. KESLER in Lexington Dist., before GEORGE
M. FULMER, Q. U. Rec. 11 March 1840. R. HARMAN, R. M.C.

Pp. 47-48: S. C.: Whereas BARNET LYBRAND, late of Lexington Dist., died seized of a consi-
          derable Real Estate leaving a widow to whom by his L. W. & T. devised said
Real Estate during her natural life, and the sd. Widow having recently departed this life
leaving six daughters to wit, ELIZABETH intermarried with JOHN COOGLE, SALLY intermarried
with DANIEL SMITH, MARY intermarried with FREDERICK GABLE, REBECCA LYBRAND, CATHARINE ADDY,
widow, formerly CATHARINE LYBRAND, and CHRISTENA LYBRAND...heirs sell for $391, 229 A to
FREDERICK GABLE adj. JOHN S. SWYGERT, JOHN DREHR, the Heirs of VALENTINE GABLE, and others.
1 Oct 1837...JOHN T. COOGLE (LS), DANIEL SMITH (LS), SALLY SMITH (X) (LS), KATHARINE ADDY
(LS), REBECCA LYBRAND (LS), CARISTENAH LYBRAND (LS), Wit: SAMUEL LORICK, DAVID GABLE.
Lexington Dist.: Proven by SAMUEL LORICK and DAVID GABLE 30 Oct 1837, before A. H. FORT,
Qu. Ex offo. SARAH SMITH, wife of DANIEL, relinquished dower 9 Nov 1837 before WILLIAM
QUATTLEBUM. Rec. 11 March 1840, R. HARMAN, R. M. C.

Pp. 48-49: Two plats referring to the preceding deed showing adj. to "Rev. J. Drehers or Bartharts Land," " Rev. John Drehers Land" "the estate of Barnet Lybrand", Surveyed 31 Aug 1837. Rec. 11 March 1840. The second plat shows heirs of BARNET LYBRAND and heirs of VALENTINE GALBES. Surveyed 31 Aug 1837, Rec. 11 March 1840, by WILLIAM QUATTLEBUM, Dept. Sur.

Pp. 49-50: S. C., Lexonton [sic] Dist.: CHRISTIAN WEED of Lexonton Dist., gentleman, to son in law JACOB STACK, for love and affection, 31 A on waters of Brod [sic] River, one mule, one waggon, one clock...CHRISTIAN WEED (X) (LS), Wit: GODFREY STACK, DANIEL METZ. Lexington Dist.: Proven by GODFREY STACK before L. BOOZER, Q. U. Deed dated 3 Mar 1840. Rec. 11 Mar 1840.

Pp. 50-51: S. C. Lexington Dist.: HARMAN SEE of Dist. aforesd., for $250 pd. by JOHN LOWN of same....904 A, the greater part of a tract granted to STEPHEN DICKSON 6 June 1814 for 1000 A on Red bank Creek, waters of Congaree adj. at time of grant to HENRY WEAVER, ARTHUR HOOD, and unknown lands...resurvey made by WILLIAM QUATTLEBUM 22 Mar 1839 7 Oct 1839...HARMON SEE (LS), Wit: ISAAC VANSANT, JOHN J. FRANCKLON. Lexington Dist.: Proven by JOHN J. BRANCKLON 7 Oct 1839. MARY SEE, wife of HARMON, relinquished dower 9 Oct 1839. Rec. 12 Mar 1840, R. HARMAN, R. M. C.

Pp. 51-52: S. C.: FELIX MEETZE of Town of Columbia, for $1000 pd. by HENRY MEETZE of Lexington Dist., two adjoining tracts on S side Saluda, on twenty mile branch... (1) 170 A adj. T. K. POINDEXTER, AMOS HENDRIX, HENRY MEETZE (2) 9 1/2 A granted to JACOB HARMAN for 51 A adj. GODFREY HARMAN, DENNIS GIBSON, T. K. POINDEXTER...conveyed to sd. FELIX MEETZE by his father YOST MEETZE, 19 July 1821; conveyed to him by GEORGE, JACOB, and FREDERIC HARMAN, 16 Sept 1831 [apparently the 9 1/2 A tract]... 1 Feb 1840...FELIX MEETZE (LS), Wit: EDWIN J. SCOTT, W. F. ANDERSON. S. C., Richland District.: Proven by WILLIAM F. ANDERSON before SAM. WEIR[?], J. Q., 3 Mar 1840. Richland District: JANE MEETZE, wife of FELIX, relinquished dower 3 Mar 1840 before SAMUEL WIER. Rec. 30 March 1840, R. HARMAN, R. M. C.

Pp. 52-53: S. C.: JOHN J. SEE of Lexington Dist., for $60 pd. by HENRY H. SEE of same, 20 A on S side Saluda River, Beech branch of Rocky Creek adj. JACOB KYZER, GEORGE CAUGHMAN...part of 150 A granted to JOHN BOYD...JOHN J. SEE (LS), Wit: JOHANNES L. SCHNEIDER [signed in German], HENRY SNIDER. Deed dated 3 Apr 1840. Proven 3 Apr 1840 by JOHANNES SCHNIDER, before L. BOOZER, Q. U. Rec. 3 Apr 1840.

Pp. 53-54: S. C., Lexington Dist.: JOHN H. JONES of Dist. aforesd., for $240 pd. by ANDREW SHEALY, 127 A adj. HENRY BATES, MARTIN GUNTER, and the BARNET LEVINGSTON old place, ANTOINAS WATSON, HEZEKIAH PRAYTOR...24 Jan 1840...JOHN H. JONES (LS), Wit: JOHN SHEALEY (X), JASPER SAWYER. Lexington Dist.: Proven by JASPER SAWYER 21 Jan 1840 before GEORGE SAWYER, Q. U. Rec. 6 Apr 1840.

Pp. 54-55: S. C.: ARTEMUS WATSON of Edgefield Dist. and WILLIS HARTLEY of Lexington Dist., for $25 pd. by ANDREW SHEALY of Lexington Dist....10 A granted to JAMES FREDERICK 17 Apr 1787 on waters of Chinquepin Creek, waters of North Edisto...4 Mar 1840 ...ARTEMUS WATSON, WILLIS HARTLEY, Wit: JOHN KNOX, WM HALL. Lexington Dist.: Proven by JOHN KNOX 6 Apr 1840 before GEORGE SAWYER, Q. U. Rec. 6 Apr 1840.

Pp. 55-56: S. C., Lexington Dist.: WILLIAM HARRIS of Dist. aforesd., for $124 pd by G. & W. M. BATES of Edgefield Dist...80 A in Lexington Dist., on waters of South Edisto adj. JOSEPH BARTONs now ELISHA JONES line, ARTHUR JACKSON, below the old bridge... 18 Dec 1838...WILLIAM HARRIS (LS), Wit: JAS E. LEE, JAMES CREED (X). Lexington Dist.: Proven by JAMES E. LEE 18 Dec 1838 before NATHL JONES JO. Rec. 6 Apr 1840, R. HARMAN.

Pp. 56-57: S. C. Lexington Dist.: SION WATERS of Lexington Dist., for love and affection I bear to my Grand children, SARY WATERS, ELLIN WATERS & GAIN WATERS, 150 A on hell hole Creek adj. ISAAC VANSANT, HARTLEY HALLMON, ISAAC ALEWINES, SION WATERS & kitchen and household furniture and personal property...2 Jan 1840...SCION WATERS (+) (LS), Wit: JOHN WATERS, MARTHEY LEE (X), JAMES WATERS (+). Lexington Dist.: Proven by JAMES WATERS 10 Mar 1840 before ANDERSON ATEEDMAN, J. P. Rec. 6 Apr 1840.

Pp. 57-58: S. C.: WILLIAM BAKER, planter, of Lexington Dist., for $50 pd by JOHN SIGHTLER SR., 100 A part of a tract surveyd for MESSER FRANCIS GOODWIN, JOHN MOORE & FRANCIS TROTTE, 13 Aug 1786 for 10,000 A in Lexington Dist., granted to them 5 Feb 1787 on Head Springs of Big Sandy Rich, waters of the Congaree River adj. JEREMIAH BROWER, JOHN SIGHTLER...1 Nov 1839....WILLIAM BAKER (LS), Wit: WILLIAM WATSON, GEORGE W. SIGHTLER. [Plat included in deed.] Proven by GEORGE W. SIGHTLER 6 Apr 1840 before MICHAEL WISE, J.P. Rec. 6 Apr 1840.

Pp. 58-59: S. C.: WILLIAM G. LOWMAN of Newbury [sic] Dist., for $550 pd. by GEORGE SCOTT
of Lexinton [sic] Dist....93 A sold by JOHN UNGER to JOHN LOWMAN, originally
granted to AVIN MARY ZWILFORD 7 Nov 1752 on S side Congree [sic] River between beaver
creek and Sandy run adj. ESAIAS SAYLOR, GEORGE SCOTT, JOHN CRAPS...5 Jan 1822...WILLIAM
G. LOWMAN (LS), Wit: VALENTINE CORLEY, J. J. LOWMAN. Edgefield Dist: Proven by JOHN J.
LOWMAN before VALE. CORLEY J. P. 12 Jan 1822. Edgefield Dist.: Before WILLIAM FORGUSON
J. Q., LUCY V. LOWMAN, wife of WILLIAM, relinquished dower, 15 Jan 1822. Rec. 6 Apr 1840.

Pp. 60-61: S. C.: JOHN CRAPS, planter, of Lexington Dist. for $525 pd. by GEORGE CRIM SENR.
of same...186 A between Sandy Run Creek and Beaver Creek adj. GEORGE SCOTT (deceased), heirs of JACOB SAYLOR, GEORGE KAIGLER, originally granted to ANN MARY ZWILFORD
7 Nov 1752...27 Jan 1830...JNO. J. CRAPPS (LS), Wit: DAVID GEIGER, HENRY MILLER.
Lexington Dist.: Proven by DAVID GEIGER 27 Jan 1830, before HENRY SEIBELS, J. Q. ELIZABETH
CRAPPS, wife of JOHN, relinquished dower 3 Feb 1830. Rec. 6 Apr 1840, R. HARMAN, R. M. C.

Pp. 61-62: S. C.: GEORGE CRIM, planter, of Lexington Dist., for $500 pd. by JOSEPH A. WOLFE,
planter, of same...93 A granted to ANN MARY ZWILFORD 7 Nov 1752, for 150 A...
adj. HENRY SEIBLES, LEWIS POU, JOHN G. KAIGLER, JOSEPH A. WOLFE...8 Feb 1840...GEORGE
CRIM (X) (LS), Wit: WILLIAM APMAN[?], GEORGE KAIGLER. Proven by WILLIAM ASSMAN 22 Feb
1840 before PETER A. BUYCK, J. Q. MARGARET CRIM, wife of GEORGE, relinquished dower 22
Feb 1840. Rec. 6 Apr 1840.

Pp. 62-63: S. C.: JOHN J. KAIGLER and GEORGE KAIGLER, planters of Lexington Dist., for
$222 pd by JOSEPH A. WOLFE planter of same...74 A, part of a tract granted to
GEORGE KAIGLER 6 Dec 1794, for 322 A at the time of resurvey adj. GEORGE CRIM, ESAIAS
SAYLOR now HENRY SEIBLES, JOHN CRAPPS, DAVID KAIGLER now GERHARD MULLER, and sd. JOS. A.
WOLFE...14 Jan 1840...GEORGE KAIGLER (LS), JOHN G. KAIGLER (LS), Wit: SAML P. CORBEN, WIL-
LIAM RUCKER. Proven by WILLIAM RUCKER before PETER A. BUYCKE, J. Q. HARRIET KAIGLER,
wife of JOHN G. KAIGLER., relinquished dower 22 Feb 1840. Rec. 6 Apr 1840.

Pp. 64-65: S. C.: PHILLIP GUISE of Lexington Dist., for $150 pd. by THOMAS SMITH of same...
tract in fork of Broad & Saluda, 25 A, originally granted to BARBARA NATES for
100 A as bounty land adj. THOMAS SMITH, JESSE BOUKNIGHT...14 Dec 1839...PHILLIP GUISE (LS)
Wit: DAVID WEED, WILLIAM T. SMITH. Proven by DAVID WEED 16 Dec 1839 before SAMUEL BOUK-
NIGHT, Q.U. ELIZABETH GUISE, wife of PHILLIP, relinquished dower 23 Dec 1839. Rec. 6
Apr 1840.

Pp. 65-66: S. C.: JEREMIAH EDWARDS of Lexington Dist., for $75 pd. by JOHN EDWARDS of Union
Dist., S. C....200 A in Lexington Dist on the head of three pond branch, waters
of Big Black Creek, waters of N Edisto River, part of a tract surveyed for JEREMIAH EDWARDS
for 700, 85 A it being taken off the south end adj. JACOB SEGRIST &c...19 Aug 1816....
JEREMIAH EDWARDS ( ) (SEAL), Wit: DVD. KING, WILLIAM STRICKLIN (+). Lexington Dist:
Proven by DAVID KING before LEW. POU, Q. U. 17 Oct 1816. Rec. 6 Apr 1840. R. HARMAN.

Pp. 66-67: S. C.: JOHN EDWARDS of Lexington Dist., for $100 pd. by JOHN BOUKNIGHT SENR. of
Lexington Dist., 200 A on the head of three pond branch [same tract in preced-
ing deed]...4 Dec 1817...JOHN EDWARDS ( ) (LS), Wit: THOMAS SHEPPARD, JOHN ELLISON (E).
S. C. Lexington Dist.: FERABY EDWARDS, wife of JOHN, relinquished dower, 11 Dec 1817 before
THOS BOYD, Q. U. Proven by THOMAS SHEPPARD, 11 Dec 1817. Rec. 6 Apr 1840.

Pp. 67-68: S. C.: SAML. P. CORBEN of Lexington Dist., for $300, to ADAM WACTER, planter,
living in Lexington Dist....land in the junction of Beaver Creek and the Congree [sic] River, part of a tract granted to JOEL SPIGUES and DAVID RUMPH on 6 Jan 1823,
resurveyed and divided by N. C. D. CULCLASURE, S. D. on 3 Jan 1833...1 Jan 1838...SAML P.
CORBEN (LS), Wit: LEW. POU, JOHN J. KIRSH. Lexington Dist.: Proven by LEWIS POU before
PETER A. BUYCK, J. Q. 13 Jan 1840. CAROLINE M. CORBIN, wife of S. P. CORBIN, relinquished
dower , 13 Jan 1840. Rec. 6 Apr 1840.

Pp. 68-69: S. C. Lexington Dist.: CHRISTENA AMICK of Lexington Dist., to daughter MARY ANN
AMICK of same, for love and affection...all household and kitchen furniture,
pottery of various kinds [may be meant for poultry]...6 Sept 1839...CHRISTENER AMICK (+),
Wit: PATRICK TODD, GASPER AMICK (X), LEVI AMICK (X). Newberry District: Proven by GASPER
AMICK, 9 Nov 1839, before BENJAMIN LINDSAY, J. Q. Rec. 6 Apr 1840.

Pp. 69-71: S. C.,Lexington District: CHRISTENER AMICK, J. J. AMICK, J. H. AMICK, and MARY
A. AMICK for $150 pd. by EMANUEL HOLMAN [HALLMAN], all of Lexington Dist....
part of a tract of 300 A originally granted to JACOB WARNE, 49 A on Camping Creek, waters
of Saludy, adj. GASPER AMICK, MARY A. AMICK.... ____ 1839. CHRISTENER AMICK (X) (LS), JOHN
J. AMICK, MARY A. AMICK (X) (LS), JOHN H. AMICK (X) (LS), Wit: PATRICK TODD, GASPER AMICK
(X). Lexington Dist: BENJAMIN LINDSAY, Justice for Newberry Dist., certify that CHRISTINA

AMICK, wife of JOHN H. AMICK, relinquished dower...9 Nov 1839, CHRISTINA AMICK (X). Newberry Dist.: Proven by GASPER AMICK 9 Nov 1839. Lexington Dist.: GEMIAH AMICK and CURTINE
AMICK, wifes [sic] of JACOB AMICK and JOHN H. AMICK, relinquished dower 9 Nov 1839. Rec.
6 Apr 1840.

Pp. 71-72: S. C. Lexington Dist.: CHRISTENA AMICK, J. J. AMICK, MARY A. AMICK, EMANUEL
HOLMAN and CHRITENER [sic] his wife of Lexington Dist., for $150 pd. by J. H.
AMICK, have sold part of a tract granted to JACOB WARNE on Camping Creek...CHRISTENER
AMICK (X), MARY A. AMICK (X), EMANUEL HOLMAN (LS), CHRISTENER HOLMAN (X). Wit: PATRICK
TODD, GASPER AMICK (X). CHRISTENA AMICK, wife of JOHN H., relinqushed dower 9 Nov 1839.
Deed dated ____ 1839. Proven by GASPER AMICK. JEMIAH AMICK & CHRISTENA HAWLMON relinquished
dower 9 Nov 1839 before BENJAMIN LINDSEY J. Q. Rec. 6 Apr 1840.

Pp. 72-74: CHRISTENER AMICK, JACOB AMICK, J. H. AMICK, EMANUEL HOLMAN & wf, to MARY ANN
AMICK, for $150...part of tract granted to JACOB WARNE...____ 1829. Same sign.
& wit. Rec. 6 Apr 1840.

Pp. 74-75: S. C. Lexington Dist.: GEORGE M. SUMMER for $375 pd. by CHRISTIAN KUNKLE, both
of Dist. aforesd...133 A on head waters of Wateree Creek, part of tract granted
to MAJ. WILLIAM SUMMER adj. WILLIAM EPTING, ANDREW KUNKLE, heirs of WILLIAM SUMMER, decd...
1 Nov 1837...GEORGE M. SUMMER (LS), Wit: G. M. FULMER, J.A. FULMER. Proven by JNO. A.
FULMER 1 Nov 1837 before G.M. FULMER. MARY SUMMER, wife of GEORGE M., relinquished dower
28 Nov 1837. Rec. 7 Mar 1840.

Pp. 75-76: S. C. Lexington Dist.: JOHN BATES of Edgefield Dist., For $1500 pd. by WILLIAM
C. MITCHELL of Lexington Dist...land on both sides the road to Augusta, on the
middle ground between branches of North Edisto and Saluda River, 346 A adj. lands of
THOMAS H. SIMMONS, JOHN W. LEE, JOHN W. LEE, DANIEL WILLIAMS...31 Jan 1826...JOHN BATES
(LS), Wit: THOS. H. SIMMONS, JOHN BURTON [BENTON?]. Edgefield Dist.: HEPSEBAH E. BATES,
wife of JOHN, relinquished dower before NATHAN NORRIS, J. Qu., 31 Jan 1826. Proven by
THOS. H. SIMMONS, 1 July 1826. Rec. 7 Apr 1840. R. HARMAN, R. M. C.

Pp. 77-78: JOHN W. LEE of Edgefield Dist, for $1000 pd. by WILLIAM C. MITCHELL of Lexington
Dist....201 1/4 A by a resurvey, originally granted to STEPHEN NORRIS adj.
JOHN BATES, ELEANOR LEE, WM. C. MITCHELL, ANDREW BATES...17 Oct 1839...JNO. W. LEE (LS),
Wit: AMOS BANKS, HENRY H. SPAUN. Edgefield Dist.:MARY L. LEE, wife of JOHN W. LEE, relin-
quished her dower, 17 Oct 1839 before AMOS BANKS, Q. U. Deed proven by HENRY SPANN 17
Oct 1839. Rec. 7 Apr 1840.

Page 78: Lexington Dist.: JESSE MATTHIAS of Lexington Dist., for $160 pd. by GEORGE W.
CLARK of Lexington...84 A, part of a tract originally granted to MICHEAL LITNER
for 300 A on Six mile creek adj. land granted to JACOB SENR [sic], RICHLAND HAMPTON, part
of the original tract laid out for ADAM EPTING now in possession of the above named JESSE
MATHIAS, and land originally sold to WILLIAM BRAZEAL now in possession of the heirs of
JONAS MATTHIAS, decd...with the exception of the claim of JESSE HOOK, one of the heirs...
21 Feb 1839...JESSE MATHIAS (LS), Wit: DAVID WILSON, SAMPSON BUFF. Proven by SAMPSON BUFF
9 Apr 1840. Rec. 9 Apr 1840.

Pp. 79-80: GEORGE W. CLARK of Lexington Dist., for $160 pd. by JOHN MEETZE of same,86 A
except for 6 A where D. HOOTEN now lives, part of a tract originally granted
by the State of MICHAEL LIEGHTER adj. JOSHUA MORE, JOHN ____, JNO. ROOF, MO. KINSLER and
others on branches of six mile creek...17 June 1839...GEORGE W. CLARKE (LS), Wit: MARTIN
LYBRAND, FRANKLIN CORLEY. Lexington Dist.: Proven by FRANKLIN CORLEY before L. BOOZER,
Q. U. 23 June 1839. Plat included in deed surveyed 12 Mar 1839 by JOHN D. SHARP, Dep. sur.
Deed & plat rec. 9 Apr 1840. R. HARMAN, R. M. C.

Pp. 80-81: JESSE HOOK of Lexington Dist., for $5, pd. by JOHN MEETZE of Lexington Dist....
86 A, except for 6 A where MRS. D. HOOTEN now lives, originally granted to
MICHAEL LIGHTNER, adj. JNO ROOF, SENR., JNO. ROOF, JOSHUA MORE, JOHN KINSLER...11 Oct 1839
JESSE HOOK (LS), Wit: JOHN FOX, WM. L. MILLER. Proven by WILLIAM L. MILLER 9 Apr 1840.
Rec. 9 Apr 1840.

Pp. 81-83: S. C. Lexington Dist.: Whereas ADAM STOUDEMIRE, one of the Heirs and distributees of A. M. STOUDEMIRE, decd, filed a petition in the Court of Ordinary, a-
gainst MARY S. BOLAND, WILKS F. WATERS & wife, & others in conjunction with the petition
of 14 Feb 1840 stating that A. M. STOUDEMIRE died Intestate leaving a tract that has not
been partitioned... to be sold by Coroner 12 Mar 1840...50 A purchased by WILLIAM MOREHEAD
for $540...57 A on Crims Creek adj. lands of A. STUCKMAYERS, R. C. BUSBY, half of original
tract surveyed for BARBARA KEISELHART for 100 A...18 Mar 1840...GEO. J. HOOK (LS), Cor.
L. D. Wit: DANIEL LEAPHEART, STANMORE LANGFORD. Proven by DANIEL LEAPHART before A. M.

FORT, Q. U. Rec. 13 Apr 1840. Plat included certified 29 Feb 1840, P. DICKERT. Rec. 13 Apr 1840.

Pp. 83-84: S. C.: AMBROSE SANDERS of Orangeburgh Dist.,for $20 pd. by BENJAMIN COOPER, SR. of same...100 A in Dist. of Orangeburgh in fork between the South and North Eidsto River,part of 905 A granted to JOHN J. COMBAA in 1785...29 Jan 1816...AMBROS SANDERS (+) (SEAL), Wit: J. J. CAMBAA, MARY CUMBOO. Orangeburg Dist.: Proven by JOHN J. COMBAA before J. J. JOHNSTON JP 18 Dec 1816. Rec. 29 Apr 1840, R. HARMAN, R. M. C.

Page 84: S. C. Oringburgh Dist.: BENJAMIN CUPPER [sic] of Orangburgh Dist., for $30 pd. by GARRA KISH of same, land between North and South Edisto, on a branch of Chalk Hill Creek waters of N Edesto [sic], part of 905 A granted to JOHN J. CUMBAA in 1788... 20 July 1818...BENGAMON CUPPER (+) (SEAL), Wit: WILLIAM ADAMS, GINEY HALL. Orangeburgh Dist.: Proven by WILLIAM ADAMS before RICHD WILLIAMS, J. Q. 4 Sept 1818. Rec. 29 Apr 1840.

Pp. 85-86: S. C.: JACOB KAMMINER of Lexington Dist., for $1500, pd. by JOHN LOWN of same, several tracts containing 1912 A....(1) 132 A part of 250 A granted to ROBERT SPENCE, 15 Mar 1785 (2) 240 A part of 316 A granted to GEORGE RALL and JOHN GARTMAN, 30 July 1805 (3) 320 A part of 480 A from the Estate of JOHN HENDRIX sold by writ of partition from Court of Equity between his Heirs &C. (4) 533 A granted to HENRY WEAVER 7 Sept 18__ (5) 687 A granted to HENRY WEAVER 6 Mar 1815, all adj. each other on which is a saw mill & Grist Mill on Twelve Mile Creek waters of big Saluda....14 Oct 1837...JACOB KAMINER (LS), Wit: THOMAS J. LEE, DAVID ARNELD. Proven by THOMAS LEE 30 Apr 1838.before WILLIAM QUATTLEBUM, Q. U. Ex officio. NANCY KAMINER, wife of JACOB, relinquished dower 30 Apr 1838 NANCY KAMINER (N). Rec. 4 May 1840. R. HARMAN, R. M. C.

Pp. 86-87: S. C. Lexington Dist.: SARAH and WILLIAM HALL heirs of NANCY HALL, formerly NANCY HOOKER of Lexington Dist., for $23 pd. by JOHN & WILLIAM HARTH...212 A on Caney Branch, a branch of Cedar Creek, a branch of the North Edisto River, 1/9 and 5/9 of a tract granted to HENRY H. H. HOOKER 26 Feb 1814...11 Mar 1840...SARAH HALL (LS), for WM. M. HALL (LS), Wit: JOHN C. JEFCOAT, WILLIAM HOOKER. Proven by JOHN C. JEFCOAT 11 Apr 1840, before ELIJAH JEFCOAT, J.P. Rec. 5 May 1840.

Pp. 87-88: S. C.: CHARLES WILLIAMSON of Lexington Dist., for $300 pd. by JOHN & WILLIAM HARTH of same, and of Orangeburg Dist...1261 A in three parcels in Lexington Dist., on Head waters of Little Pond Branch and Ceder [sic] Creek waters of North Edisto River (1) 234 A, part of 1000 A granted to EDWARD EVANS, sruveyd. 3 Feb 1792 (2)212 A surveyed for HENRY H. H. HOOKER 26 Feb 1814 on Cane Branch, a branch of Ceder Creek (3) 863 A, part of 1000 A granted to EDWARD EVANS 3 May 1792 also my interest in the saw mill which is now owned by myself, DAVID WILLIAMSON and WILLIAM MALPASS...the 6d. DR. JOHN and WILLIAM HARTH...CHARLES WILLIAMSON (SEAL), Wit: JESSE M. MALPASS, JOHN WILLIAMSON, DAVID WILLIAMSON. Dated 2 Feb 1840. We relinquish our right to JOHN and WILLIAM HARTH, ...DAVID WILLIAMSON, J. WMSON. THOS. WILLIAMSON, Wit: ELIJAH JEFCOAT, CRAWFORD E. WILLIAMSON, 22 Feb 1840. Lexington Dist.: MARY WILLIAMSON, wife of CHARLES, relinquished dower 14 Mar 1840, before SIDNEY M. DAVID, Q. U. (LS), Proven by JESSE MALPASS, CRAWFORD E. WILLIAMSON, 13 Apr 1840. Rec. 5 May 1840.

Pp. 89-91: [Pages 89-90 plat made by J. D. A. MURPHY, Dep. Surveyor, made Sept 1834, for several tracts totalling 1640 A.]
S. C. JOHN D. A. MURPHY & JOHN N. BARRILON of Orangeburgh Dist., for $375 pd. by SAMUEL FELDER & FRANKLIN J. FELDER of Orangeburgh Dist....1640 A in Lexington Dist on S side Cedar Creek, waters of North Edisto adj. WILLIAMSON,L. FERTIG, OHANEY, WALKER & LEWIS, BARR & HOOKER... A 132 A, B 163 A, C 148 A & contg. 463 A is part of three tracts of 200 A each originally granted to PETER ____ 29 May 1736, conveyed by ANN BUYCK to J. D. A. MURPHY & J. N. BARRILLON 2 Sept 1834...Part D is a tract of 39___ A granted to R. STARKE 5 Aug 1793 and contains 1177.A which with the parts A B & C make 1640 A...10 Nov 1834...JOHN D. A. MURPHY (LS), JOHN N. BARRILLON (LS), Wit: M. C. POOSER, C. ARANT. Orangeburgh Dist.: Proven by C. ARANT, 23 Mar 1840, before SIDNEY M. DAVIS, Q. U. Rec. 5 May 1840.

Pp. 91-92: S. C. JOHN M. FELDER, Planter, and SAMUEL FELDER both of Orangeburgh Dist., for $9500 pd. by WILLIAM HARTH SENR, & DR. JOHN HARTH of Orangeburgh Dist....two plantations (1) 734 A, the other (2) 1640 A with a saw mill adj. DANIEL RAMBO, MAJR. J. M. FELDER, LEWIS BARR, CHANEY, LEWIS FERTICKS, WILLIAMSON, and MOLPHUS [sic]...conveyed by JOHN D. A. MURPHY on 9 Sept 1833 to SAMUEL & F. J. FELDER...14 Oct 1839...JOHN M. FELDER (LS), SAMUEL FELDER (LS), Wit: JOHN D. A. MURPHY, JOHN J. SALLY. Orangeburgh Dist.: Proven by JOHN D. A. MURPHY 23 March 1840, before D. S. DANNELLY, Q. U. Rec. 5 May 1840.

Pp. 93-95: [plat on pp. 93-94]. S. C. JOHN D. A. MURPHY of Orangeburgh Dist., for $750
           pd. by SAMUEL & FRANKLIN J. FELDER of Orangeburgh Dist...1734 A on Cedar Creek
on both sides the road leading from WMSONS Bridge to Columbia and Granby part of the tract
originally granted to DAVID COALTER & JAMES STUART 5 Aug 1793 for 2000 A conveyed by
the Exrs. of DAVID COALTER (anmely WM HARPER, DAVID H. MEANS & DAVID RUMPH) to WM. C.
PRESTON 6 May 1829, conveyed by sd. PRESTON to JOHN D. A. MURPHY 24 June 1833...the moiety
or half part of the grant which was vested in JAMES STUART was conveyed by sd. STUART to
D. COALTER, Recorded in Orangeburgh...9 Sept 1833...JOHN D. A. MURPHY (LS), Wit: EDM. J.
FELDER, J. B. McMICHAEL. Orangeburgh Dist.: Proven by EDMUND J. FELDER 9 Sept 1833, before JOHN N. BARRILLON, Natary Public & Q. U. Ex off. ANN C. MURPHY, wife of JOHN D. A.,
relinquished dower 9 Sept 1833. Rec. 5 May 1840.

Page 96: S. C. Lexington Dist.: GEORGE BOWERS OF Edgefield Dist., for ___ [not stated],
         to ALLEN PARMER, 91 A adj. JOHN BATES, HENRY H. SPANN, and others...lease for
10 years...14 Feb 1840...GEORGE BOWERS (B) (LS), ALLEN PARMER (R) (LS), Wit: ABHM JONES,
WM. R. SPANN. Proven by ABRAHAM JONES 20 Feb 1840 before HENRY A. SMITH, Q. U. Rec. 11
May 1840.

Pp. 96-97: S. C.: THOMAS RISINGER of Lexington Dist., in consideration of my weight of
                  years, my beloved wife likewise being aged, therefore for the partial
purpose of compensation for care, to my beloved daughter REBECCA RISINGER, do give her
half of my plantation, tract originally granted to JOSEPH WILLIAMS and by him on 10 Sept
1799 conveyed to STEPHEN WILLIAMS & sd. STEPHEN WILLIAMS to me on 29 Aug 1806, 100 A on
waters of Saluda River on a Branch called Caney Branch...19 May 1837...THOMAS RISINGER
(LS). Wit: DAVID CROUT, AZARIAH CROUT, A. H. FORT. Lexington Dist.: MRS. ELIZABETH RIS-
INGER, wife of THOMAS, relinquished dower 19 May 1837, before A. H. FORT. Proven by
A. H. FORT 11 May 1840. Rec. 11 May 1840.

Pp. 97-98: S. C. THOMAS RISINGER of Lexington Dist., in consideration of weight of years
           ...to daughter BARBARA RISINGER, half of tract [other half of tract mentioned
in preceding deed]...19 May 1837...[same sign & wit.]

Pp. 99-100: S. C.: DAVID EWART, President of the Saluda Manufacturing Company, as Trustee
            for sd. company, for $60,100 pd by ABRAM D. JONES, JOHN FISHER, EDWARD R.
FISHER, BENJAMIN F. TAYLOR, WILLIAM F. DeSAUSSURE, HUGH H. TOLAND, DAVID McDOWELL, JOHN
B. ONEALL, R. W. GIBBS, JAMES ROGERS, JOEL ADAMS SENIOR, and JOHN ENGLISH ...all those
tracts on the Saluda near the mouth thereof, two tracts adj. to each other on the S side
of the river, designated as AB on a resurvey made 21 Nov 1789 by GASPER TROTTE of a large
body of land near the confluence of the said river with Broad River, A having been granted
to GASPER GRY and B to GASPER FAUST, 105 A...and tract originally granted to ZEBULON RU-
DOLPH and the heirs of THOMAS BROWN 11 A 1809, 14 A in the Rocky part of Saluda River
known as Beard's falls, and a tract granted to WILLIAM HUNTER...1840...DAVID EWART (SEAL),
Wit: N. RAMSAY, JAMES L. CLARK. S. C. Richland, Proven by J. L. CLARK, before R. H.
GOODWYN, Town Warden. [Plat included], Rec. 21 May 1840. R. HARMAN, R. M. C.

Pp. 101-102: CHRISTIAN RISTER & MARY ANN RISTER of Lexington Dist., for love & good will
             & affection to our loving children ABRAHAM RISTER & ADAM RISTER & ELIAS
RISTER...tract where we now live 219 1/2 A adj. MICHAEL WISE, on Road leaving from Columbia S. C. to Augusta Georgia on the head branches of Cedar Creek, waters of N Edisto River
...23 Sept 1837. CHRISTIAN RISTER (SEAL), MARY ANN RISTER (X) (SEAL), Wit. Dvd. KING,
ISABELLA RING. Proven by DAVID KING 2 Jan 1838. Rec. 23 May 1840.R. HARMAN, R. M. C.

Pp. 102-103: S. C. Lexington Dist.: TIMOTHY TONEY of Lexington Dist., for $750 pd. by
             GEORGE TONEY of same, Felder tract, 1500 A in the fork of Edisto on McTier
Creek, waters of S Edisto River, in a line of land granted to HAMPTON & BYNUM...PETER
GALLOWAYs line...JOHN P. CULLUMS line on JAMES PROTHRS[?]...26 Apr 1838...TIMOTHY TONEY
Wit: BARZILLE CULLUM, G. W. BOATWRIGHT. Proven by CULLUM 21 Apr 1839 before NATHL. JONES
JP. Rec. 25 May 1840. JOHN FOX,R. M. C.[note change].

Pp. 103-105: S. C. Lexington District: TIMOTHY TONEY of Lexington Dist., for $750 pd. by
             WILLIAM TONEY of same...1/ 4 of what he now has, and cultivateable part which
he may clear, part of Felder tract [part of tract mentioned in preceding deed]...26 Apr
1838...TIMOTHY TONEY (SEAL), Wit: BARZILLE CULLUM, G. W. BOATWRIGHT. Proven by BARZILLA
CULLUM 29 Apr 1839. Rec. 25 May 1840. JOHN FOX, R. M. C.

Pp. 105-106: S. C.: JOHN KNOX and JOHN K. JOHNSTON of Lexington Dist., for $65 pd. by
             JESSE FOX of same...65 A on Chinquepin Creek, waters of N Edisto River,
Graney's Branch...land originally granted to THOMAS FOX in 17__, for 390 A...7 Apr 1840
JOHN KNOX (LS), JNO. K. JOHNSTON (LS), Wit: ANDERSON STEEDMAN, GEORGE STEEDMAN. Proven
by GEORGE STEEDMAN, 8 Apr 1840. REC. 25 May 1840, JOHN FOX, R. M. C.

Pp. 106-107: S. C., Lexington Dist.:Whereas WILLIAM B. JONES assignee Applicants, one of the heirs of JEREMIAH GIST alias KISH deceased, filed a petition in the Court of Ordinary, against NANCY TITSHAW, AARON CHRISTMAS & wf and CELIA KISK on 19 Apr 1840 stating that JEREMIAH KISH or GIST died intestate, leaving certain parcels of land that has not been partitioned...to be partitioned and sold by sheriff...CELIA GIST became the purchaser for $80, 100 A on chalk Hill Creek...WILLIAM L. MILLER, Sheriff, 1 June 1840. Wit: PETER ROWE, JOHN FOX. Proven by JOHN FOX, before L. BOOZER, Q. U. 2 June 1840. Rec. 2 June 1840. Delivered to AARON CHRISTMAS, 31 Oct 1842.

Pp. 108-109: S. C., I, PAUL JAMES SIMONS of Newberry Dist., for $400 pd by JOHN FOX of Lexington Dist.,have sold 1/4 A, part of a grant to LAWRENCE CORLEY, 4 June 1804, lot in Village of Lexington by the main street or road leading from Columbia to Augusta adj. tracts now held by MRS. BARBARA CORLEY, SILAS MILTON SIMON, but now sd. JOHN FOX...15 May 1840...P. J. SIMONS (LS), Wit: WM. L. MILLER, LEROY HENDRIX, Lexington Dist: Proven by HENDRIX 3 June 1840, beofre L. BOOZER, Q. U. Newberry Dist.: NANCY G. SIMONS, wife of P. J. SIMONS, relinquished dower 19 May 1840, before H. K. BOYD, Q. U. Rec. 3 June 1840, JOHN FOX, R. M. C.

Pp. 109-111: S. C. THOMAS A. GREEN, SUSANNAH GREEN, ANDREW PLYMALE, CHRISTIAN PLYMALE, MARY ANN PLYMALE, BARBARA PLYMALE, and PETER PLYMALE of Lexington Dist., for $526...pd. by HENRY J. DRAFTS of same...379 A in Lexington and Edgefield Dists., on Rocky Creek, waters of Saluda River being land devised by MICHAEL PLYMALE SNR by his L. W. & T. to the sd. SUSANNAH GREEN (then the wife of the testator)...100 A to SUSANNAH for life and the balance to be divided between JOHN PLYMALE, ANDREW PLYAMLE, CHRISTINA PLYMALE, PETER PLYMALE, and MICHAEL PLYMALE, 379 A granted to sd. THOMAS A. GREEN 23 Nov 1835 adj. JOHN HOLLEY, SAMUEL SNELGROVE, WILLIAM FORTNER, PETERPLYMALE and lands formerly owned by DENNIS G. HAYES...4 Oct 1839...THOMAS A. GREEN (X) (LS), SUSANNAH GREEN (+) (LS), ANDREW PLYMALE (LS), CHRISTIAN PLYMALE (LS), MARY ANN PLYMALE (X) (LS), BARBARA PLYMALE (X) (LS), PETER PLYMALE (LS), Wit: L. BOOZER, DANIEL DRAFTS. Proven by DANIEL DRAFTS before GEORGE SAWYER, 11 Oct 1839. SUSANNAH GREEN relinquished dower 11 Oct 1839, before GEORGE SAWYER. Rec. 3 June 1840.

Pp. 111-112: S. C.: JACOB RAWL of Lexington Dist., for $1300 pd. by WILLIAM RALL of same... 231 1/2 A on branches of Beaver Dam Creek, waters of Saluda adj. JOHN LOWN, DANIEL RALL, HENRY HENDRIX, CALEB LITES, JOSEPH LITES, WILLIAM GARTMAN and SAMUEL RAWL, granted to GEORGE GARTMAN 6 Nov 1786...13 Jan 1840...JACOB RALL (LS), Wit: WILLIAM GARTMAN, DANIEL RAWL. Proven by DANIEL RALL, 28 Mar 1840 before GEORGE SAWYER, Q. U. SARAH RAWL, wife of JACOB, relinquished dower before L. BOOZER. 3 Feb 1840. Rec. 13 June 1840.

Page 113: S. C.: WILLIAM RAWL of Lexington Dist., for $33 pd by SAMUEL RAWL of same...7 A, part of a tract granted to GEORGE GARTMAN 6 Nov 1786 for 680 A on a branch of Beaver Dam Creek waters of big Saluda River adj. WILLIAM RAWLS, SAMUEL RAWLS land...28 Mar 1840...WILLIAM RAWL (LS), Wit: JOHN FOX, LEROY HENDRIX. Lexington Dist.: Proven by LEROY HENDRIX before JOHN FOX, 13 June 1840. Rec. 13 June 1840.

Pp. 114-115: S. C., Lexington Dist.: HENRY FRAYSURE (FRAZIER) for $80 pd by WILLIAM EPTING ....57 A on Dunbare branch of big Saluday [sic] River...part of tract granted to JOHN HENRY SUMMER for 114 A on W side of sd. tract, the same parcel which ALEXANDER JENKINS sold to JAMES HENDRIX, also being part of the tract which I bough when it was sold as part of the real estate of WILLIAM HOLEMAN decd by writ of partition &c. &c....30 June 1838...HENRY FRAZIER (LS), Wit: BENJAMIN LINDSAY, ABERHART FULMER (E), DAVID HOLEMAN. Newberry Dist.: Proven by DAVID HOLEMAN 30 June 1838. Lexington Dist.: MARY FRAYSURE, wife of HENRY, relinquished dower 30 June 1838 before BENJAMIN LINDSEY, J. Q.

Pp. 115-117: S. C. _____ 1840, FREDERICK W. GREEN of Richland Dist and _____ ANDERSON of Lexington Dist of one part, and JAMES S. GUIGNARD of Town of Columbia of the other part...Whereas, FREDERICK W. GREEN with one WILLIAM JENKS by certain obligation joint with SAMUEL GREEN decd, bearing date 3 Feb 1836 were bound to JAMES S. GUIGNARD and EDWARD FISHER Trustees of CAROLINE HERBEMONT in the sum of $4000 on or before 1 Jan next thereafter with Interest from 26 July 1838, transfered by JAMES S. GUIGNARD the Surviving trustee to the Exrs. of sd. CAROLINE HERBEMONT,on 27 Feb 1839 transfered by WILLIAM F. DESAUSSURE, Exr. to the sd. JAMES S. GUIGNARD who is now the real and bond fide owner of sd. Bond the principal of which is still due and interest from 27 Feb 1839...and whereas the sd. WILLIAM JENKS hath removed from the State and FREDERICK W. GREEN and JOHN P. ANDERSON have taken upon themselves the sd. debt of $2000 with interest...for $1 convey tract of 1618 A in Lexington Dist on Red Bank Creek with the use of timber on 672 A adjoining, adj. TURPIN, DAVID BOOZER, GODFREY HENDRIX, THOMAS POINDEXTER, JOSEPH LYBRAND and Est. of WILLIAM KINSLER which tract was conveyed on 13 Feb 1836 by DANIEL RALL to F. W. GREEN and WILLIAM JENKS, also tract of 63 A adj. to KINSLER and DAVIS BOOZER, conveyed by DAVID

BOOZER on 13 Feb 1836 to sd. GREEN & JENKS...FRED. WM. GREEN (LS), JOHN P. ANDERSON (LS), Wit: JAS. S. ANDERSON, W. F. ANDERSON. Richland District: Proven by JAMES S. ANDERSON before EDWARD A. SEYMOUR, J. P. Rec. 20 June 1840.

Pp. 117-119: S. C.: Whereas COL. JOHN W. LEE in his life time affected a bargain in which he contracted to purchase a certain tract of land the title of which was vested in one H. C. KELLER and the sd. LEE departed this life without accomplishing said object by reason no title had been executed and in pursuance of said bargain, since his death, MRS. ELEANOR LEE, widow and admr. of JOHN W. LEE decd, obtained a titled which was executed on 5 Jan 1831 by sd. H. C. KELLER for use of sd. LEE's estate, also application for partition was made and had for partition of Real Estate by the Court of Equity.... PATRICK LEE one of the sons and heir at Law of the sd. JOHN W. LEE decd, and ELEANOR made guardian for sd. PATRICK...now ELEANOR as guardian, for $305 pd by GEORGE SAWYER EQR., 122 A on branches of Hollow Creek, waters of Saluda River, conveyed by MICHAEL KELLER to H. C. KELLER, adj. EMANUEL RICE, ADAM RISH, DANIEL LOMANACK, JACOB VANZANT, ____ OXNER...20 June 1839...ELEANOR LEE (LS), Wit: JOHN T. LLOYD, JAS. E. LEE. Lexington Dist.: Proven by JAMES E. LEE 3 Oct 1839 before WILLIAM QUATTLEBUM, Q. U. Ex. off. Rec. 20 June 1840.

Page 119: Lexington Dist.: ALLEN PARMER for $100 pd. by GEORGE BOWERS of Edgefield Dist., 90 A in Lexington Dist., lease for 10 years...adj. JOHN BATES, HENRY H. SPANN, & others...23 June 1840...ARRLEN PARMER (R) (LS), Wit: AMOS BANKS, GEORGE L. BANKS. Edgefield Dist.: Proven by GEORGE L. BANKS, before AMOS BANKS, Q. U. 23 June 1840. Rec. 26 June 1840.

Pp. 120-121: S. C.: HARMAN GEIGER of Lexington Dist., for $968.33 pd by JOHN METZ JUNIOR of same, 145 A on S side Eighteen Mile Creek adj. lands of THOS WINGARD, JOHN A. ROBERTS, DANIEL WAY[?], and others, part of a tract granted to JOHANNAS KIMSE[?] 13 Apr 1750....plat executed by WILLIAM QUATTLEBUM, D. S., 3 Apr 1838, rec. in Office of Register of Mesne Conveyance, Lexington Dist., Book L, p. 267...also tract of 25 A adjoining land of JOHN FREY, JOHN A. ROBERTS, GEORGE ROBERTS, MARTIN CAUGHMAN, also on 18 Mile Creek, conveyed by CHRISTENA WINGARD and IZAIAH WINGARD to sd. HARMAN GEIGER...27 June 1840...HARMAN GEIGER (LS), Wit: WILLIAM L. MILLER, REUBEN BROSS. Lexington Dist.: Proven by WILLIAM L. MILLER before L. BOOZER, Q. U. 27 June 1840. Lexington Dist.: BARBARA GEIGER, wife of HARMAN, relinquished dower 27 June 1840, before LEMUEL BOOZER, Q. U. "delivered to JOHN METZ." Rec. 29 June 1840.

Pp. 121-123: S. C.: A. H. FORT of Lexington Dist., for $100 pd. by MARY WING & ELIZA-BETH WING of same...100 A on waters of Twelve Mile Creek adj. MARTIN LYBRAND, WIDOW WARREN, and others...granted to DIONASIOUS BLAKELY and conveyed to JOHN EDDINGS, who died intestate, after whose death the widow, who had intermarried with DAVID WINCHEL, petitioned the Court of Ordinary to affect partition, and J. A. H. FORT was the purchaser ...A. H. FORT (LS), Wit: WM FORT, LYDIA FORT. Lexington Dist.: Proven by WILLIAM FORT 3 July 1840. Deed dated 14 Jan 1840. Lexington Dist.: MRS. PHEBE FORT, wife of A. H. FORT, relinquished dower 3 July 1840 before L. BOOZER. Rec. 3 July 1840. [Plat included in deed showing land adj. to GEORGE SOUTER, WEST CAUGHMAN, MARTIN LYBRAND.] Plat dated 17 Feb 1837, JOHN D. SHARP, Dep. Sur.

Pp. 123-124: S. C., Lexington Dist.: JACOB R. COOK for $230 pd by LEWIS COOK, both of Dist. aforesd....200 A on horsepen or Adams Branch adj. CLEMENT JACKSON, CHARLES COOK mill path...part of three tracts, one part granted to JACOB ADAMS and one to JEREMIAH WEB and one to ELIGAH ADAMS and ELISHA GANTT...10 Jany 1840...JACOB R. COOK, Wit: FRANCIS L. WALKER, CHARLES COOK. Proven by CHARLES COOK, before NATHL. JONES, J. P. 15 May 1840 Rec. 6 July 1840. Delivered to PETER READHIMER for CHARLES COOK, May 22, 1849.

Pp. 124-125: S. C., ELIAS HARPER for $300 pd. by CHRISTIAN RISTER both of Lexington Dist., 700 A in three separate tracts & whereon I now dwell on or near the head branches of Bull Swamp, waters of N. Edisto River adj. HARBERT SPIRES, JOHN H. WISE, ABRAHAM GEIGER, the first tract 441 A granted to JOHN WISE, the 2nd 184 A granted to JOHN SMITH, the 3rd to ELIAS HARPER...25 May 1840...ELIAS HARPER (X) (SEAL), Wit: DAVID KING, BURREL BAYLES. Lexington Dist.: Proven by DAVID KING 4 July 1840, before ELIJAH JEFCOAT, J.P. Rec. 18 July 1840. Delivered to ELIAS HARPER 18 Sept 1840.

Pp. 125-26: S. C., Lexington Dist.: ELIAS HARPER to CHRISTIAN RISTER, Bill of Sale for bay mare branded EB, also cattle, hogs, for $200...25 May 1840...ELIAS HARPER (X). Wit: ABRAHAM RISTER, DAVID KING. Proven by DAVID KING, 4 July 1840. Rec. 18 July 1840. Delivered to ELIAS HARPER 18 Sept 1840.

Pp. 126-127: S. C. Lexington Dist.: CHRISTIAN RISTER for love, good will & affection to my loving daughter REBECCA HARPER and her children WILL HARPER & MARY HARPER two tracts adj. each other 700 A on a branch of Bull Swamp, also cattle...CHRISTIAN RISTER

(SEAL), Wit: BURREL BAYLIS, JOHN J. HOOVER. Proven by JOHN HOOVER before ELIJAH JEFCOAT, J.P., 14 July 1840. MARY ANN RISTER, wife of CHRISTIAN, relinquished dower 18 July 1840 before JOHN FOX, Clk. Rec. 18 July 1840. Delivered to ELIAS HARPER, 18 Sept 1840.

Pp. 127-128: S. C., GEORGE SAWYER of Lexington Dist., for $360 pd. by SIMON RIDLEHOVER of same, 181 A on Lightwood Creek, part of a tract originally granted to WILL BURGESS in 1802, and by deed 1 Jan 1829, conveyed by WILLIAM BURGEES to JACOB KINARD, and then on 17 Feb 1832 to MICHAEL KINARD by JACOB KINARD, and on 20 July 1839 by JOHN FOX, Sheriff to GEORGE SAWYER, adj. JOHN DENT, JAMES CRIM, JACOB KINARD, WILLIAM ALLEN...4 July 1840...GEORGE SAWYER (LS), Wit: AMOS BANKS, JASPER SAWYER. Proven by JASPER SAWYER before AMOS BANKS, Q. U. 4 July 1840 in Lexington Dist. CATHARINE SAWYER, wife of GEORGE, relinquished dower before AMOS BANKS, a Justice of the Quorum for Edgefield District, 4 July 1840 in Lexington District. Rec. 20 July 1840. Delivered to SIMEON RIDLEHOVER __ Oct 1840.

Pp. 129-130: S. C., Lexington Dist.: JOSHUA MILLER for $600 pd. by ASA LANGFORD, both of Dist. aforesd...173 A on S side Saluda adj. Estate of WILLIAM CALK, Decd, MRS. SARAH SHIREY, ASA LANGFORD, and Saluda River...24 Aug 1839...JOSHUA MILLER (LS), Wit: WM. L. MILLER, STANMORE LANGFORD. Proven by MILLER 15 July 1840 before JOHN FOX. DOROTHY MILLER, wife of JOSHUA, relinquished dower 22 July 1840 before JOHN FOX. Rec. 22 July 1840. Delivered to ASA LANGFORD 14 Oct 1840.

Pp. 130-131: S. C.: JAMES S. GUIGNARD of Twon of Columbia, for $400 pd. by DANIEL ROOF of Lexington Dist...400 A on Lexington Dist. on Savannah Branch adj. JESSE FLOYD, JOHN RAMICK, land granted to HENRY P. HAMPTON, land belonging to the estate of KINSLER, and sd. GUIGNARD...13 Jan 1838...JAMES S. GUIGNARD (LS), Wit: EDWARD A. SEYMOUR, EDWARD J. ARTHUR. Richland Dist.: Proven by EDWARD L. ARTHUR before H. MAXEY, Q. U. Rec. 25 July 1840.

Pp. 131-132: S. C. HENRY MULLER of Lexington Dist., for $900 pd. by REV. DAVID BERNHARD of same...tract called the White house, 300 A on waters of Beaver Creek adj. JOHN MURPH, LAURENCE CRIM, RUCKER, and others formerly occupied by WILLIAM TAYLOR...1 July 1840...HENRY MULLER (LS), Wit: JOSEPH WINGARD, HENRY MULLER, JR.. Proven by JOSEPH WINGARD before JOHN FOX 28 July 1840. Rec. 28 July 1840. Delivered to JOSEPH WINGARD.

Pp. 132-133: S. C., Lexington Dist.: MARTIN WHITE, planter, for $130 pd. by GEORGE WHITE planter, both of Dist. aforesd....104 1/2 A on waters of Wateree Creek, waters of Broad River adj. MICHAEL SLICE, RACHEL SLICE, ADAM MAYER, & MICHAEL CHARLES, part of 200 A originally granted to CHRISTIAN TISTER, who conveyed 104 1/2 A to MARTIN WHITE ...30 Dec 1837 MARTIN WHITE (LS), Wit: JOHN G. METZE, HENRY ADDY. Proven by HENRY ADDY before STERLING C. WILLIAMSON, J. @. 9 Mar 1840. Rec. 8 Aug 1840. Belivered to GEORGE WHITE.

Pp. 133-135: S. C. Lexington Dist.: JOSHUA WOOD for $100 pd. by JAMES W. E. STALEY, and JOHN JORDAN of Orangeburgh Dist...1/2 of three several tracts (1) originally granted to ENOCH RILEY, 1000 A and by a resurvey plat made by H. J. SALLEY, found to contain 1519 A on N side Giddy Swamp adj. lands granted to JAMES LYNCH, WM GEIGER, BENJAMIN HUTTO, SALLY JOHNSON and JOSEPH HUTTO, the same where JOHN ALTMAN formerly lived...1/2 of tract on S side Giddy Swamp containing 500 A granted to HUTTO adj. above tract and land of estate of SOLOMON ALTMAN and GARVIN...one half of 50 A part of tract granted to JOHN KEADLE[?] and now known as the Estate land of SOLOMON ALTMAN...the whole 1593 A...25 Feb 1840...JOSHUA WOODWARD (LS), Wit: JOHN JORDAN SENR., JOHN D. WILLIAMS. Lexington Dist.: Proven by JOHN D. WILLIAMS before JAMES GARVIN, J. Q. SARAH WOOD, wife of JOSHUA, relinquished dower 25 Feb 1840. Rec. 11 Aug 1840. Delivered to J. W. E. STALEY.

Pp. 135-136: S. C.: JOHN KNOX of Lexington Dist., for $1200 pd. by JOHN LOWERMAN of same, 530 A on Horsepen Branch, waters of North Edisto River adj. SCION WATERS, JAMES E. LEE, ANDREW SHEALY, WILLIS HARTLEY, LOWERMAN, Heirs of JOHN W. LEE, decd, A. H. FORT, Esqr...made up of several small tracts one of 50 A sold by W. J. TURNER to sd. KNOX 2 May 1833; one of 180 A conveyed to the sd. KNOX by J. T. DUNKINS by a power of attorney to STEPHEN G. SMITH, also one tract 100 A conveyed by sd. DUNKINS by SMTTH 9 Oct 1834 and one tract of 200 A conveyed to KNOX by WM. PRITCHETT by deed 6 Apr 1836...8 Oct 1839...JOHN KNOX (LS), Wit: DANIEL LOWERMAN, WILLIS HARTLEY. Proven by WILLIS HARTLEY 23 Oct 1839, before ISAAC VANSANT J: P. Rec. 14 Aug 1840.

Pp. 136-137: S. C.: JACOB KAMINER of Lexington Dist., for $150 pd. by SAMUEL RAWL of same, 48 A on dreans [sic] of Beaver Dam and Rocky Creek, waters of Saluda River adj. DENNIS G. HAYES, GEORGE OSWALT, SAMUEL TAWL, which will be seen by reference to a plat dated 17 Dec 1835...7 Apr 1840...JACOB KAMINER (LS), Wit: HENRY HENDRIX, GEO. J. HOOK. Proven by HENRY HENDRIX 13 June 1840. NANCY KAMINER, wife of JACOB, relinquished dower 15 Aug 1840 before JOHN FOX. Delivered to SAML RAWL. Rec. 15 Aug 1840.

Pp. 137-138: S. C., WM L. MILLER, Sheriff of Lexington Dist...Whereas, by four writs of
Fiere Facias issued out of the Court of Common Pleas...HARMAN CORLEY & Co.
vs. JESSE HARMAN tested 9 Sept 1839, REUBEN GROSS vs JESSE HARMAN tested 9 Sept 1839,
WILLIAM BROWN vs JESSE HARMAN tested 9 Sept 1839, HARMAN & LOWERMAN vs JESSE HARMAN, 9
Sept 1839...50 A adj. GEO. YOUNGINER, EMANUEL GEIGER, HENRY MEETZE, & others, for $151
pd by JOSEPH J. CORLEY...WM. L. MILLER, (LS, S. L. D. Wit: J. N. BOOZER, L. BOOZER. Proven by JACOB N. BOOZER before JOHN FOX 17 Aug 1840. Deed dated 17 Aug 1840. Rec. 17 Aug
1840. Delivered to JOSEPH J. CORLEY.

Pp. 138-139: S. C. ELIZABETH STEEDMAN, wife of GEORGE STEEDMAN, decd of Lexington Dist.,
to ANDERSON STEEDMAN, for $1200...all right and title in Estate of GEORGE
STEEDMAN...4 Jan 1839 ELIZABETH STEEDMAN (X) (LS), Wit: JESSE FOX, FELIX FOX. Proven by
FELIX FOX, 7 Sept 1840. Rec. 7 Sept 1840. Delivered to ANDERSON STEEDMAN.

Pp. 140-141: Plat resurveyed at request of JOHN ROOF, part of a tract originally granted
to J. S. GUIGNARD also 132 A part of a tract granted to RICHARD HAMPTON also
50 A purchased from HENRY SHULL and one other tract of 25 A purchased from URIAH SENN &
which I find to contain in the whole 364 A on branches of Six Mile Creek waters of Congaree
River adj. to Church Land, JOHN SHULL, DAVID WILSON, GEORGE CLARK, KINSLER, land formerly
belonging to CANTY, GEORGE CLARK, SAMUEL SOCKS, JOHN MURPH, HENRY SHULL, CONROD SHULL,
WILLIAM SHULL, JOHN KINSLER...13 Mar 1839 JOHN D. SHARP, Dep. Surv. Chain Carriers,
SAMUEL SOCKS, DAVID WILSON. Rec. 24 Sept 1840. Delivered to JOHN ROOF SEN. 13 Apr 1842.

Pp. 141-142: S. C. Lexington Dist.: JACOB EAREHART for $140 pd. by HENRY J. DRAFTS...50 A
part of 170 A on Hollow Creek adj. JOHN KELLEY, DAVID FIKE...23 Sept 1840...
JACOB EAREHART (LS), Wit: JESSE HOLMAN, JOHN P. EAREHART,. Proven by JOHN P. EAREHART,
24 Sept 1840, JOHN FOX, Clk. Rec. 24 Sept 1840. Delivered to HENRY J. DRAFTS.

Pp. 142-143: S. C., Lexington Dist.: DANIEL GUNTER & wf DEBORAH for $800 pd. by GIDEON
JONES...one tract granted to WADSWORTH, 250 A and one tract granted to BALAAM
GUNTER for 450 A and one tract granted to RIVERS GUNTER JR. for 630 A and a tract called
the Dent tract for 500 A and the JACKSON tract of 86 A...formerly belonging to the estate
of BALAAM GUNTER decd...29 Sept 1837...DANIEL GUNTER (LS), DEBORAH GUNTER, Wit: BENJAMIN
GUNTER, RUTHA GUNTER (+). Proven by BENJAMIN GUNTER 25 Oct 1837, before JACOB GANTT, J.P.
Rec. 28 Sept 1840. Delivered to JOSEPH C. FANNING 30 Dec 1842.

Pp. 143-144: S. C.,18 Apr 1840, WILLIAM MERITT of Lexington Dist., to WILLIAM H. GEIGER of
same, for $1500;payable on 1 Jan now last past for $750, the other payable
1 Jan...both notes dated 15 July 1839...debt owed to JOHN J. ABLE [mortgage] 600 A on
N edisto River adj. WAIN ABLE,the WIDOW ABLE, JOHN J. ABLE, DANIEL RAMBO, ISRAEL GAUNTT
JUNR., WILLIAM MERRITT (LS), Wit: A. H. FORT, GEORGE SAWYER. Proven by A. H. FORT,
before JOHN FOX. Rec. 2 Oct 1840. Delivered to WM. H. GEIGER 16 Oct 1841.

Pp. 145-147: S. C., Charleston District: HENRY HORLBECK, DAVID GEIGER & wf ELIZABETH, formerly ELIZABETH HORLBECK, ELIAS HORLBECK, LOUISA MARGARET HORLBECK, DANIEL
HORLBECK, EDWARD HORLBECK, PETER HORLBECK JUR, CHARLES BLUM & wf ESTER formerly ESTER
HORLBECK, ANN GEIGER HORLBECK, JOHN HORLBECK JR and BUCKINGHAM HORLBECK, children of MAR-
GARET BUCKINGHAM HORLBECK, decd who was the grand daughter of ESTER STOUT, for $100 pd.
by HENRY MULLER of Lexington Dist...100 A in Lexington Dist., on S side Congaree River,
granted to STEPHEN KEIRLING 26 Aug 1776 for 100 A and resurveyed by HENRY SMITH on 7 Apr
1790 for 108 A afterwards conveyed by STEPHEN KEIRLING to CONROD KYSELL on 16 Oct 1770
[sic], who devised the same to his wife ESTER afterwards ESTER STOUT who devised the same
to her granddaughter MARGARET BUCKINGHAM afterwards HORLBECK...1 Aug 1840...[all parties
signed], Wit: JOHN T. HENREY, JAMES B. FREEMAN. Plat included showing adj. to WARD, JACOB
SAYLOR, GOODWIN, ZACHARIAH GRIMES. Resurveyed 7 Apr 1790 for 108 A . Dowers relinquished
13 Aug 1840 in Charleston Dist by ELIZABETH H. GEIGER, ESTER BLUM. Dowers of HARRIET P.
HORLBECK, wife of ELIAS HORLBECK and AINSLEY H. HORLBECK wife of EDWARD HORLBECK all of
City of Charleston relinquished dower, 13 Aug 1840 before DANIEL HORLBEKC, Q. U. Proven
by JOHN J. HENRY. Rec. 3 Oct 1840.

Page 148: S. C.: GEORGE EPTING SENR of Newberry Dist, S. C. for $125 pd by DAVID LONG of
Lexington Dist...125 A,a part of tract originally surveyed for JACOB EPTING
SENR in Myrtle Branch adj. FREDERICK BOLAND, URIAH WESSINGER, GEO. EPTING, JOHN SHEELY...
3 Oct 1840. GEORGE EPTING SENR(LS), Wit: ADAM SETSLER, P. DICKERT. Newberry Dist.: Proven
before P. DICKERT J. Q, by ADAM SETSLER. Rec. 5 Oct 1840. Delivered to DAVID LONG Dec.
16, 1842.

Page 149: S. C., Lexington Dist.: JAMES CARR for $60 pd. by SARAH WINGARD, all of Lexing-
          ton Dist...106 1/4 A on Juniper Branch adj. JOSEPH LYBRAND, JOHN DERICK, BARTON
TAYLOR, WM. SEIBLE, JOSEPH LYBRAND...24 Sept 1840...JAMES CARR (X) (LS), Wit: JOHN G. TAY-
LOR, DANIEL M. CLARK. Proven by JOHN G. TAYLOR before JAMES J. CLARK, J. P. Rec. 21 Oct
1840. Delivered to JAMES CARR.

Pp. 150-151: JOHN BAUKNIGHT SENR of Lexington Dist., for $87 pd. by JETHRO HARMAN of same
             ...35 A on fork of Broad and Saluda on main Road from Columbia to the Moun-
tains, part of a tract originally granted to SEIBLES & BRAZELMAN and by a division was
allotted to THOMAS J. BRAZELMAN now decd and conveyed by NATHAN SIMS, Exrs. of T. J.
BRAZELMAN to JOHN BAUKNIGHT 1 Mar 1837, and conveyed to JOHN BAUKNIGHT JR to JOHN BAUK-
NIGHT SENR for 58 A...sd. 35 A at the south end, adj. HENRY BAUKNIGHT, SAMUEL BAUKNIGHT,
DERRICK, ...35 A already sold to sd. JETHRO HARMAN by deed 2 Dec 1839...24 Oct 1840...
JOHN BAUKNIGHT (LS), Wit: SAMUEL BAUKNIGHT, __ BAUKNIGHT. Proven by JOEL BAUKNIGHT before
SAMUEL BAUKNIGHT, Q. U. 24 Oct 1840. Rec. 30 Oct 1840. Delivered to JESSE BOOKMAN per
order of JETHRO HARMAN. JOHN FOX, Reg.

Pp. 151-152: S. C., Lexington Dist.: ELIZABETH M. BLEWER for $1500 pd. by JOHN P. BLEWER
             both of Lexington Dist...240 A and 1/2 of my claim in the Saw Mills on Rocky
Spring Creek, branch of South Edisto adj. lands of JOHN P. CULLUM, JOHN JOHNSON, DAVID
COOK, L. D. JOHNSON, PETER READHEIMER...5 Mar 1838...ELIZABETH M. BLEWER (LS), Wit: PETER
READHIMER, FRANCIS L. WALKER. Proven by READHIMER 2 Nov 1840. Rec. 2 Nov 1840. Delivered
to JOHN P. BLEWER.

Pp. 152-153: S. C, Lexington Dist.: ELIZABETH M. BLEWER for $500 pd. by JOHN P. BLEWER...
             1/2 of tract of 700 A adj. lands of PETER READHIMER, L. D. JOHNSON, and
Edisto River...5 Mar 1838. Same Sign, wit., and probate.

Pp. 153-155: S. C., Lexington Dist.: IVY DANSBY for $26 pd. by JOHN A. FULMER...5 1/5 A
             waters of Crims Creek adj. MICHL. FULMER, sd. JOHN A. FULMER...21 Dec 1839...
IVY DANSBY (LS), Wit: GEORGE M. SUMMER, JOHN O. MARTIN. Plat included in deed, showing
lands of MICHL. & JOHN A. FULMER made 12 Feb 1839 by THOMAS FRKAR, Dep. Sur. Proven by
G. M. SUMMER 31 Dec 1839, before G. M. FULMER,Q. U. ELIZABETH DANSBY, wife of IVY,
relinquished dower...31 Dec 1839, before G. M. FULMER. Rec. 2 Nov 1840. Delivered to
J. A. FULMER, 1 Jan 1844.

Pp. 155-156: S. C., Lexington Dist.: JOHN MATHIS for $550 pd. by JOHN A. FULMER, JR...
             77 A, part of a tract belonging to NELSON SUMMER and part of a tract surveyed
for COL. JOHN A. SUMMER in Dist. aford. on head Branches of Crims Creek, waters of Broad
River adj. INVY DANSBY, CONRAD FARR, JOHN G. KESSLER, GEORGE M. FULMER...9 Jan 1839...
JOHN MATHIS (LS), Wit: JOHN MILLER, G. A. FIKE. Proven by GEORGE A. FIKE before G. M.
FULMER, Q. U. 9 Jan 1839. MARY MATHIS, wife of JOHN, relinquished dower, 30 Jan 1839
before GEORGE M. FULMER. Rec. 2 Nov 1840.

Pp. 156-157: JOHN WILLIAMS of Lexington Dist. for $200 pd. by HENRY GRUBBS ...300 A on
             head of Sedar [sic] Creek, part of a tract granted to EVAN HOWARD in 1807,
known as Walker tract on road leading from Barnwell to Columbia binding on the STACK line
...13 Feb 1840...JOHN WILLIAMS (LS), Wit: WILLIAM SCOFIELD, CHARLES LUCAS (+). Proven by
WILLIAM SCOFIELD before MICHAEL WISE, J. P. Rec. 2 Nov 1840.

Pp. 157-158: S. C.: MICHAEL WISE, planter, of Lexington Dist., for $75 pd. by NICHOLAS
             COALMAN, planter, of same...398 A granted to HARMAN SIGHTLER, 2 Aug 1820...
conveyed to DAVID SENN 22 Jan 1831...on head springs of Cedar Creek, waters of North Edisto
adj. to land granted to DANIEL KING, EVAN HOWARD, and HOWARD now MICHAEL WISE...8 July
1840...MICHAEL WISE (LS), Wit: HENRY GRUBS, WILLIAM SHIVERS (+). Proven by HENRY GRUBS
before ISAAC VANSANT 2 Nov 1840. Rec. 2 Nov 1840.

Pp. 159-160: MICHAEL WISE to HENRY GRUBS for $100...600 A granted to HARMAN SIGHTLER
             2 Aug 1830, conveyed to DANIEL SENN, 22 Jan 1831 on head springs of Cedar
Creek, adj. JOSEPH & JOHN SIGHTLER, CONRAD NEESE, HOWARD now MICHAEL WISE, JACBO HAUGA-
BOOK now CHRISTIAN RISTER and adj. to land granted to JOHN WISE...8 July 1840...MICHAEL
WISE (LS), Wit: NICHOLAS COLEMAN, WILLIAM SHIVERS (+). Proven by NICHOLAS COLEMAN before
ELIJAH JEFCOAT, J.P. 31 Oct 1840. Rec. 2 Nov 1840. Delivered to HENRY GRUBBS 4 June 1841.

Pp. 160-161: Articles of Agreement. S. C. Lexington Dist.: HENRY H. SPANN and ABRAHAM
             JONES have agreed to erect at the joint equal exepnse on a tract of land
owned by sd. SPANN on Lick Creek a house to be used as a Grist Mill and Cotton Gin and a
screw for packing cotton and to complete the dam for sd. mill and gin a part of which has
been erected...29 Oct 1840. HENRY H. SPANN, ABRAHAM JONES. Wit: JESSE THOMAS, JOSEPH
WM. FULMER. Proven by FULMER before HENRY A. SMITH 31 Oct 1840. Rec. 2 Nov 1840.

Pp. 162-163: S. C. BENJAMIN H. GRAY of Aiken, for $150 pd. by AMOS BANKS of Edgefield
Dist...700 A surveyed for PHILLIP SPILLERS 10 Jan 1813 in Lexington Dist. on
branches of Twelve Mile Creek waters of Saluda adj. land surveyed for CAGE MARTIN, SAMUEL
MORRIS, GEORGE RALL & vacant land...3 Nov 1836...B. H. GRAY (LS), Wit: GEORGE L. BANKS,
DANL. MOORE. Lexington Dist.: Proven by GEORGE L. BANKS 23 June 1837, before HENRY A.
SMITH, J. P. Rec. 2 Nov 1840.

Pp. 163-165: S. C. Lexington Dist.: Whereas URIAH INABNET, one of the heirs and distributees of KATHARINE BANKS, decd filed a Petition in Court of Ordinary for Lexington Dist against AMOS BANKS, CHARLES BANKS, MARTIN BANKS on 25 Nov 1833...CATHARINE
BANKS decd died Intestate leaving a tract of Land and it has not been partitioned...on
14 Dec 1833 ARTHUR H. FORT, Esq. Ordy., did order that it be sold by the Sheriff on the
1st Tues in Jan 1834...Sheriff REUBEN HARMAN sold the 204 A for $250 to AMOS BANKS...land
on big hole branch, waters of big How Creek waters of Saluda adj. AMOS BANKS, CHRISTIAN
GABLE, GEORGE PRICE, DANIEL DERRICK...12 Feb 1823...REUBEN HARMAN S. L. D. Wit: JACOB
RALL, JR., ANDREW SHEALY (S). Rec. 2 Nov 1840. Delivered to JACOB LONG SR., Admr. of
AMOS BANKS decd by the hand of JAMES FULMER 5 Feb 1845. JOHN FOX. Plat included showing
lands of GEORGE PRISE, JOHN BENTON, JOHN SAWYER, JACOB FULLMER, GEORGE LONG, REBECKAH
HAIGLER. Plat made by request of MR. CHARLES BELL & MR. GEORGE LONG with their old plat
and grant dated 4 Mar 1790...resurveyed 23 Feb 1814, DVD KING, D. S. Deed proven by
JACOB ROLL before J. A. ADDISON, Q. U.

Pp. 166-167: S. C., DAVID CULCLAZUR of Orangeburgh Dist., planter, for $258 pd. by ALLEN
NEESE of Lexington Dist, planter...258 A part of 607 A on one prong of the N
fork called bullswamp adj. GUSSENDANNES [sic] land, originally granted to PETER HOFFMAN...
DAVID CULCLASURE (LS), Wit: JAMES LEONARD, JACOB NEESE. Proven by JAMES LEONARD 1 Apr
1840. Deed dated 6 Dec 1838. Proven before MICHAEL WISE, J.P. Rec. 3 Nov 1840. Delivered
to ALLEN NEESE 9 Nov 1842.

Pp. 167-168: Georgia, Jefferson County: ALEXANDER HARRELL of Jefferson Co., Ga., heir of
THOMAS CLARKs estate, for $100 pd. by JAOSEPH GANTT of South Carolina...land
surveyed for THOMAS CLARK in Orangeburgh Dist, on persimon Creek, 500 A now Lexington Dist.
on Chinquapin Creek sometimes called Edisto River on a branch now called Caney Branch...
surveyed for THOMAS CLARK in the year 1775, 18 May adj. to an old surveyethe owner not
known...ALEXANDER HARRELL, the heir and only proper heir of sd. CLARK...21 Jan 1840...
ALEXANDER HARRELL (LS), Wit: GEORGE JERNIGAN, C. D. BYNUM, MARY HARRELL (+). Proven by
GEORGE JERNIGAN before L. BOOZER, 2 Nov 1840. Rec. 3 Nov 1840. Delivered to JOSEPH
GANTT.

Pp. 168-170: S. C., 14 Oct 1839, J. A. ADDISON, Comr. of the Court of Equity of Lexington
Dist. to JACOB LORICK...Whereas JOHN LOWN and ANNA his wife on or about the
8 July 1839 exhibted their bill of complaint at the Court of Equity against MARY M. BOUK-
NIGHT et al stating that DANIEL BOUKNIGHT late of Lexington Dist. was in his lifetime
seized of considerable property...for $879.85 sold to sd. JACOB LORICK 90 A on Bookmans
Creek adj. SAMUEL BOOKMAN, G. LORICK, and other lands of sd. DANIEL BOUKNIGHT decd...plat
executed by SAMUEL ALSTON 22 Sept 1830...J. A. ADDISON Comr. (LS), Wit: HENRY BOUKNIGHT,
JACOB BOUKNIGHT. Proven by JACOB BOUKNIGHT before LEVI METZ, Q. U., 2 Nov 1840. Rec.
3 Nov 1840. Delivered to SAML. T. LORICK 19 June 1848.

Page 171: Plat of JOEL RIDGELs land deeded to JEREMIAH WATERS, resurveyed by JOSEPH QUATTLE-
BUM, 15 Aug 1840. Rec. 3 Nov 1840. Shows adj. lands of ANDREW SHEALY, JAMES E.
LEE, LEON HARTLEY.

Pp. 171-172: S. C. Lexington and Edgefield District. A contract made between TIMOTHY TONEY
and PENNY WILLIAMSON, agreeing in a marriage contract...PENNY WILLIAMSON
agrees to give all real estate, etc. to sd. TONEY...20 Jan 1835...TIMOTHY TONEY (SEAL),
PENNY WILLIAMSON (X) (SEAL), Wit: WILLIAM MERRITT, JOHN P. CULLUM, JOHN GALLOWAY. Barnwell
Dist.: PROVEN BY WM. MERRITT before S. H. WEEKS, J. P., 31 Aug 1840. Rec. 4 Nov 1840.
Delivered to WILLIAM TONEY.

Pp. 173-174: S. C., ADAM SHEALY SENR of Edgefield Dist., for $275 pb. dy EPHRAIM SHELEY of
same...130 A part of 376 A granted to JOHN TAYLOR in Lexington Dist. on the
road from Lees Ferry & on the Whitstone branch to Charleston, on waters of Saluda River
adj. land conveyed to JOHN W. SHEALY, and by that which I now conveye to ABRAHAM HHEALY,
and adj. to where I now live...14 Nov 1840...ADAM SHEALY SENR (X) (LS), Wit: GEORGE L.
BANKS, BJN. HARTLEY. Edgefield Dist.: ANNA MARY SHEALY, wife of ADAM, relinquished dower
14 Nov 1840 before AMOS BANKS, Q. U. Proven by BENJAMIN HARTLEY before AMOS BANKS. Rec.
24 Nov 1840. Delivered to EPHRAIM SHEALEY.

Pp. 174-176: S. C.: JOSEPH SOUTER of Lexington Dist., for $500 pd. by JOHN LOWN of same...
178 A, part of a tract granted to HENRY P. HAMPTON in Feb 1807, for 1000 A
and conveyed to JESSE ARTHUR 5 Feb 1816, from ARTHUR to CASPER SOUTER & 200 A conveyed
from ELIZABETH SOUTER to JOSEPH SOUTER 21 Feb 1835, which sd. 178 A is in Lexington Dist.
on Savannah Branch, waters of Congaree River adj. JOHN RAMICK, JOHN MEETZ, DAVID LEETH,
JOHN J. KINSLER...15 Jan 1839...JOSEPH SOUTER (LS), Wit: JOHN D. SHARP, DAVID BOOZER.
Proven by JOHN D. SHARP before J. A. ADDISON, J. P. JEMIAH SOUTER, wife of JOSEPH, relinquished dower 11 May 1840. Rec. 30 Nov 1840. Delivered to JOHN LOWN.

Pp. 176-177: S. C., JOHN RAMICK of Lexington Dist., for $209 pd. by JOHN LOWN of same...
104 1/2 A, part of a tract granted to HENRY P. HAMPTON on Savannah Branch,
waters of Congaree Creek & waters of Congaree River adj. DANIEL ROOF, JOHN RAMICK, JOSEPH
SOUTER...15 Jan 1839...JOHN RAMICK (X) (LS), Wit: JOHN D. SHAPR, DAVID BOOZER. Proven by
JOHN D. SHARP, 3 Nov 1840. SARAH RAMICK, wife of JOHN, relinquished dower 16 Nov 1840.
Rec. 30 Nov 1840. Delivered to JOHN LOWN.

Pp. 177-179: S. C.: WM L. MILLER Sheriff of Lexington Dist...whereas a writ of fiere facias
issued out of Court of Common Pleas 10 Nov 1838...goods and chattels of
JOHN DAVIDSON to levy sum of $50...1/4 A on Village of Lexington whereon the defendant
now lives on N side Main Street or Augusta Road adj. JOHN MEETZE Lot, EPHRAIM CORLEYs lot,
JOHN HENDRIX lot for $260 sold to MICHAEL DRAFTS...21 Nov 1840...WM. L. MILLER (LS), Wit:
JOHN HOOK, G. A. LEWEY. Proven by JOHN HOOK 1 Dec 1840 before JOHN FOX. NANCY EMILINE
DAVIDSON, wife of JOHN, relinquished dower 1 Dec 1840. Rec. 1 Dec 1840. Delivered to
MICHAEL DRAFTS.

Pp. 179-181: S. C., 14 Jan 1840, J. A. ADDISON, Comr. of Court of Equity to JOHN KAIGLER,
whereas sd. KAIGLER stands indebted to sd. ADDISON by bond for $24,000 con-
ditional for payment of $12,300...for said debt to J. A. ADDISON...tract on Congaree River
as mortgage, 1617 A adj. lands of sd. KAIGLER, HENRY SEIBLES, & others by two resurvey
plats one executed by S. H. BOYKIN 12 May 1827 and the other by JOHN SIGHTLER on 1 Jan
1839, except 150 A on W side of the State Road...JOHN G. KAIGLER (LS), Wit: J. A. WOLFE,
GEORGE KAIGLER. Proven by JOSEPH A. WOLF, 2 Dec 1840. By virtue of the decretal order
of Chancellor Johnson made 19 July 1839 in the case of S. P. CORBIN & wf vs. MARY PARR,
S. S. SAYLOR & others, I hereby assign to MARY PARR the within mortgage 26 Feb 1840.,
Wit: L. BOOZER, SAML. P. CORBIN. Rec. 2 Dec 1840. Delivered to JAMES PARR for his mother
MARY PARR.

Pp. 181-183: WILLIAM L. MILLER, Sheriff, to HENRY MARTIN GROSS...by writ of fiere facias
issued out of Court of Common Pleas held for Lexington Dist., 3 Apr 1840
at the suit of JOHN METZE JR vs J. &.R. GROSS et al;to sell goods and chattels of REUBIN
GROSS, JOHN GROSS, H. J. CAUGHMAN and WILLIAM L. MILLER to levy to sum of $450...sold land
of JOHN GROSS, 1 3/4 A whereon REUBIN GROSS now lives in Village of Lexington adj. Main
Street or Augusta Road adj. JACOB HARMANs lot, and lot upon which DR. ISAIAH CAUGHMAN now
lives...land exposed to public sale and purchased by EPHRAIM CORLEY for $205, and who
directs me to make title to HENRY MARTIN GROSS...4 Dec 1840... WM. L. MILLER (LS), Wit:
J. A. ADDISON, GEORGE L. BANKS. Proven by GEORGE L. BANKS, 5 Dec 1840. Rec. 5 Dec 1840.
Delivered to HL M. GROSS 8 Dec 1845.

Pp. 183-184: BENJAMIN POINDEXTER of Shelby Co., Alabama, for $160 pd. by A. H. FORT of
Lexington Dist....40 A on Rocky Creek adj. A. H. FORT, JOHN GARTMAN, SAMUEL
RALL & DAVID KYZER, being part of a tract granted to WILLIAM CALDWELL for 450 A...9 Jan
1840. BENJAMIN POINDEXTER (LS), Wit: THOS K. POINDEXTER, D. WINCHELL. Proven by POINDEX-
TER 7 Dec 1840, before JOHN FOX. Plat included made 4 Feb 1815 by JOHN HORSEY, D. S.
made at request of SARAH TAYLOR, showing adj. to MARTHA SNIDER, GEORGE WICE, JOHN GARTMAN,
WM. HOWARD.

Page 185: S. C., Lexington Dist.: URIAH CROUT bound to JOHN CROUT SR.!...26 Aug 1840 to
see that JOHN CROUT & wf ELIZABETH are taken care of and to have the privilege
of remaining on the premises and have the use of a negro boy...URIAH CROUT (LS), Wit:
JNO W. LEE, CALEB INABNET. Proven by JOHN W. LEE 26 Aug 1840, before AMOS BANKS. Rec.
7 Dec 1840.

Pp. 186-187: S. C., JOHN CROUT SR of Lexington Dist, for natural love & affection to my
son URIAH CROUT...100 A where I now live on Caney Branch, waters of big
Hollow Creek adj. DANIEL OXNER, THOS RISSINGER, URIAH CROUT, WILLIAM BRYSON...26 Aug 1840.
JOHN CROUT SR (X) (LS), Wit: JNO W. LEE, CALEB INABNET. Also a deed of gift for a negro
Aaron aged 5 years, same dates and wit. Proven by JOHN W. LEE. Rec. 7 Dec 1840.

Pp. 187-188: S. C., CHARLES WILLIAMSON and DAVID WILLIAMSON of Lexington and Orangeburgh
Districts, for $186 pd. by JOHN H. LIVINGSTON of Orangeburgh Dist...593 A

on N side N Edisto River, one tract of 413 A, and the other 180 A...11 Feb 1840...CHARLES
WILLIAMSON (SEAL), DAVID WILLIAMSON (LS), Wit: FREDERICK LIVINGSTON, HILLIARD OLIVER.
Proven by HILLIARD OLIVER, 14 Mar 1840 before SIDNEY M. DAVIS, Q. U. MARY WILLIAMSON,
wife of CHARLES, relinqsuiehd dower, 14 Mar 1840 before SINDEY M. DAVIS. Rec. 7 Dec 1840.

Pp. 189-190: S. C., CORNELIUS SENN of Lexington Dist., for $120 pd. by JOHN LEBRECHT MUL-
LER of same...115 A, half of tract of 194 A granted 21 Nov 1808 to WILLIAM
TAYLOR, sold by the Sheriff AMOS BANKS on 17 Apr 1826 to JOHN MEETZE of Lexington Dist,
and conveyed by him to CORNELIUS SENN and HENRY ROWLAND, both of Lexington Dist on Congary
[sic] Creek adj. lands of HENRY ROWLAND, WADSWORTH BLACKLY now HENRY MULLERS, and vacant
land...plat executed by DAVID KING, D. S. 29 Nov 1838...7 Nov 1840...CORNELIUS SENN (LS),
Wit: HENRY MULLER, CHARLES F. BONDMER[??]. Proven by HENRY MULLER who swore to his and
the signature of CHARLES F. BANSIMER 7 Dec 1840. MARY SENN, wife of CORNELIUS, relinquished
dower 7 Dec 1840. Rec. 8 Dec 1840. Delivered to HENRY MULLER.

Pp. 190-191: S. C. Lexington Dist.: ELISHA JONES & wf ELIZABETH for $26 pd. by THOMAS J.
RAWLS...51 A, part of a tract of 179 A granted to JAMES DUNBAR SENR, part of
the west end of sd. tract....10 May 1837...ELISJAH JONES, ELIZABETH JONES (X) (LS), Wit:
BENJAMIN GUNTER, WILLIAM B. JONES. Proven by BENJAMIN GUNTER 21 Oct 1837, before JACOB
GANTT, J. P. Rec. 9 Dec 1840. Delivered to THOS J. RAWLS 6 Mar 1843.

Pp. 191-192: S. C., Lexington Dist.: JOHN MEETZE and COLLY SOUTER agree to build a saw
mill on Congaree Creek on the Lick fork branch...21 Oct 1839...JOHN MEETZE
(LS), Wit: H. A. MEETZE. Proven by HENRY A. MEETZE, 9 Dec 1840, before A. H. FORT. Rec.
9 Dec 1840. Delivered to COLLY SOUTER 6 Sept 1841.

Pp. 192-193: S. C., THOMAS H. BUTLER of Lexington Dist, for $355 pd. by ADAM BUFF of same,
30 A, part of a tract of 451 A, granted to PETER LEGOR in 1795 in the Fork
of Broad and Saluda Rivers on the main road leading from Columbia to the mountains...13
Mar 1840...THOMAS H. BUTLER (LS), Wit: DANIEL NATES, LEWIS METZ. Richland Dist.: CATHERINE
BUTLER, wife of THOMAS H. BUTLER, relinquished dower 10 Mar 1840 before JAMES S. GUIGNARD,
Q. U. and Clerk. Lexington Dist: PROVEN by DANIEL NATES 12 Dec 1840. Rec. 12 Dec 1840.
Delivered to LEWIS METZ 1 Nov 1841.

Pp. 194-195: S.C., DANIEL ROOF of Lexington Dist., for $194.50 pd. by JOHN LOWN of same...
97 1/4 A, part of a tract granted to HENRY P. HAMPTON on the Savanah Branch
and on poplar branch, waters of Congaree Creek & waters of Congaree River adj. DANIEL
ROOF, JOHN REMICKS, Heirs of WILLIAM KINSLER decd...1 Jan 1839...DANIEL ROOF (LS), Wit:
JOHN D. SHARP, DAVID BOOZER. Proven by JOHN D. SHARP, 3 Nov 1840, before J. A. ADDISON,
J.P. NANCY ROOF, wife of DANIEL, relinquished dower 8 Dec 1840. Rec. 16 Dec 1840.
Delivered to JOHN LOWN.

Pp. 195-197: S. C.: JOHN J. KINSLER of Columbia, for $2000 pd. by JOHN LOWN of Lexington
Dist...3015 A on Red Bank and Lick Fork Creek, granted to HENRY P. HAMPTON for
1000 A and two other tracts adjoining, surveyed for HENRY P. HAMPTON, adj. BRAZELMAN,
KINSLER, FELLERS, Estate of WM KINSLER, COLLY SOUTER, Estate of SAMUEL RAMICK, JOSEPH
SOUTER, and ROOFs land now the property of MR. LOWN...22 Jan 1839...JOHN J. KINSLER (LS),
Wit: G. P. HUSSEY, SAMUEL J. KENNERLY, EMANUEL FRIDAY. Richland Dist.: Proven by EMANUEL
FRIDAY 4 Dec 1840 before A. FITCH, Q. U. AMELIA KINSLER, wife of JOHN J., relinquished
dower 12 May 1840. Rec. 2 Jan 1841. Delivered to JOHN LOWN.

Pp. 197-198: S. C., Lexington Dist.: 21 Sept 1840, J. J. SLIGH to JESSE SWYGERT...mortgage
for note of $1035.94...one gig, one set of carpenters tools, Beas and Bead-
ing...J. J. SLIGH, Wit: DAVID UNGHER, DAVID LOWMAN. Proven by DAVID UNGER, 4 Jan 1840.
Rec. 4 Jan 1841. Delivered to JESSE SWYGERT.

Pp. 198-200: S. C., A. H. FORT & CHARLES DUNKIN of Lexington and Edgefield Dists., for
$500 pd. by EPHRAIM SHEALLY of Lexington Dist...426 A, part of a tract granted
to SAMUEL BROOKS on 4 Feb 1792, conveyed by sd. BROOKS to SIMPSON LAWYER on 1 Jan 1817,
then to A. H. FORT & ANSEL SAWYER jointly, and ANSEL SAWYER conveyed his part to CHARLES
DUNKIN...land in Lexington & Edgefield Dists., plat made by JOHN KNOX, Esqr, Surveyor...
19 Dec 1840....A. H. FORT (LS), CHARLES DUNKIN (D) (LS), Wit: JOHN KNOX, WILSON SHEALY.
Edgefield Dist.: Proven by WILSON SHELEY 31 Dec 1840 before AMOS BANKS, Q. U. Edgefield
Dist: REBECCA DUNKIN, wife of CHARLES, relinquished dower 31 dec 1840 before AMOS BANKS.
Lexington Dist.: PHEBE FORT, wife of A. H. FORT, relinquished dower 4 Jan 1841 before
AMOS BANKS. Rec. 4 Jan 1841. Delivered to EPHRAIM SHEALLY. Plat recorded on page 201.

Page 201: E. SHEALEYS Plat for 426 Acres, made by JOHN KNOX 19 Dec 1840, showing adj.
land of DANA SHEALEY, A. SHEALEY, MAR. SHEALEY, SAML MORE[?], and SHEALYS land.

Pp. 201-202: S. C., Lexington Dist.:Whereas MARY SAWYER, JOHN V. SAWYER, MARY SAWYER,
          GEORGE R. SAWYER, & WILLIAM THURLKILL & wf has[sic] satisfied me for all
the property at the sale of the property of GEORGE SAWYER decd for which a bill in possession of JAMES TERRY Commissioner in Equity for Edgefield District will show...relinquish
of interest...28 Aug 1829...SAMUEL WINGARD (X). Wit: JAMES J. BLAIR, TIMOTHY TONEY.
Lexington Dist.: Proven by JAMES J. CLARK, Esqr. who made oath to signature of SAMUEL
WINGARD JR, 4 Jan 1841...JAMES J. CLARK. Rec. 4 Jan 1841. Delivered to JOHN V. SAWYER,
8 Sept 1845.

Pp. 202-203: S. C., Lexington Dist.: WM LUCAS SENR for $10 pd. by DANIEL M. LUCAS all of
          Lexington Dist...50 A, part of a tract granted to GEORGE STEEDHAM 4 June
1813 for 1000 A on a Road leading to Charleston and between the head of Scouter Creek
and the waters of Big Black Creek...7 Nov 1837...WM LUCAS (LS), Wit: DANIEL J. LUCAS,
WILLIAM QUATTLEBUM. Proven by DANIEL J. LUCAS, 7 Nov 1837. Rec. 4 Jan 1841. Delivered
to ANTHONY SPIRES JR, 10 Feb 1851.

Pp. 203-204: S. C., Lexington Dist.: GEORGE J. TONEY of Lexington Dist.: for $1500 pd. by
          WILLIAM TONEY of same...one fourth part of what he has in cultivation also
1/4 part of Woodin land of that tract, called the Felder tract...2 Jan 1841...GEORGE J.
TONEY (LS), Wit: JOHN P. CULLUM, BARZELLE CULLUM. Proven by JOHN P. CULLUM, 4 Jan 1841.
rec. 5 Jan 1841. Delivered to WILLIAM TONEY.

Pp. 204-206: S. C., Lexington Dist.: JESSE HALLMAN for $576 pd. by CHRISTIAN PRICE , both
          of Dist afresd....276 A on S side of the Main road leading from Columbia to
Augusta on the head waters of Twelve Mile Creek and other small branches of Horse branch,
waters of Saluda adj. WILLIAM A. LAMINACs, DANIEL LAMINACs, unknown lands, heirs of SAM-
UEL KENNERLEY decd...plat made by WILLIAM QUATTLEBUM 12 & 13 Mar 1838...9 Nov 1839...
JESSE HOLMAN (LS), Wit: JOHN W. HOLMAN, LEVI HOLMAN. Proven by LEVI HOLMAN, 7 Dec 1839,
before WILLIAM QUATLEBUM, Q. U. Ex off. HEPSIBAH HOLMAN, wife of JESSE, relinquished dower
5 Dec 1839. Rec. 8 Jan 1841.

Pp. 206-208: S. C., Lexington Dist.: Whereas MARY ANN RAWL, one of the Heirs and distri-
          butees of DANIEL RAWL decd filed a petition in the Court of Ordinary for
Lexington Dist, against ELIZABETH RAWL and JOHN SANDERS RAWL on 12 Nov 1840...land has
not been partitioned...land to be sold by sheriff...WM. L. MILLER, Sheriff sold on 15
Dec 1840, 156 1/2 A to JOHN H. DRAWFTS, the highest bidder for $881, 156 A on Beaver Dam
Creek, waters of Saluda adj. HENRY HENDRIX, WILLIAM LEAPHART, JOHN LOWN, JACOB RAWLS...
WM. L. MILLER (LS), Wit: WM. FORT, JEREMIAH CRAPS.
          Lexington Dist.: DANIEL RAWL did in his lifetime did bargain and pay for sic
acres from me, but no deed was executed, do vest the title to JOHN H. DRAFTS...23 Dec 1840
SAMUEL RAWL (LS), Wit: G. A. LOWEY[?]. Proven by GEORGE A. LEWEY[?], 11 Jany 1841, before
JOHN FOX. Preceding deed proven by WILLIAM FORT, 11 Jan 1841. Rec. 9 Jan 1841. Delivered
to W. L. MILLER 21 Jan 1843.

Pp. 208-209: S. C., Lexington Dist.: JOHN H. DRAFTS for $881 pd by WILLIAM L. MILLER...
          156 A [same land in preceding deed]...JOHN H. DRAFTS (LS), 26 Dec 1840...
Wit: WM FORT, JEREMIAH CRAPS. Proven by WILLIAM FORT. Rec. 9 Jan 1841 Delivered to W.
L. MILLER 21 Jan 1843.

Pp. 209-210: S. C., Lexington Dist.: JOHN EARGLE for $200 pd. by JOHN J. EARGLE...175 1/2
          A on S side Saluda River adj. ASA LANGFORD, MRS. ELIZABETH LEWEY, JAMES HUFF,
HONORIAH STEEL...2 Feb 1839...JOHN EARGLE ( ) (LS), Wit: F. J. HOOK, PATRICK TODD.
Proven by G. J. HOOK 5 July 1839. Rec. 9 Jan 1841. Delivered to JOHN J. EARGLE 29 Jan
1842.

Pp. 211-212: S. C., By virtue of a writ of fiere facias issued out of Court of Common
          Pleas, tested 12 Apr 1839, at suit of HO. L. HENDRIX to me directed command-
ing to levy $27.53 from goods and chattels of JOHN W. SHEALEY...sold 100 A where the Deft.
now lives on Whtestone Branch, waters of Rocky Creek, waters of Saluda River adj. MARTIN
SHIREY, LUKE NICHOLS, ADAM LOMINACK...purchased by URIAH CROUT AND JOHN FOX, for $160...
___ Aug 1840...WILLIAM L. MILLER (LS), Wit: LEROY HENDRIX, W. H. FOX. Proven by LEROY
HENDRIX, 13 Jan 1841. Rec. 13 Jan 1841.

Pp. 212-213: MICHAEL PLYMALE for $100 pd by HENRY J. DRAFTS...50 A on Big Rocky Creek,
          waters of Saluda River adj. JOHN LANGFORD, BRIDGES, STEPHEN CUMBO, by the
original tract now belonging to H. J. DRAFTS...MICHAEL PLYMALE (LS), Wit: DANIEL LEAPHART,
G. J. HOOK. Dated 11 Jan 1841. Proven by DANIEL LEAPHART, 14 Jan 1841, before L. BOOZER,
Q. U. Rec. 14 Jan 1841.

Pp. 213-214: S. C. , Lexington Dist.: JACOB PRICE SENR for $400 pd. by JOHN PRICE, both
of Lexington Dist.:...200 A on waters of little Hollow Creek and Horse Creeks
waters of Big Saluda, adj. JOHN MEETZES, SAMUEL LEWEY, JESSE HALMAN, COL. H. J. CAUGHMAN,
in Lexington Dist, crossing the road leading from Waters ferry on Saluda to Charleston,
granted to HENRY CENTERFIT 7 June 1790...15 Mar 1838...JACOB PRICE (X) (LS), Wit: SAMUEL
LEWIS, CHRISTIAN PRICE, JR, Test. Proven by CHRISTIAN PRICE JUNR 23 Oct 1838 before
WILLIAM QUARTLEBUM, Q. U. Ex off. ANNA KATHERINE PRICE, wife of JACOB, relinquished dower
23 Oct 1838. Rec. 19 Jan 1841. Delivered to JOHN PRICE.

Pp. 215-217: S. C., Lexington Dist.: ANNA ARTHUR, KEZIAH ARTHUR & CAROLINE E. ARTHUR for
$53 pd. by JOSEPH H. MORGAN of Orangeburgh Dist, Trustee of MRS. MARY MOR-
GAN, all that plantation whereon the sd. MARY MORGAN now lives, 17 A in Lexington Dist.
adj. lands belonging to the Estate of JOHN TAYLOR decd, Lands of the sd. ANNA, KEZIAH,
& CAROLINE E. ARTHUR, GENERAL HENRY ARTHUR, and my Monkey Spring Branch, as pr survey
by E. J. ARTHUR, D. S. in Jan 1840...by a decree of the Court of Equity dated 15 June
1840...land of sd. MARY MORGAN free from control of her husband DANIEL MORGAN...22 Jan
1841...ANNA ARTHUR (LS), KEZIAH ARTHUR (LS), CAROLINE E. ARTHUR (LS), Wit: JOHN SHULL,
JAMES BELL. Proven by JOHN SHULL 26 Jan 1841, before A. FITCH, Q. U. Rec. 1 Feb 1841.
Delivered to DANIEL MORGAN 1 Feb 1841.

Pp. 217-219: S. C., By virtue of a writ of Fiere facias issued out of the court of Common
Pleas held of Lexington Dist, tested 12 Apr 1839, on goods and chattels of
TIMOTHY TONEY to levy $7345...3360 A on McTier Creek and Boggy Gulley waters of S Edisto
adj. JOHN P. CULLUM, KIRKLAND, and lands of the Deft. TIMOTHY TONEY, Alman tract including
a saw mill...sold to JOHN P. CULLUM...WM L. MILLER (LS), S. L. D., Wit: JOSEPH R. MILLER,
JOHN HOOK. Proven by JOHN HOOK 2 Feb 1841. Rec. 2 Feb 1841. Delivered to WILLIAM TONEY.

Pp. 219-220: S. C.: By virtue of a writ of fiere facias out of court of Common Please
held for Lexington Dist....tested 12 Apr 1839, at the suit of the President
and dircetors of the Bank of the State of S. C. to levy $7345, from lands and tenements
of TIMOTHY TONEY, 1/2 of saw mill...land adj. JOHN P. CULLUM, sold to WILLIAM TONEY...
4 Jan 1841...WM. L. MILLER (LS), S. L. D. Wit: JOHN HOOK, JAMES LANGFORD, JR. Proven
by JOHN HOOK before JOHN FOX, 2 Feb 1841. Rec. 2 Feb 1841, Delivered to WILLIAM TONEY.

Pp. 220-223: JOHN P. CULLUM and WILLIAM TONEY to the President and directors of the Bank
of the State of South Carolina...by bond bearing date 4 Jan 1841 in penal
sum of $365.78 conditioned for full sum of $8182.89...mortgage of tracts (5) resurveyed
and connected by WILLIAM BUCKHALTER, D. S. on 2 July 1839 3360 A on McTier Creek, waters
of S Edisto...also Felder tract of 2016 A including a saw mill...4 Jan 1841...JOHN P.
CULLUM (LS), WILLIAM TONEY (LS), Wit: THO R. WARING, FISHER GADSDEN. Proven by THOMAS
R. WARING 22 Jan 1841 before WM. R. FOSTER, Notary Public & Q. U. Ex. off. Rec. 2 Feb
1841. Sent by mail to Edgefield Court House in according to directions on opposite side
directed to DR. R. T. MIMS 17 Feb 1854. MARY CULLUM and HARRIET TONEY, wifes of aforesd.,
relinquish dower 29 Jan 1841. Letter attached dated 11[?] Feb [?] 1853, to Court Clerk
Lexington Dist, from THOS WARING instructing to mail deed to R. T. MIMS.

Pp. 223-225: S. C., Lexingonn Dist.: GEORGE M. SUMMER for $550 pd by ANDREW SHEALY, both
of Lexington Dist.:...land on Watteree Creek and waters of Broad River adj.
CHRISTIAN KUNKLE, Estate of WILLIAM SUMMER decd, JOHN SUMMER...19 Jan 1841...GEORGE M.
SUMMER (LS), Wit: G. M. FULMER, GEORGE H. CHAPMAN, JOHN SEAS. Proven by JOHN SEAS 19
Jan 1841 before GEORGE M. FULMER, Q. U. MARY M. SUMMER, wife of GEORGE, relinquibhed
dower 21 Jan 1841. Rec. 3 Feb 1841. Delivered to JOHN SEAS, 18 Jan 1842.

Pp. 225-228: S. C. Lexington Dist.: 28 Dec 1840, JOHN SIGHTLER to HENRY SIGHTLER, GEORGE
W. SIGHTLER, DANIEL SENN and SYDNEY CRANE for $1...plantation embracing the
following parcels, the undivided moiety of the Plantation on which the said JOHN SIGHTLER
resides 400 A, more or less, the same being part of a tract of 880 A granted to sd.
SIGHTLER on 2 Dec 1815, designated in Grand Plat of the said JOHN SIGHTLERs father real
estate No. 5, also the undivided moiety of one other plantation containing 880 A composed
of three several tracts (1) 308 A being part of a tract of 715 A granted to HENRY SIGHT-
LER 2 Dec 1816 (2) a tract granted to ABRAHAM HARRIS 6 Nov 1816 for 504 A (3) a tract of
44 A granted to JOSEPH SIGHTLER 6 Dec 1826...also for two mulatto women Slaves named
Keziah and Keren, 23 and 20 years old...JOHN SIGHTLER (LS), HENRY SIGHTLER (LS), GEORGE
W. SIGHTLER (LS), DANIEL SENN (LS), SIDNEY CRANE (LS), Wit: P. B. SMITH, JACOB HENDRIX.
Richland Co.: Proven by PETER B. SMITH, 28 Dec 1840 before JAMES S. GUIGNARD. Rec. 2
Feb 1841. Delivered to HENRY SIGHTLER.

Pp. 229-230: 1 Feb 1841, NATHANIEL KLECKLY of Lexington Dist. to DANIEL DRAFTS SENIOR &
GEORGE CAUGHMAN for $608.66...made payable to WEST CAUGHMAN as Guardian...
mortgage, 98 A near the Eighteen mile Branch, waters of Saluda adj. JOSEPH CORLEY, GEORGE
ROBERTS, M. CAUGHMAN, JACOB RAUCH, SAMUEL WINGARD SR, THOMAS POINDEXTER....NATHANIEL

KLECKLEY (LS), Wit: WEST CAUGHMAN, SAMUEL DRAFTS. Proven by WEST CAUGHMAN 5 Feb 1841, before J. A. ADDISON J.P. Rec. 5 Feb 1841. JOHN FOX, Regr.

Pp. 231-232: S. C., Lexington Dist.: GEORGE LINDLER JUNR of $250 pd. by JNO HENRY ERRIGLE (both of state and dist. aforesd.)...land on E side Wateree Creek, a branch of Broad River, bounded by lands of my sisters, by lands of my own, and by other lands belonging to the said HENRY ERRIGLE, 50 A...18 Dec 1839, part of a tract granted to J. M. ERRIGLE, 200 A A. D. 1752, which I have received by the will of my late father JACOB LINDLER as his legacy to me...GEORGE LINDER JUNR, Wit: THOMAS FRIAR, WILKS F. WATERS. Proven by WILKS WATERS 2 Jan 1840 before G. M. FULMER, Q. U. ANNE SYBIL LINDLER, wife of GEORGE, relinquished dower 18 Dec 1839 before THOMAS FREAN, J. Q. Rec. 8 Feb 1841. Delivered to HENRY ELEAZER 22 Nov 1845. Plat included in deed made 18 Dec 1839 showing land adj. to GEO. LINDLER, MISS LINDLER, HENRY ERRIGLE.

Pp. 232-233: S. C. Lexington Dist.: JOHN HOLMAN for $400 pd. by ADAM RISH both of Lexington Dist...450 A granted to ROBERT CRAIG 6 Oct 1806 on horsepen Branch, waters of No Edisto River adj. A. R. ABLES, RAMBO, JOHN CATTLE, Z. GAUNTT...JOHN HOLMAN (LS), Wit: ZABULON GALNTT, HENRY GANTT. Proven by HENRY GAUNTT 29[?] Oct 1823. Dated 16 Apr 1823. Rec. 8 Feb 1841. Delivered to D. J. AUSTIN 8 Dec 1841.

Page 234: S. C., Lexington Dist.: JAMES COOK, BARBY COOK of Lexington Dist, for $45 to GEORGE RISH...70 A on waters of North Edisto, be the place where PHILIP GRUBS did live adj. lands formerly belonging to ZEB GANT, which at preasant[sic] belongs to JOHN RISH, Land E. STARKS decd and JOHN M. FELDER together...28 Nov 1840...JAMES COOK (LS), BARBRY COOK (X) (LS), Wit: DAVIS J. AUSTIN, LEVI RISH. Proven by LEVI RISH 8 Feb 1841. Rec. 8 Feb 1841. Delivered to D. J. AUSTIN 8 Dec 1841.

Page 235: S. C., Lexington Dist.: GEORGE RISH & wf MARY for $150 pd. by DAVID J. AUSTIN... 195 A in Lexington Dist. on N Edisto River granted to JOHN QUATTLEBUM 23 Mar 1818 adj. ELIZABETH ABLE, JOHN J. ABLE...9 Oct 1840...GEORGE RISH (X) (LS), MARY RISH (X) (LS), Wit: LEVI RISH, JAMES COOK. Proven by LEVI RISH 8 Feb 1841 before JOHN FOX, Clerk. Rec. 8 Feb 1841. Delivered to D. J. AUSTIN 8 Dec 1841.

Pp. 236-237: S. C. Lexington Dist: GEORGE & MARY RISH to DAVIS J. AUSTIN for $850...550 A, with part in a saw mill adj. JOHN RISH, JOHN M. FELDER, DANIEL RAMBO, on waters of North Edisto...9 Oct 1840...[Same sign & wit.]. Rec. 8 Feb 1841.

Pp. 237-238: S. C., Lexington Dist.: JOHN P. FRANKDOW, JOHN H. FRANKLOW, EPHRAIM CORLEY for $450 pd. by JACOB KLECKLEY...part of a tract grandted & surveyed for GEORGE P. DRAFTS 5 Oct 1812 on granches of Big Saluda River on S side of sd. River adj. land laid out to KLECKLEY, JONAS BEARD, 165 A...15 Apr 1828...JOHN P. FRANKLOW (LS), J. H. FRANKLOW (LS), EPHRAIM CORLEY (LS), Wit: WEST CAUGHMAN, WESTLEY MERCHANT. Proven by WEST CAUGHMAN before M. HOOK, J. P. 11 Nov 1828. SARAH FRANKLOW, wife of JOHN P., relinquished dower 27 Oct 1828 before WEST CAUGHMAN, Q. U. Rec. 12 Feb 1841. Delivered to DANIEL DRAFTS SR. 5 June 1843.

Pp. 238-239: S. C., THE SALUDA MANUFACTURING COMPANY for $258 pd. by ISAAC WALKER, a tract which contains 113 A, part of tract granted in 1785 to LEONARD MARTIN in the forks of Broad and Saluda on the Branches of Kennerlys Creek, waters of Saluda adj. EMANUEL GEIGER, DOCTOR WALLACE, GEORGE LORICK...9 Dec 1839...DAVID EWART (SEAL), President of the Saluda M. Co. Wit: J. A. CRAWFORD, ALEXR CAMPBELL. Richland Dist.: Proven by JOHN A. CRAWFORD, before JOHN J. SEIBLES, Not Pub. 3 Jan 1841. Rec. 25 Feb 1841. Delivered to HENRY SCOTT 28 Aug 1841.

Pp. 240-241: GEORGE V. SAWYER vs HENRY SAWYER, Real & Personal Estate. GEORGE V. SAWYER of Lexington Dist., to secure HENRY SAWYER of Edgefield Dist my security for the dollowing Debts. $1000 to the Estate of JOHN EIDSON Decd, $1795 to the Estate of GEORGE SAWYER Decd, $120 to CANADA & PROTHRO, $200 to DANIEL QUATTLEBUM for MCKEY...the following tracts: one half of the saw mill on boggy gully, waters of South Edisto; another adj. lands of WILLIAM E. SAWYER, part of the same survey; another tract of 73 A surveyed to the sd. GEORGE V. SAWYER adj. lands of NATHAN JONES SR; conveyed to sd. SAWYER by ARTHUR JACKSON, 500 A on the two notched Road adj. lands of NATHAN JONES SR., MICHAEL & ARTHUR JACKSON: also 375 A adj. lands of ELISHA JONES, Heirs of JOHN WARREN decd, and lands of WILLIAM E. SAWYER...also one negro boy Isaac 26 years old, and other negroes [named], horse, mule, etc...16 Oct 1840...GEORGE V. SAWYER (LS), Wit: JOHN V. SAWYER, NATHANIEL JONES. Lexington Dist: Proven by JOHN V. SAWYER 16 Oct 1840 before NATHANIEL JONES J.P. Rec. 13 Mar 1841. Delivered to HENRY SAWYER.

Pp. 241-242: S. C. Lexington Dist.: GEORGE YOUNGINER of Lexington Dist. for $200 pd. by ADAM & DANIEL YOUNGINER of same...160 A by resurvey of 12 Sept 1838 on waters of the Eighteen Mile Creek adj. THOS K. POINDEXTER, SAMUEL WINGARD, SAMUEL CAUGHMAN & others...22 Oct 1840...GEORGE YOUNGINER (X) (LS), Wit: REUBEN GROSS, HENRY M. GROSS. Proven by REUBEN GROSS 1 Mar 1841 before JOHN FOX. Rec. 1 Mar 1841. Delivered to ADAM YOUNGINER 15 Feb 1843.

Pp. 242-243: JACOB LITES of Lexington Dist. for $1030 pd. by URIAH HENDRIX of same...103 A on S side Saluda River on Rockey Creek adj. lands of HENRY HENDRIX, WILLIAM RALL, JOSEPH LITES, Heirs of HENRIX, the north side of a tract surveyed for MICHAEL OSWALT 2 Mar 1773 for 150 A...plat dated 9 & 16 Apr 1836...1 Mar 1841...JACOB LITES ( ) (LS), Wit: JOSEPH LITES, CALEB LITES. Proven by JOSEPH LITES 1 Mar 1841 before JOHN FOX. Plat included. Rec. 1 Mar 1841, delivered to URIAH HENDRIX. Plat made by WM QUATTLEBUM.

Pp. 244-245: S. C.: JOHN SETZLER SR & wf MAGDALENE of Lexington Dist, for $2500 pd. by JOHN C. HOPE of same...the following parts or original tracts of land 207 A being in part an original tract of 150 A laid out to ULRICK ULRICK [sic] dated 1753, owned by JOHN ADAM SETZLER decd and willed to the above said JOHN SETZLER SENR and in part a tract of land originally granted to NICHOLAS PRESSLER [PRIESTER--BHH] on Crims Creek, a branch of Broad River adj. to JOHN C. HOPE, WIDOW MAUGH, ADAM MILLER, GEORGE EPTING, ADAM EPTING...16 Feb 1841...JOHN SETZLER SR (LS), MARDALENA SETZLER (X) (LS), Wit: LEMUEL LANE, DAVID ENGLISH. MAGDALENA SETZLER relinquished dower 24 Feb 1841 before G. M. FULMER. Proven by DAVID ENGLISH 28 Feb 1841. Rec. 3 Mar 1841. DElivered to JOHN C. HOPE.

Pp. 245-247: S. C.: 3 Feb 1841, MARY ANN DRAFTS of Lexington Dist. to GEORGE CRAPS of same...mortgage...indebted to sd. CRAPS for $400...250 A on big Horse Creek waters of Saluda adj. lands of JOHN JACKSON, JOSEPH HUSE, CATHARINE LONG & others...MARY ANN DRAFTS (X) (LS), Wit: HENRY CRAPS, J. H. CAUGHMAN. Proven by H. J. CAUGHMAN...6 Mar 1841. Rec. 6 Mar 1841. Delivered to GEORGE CRAPS.

Pp. 247-248: S. C., Lexington Dist.: JULIUS SNELGROVE planter for $400 pd. by JACOB PRICE planter, both of Lexington Dist...200 A on branches of big Saluda called little hollow and horse Creeks on the Road from Waters Ferry to Charleston, granted to HENRY CONTERFIT adj. JOHN MEETZE, SAMUEL LOVEY, JACOB PRICE, JACOB DRAFTS...24 Sept 1834 ...JULIUS SNELGROVE (SEAL), Wit: JOHN PRICE, JOEL KEISLER, CHRISTIAN PRICE, JR. Proven by JOHN PRICE 8 Oct 1834, before WM. QUATTLEBUM, Q. U. Exoff. SUSANNAH SNELGROVE, wife of JULIUS, relinquished dower 8 Oct 1834. Rec. 6 Mar 1841. Delivered to JOHN PRICE.

Pp. 248-249: S. C.: HENRY J. DRAFTS of Lexington Dist. for $1200 pd. by THOMAS DERRICK of same...430 A granted to THOMAS A. GREEN and others on S side of big Saluda...23 Jan 1841...HENRY J. DRAFTS (LS), Wit: JOHN S. ADDY SENR, DANIEL LEAPHART. Proven by JOHN S. ADDY SENR 20 Feb 1841. Rec. 8 Mar 1841. Delivered to THOS DERRICK 16 Aug 1841.

Pp. 249-250: S. C., Lexington Dist.: ELIZABETH M. BLEWER of Lexington Dist. for $1 pd. by JOHN P. BLEWER "my son"...negro male slave Francis...21 Aug 1838...ELIZABETH M. BLEWER (LS), Wit: FRANCIS L. WALKER, CHARLES GRANDY. Proven by FRANCIS L. WALKER 9 Mar 1841. Rec. 9 Mar 1841. Delivered to JOHN P. BLEWER.

Pp. 250-252: S. C.: By virtue of three writs of Firi Facias issued out of Court of Common Pleas for Lexington Dist, 12 Apr 1839 MEETZE & HENDRIX vs LEWIS FURTICK & ANTHONY SPIRES; 13 Apr. 1840, R. HARMAN & CO. vs LEWIS FURTICK; 18 Apr 1840 ISAAC LYONS & son vs. CAROLINE FURTICK...goods and chattels of LEWIS & CAROLINE FURTICK to levy $149. 86 & damages...land granted to HARRIS WHEAT surveyd 31 Jan 1784 and 61 A PART OF A TRACT surveyed for JESSE KINARD granted to him ___ 1802, 196 A; also part of a tract of 209 A laid out by ROBERT B. STARK to SAMUEL STEEDMAN 26 Sept 1793, also part of 289 A laid out to EDWARD EVANS by ROBERT STARK, also part of a tract conveyed to LEWIS FURTICK by BENJAMIN JEFCOAT 13 A all lying on or near Bee hunter branch, waters of North Edisto R, adj. land held by ISAAC CHANEY, the widow CHANEY, BENJAMIN JEFCOAT SR & JR, & others...purchased by JOHN MEETZE & CALEB BOUKNIGHT, for $103...31 July 1840...WM L. MILLER, S. L. D. (LS), Wit: SAML LOWMAN, FRANKLIN CORLEY. Proven by FRANKLIN CORLEY, 3 Aug 1810 before L. BOOZER. Rec. 9 Mar 1841. Delivered to C. BOUKNIGHT 4 Oct 1842.

Pp. 252-253: By a writ of Fiere Facias from Court of Common Pleas for Lexington Dist, 18 Apr 1840 commanding WM. L. MILLER of levy $27.37 from goods and chattels of ZEBULON GAUNTT...516 A on Giddy Swamp, waters of North Edisto River adj. SARAH JOHNSON, BENJAMIN HUTTO, JOSHUA WOODWARD...sold to JOHN MEETZE & CALEB BOUKNIGHT...16 Aug 1840... WM. L. MILLER (LS), S. L. D., Wit: D. J. HARMAN, H. J. CAUGHMAN, Proven by HENRY J. CAUGHMAN 9 Mar 1841 before JOHN FOX. Rec. 9 Mar 1841. Delivered to C. BOUKNIGHT, 4 Oct 1842.

Pp. 253-255: JOHN WESSINGER of Lexington Dist., for $100 pd. by JOHN MEETZE & C. BOUKNIGHT 167 A on head branches of Lick Fork, waters of Red Bank Creek, waters of

Red Bank creek, waters of Congaree River part of tract granted to HENRY P. HAMPTON for 935 A in 1807 adj. WEST CAUGHMAN, JOHN MEETZE, and lands supposed to belong to TERPIN or BRASELMAN, heirs of MATHIAS WESSINGER and COLLY SOUTERS...7 May 1840...JOHN WESSINGER (X) (LS), Wit: HENRY A. MEETZE, RIGNAL O. WILLIAMS. Proven by HENRY MEETZE 9 Mar 1841. Plat included in deed showing adjacent land owners mentioned in deed, made 27 Apr 1840 by JOHN D. SHARP, Dept. Surv. Delivered to C. BOUKNIGHT 4 Oct 1842.

Pp. 255-256: S. C., JONATHAN TAYLOR of Lexington Dist., for $151 pd. by JOHN MEETZE & CALEB BOUKNIGHT...two tracts, (1) 963 A conveyed by State of S. C. 17 Jan 1822 on Scouter Creek, waters of Congaree Creek, waters of Congaree River adj. A. J. CLARK, THOMAS SHARP, JOHN D. N. MURPHY,DANIEL SMITH (2) 230 A on waters of Congaree Creek adj. W. L. TAYLOR, JOSEPH A. TAYLOR, JNO. MEETZE, JNO MILLER, BATON TAYLOR, J. SWYGERT, 35 A of which was conveyed on 11 Jan 1811 by DANIEL HOVREY[?], to him by SARAH ALMAN: to her by FRANCIS BELL, and to him by State of S. C., and 38 A by FRANCIS BELL on 29 Mar 1816 and to him by State of S. C. and the ballance was conveyed to me by the State of S. C. on 9 Jan 1816...5 Jan 1841 JONATHAN TAYLOR (X) (LS), Wit: JACOB SWIGART, JOSHUA TAYLOR. Proven by JACOB SWYGERT, 12 Mar 1841. Rec. 12 Mar 1841 Delivered to C. BOUKNIGHT 4 Oct 1842.

Page 257: S. C. Lexington Dist.: H. J. CAUGHMAN for $1200 mortgage to JOHN MEETZE and MARTIN CAUGHMAN one negro slave Lewis about 30 years old to be paid by 14 Oct 1841...16 Oct 1840. H. J. CAUGHMAN (LS), Wit: REUBEN HARMAN. Proven by REUBEN HARMAN, 12 Mar 1841. Rec. 12 Mar 1841. DELIVERED TO JOHN MEETZE Feb 5, 1842.

Pp. 257-259: H. J. CAUGHMAN to JOHN MEETZE & MARTIN CAUGHMAN, For $4752...mortgage...notes payable to H. J. DRAFTS dated about 1 Nov 1839, due 1 Nov 1840, one payable to JOHN BLACK due 14 Oct 1841, dated 14 Oct 1840, a third note of same date payable 12 months after...tract of 200 A on Saluda River adj. MARTIN CAUGHMAN, EMANUEL GEIGER, SAMUEL P. CAUGHMAN...16 Oct 1840...H. J. CAUGHMAN (LS), Wit: REUBEN HARMAN, C. BOUKNIGHT. Proven by REUBEN HARMAN, 12 Mar 1841. Rec. 12 Mar 1841. Delivered to JOHN MEETZE 5 Feb 1842.

Pp. 259-261: S. C. Lexington Dist.: HENRY SENN for $350 pd. by ADAM & DAVID CROMER...180 A on waters of Twelve Mile Creek...granted 1 Oct 1787 to WILLIAM KELLEY for 768 A adj. BENJAMIN ROOF, GEORGE LEAPHART, JOHN ROOF...HENRY SENN (SEAL), Dated31 July 1822, Wit: ANDREW CROMER, HENRY SHULL (X). NANCY SENN, wife of HENRY relinquished dower 31 Mar 1823 before WEST CAUGHMAN. NANCY SENN(X). Proven by ANDREW CROMER 31 Mar 1823. Rec. 19 Mar 1841. Delivered to ADAM CROMER.

Pp. 261-263: S. C., 12 Mar 1841, SAMUEL CORLEY to JACOB SWYGERT...sd. CORLEY is indebted to SWYGERT for $315.98 note due in 3 years...mortgage 178 A whereon sd. SAMUEL CORLEY now lives on Twelve Mile Creek adj. JOHN MEETZE, JESSE CORLEY, DAVID BOOZER, made up of four parcels adj. each other, one of 40 A, one 58, one 30, and the other 50...SAMUEL CORLEY (LS), Wit: JOHN FOX, SAMUEL HALLMAN. Proven by JOHN FOX, before L. BOOZER, Magistrate 13 Mar 1841. Rec. 13 Mar 1841. Delivered to JACOB SWYGERT 24 July 1841.

Pp. 263-264: S. C., Lexington Dist.: ANDREW J. CLARK for $155 pd. by JOSEPH LYBRAND... 155 A, part of a grant to MICHAEL SEE 2 July 1806 for 1000 A on beaver dam Creek, waters of Congaree...25 Feb 1841...ANDREW J. CLARK (LS), Wit: JOHN C. LYBRAND,[other wit. illegible]. Proven by JOHN C. LYBRAND before J. A. ADDISON, J. P. 13 Mar 1841. Rec. 13 Mar 1841. Delivered to JOSEPH LYBRAND 4 Feb 1850.

Pp. 264-265: S. C., Whereas CLARA JONES, late of Lexington Dist., by her L. W. & T. dated 6 Aug 1840, in the second clause, gave to her son ISAAC JONES "my undivided half of the plantation or tract of Land on which I reside including the small tract recently purchased of MR. HALLMAN together with the mill...."for $5 pd. by LEWIS JONES, sell sd. tract... 15 Mar 1841...ISAAC JONES (LS), Wit: JOHN K. JOHNSTON, WM. FORT. Proven by WILLIAM FORT before JOHN FOX, Clk, 16 Mar 1841... Rec. 16 Mar 1841. Delivered to COL. P. QUATTLEBUM 21 June 1842.

Page 266: S. C., Lexington Dist.: WALTER GANTT for $150 pd. by JAMES P. RANKIN...266 A, the lower part of a tract granted to FRANCIS DAVIS 1773 at the head of one of the prongs of Jumping branch...23 Dec 1837...WALTER GANTT (LS), Wit: WILLIAM RANKIN, MARY RANKIN. Proven by WILLIAM RANKIN 16 Mar 1841, beofre NATHANIEL JONES J. P. Rec. 17 Mar 1841. Delivered to WM. HOWARD 7 Jan 1851.

Page 267: S. C. Orangeburgh Dist.: THOMAS CATO of Dist. aforesaid, for $100 pd. by STEPHEN BUSBY of same...300 A surveyed for GODFREY[sic] HOOKER and Relapsed by JACOB RUMPH JUNR and sold at publick sale for the benefit to sd. RUMPH situate in Dist. aforesd. between THOMAS CATO and GEORGE SAWYER SENR on the WAggon Road from Charleston to Camebridge [sic]...2 Dec 1820...THOMAS CATO (T) (SEAL), DELPH CATO (+),(Wit: FREDERICK JACOSON (ab), JOSEPH BARTON. Proven by JOSEPH BARTON 19 Mar 1841 before WILLIAM DAILEY, Q. U. Rec. 17 Mar 1841.

Page 268: S. C., Orangeburgh Dist.: STEPHEN BUSBY of State aforesd., for $250 to ARTHUR
          JACKSON, 300 A surveyed for GODFREY HOOKER and relapsed by JACOB RUMPH JUNR...
[same tract as in preceding deed]...20 Dec 1821...STEPHEN BUZBEE (LS), Wit: JOHN KINARD,
SAMUEL RICHARDSON. Proven by SAMUEL RICHARDSON 10 Apr 1822 before WILLIAM DAILEY, Q. U.
Rec. 17 Mar 1841.

Page 269: S. C. Orangeburgh Dist.: WHEATON JONES of Dist aforesd., for $30 pd. by FREDERICK
          JACKSON of same...89 A in Orangeburg Dist on waters of South Edisto on Boggy
Gulley on the broad gully branch adj. JOSEPH BARTON, ARTHUR JACKSON...5 Mar 1829...WHEATON
JONES (LS), Wit: WILLIS HARTLEY, JOSEPH BARTON. Proven by WILLIS HARTLEY. 14 Dec 1832,
before NATHL. JONES, J. P. Rec. 17 Mar 1841.

Page 270: S. C., Orangeburgh Dist.: CHARLES J. RICHARDSON for $150 pd. by THOMAS JONES
          ...150 A in Orangeburgh Dist on the boggy gulley, on waters of South Edisto
River part of a tract granted to WM. CATO surveyed for him 29 Jan 1810, adj. TIMOTHY
TONEY, JACKSONS land, Jacksons spring branch...13 Jan 1832...CHARLES J. RICHARDSON (LS),
Wit: JAMES READY, WHEATON JONES. Proven by WHEATON JONES, _____.

Page 271: EPHRAIM SHEALEY Resurvey Platt, 133 A, made by GEORGE P. DRAFTS, D. S., 15 Feb
          1841, adj. MICHAEL SHEALY, CROUTS, JESSE SHEALEY, shows Lees Road, Whetstone
Creek, waters of SALUDA. Rec. 18 Mar 1841. Delivered to EPH. SHEALEY, 5 Sept 1842.

Pp. 271-273: S. C., JOHN J. MURPH, to JOHN MEETZE...mortgage 3 Oct 1837...indebted to sd.
             MEETZE for $750 notes due 1 Jan 1840, 1 Jan 1841.....379 A on Six Mile Creek,
conveyed to sd. MURPH by MICHAEL WESSINGER...JOHN J. MURPH (LS), Wit: FRANKLIN CORLEY, J.
N. BOOZER. Proven by FRANKLIN CORLEY, 22 Mar 1841. Rec. 22 Mar 1841. Delivered to C.
BOUKNIGHT 4 Oct 1822.

Pp. 273-274: S. C., Lexington Dist.: ADAM SHEALY SENR for $200 pd. by MICHAEL SHEALEY...
             256 A adj. JEREMIAH RAWLS, MOORE, EPHRAIM SHEALY, CHRISTANAH HALLMAN...8 Mar
1841...ADAM SHEELEY (I) SR (LS), Wit: JEREMIAH RAWL, EPHRAIM SHEALY. Proven by JEREMIAH
RAWL, 27 Mar 1841. Plat included in deed, made 15 Feb 1841 by GEO. P. DRAFTS, D. S.
Rec. 29 Mar 1841. Delivered to MICHAEL SHEALY 4 June 1841.

Pp. 275-276: S. C., MICHAEL KELLER of Orangeburgh Dist, planter, for $60 pd. by JACOB
             OXNER SENR of Newberry Dist, farmer...land on Hollo Creek, waters of
Saluda River adj. WEST ALLEN, GEORGE FIKE, MRS. SAULSTER, ADAM BLACK, Part of a tract
granted to WEST ALLEN, 470 A dated 17 June 1803...6 Nov 1803...MICHAEL KELLER (M) (SEAL),
Wit: JEREMIAH WILLIAMS, JONADAB NETTLES. Orangeburgh Dist.: Proven by JONADAB NETTLES,
14 Nov 1803 before JEREMIAH WILLIAMS, J. Q. BARBARA KELLER, wife of MICHAEL relinquished
dower 14 Nov 1803 before JEREMIAH WILLIAMS, J. Q. Rec. 29 Mar 1841. Delivered to GEORGE
SAWYER, 21 June 1841.

Pp. 276-278: Lexington Dist: GEORGE OXNER of Newberry Dist., for $103 pd by GEORGE SAWYER
             Of Lexington Dist....62 A on Hollow Creek, waters of Saluda, adj. lands now
held by JACOB VANSANT, JOHN BLACK, DAVID BLACK, DANIEL LOMANACK, GEORGE SAWYER, originally
granted to WEST ALLEN 17 June 1790...27 Mar 1841...GEORGE OXNER (LS), Wit: WM. L. MILLER,
ADAM RISH. Proven by WILLIAM L. MILLER 29 Mar 1841. Rec. 29 Mar 1841, Delivered to
GEORGE SAWYER, 21 June 1841.

[N. B. There is no page numbered 277.]

Pp. 278-279: S. C., WILLIAM MOREHEAD of Lexington Dist., for $60 pd. by NATHANIEL W. BUSBY
             of same...land known as William Morehead land on South of the Wateree Creek,
on the road Leading from Spring Hill to Freshleys Mill adj. NATHANEIL W. BUSBY, SUMMERS,
ELI FRESHLEY, 31 A according to a survey of WILLIAM B. ELKIN, D. S., dated 16 Nov 1840...
8 Mar 1841...WILLIAM MOREHEAD (+) (LS), Wit: ADAM STOUDEMIRE, NANCY J. BARKER. Proven by
ADAM SOUTEMIRE 8 Mar 1841, before LEVI METZ, Q. U. JUDITH MOREHEAD, wife of WILLIAM,
relinquished dower 8 Mar 1841. Rec. 5 Apr 1841. Delivered to NATHL. W. BUSBY 20 Oct 1845.

Pp. 279-281: S. C., WILKES F. WATERS of Lexington Dist., for $300 pd. by ADAM SWARTZ of
             same, 82 A part of land belonging to CAPT. JOHN LINDLER decd in Lexington
Dist., on drains of wateree Creet, waters of Broad River, adj. lands held by SD. ADAM
SWARTZ, MICHAEL SLICE...18 Dec 1840...WILKS F. WATERS (LS), Wit: ADAM STOUDEMIRE, JACOB
BUSBY. Proven by ADAM STOUDEMIRE 19 Jan 1841. ELIZABETH WATERS, wife of WILKS F.
WATERS, relinquished dower 22 Jan 1841. Rec. 5 Apr 1841. Delivered to ADAM SWARTZ, 12
Apr 1844.

Page 281: JOHN ELLISOR plat, made 18 Feb 1837 by THOMAS FREAN, Dep. Surv. 86 1/4 A in the
          forks of Broad and Saluda adj. THOMAS SMITH, JACOB DERRICK, GEORGE ELLISOR, heirs
of ADAM ZEIGLER, other lands of JOHN ELLISOR, land laid out for DEMPSEY BUSBY. Rec.

5 Apr 1841. Delivered to JOHN M. BOUKNIGHT 4 Nov 1844.

Page 282: S. C., Lexington Dist.: JACOB SWYGERT, EVE M. SWYGERT, and BARNET H. RAWLS, for
    love, good will and Sungry other good causes, gáve to DAVID COUNTZ & wf MARY E.
his wife...185 A on small branches, waters of Broad River, originally granted to ___
and by legal transactions became the property of COL. JOHN A. SUMMER & by his L. W. & T.
became the property of the present donors...plat by WM. B. ELKIN, D. S. 4 Feb last adj.
land at present owned by J. SWYGERT, GEORGE A. EIGLEBERGER, JOHN SUMMER JUNR., THOMAS
BOYD, BARNET H. RAWLS...2 Mar 1841...J. SWYGERT (SL), EVE M. SWYGERT (LS), BARNET H. RAWLS
(LS), Wit: OZRO H. SYWGERT, FRANCIS H. SWYGERT. Proven by OZRO H. SWYGERT 5 Apr 1841,
before JOHN FOX, Clk. Rec. 8 Apr 1841

Pp. 283-284: S. C.: DAVID AMICK of Lexington Dist., for $158 pd. by WILLIAM RISH of same...
    80 A, part of a tract granted to FRED. JOS. WALLERN, 5 Mar 1792 on wateree
branch, waters of Saluda, adj. lands held by JOHN SHEELY, JERED WIGGIES, DAVID AMICK, &
land unknown...4 Feb 1841...DAVID AMICK (LS), Wit: JOHN SHEELY, JR., DAVID AMICK, JR.,
P. DICKERT. Newberry Dist.: Proven by JOHN SHEELY JR, before P. DICKERT, J. Q. ANNA
AMICK, wife of DAVID, relinquished dower 5 Feb 1841, before P.DICKERT. Rec. 6 Apr 1841.
Delivered to JOHN H. SULTON, Esq., 4 Oct 1841.

Pp. 284-285: S. C., ANDREW RISH of Lexington Dist., for $200 pd. by ROSANA B. RISH, WIL-
    LIAM RISH, MARY M. RISH, and ELIZABETH RISH, all of same...86 A part of a
tract including three different tracts granted to JOHN WARREN[?], NICHOLAS HAMITER, and
FRED. JOS. WALLERN, on Wateree Branch, waters of Saluda River adj. Estate of HENRY
SHEELY, F. J. WALLERN, & JERED WIGGIES, and the original...6 Oct 1840...ANDREW RISH (LS),
Wit: DAVID LONG, P. DICKERT. Proven by DAVID LONG in Newberry Dist., 6 Oct 1840 before
P. DICKERT, J. Qu. Newberry Dist.: MARY MAGD. RISH, wife of ANDREW, relinquished dower
6 Oct 1840 before PETER DICKERT, Rec. 6 Apr 1841. Delivered to JOHN H. SULTON, Esq.,
4 Oct 1841.

Pp. 286-287: S? C., Banks GUNTER of Lexington Dist., for $50 pd. by PAUL QUATTLEBUM of
    same...land on E side of Lightwood Creek waters of North Edisto River adj.
land originally granted to WILLIAM BURGESS, land originally granted to BANJ. TARRANT,
granted for 39 1/2 A, to SAMUEL FLEMING 4 March 1822...17 Oct 1838...BANKS GUNTER (+)
(LS), Wit: JNO. K. JOHNSTON, LARKIN GUNTER. Lexington Dist.: Proven by JOHN K. JOHNSTON,
before ANDERSON STEEDMAN 6 Apr 1841. Rec. 7 Apr 1841. Delivered to COL. P. QUATTLEBUM,
21 June 1842.

Pp. 287-288: S. C., PETER ROWE of Lexington Dist., for $6000 pd. by CLARA JONES and ISAAC
    JONES, late of Edgefield District...land on Lightwood and Chinquepin Creeks,
waters of North Edisto River, by resurvey of WILLIAM QUATTLEBUM 28 Aug 1839, 2323 A, called
the Mill tract, also half of a tract granted to ROBT. STARK, 2 June 1817, transfered from
JOHN D. A. MURPHY to PETER ROWE 22 Oct 1834...6 Sept 1839...PETER ROWE (LS), Wit: PAUL
QUATTLEBUM, JOHN M. FELDER. Lexington Dist.: Proven by PAUL QUATTLEBUM, 8 Apr 1841,
before JOHN FOX. Rec. 8 Apr 1841. D-livered to J. A. ADDISON, Atty for ISAAC JONES, 25
Oct 1841.

Pp. 288-289: S. C., JOHN KOON of Newberry District, for $1300 pd. by FREDERICK DERRICK
    of same...150 A, part of two separate tracts the one originally granted to
MICHAEL BOUKNIGHT, the other to THOMAS GIBSON in Lexington Dist on Saluda River adj.
DAVID EPTING, DAVID FULMER DREHR [not clear if DAVID FULMER DREHR is one name]...24 Aug
1840...JOHN KOON (LS), Wit: GEORGE WISE, MICHAEL SHEALEY, Newberry Dist.: Proven by
GEORGE WISE before P? DICKERT, 24 Augt 1840. Newberry Dist.: BARBARA KOON (X), wife of
JOHN KOON, relinquished dower 24 Augt 1840, before PETER DICKERT. Rec. 9 Apr 1841.

Pp. 290-291: S. C., Lexington Dist.: DAVID FULMER of Lexington Dist., for $725 pd. by
    GEORGE W. BOWERS of Newberry Dist....150 A in Lexington Dist on N side of
big Saluda beginning on a willow corner made by DAVID FULMER & JOHN FULMER, plat made
by Dept Sury. SAMUEL CANNON, except 24 A and 3/4 which WILLIAM HOLEMAN took out of sd.
platt by an older grant at the NE corner...5 Sept 1840...DAVID FULMER (X) (LS), Wit:
MICHAEL SHEELY, JACOB WHEELER, WILLIAM EPTING. Newberry Dist.: Proven by JACOB WHEELER
5 Sept 1840 before JOHN P. STOCKMAN, J. P. Lexington Dist.: ONNY FULLMER (+), wife of
DAVID, relinquished dower 13 Nov 1840 before J. H. COUNTS, J. Q. Rec. 9 Apr 1841.
Delivered to GEORGE W. BOWERS 2 Jan 1843.

Page 292: S. C.: JOHN HENDRIX of Lexington Dist., for $350 pd. by EDWIN J. SCOTT of same
    [deed not completed].

Pp. 293-293: S.C., Lexington Dist.: WILLIAM L. MILLER for $250 pd. by ELIAS SLICE & ADAM
    HALTIWANGER of same...250 A on waters of Wateree Creek, waters of Saluda, adj.

SIMEON MILLER, HENRY F. HALTIWANGER & others...19 Apr 1841...WM. L. MILLER (LS), Wit:
L. BOOZER, JOHN HOOK. Proven by JOHN HOOK 19 Apr 1841 before JOHN FOX. GRACY H. MILLER,
wife of WILLIAM L. MI_LER, relinquished dower 19 Apr 1841 before LEMUEL BOOZER, Magt.
Rec. 19 Apr 1841. Delivered to ADAM HALTIWANGER 24 May 1842.

Pp. 294-295: S. C., WM. L. MILLER, Sheriff, by virtue of a writ of fiere facias issued
out of the Court of Common Pleas of Lexington Dist., tested 9 Nov 1840,
at the suit of R. HARMAN vs HENRY KLECKLEY to sell goods and chattels of HENRY KLECKLEY to
levy the sum of $178.59...150 A adj. DANIEL KLECKLEY, T. LORICK, & others..purchased by
MICHAEL DRAFTS and DANIEL DRAFTS SENR for $50...21 Apr 1841...WILLIAM L. MILLER, S. L. D.
(LS), Wit: JOSEPH R. MILLER, JOHN HOOK. Proven by JOSEPH R. MILLER 21 Apr 1841 before
JOHN FOX. Rec. 21 Apr 1841.

Pp. 296-297: S. C., Lexington Dist.: Whereas CATHARINE FRAZIER one of the Heirs and Distributees of WILLIAM FRAZIER decd, filed a petition in the Court of Ordinary
for Lexington Dist against HENRY FRAZIER & Others Heirs and distributees of the sd. WM.
FRAZIER on the 13 Nov 1840 stating that the sd. WM. FRAZIER died intestate leaving a tract
that has not been partitioned on 23 Mar 1841, ARTHUR H. FORT, Ordinary decreed that sd.
land be sold...WILLIAM L. MILLER exposed it to public sale and CATHARINE FRAZIER became
the purchaser...land adj. WILLIAM LYBRAND, REBECCA FRAZIER, ABSALOM HENDRIX...26 Apr 1841
...WM. L. MILLER (LS), S. L. D. Wit: PATRICK TODD, JOHN HOOK. Proven by JOHN HOOK 26
Apr 1841. Rec. 26 Apr 1841. Delivered to FREDERICK SEAS 10 Nov 1841.

Pp. 297-299: WILLIAM L. MILLER, Sheriff, by virtue of writ of Fiere Facias from Court of
Common Pleas tested 3 Nov 1838 at the suit of MEETZE & HENDRIX against the
goods and chattels of DANIEL JACKSON to levy $128.70...tract of 200 A on Big Hollow Creek,
waters of Saluda adj. lands of FREDERICK SEAS, KESIAH HAYES, DANIEL LEAPHART...for $11
sold to DANIEL LEAPHART...27 Apr 1841...WM. L. MILLER, S. L. D. (LS), Wit: WILLIAM FORT,
JOHN HOOK. Proven by WM. FORT 27 Apr 1841 before JOHN FOX. Delivered 7 June 1841 to
D. LEAPHART.

Pp. 299-301: WILLIAM L. MILLER, Sheriff, whereas DAIVD BOOZER one of the Heirs and Distributees of JACOB BOOZER decd filed a petition in the Court of Ordinary of
Lexington Dist., against WILLIAM BOOZER, HENRY BOOZER, NANCY BOOZER, DAVID HENDRIX & wf
ELIZABETH, LEMUEL BOOZER, JACOB N. BOOZER, SAMUEL P. CAUGHMAN & BETHANY his wife, on 10
Aug 1840., stating that the sd. JACOB BOOZER SENR decd died intestate leaving a tract
that has not been partitioned on 8 Feb 1841, ARTHHR FORT, Ordinary decreed that the land be
sold...217 A, but later found by survey to be 333 A and HENRY HENDRIX became the purchaser
for $173...26 Apr 1841...WM. L. MILLER, S. L. D. (LS), Wit: W. H. FOX, H. J. CAUGHMAN.
Proven by WASHINGTON H. FOX. 27 Apr 1841. Plat made by JOHN D. SHARP, 26 Feb 1841 showing Hogpen Branch add land adj. to THOMAS TALLS, HENRY HENDRIX, "supposed to be vacant,"
GEORGE CAUGHAM, land formerly SPENCE, now LITES, "supposed to be KISERS"...Rec. 27 Apr
1841. Delivered to HENRY HENDRIX, 29 DEc 1841.

Page 302: Blank.

Pp. 303-304: S. C., GEORGE C. POOSER of Lexington Dist. by a bond or obligation bearing
date 1 Dec 1840 stands bound to JOHN D. A. MURPHY, Planter, of Orangeburgh
Dist, in the penal sum of $15,380.66 for the payment of $7684.30...mortgage of land on
Cedar Creek with two saw mills adj. lands of WILLIAM and JOHN HARTH, MAJR. JOHN M. FELDER,
SCOFIELD, JOHN RISH now claim by WILLIAM ALTMAN and LUCAS, JOHN WILLIAMS, HENRY GRUBBS,
unknown land, BENJAMIN JEFCOAT JUR., LEWIS BARR, whereon LEWIS BARR now lives, 2100 A...
1 Dec 1840...G. C. POOSER (LS), Wit: A. E. GLOVER, P. S. FELDER. Orangeburgh Dist.:
Proven by A. E. GLOVER before M. GRAMBURY, Q. U. Ex off. 9 Apr 1841. Rec. 13 Apr 1841.

Pp. 305-306: S. C., Lexington Dist.: GEORGE KREPS for $275 pd by WILLIAM KREPS of same...
87 A on drains of Horse Creek of Hollow Creek,waters of Saluda River adj.
CHRISTIAN PRICE, JOEL KEASLER, GEORGE PRICE, JACOB PRICE, part of tract originally granted
to MICHAEL WISE and THOMAS C. WARNER...plat made by WILLIAM QUATTLEBUM 15 Mar 1839...5
Dec 1839...GEORGE KREPS (+) (SEAL), Wit: JOHN PRICE, JOEL KEISLER SR[?]. Proven by JOHN
PRICE 5 Dec 1839 before WILLIAM QUATTLEBUM. BARBARA KREPS, wife of GOERGE, relinquished
dower 5 Dec 1839. Plat included in deed. Rec. 28 Apr 1841. Delivered to WILLIAM KREPS
14 June 1841.

Pp. 307-309: WILLIAM MILLER Shff, by virtue of two writs of Fiere Facias, one issued out
of the Court of Common Pleas for Lexington Dist., tested 10 Apr 1839 at the
suit of C. D. FOX and the other issued out of Court of Common Pleas for Charleston Dist.,
tested on 13 Jan 1841 at Charleston to levy $1311.87 from goods and chattels of JEREMIAH
WINGARD...land 134 A, originally granted to ANDREW KELLEY 25 May 1774 for 100 A and resurveyed by JOHN W. SEE, Dept Sury. on 2 Feb 1830 on Beach Creek, waters of Rocky Creek

waters of Saluda River adj. DAVID HENDRIX, JACOB LITES, JEREMIAH WINGARD, JACOB KYZER...
purchased by JOHN MEETZE & BOUKNIGHT for $488 and directed to execute titles to JEROME
BONAPARTE SEE and WILLIAM ERVIN SEE, son of WM. SEE, all of Lex. Dist...8 Mar 1841...
WM. L. MILLER (LS), S. L. D. Wit: A. H. FORT, JOHN HOOK. Proven by JOHN HOOK, before
JOHN FOX, 1 May 1841. MARGARET WINGARD, wife of JEREMIAH, relinquished dower, 1 May
1841. Plat included made by JOHN W. SEAY, 2 Feb 1830. Rec. 1 May 1841. Delivered to
WM. SEE 11 Oct 1841.

Pp. 310-311: S. C., Lexington Dist.: Whereas MARY JONES, one of the Heirs and Distributees
        of GIDEON JONES decd., filed a petition in the Court of Ordinary for Lexing-
ton Dist. against SIMPSON JONES, JOHN E. JONES, WILLIAM W. JONES, and ELI JONES on 28
Sept 1840 stating that sd. GIDEON JONES died Intestate leaving a tract that has not been
partitioned...on 30 Oct 1840, ARTHUR FORT made decree to sell on 2 Nov 1840...958 A pur-
chased by JOHN A. SALLY for $702 on Marrow bone Creek, waters of North Edisto adj. JOHN
A. SALLY, WILSON GUNTER, JACOB GAUNTT...30 Apr 1841... WM. L. MILLER (LS), S. L. D. Wit:
JOHN HOOK, LEROY HENDRIX. Proven by JOHN HOOK 3 May 1841. Rec. 3 May 1841. Delivered to
JOSEPH C. FANNING 30 Dec 1842.

Pp. 311-312: S. C., JACOB BICKLEY of Lexington Dist., for $500 pd. by JOHN HILLER of same,
        ...144 A, the NW part of a tract resurveyed by J. W. SEAY for sd. BICKLEY
in Lexington Dist adj. MICHL. RAUCH, JOHN SMITH, MRS. LOWMAN, GEORGE STINLEY[?], & sd.
JOHN HILLER...19 Dec 1840...JACOB BICKLEY (LS), Wit: HENRY STINILEY[?], GEORGE P. DRAFTS.
Proven by HENRY STINGILEY, 19 Dec 1840 before J. H. COUNTS, J. Q. Rec. 6 May 1841.
Delivered to JOHN HILLER.

Pp. 313-314: S. C., Lexington Dist.: Whereas CHRISTIAN PRICE, one of the heirs and Distri-
        butees of HENRY OSWALT decd, filed a petition in Court·· of Ordinary·of
Lexington Dist., against HARMAN SEE & wf MARY, and others on 24 Dec 1841[sic]...said
HENRY OSWALT died intestate leaving a tract of land that has not been partitioned...on 23
Mar 1841, ARTHUR H. FORT, Eqr., Ordinary, decreed that sd. land be paritioned & sold by
Sheriff of Lexington Dist., 1st Mon in May 1841...JOHN KEASLER became purchaser for $90,
being the highest bidder...10 A adj. JOHN KEASLER, HARMAN SEE & others...8 May 1841...WM.
L. MILLER (LS), S. L. D. Wit: J. R. MILLER, JOHN HOOK. Proven by JOHN HOOK 20 May 1841.
Rec. 24 May 1841. Delivered to JOHN KEASLER Dec 6, 1841.

Pp. 314-316: JOHN SON of Lexington Dist., for $600 pd. by MICHAEL BARR...land on E side
        Lick Creek, waters of Saluda, 221 A adj. GASAWAY BOWERS, DANIEL RAMBO,
MICHAEL BARR, with the exception that DANIEL RAMBO & his heirs, etc. shall at all times be
at liberty to build a Mill Dam across the sd. Lick Creek...6 May 1839...JOHN SON (LS), Wit:
WM. J. BARR, J. J. BARR. Proven by W. J. BARR 17 May 1834 before HENRY A. SMITH, Q. U.
MALINDY SON, wife of JOHN, relinquished dower 17 May 1839 before HENRY A. SMITH. Rec. 29
May 1841. Delivered to WM. BARR, 2 Apr 1842.

Pp. 316-317: S. C., MICHAEL BARR of Lexington Dist., for $600 pd. by WM. J. BARR of same...
        221 A on E side Lick Creek [same land as in preceding deed]...18 Feb 1841...
MICHAEL BARR (LS), Wit: D. WINCHELL, JOHN J. BARR. Proven by JOHN J. BARR 23 Mar 1841.
MARY A. BARR relinquished dower 23 Mar 1841, before HENRY A. SMITH; Rec. 29 May 1841.
Delivered to WM. BARR, 2 Apr 1842.

Pp. 317-318: S. C., JOHN P. CULLUM of Lexington Dist., for $2318 pd. by BARZILLA CULLUM of
        same...1/4 part of FELDER survey whereon the saw mill is situated , 1/2 of
one saw, 1/4 of ALMAN survey, plat made by WILLIAM BUCKHALTER, D. S., 2 July 1839...15 May
1841...JOHN P. CULLUM (LS), Wit: W. E. CULLUM, NATHANIEL JONES. Proven by WM. E. CULLUM
15 May 1841, before NATHANIEL JONES, J. P. Rec. 7 June 1841. Delivered to BARZILLA
CULLUM, Dec. 21, 1851.

Pp. 318-320: S. C.: Whereas by virtue of a writ of Fiere Facias from the Court of Common
        Pleas held for Fairfield District, tested 19 Nov 1839 at the suit of SMITH &
ELKIN against THOMAS A. CRUMPTON to me directed to WILLIAM L. MILLER, Shff to sell the
goods and chattels of sd. CRUMPTON to levy $47...127 A in Lexington Dist., adj. lands now
held by ELIZABETH SUMMER, MARY BRIGHT, JOHN SUMMER SENR, BENJ. BUSBY, for $60 pd. by JAMES
WILSON...1 Feb 1841...WM. L. MILLER (LS), S. L. D. Wit: JOSEPH GANTT, JOHN HOOK. Proven
by JOHN HOOK, 1 Feb 1841. Fairfield Dist.: ELIZABETH E. CRUMPTON, wife of THOS A., relinquished dower 2 March 1841, before DANIEL B. KIRKLAND, J. P. Rec. 7 June 1841. Delivered to JAMES WILSON Sept 6, 1841.

Pp. 320-321: S. C. Lexington Dist.: JONATHAN V. PETT & MARIA PETT for $600 pd. by JAMES
        D. BOUKNIGHT of Edgefield Dist...253 A with the exception of one acre around
the graveyard in Lexington Dist., on N side of long branch, waters of Saluda River, adj.
ELIAS BOUKNIGHT, ELEANOR LEES, GEORGE BOWERS...13 Dec 1839...JONATHAN V. PELT (LS),

MARIA PELT (+) (LS), Wit: MARY BOUKNIGHT (X), DANIEL BOUKNIGHT. Edgefield Dist.: Proven by DANIEL BOUKNIGHT, 5 June 1841. before R. B. BOUKNIGHT, Magist. Lexington Dist.: MRS. MARIA PELT relinquished dower 5 June 1841 before R. B. BOUKNIGHT. Rec. 7 June 1841. Delivered to JAMES D. BOUKNIGHT, 3 July 1841.

Pp. 322-324: Plat Surveyed 8 May 1822 by SAML CANNON, D. S. at request of MR. DRURY DAVIS 619 A being part of several tracts on N side Saluda River, shows adj. land-owners: SAMUEL KENNERLY, MRS. GEIGER, TARRES, TANKERS[?], and shows Saluda River and Road to Columbia.
BARTHOLOMEW TURNIPSEED & wf NANCY and sister of one of the Distributees of the late WILLIAM J. GEIGER, for $6600 pd. by SAMUEL HUFF...all right and interest to the land of which the sd. WILLIAM J. GEIGER was seized and possessed on 3 Jan 1830, the un-divided half or moiety of tract in Lexington Dist., containing about 616 A...3 Mar 1841... BARTHOLOMEW TURNIPSEED (LS), NANCY TURNIPSEED (X) (LS), Wit: GEORGE LEAPHART, J. GREGG. Richland Dist.: NANCY TURNIPSEED, wife of BARTHOLOMEW, relinquished dower 5 June 1841, before EDWARD J. ARTHUR. Richland Dist.: Proven by J. GREGG, before JAMES S. GUIGNARD, 5 Mar 1841. Memorandum, the Deed was Executed on the 4th of March & that should have been the date instead of the 3rd. Rec. 7 June 1841. Delivered to SAMUEL HUFFMAN 5 July 1841.

Pp. 324-326: BARTHOLOMEW TURNIPSEED of Richland Dist., for $50 pd. by SAMUEL HUFFMAN of Lexington Dist...half of 6 3/4 A originally sold by sd. HUFFMAN to WILLIAM J. GEIGER on both sides of the Bush River adj. to SAMUEL HUFFMAN, WILLIAM J. GEIGER, conveyed to SAMUEL HUGGMAN by GEORGE LEAPHART agent for sd. GEIGER on 5 Mar 1830...B. TURNIPSEED (LS), Wit: HENRY TURNIPSEED, GEORGE LEAPHART. Richland Dist.: Proven by HENRY TURNIPSEED, 26 Apr 1841., before DANIEL D. FENLY, Magist. of R. D. ANNY, wife of B. TURNIPSEED, relinquished dower 23 Apr 1841 before HENRY TURNIPSEED. Rec. 7 June 1841. Delivered to SAMUEL HUFFMAN 5 July 1841.

Pp. 326-327: S. C., EDWIN J. SCOTT of Lexington Dist., for $100 pd. by JOHN HENDRIX of same...land near Lexington Village adj. lands of JOHN H. SOUTER, DR. SOUTERs lot...2 A excluding the Street...2 Nov 1840...EDWIN J. SCOTT (LS), Wit: CYRENIUS LOOMIS, SAML LOWMAN. Lexington Dist.: Proven by SAMUEL LOWMAN 8 June 1841 before L. BOOZER, Magistrate. REBECCA, Wife of Edwin J. SCOTT, relinquished dower 28 May 1841, before LEMUEL BOOZER. Rec. 8 June 1841. Delivered to JOHN HENDRIX, 7 Augt 1841.

Page 328: S. C., Lexington Dist.: BENJAMIN GUNTER & wf RUTH for $80 pd. by GILPIN GUNTER all of Lexington Dist...80 A, part of 200 A granted to EDWARD WATTS 7 June 1786 adj. THOMAS J. RALLS, BENJAMIN GUNTER...23 Sept 1837...BENJAMIN GUNTER (LS), RUTH GUNTER (X), Wit: WILLIAM GUNTER, LEAH GUNTER. Proven by WILLIAM GUNTER 18 Oct 1837, before JACOB GAUNTT.

Pp. 329-331: S. C., EMANUEL GEIGER of Lexington Dist., for [amt: not stated] pd. by SAMUEL HUFFMAN...land on E side Saluda River containing (according to a survey by E. J. ARTHUR, D. S. on 28 Mar 1841), 258 A adj. Saluda River, lands of SAMUEL HUFFMAN, EMANUEL GEIGER, SAMUEL KENNERLY decd, part of 619 A lately belonging to WILLIAM GEIGER decd...5 Mar 1841...EMANUEL GEIGER (LS), Wit: JAS. T. FLEMING, JAMES. R. HEISE. Richland District.: Proven by JAMES T. FLEMING 4 June 1841, before EDWARD J. ARTHUR, Magistrate. Lexington Dist.: MRS. POLLY GEIGER, wife of EMANUEL GEIGER, relinquished dower 19 June 1841, beofre JOHN FOX Clk & Magist. Ex off. Plat included showing adj. lands owners and Bush River Road to Columbia. Rec. 19 June 1841. Delivered to SAMUEL HUFFMAN, 5 July 1841.

Pp. 331-333: Plat made by EDW. J. ARTHUR, D. S. 28 Mar 1841 at the request of SAMUEL HUFF-MAN & EMANUEL GEIGER, divided a tract lately belonging to the est. of WM. GEIGER, decd, 619 1/2 A on E side Saluda...shows lands "Formerly Saml, Kennerlys,", "For-merly TARRERS," "Formerly TANKERS"....
S. C., SAMUEL HUFFMAN of Lexington Dist., for $1 pd. by EMANUEL GEIGER of same...255 1/2 A, according to a survey made by E. J. ARTHUR, 28 Mar 1841...4 June 1841... SAMUEL HUFFMAN (LS), Wit: JAS. T. FLEMING, JAMES R. HEISE. Richland Dist.: Proven by JAMES T. FLEMING 5 June 1841, before E. J. ARTHUR. Lexington Dist: MRS. SALLY HUFFMAN, wife of SAMUEL, Relinquished dower 15 June 1841. Rec. 21 June 1841. Delivered to EMANUEL GEIGER, 3 July 1841.

Pp. 333-334: S. C., EMANUEL GEIGER for $40 pd. by SAMUEL HUFFMAN...3 A in the Dutch Fork, on the Bush River Road...7 June 1841...EDMANUEL GEIGER (LS), Wit: STANSMORE LANGFORD, WM. FORT. Proven by WILLIAM FORT, 21 June 1841, before JOHN FOX. MRS. POLLY GEIGER, wife of EMANUEL, relinquished dower 19 June 1841. Rec. 21 June 1841. Delivered to SAMUEL HUFFMAN 5 July 1841.

Pp. 334-336: ADAM BUFF of Lexington Dist., for $55 pd. by LEWIS METZ of same...30 A, part
of a tract of 451 1/2 A granted to PETER LEGON in 1795, to THOMAS H. BUTLER
in 1832, to ADAM BUFF in 1840 in the fork of Broad and Saluda on the main road leading
from Columbia to the mountains adj. JOHN D SHARP, JAMES WALLACE...15 Jan 1841...ADAM BUFF
(LS), Wit: DANIEL NATS[?], SIMON YOUNGINER. Proven by SIMON YOUNG 17 May 1841, before
LEVI METZ, Magit. RACHEL BUFF, wife of ADAM, relinquished dower 18 May 1841. Rec. 21
June 1841. Delivered to LEWIS METZ 1 Nov 1841.

Pp. 336-338: Lexington Dist.: Whereas ADAM and JOHN G. HALTIWANGER, Heirs and distributees
of HENRY F. HALTIWANGER decd, filed a petition in the Court of ordinary for
Lexington Dist., against ANDREW HALTIWANGER, JACOB HALTIWANGER, MRS. M. B. HALTIWANGER,
S. MILLER & wf MILLY HALTIWANGER and ANDREW T. HALTIWANGER, on 14 April 1841 for division
of land...165 A which ADAM HALTIWANGER became the purchaser for $35, land between Broad
and Saluda adj. GEORGE HALTIWANGER, FRANCIS KOON, ANDREW HALTIWANGER...sold by Sheriff...
WM. L. MILLER (LS), S. L. D. Wit: WILLIAM HALTIWANGER, SIMEON MILLER. Proven by WILLIAM
HALTIWANGER 21 June 1841. Rec. 21 June 1841. Delivered to ADAM HALTIWANGER 24 May 1842.

Pp. 338-339: Lexington Dist.: HENRY W. AUSTIN for $400 pd/ by AZARIAH CROUT of same...42
A on Hollow Creek, waters of Saluda River, originally granted to BARNARD
LYBRAND, conveyed by him to DAVIS AUSTIN decd, and at his death fell to sd. **DAVIS** AUSTIN
by partition...HENRY W. AUSTIN (LS), Wit: URIAH CROUT, V. V. S. AUSTIN. Proven by URIAH
CROUT 27 Apr 1841, before ISAAC VANSANT, J. P. Rec. 3 July 1841. Delivered to AZARIAH
CROUT 20 Jan 1842.

Pp. 339-340: Power of Attorney to Employ an Overseer. ANN ARTHUR, KIZAH ARTHUR, & CAROLINE
E. ARTHUR of Lexington Dist., to appointed DANIEL MORGAN of same, our true &
lawful attorney to employ an overseer to take charge of our plantation below Congaree
Creek on the State Road...4 Jan 1841...ANN ARTHUR (LS), KEZIAH ARTHUR (LS), CAROLINE E.
ARTHUR (LS), Wit: CAROLINE S. MORGAN. Proven by CAROLINE S. MORGAN 10 July 1841, before
CONRAD SHULL, Magt. Rec. 12 July 1841. Delivered to D. MORGAN 12 July 1841.

Pp. 340-341: S. C., STEPHEN SENTERFIT of Lexington Dist., in the consideration of JOHN
KNOX and ANDREW SHEALY becoming my Surity[sic] for the payment of $350...
350 A on N Edisto River adj. ANDREW SHEALEY, WILLIAM REYNOLDS, WILLIS HARTLEY, WILLIAM
MALPASS...4 Mar 1840...STEPHEN SENTERFIT (LS), Wit: ARTEMAS WATSON, WILLIS HARTLEY. Pro-
ven by WILLIS HARTLEY 26 June 1841, before ISAAC VANSANT, Magistrate. Rec. 15 July 1841.
Delivered to ANDREW SHEALEY.

Pp. 341-342: CHARLES LUCAS of Lexington Dist., for $300 pd. by JACOB BARRY (BERRY)...200
A, part of 1000 A granted to GEORGE STEEDMAN on head of Congaree Creek and
big black Creek, waters of North Edisto River adj. WILLIAM LUCAS, JOHN RICHES, on the road
from Charleston...1 Jan 1840...CHARLES LUCAS (X) (SEAL), Wit: WILLIAM ALTMAN, HENRY
GRUBS. Proven by HENRY GRUBS 13 July 1841, before JOHN WILLIAMS Magist. Rec. 15 July
1841. Delivered to JACOB BERRY, 19 Sept 1848.

Pp. 324-344: S. C.: JOHN KLECKLEY, JOHN WINGARD & wf MARY, formerly MARY KLECKLEY(children
of JOHN KLECKLY the Elder ced & his wife CATHARINE who afterwards Intermarried with CHRISTIAN LONG and both have since died) of Lexington Dist., for $325 pd by
JOHN SHULER of same...40 3/4 A in Lexington Dist., in fork of Broad and Saluda on Yost
Branch, waters of Saluda River adj. lands at present held by sd. JOHN SHULER, THOMAS SHULER,
part of 200 A grant to JOHN HIPP 13 Oct 1772 (this 40 3/4 A assinged to CATHARINE LONG,
formerly the wife of sd. JOHN KLECKLEY the Elder, decd by Commissioner appointed by the
Court of Common Please for Lexington Dist. to Partition the Real Estate of sd. JOHN
KLECKLEY decd and the sd. CATHARINE LONG having since died intestate leaving as as next
of kin)...7 June 1841...JOHN KLECKLY (LS), JOHN WINGARD (LS), MARY WINGARD (LS), Wit:
SAMUEL HUFFMAN, JESSE COOGLER. Proven by SAMUEL HUFFMAN __ June 1841, before JOHN FOX,
Clk. MARY WINGARD relinquished dower 26 July 1841. Rec. 26 July 1841. Delivered to JOHN
SHULER, 16 Sept 1841.

Pp. 344-346: S. C., FREDERICK BICKLEY of Lexington Dist., for $200 pd. by JOSEPH W. WYSE,
of same...225 A on N side Saluda River adj. FREDERICK BICKLEY, JAMES BALEN-
TINE, GEORGE WYSE, HENRY LYBRAND...3 Sept 1831...FREDERICK BICKLEY (LS), Wit: FREDERICK
WYSE, JOHN W. SEAY. Proven by FREDERICK WYSE, 2 Augt 1841, before JOHN TOX. ANNA, wife
of FREDERICK BICKLEY, relinquished dower before J. H. CAUGHMAN, 4 Feb ___. Rec. 2 Aug
1841. Delivered 13 Sept 1841 to DANIEL LEAPHART. Plat made 2 Sept 1831 by JOHN W. SEAY,
shows Calks or Bickleys Road. Rec. 2 Aug 1841.

Pp. 346-348: S. C.: JACOB STACK of Lexington Dist., planter, for $100 pd. by HENRY SETS-
LER of same, planter...100 A, part of 604 A granted to LEWELLIN THREEWITS
and JOHN WOLF JR 7 May 1792 over the third branch of Big Bull Swamp...6 Feb 1806...JACOB

STACK (LS), Wit: JACOB TYLER, JOHN HOZFORD (X). Proven by JACOB TYLER 6 Feb 1806, before FRED. CLAP [CLASS?], J. P. BARBARA STACK, wife of JACOB, relinquished dower, 14 Feb 1806. Rec. 2 Aug 1841. Delivered to JACOB REDMAN, 30 Nov 1843.

Pp. 348-349: S. C. Lexington Dist.: HENRY SITELER, planter, for $80 pd. by WILLIAM
LEONARD of same, planter...100 A, part of 664 A, granted to LEWELLING THRE-WITS and JOHN WOLFE, JUR. 7 May 1792 by Gov. CHARLES PINCKNEY on a branch of Big Bull Swamp...7 Dec 1810...HENRY SITELER (X) (SEAL), Wit: JOHN BAUGHMAN, ABRAHAM BAUGHMAN. Proven by JOHN CAUGHMAN, 17 Dec 1810 before HARMAN BAUGHMAN. Rec. 2 Aug 1840. Delivered to JACOB REDMAN 30 Nov 1843.

Pp. 349-350: S. C., Lexington Dist.: JAMES LEONARD, planter, for $100 pd. by HENRY FUR-TICK, both of Lex....100 A, part of 664 A [same land in preceding deed]...
5 Feb 1834...JAMES LEONARD (LS), Wit: MATHEW C. CRAFT, PETER REDMAN. Orangeburgh Dist.: Proven by PETER REDMAN before D. S. DANNELLY, J. Q., 26 July 1841. Rec. 2 Aug 1841. Delivered to JACOB REDMAN, 30 Nov 1843.

Pp. 351-352: S. C. Lexington Dist.: HENRY FURTICK, planter, for $150 pd. by LEMUEL SENN...
100 A, part of 664 A [same land in preceding deeds]...18 Sept 1834...HENRY FURTICK (LS), Wit: DANIEL SENN, PETER REDMAN. Orangeburgh District: Proven by PETER REDMAN, before D. S. DANNELLY, 25 Feb 1841. Rec. 2 Aug 1841.

Pp. 352-353: S. C. Lexington Dist.: LEMUEL SENN, planter, for $150 pd. by SAMUEL RUCKER
...100 A part of 664 A [same land in preceding deeds]...2 Aug 1836...LEMUEL SENN (LS), Wit: HENRY A. WILLIAMS, HENRY FURTICK. Orangeburgh Dist.: Proven by HENRY FURTICK before D. S. DANNELLY, J. Q. 4 Dec 1840... Rec. 2 Aug 1841.

Pp. 353-354: S. C. Lexington Dist.: SAMUEL RUCKER, planter, for $160 pd. by ELISHA BAG-GETT...100 A, part of 664 [same land in preceding deeds]..._____ 1837...
SAMUEL RUCKER (LS), Wit: JOHN CRIM, MARTHY LEONARD (X). Lexington Dist.: Proven by MARTHA LEONARD, before D. S. DANNELLY, J. Q., 20 Feb 1841. Rec. 2 Aug 1841 Witness signed as MARTHA SCOTT (X)..

Pp. 354-356: S. C.: By virtue of two writs of Fiere Facias issued out of the Court of
Common Pleas of Lexington Dist, tested 4 Mar 1841 at the suit of DAVID HENDRIX commanding me to levy $144 from goods, chattels of Cyrenius LOOMIS...tract of 3 1/2 A where sd. LOOMIS now resides adj. lands of L. BOOZER, J. C. HOPE and the Theo-logical Seminary...3 Aug 1841, sold to REV. JOHN C. HOPE, for $200...WM. L. MILLER (LS), S. L. D., Wit: ISAIAH CAUGHMAN, JOHN HOOK. Proven by DR. ISAIAH CAUGHMAN, 3 Aug 1841. MRS. LEAH LOOMIS, wife of CYRENIUS, relinquished dower 3 Aug 1841. Rec. 3 Aug 1841. Delivered to J. C. HOPE 12 Apr 1842.

Pp. 356-357: S. C., Lexington Dist.: ADAM TAYLOR for $112 pd. by DANIEL GRIFFIN...100 A
part of two adjoining tracts contain 75 A, originally granted to JOHN LE-WEALLEN and the other 590 A, granted to JONATHAN TAYLOR, near the head waters of Congaree Creek adj. EPHRAIM EDINS, J. D. F. EDINS, JOHN MEETZE...26 Oct 1835...ADAM TAYLOR (X) (LS), Wit: G. TAYLOR, W. L. TAYLOR. Proven by G. TAYLOR, before D. ROOF, J. P. 11 Jan 1836. Rec. 17 Aug 1840.

Pp. 357-358: S. C. Lexington Dist.: DANIEL GRIFFIN, for $140. pd by. JOSEPH A. TAYLOR,
100 A[same land in preceding deed]...27 Sept 1837...DANIEL GRIFFIN (LS), Wit: G. TAYLOR, JOHN G. TAYLOR. Proven by JOHN G. TAYLOR, before A. H. FORT, 2 Dec 1837. Rec. 7 Aug 1841.

Page 359: S. C.: JOSEPH A. TAYLOR of Lexington Dist., for $75 pd. by JOHN FOX, of same...
100 A in Lex. Dist., near head waters of Congaree Creek adj. lands held at this time by EPHRAIM EDDINS, MRS. LOUISA EDDINS, JOHN MEETZE, & CALEB BOUKNIGHT...
[same tract in preceding deeds]...17 Aug 1841...JOSEPH A. TAYLOR (LS), Wit: WM.L. MILLER, JAMES DUNBAR JR (X). Proven by WILLIAM L. MILLER, 17 Aug 1841 before L. BOOZER.

Page 360: S. C.: JOSEPH C. HOOVER of Lexington Dist., for $250 pd. by JOHN J. HOOVER and
HENRY L. HOOVER, minors of Lexington Dist...250 A on pond branch, waters of N Edisto River, originally granted to DANIEL AGKILTON, 23 June 1774, conveyed 8 July 1774 to THOMAS TOD, and REcorded in the Mesne Conveyance Office in Charleston on 15 Sept 1774 and THOMAS TOD to JACOB VAULK on 9 Dec 1777 and recorded on 5 Oct 1781...18 Jan 1840...JOSEPH HOOVER (X) (LS), Wit: JOCOB LEARD, JOHN HUFFMAN. Proven by JOHN HUFFMAN, 18 Jan 1840, before MICHAEL WISE.

Pp. 361-362: S. C. Lexington Dist.:, JOHN J. MARTIN and HENRY L. HOOVER of Lexington Dist.,
for $221.87 1/2 pd. by JACOB LARD of same...142 A on Pon branch, waters of N

Edisto, adj. BENJ. JEFCOAT, HOOVER, originally granted to DANIEL AGHETTON on 23 June
1774...[same land as in preceding deed]...3 Aug 1840...JOHN J. MARTIN (LS), HENRY L.
HOOVER (LS), Wit: JOHN CRAFT, BURREL BAYLIS. Orangeburgh Dist.: Proven by JOHN CRAFT, 13
Mar 1841 before D. S. DANNELLY, J. Q. Lexington Dist.: ELIZABETH HOOVER(+), wife of
JOHN MARTIN, relinquished dower 13 Aug 1841, before ELIJAH JEFCOAT. SELENA HOOVER, wife
of LEWIS HOOVER, relinquished dower 13 Aug 1841, before ELIJAH JEFCOAT. Rec. 21 Aug 1841.
Delivered to JACOB LEARD, 15 Oct 1841.

Pp. 363-364: S. C., Lexington Dist.: GEORGE WHITES, plnater, for $300 pd. by JEREMIAH
        MILLER, planter...104 1/2 A on waters of wateree Creek, waters of Broad River
adj. MICHÆL SLICE, DANIEL AMICK, MICHAEL CHARLES, the SW part of a tract of 209 A,
granted to CHRISTIAN RISTER, who conveyed 104 1/2 A to MARTIN WHITES, the sd. MARTIN
WHITES, conveyed the same to the present grantor...17 Aug 1840...GEORGE WHITES (LS), Wit:
GEORGE SLICE, JOHN SLICE (X). Proven by JOHN SLICE 5 Sept 1840 before J. H. COUNTZ, J.
Q. KATHARINE WHITES, wife of GEORGE, relinquished dower, 14 July 1841, before LEVI
METZ, Magr. Delivered to JEREMIAH MILLER 25 Apr 1843.

Pp. 364-365: S. C., Lexington Dist.: JOHN F. LIGHTSEY for natural love and affection to
        MICHAEL KINARD and MAHALA mother of the sd. MICHAEL O. KINARD, a minor...
do give to sd. MICHAEL O. KINARD & MAHALA his mother a negro boy March, about 7 years old
...27 July 1841...JOHN F. LIGHTSEY (LS), Wit: REUBEN STEEDMAN, JONATHAN G. STEEDMAN JR.
Proven by REUBEN STEEDMAN, 27 July 1841, before ANDERSON STEEDMAN, Magistrate. Rec. 3
Sept 1841. Delivered to JACOB KINARD, 12 Oct 1842.

Pp. 366-367: S. C., DAVID COUNTS of Lexington Dist., for $425 pd. by JACOB J. BUSBY of
        same...87 3/4 A adj. JOHN SUMMER JR., THOMAS L. VEALE, adj. the Charleston
Road and hog branch, plat 25 Oct 1833, conveyed to the present on 31 Dec 1834 by ANDREW
SUMMER...7 Jan 1841...DAVID COUNTZ (LS), Wit: B. H. RAWLS, MARY A. RUTHERFORD. Proven by
B. H. RAWLS, before GEORGE M. FULMER, 14 Apr 1841. MARY ELIZABETH COUNTZ, wife of DAVID,
relinquished dower 14 Apr 1841. Rec. 6 Sept 1841. Delivered to J. J. BUSBY, 1 Nov 1841.

Pp. 367-368: S. C., MARY BUSBY, widow of the late JACOB BUSBY, decd of Lexington Dist.,
        in consideration that JACOB J. BUSBY of same, has covenanted, promised and
agreed to support, maintain, and provide for me during my natural life and for $5...all
lands and real estate of which JACOB BUSBY decd, died seized of on Broad River, the one
undivided third part [i. e., the widow's part]...27 Apr 1841...MARY BUSBY (+) (LS), Wit:
J. SWYGERT, B. H. RAWLS. Proven by JACOB SWYGERT, before B. M. FULMER. Rec. 6 Sept
1841. Delivered to J. J. BUSBY, 1 Nov 1841.

Pp. 368-370: S. C.: 6 Sept 1841, J. A. ADDISON, Esqr., Commissioner of the Hon. Court of
        Equity for Lexington Dist, to J. J. BUSBY...whereas JACOB J. BUSBY, on or
about 10 May 1841, did exhibit his bill of complaint in the Court of Equity against NATHAN
BUSBY & others, stating that JACOB BUSBY, late of Dist. aforesd. was seized of a large
real estate, consisting of several tracts...JACOB J. BUSBY, paid $1580.75...now for $80.75
207 1/2 A designated on the Platt of WM. B. ELKIN, adj.[?] JACOB SWYGERT...J. A. ADDISON
(LS), C. E. L. D. Wit: DAVID COUNTZ, JAS. WILSON. Proven by JAMES WILSON, 6 Sept 1841,
before JOHN FOX. Delivered to J. J. BUSBY, 1 Nov 1841.

Pp. 370-373: S. C., 6 Sept 1841, J& A. ADDISON, Comr. of Equity, to BENJAMIN C. BUSBY,
        [same case as in preceding deed]...for $17.35, 192 1/4 A on Broad River...
J. A. ADDISON, C. E. L. D., Wit: DAVID COUNTZ, JAMES WILSON. Proven by JAMES WILSON.
Rec. 6 Sept 1841. Delivered to BENJ. C. BUSBY, 2 Nov 1841. [Plat included on p. 373]:
Swon Chain Carriers: DAVID COUNTS, O. H. SWYGERT, BUCK BUSBY, & WEATHERSBY. Plat shows
Busby Creek, land adj. to THOMAS BRIGHT, A. STOUDEMIRE, BENJ. BUSBY, MRS. BRIGHT, J. J.
BUSBY, MAJ. SWYGERT, MAd. J. SWYGERT, and Broad River. Plat made at the joint request of
J. SWYGERT, DAVID COUNTS, and ADAM STOUDEMIRE, plat made by WM. B. ELKIN, D. S. 23 July
1841. Rec. 6 Sept 1841.

Pp. 374-375: S. C., Newberry District: WILLIAM SNELGROVE of Bib County, Georgia, for love
        and good will to my daughter PHILLISSA ANN GRAY, I give grant and release to
BENJAMIN H. GRAY of Newberry District, 700 A in Lexington Dist., on the waters of Long
Branch, waters of big Saluda River, originally granted to PHILLIP SPILLERS, 7 June 1814,
plat certified by GEORGE EIGLEBERGER, Dep. Sur. adj. CAGE MARTIN, SAMUEL MORRIS, GEORGE
RALL and on all other sides by vacant land at the time of survey...12 Mar 1824...WM.
SNELGROVE (LS), Wit: R. C. WORTHINGTON, DAVID HARMAN (N) Newberry Dist.: Proven by
DAVID HARMAN, 17 Mar 1828, before G. M. BOWERS, J. P. Rec. 6 Sept 1841. Delivered to
JACOB LONG SR., Admr. of A. BANKS, decd by the hand of JAMES FULMER, Feby 6, 1845.

Pp. 375-376: S. C., Lexington Dist.: Whereas ADAM HALTIWANGER & SIMEON MILLER two of the
        Heirs and Distributees of GEORGE HALTIWANGER, decd filed a petition in the

76

Court of Ordinary of Lexington Dist...against MARY B. HALTIWANGER, J. G. HALTIWANGER,
ANDREW HALTIWANGER, JACOB HALTIWANGER, MISS MILEY HALTIWANGER, & ANDREW T. HALTIWANGER,
on 21 June 1841 stating that the sd. GEORGE HAWLTIWANGER died intestate leaving several
tracts of land which have not been partitioned...on 3 Aug 1841, ARTHUR H. FORT did decree
that sd. lands be sold by Sheriff on the last monday in Aug. 1841...ADAM HALTIWANGER
became the purchaser, for $150, 200 A in fork of Broad and Saluda adj. lands of SIMEON
MILLER, CUMALANDER, GEORGE COON, KATHERINE WHEELER, ANDREW HALTIWANGER...6 Sept 1841...
WM. L. MILLER (LS), S. L. D. Wit: J. R. MILLER, JOHN HOOK. Proven by JOHN HOOK, 6 Sept
1841. Rec. 6 Sept 1841.

Page 377: S. C. Lexington Dist.: JESSE SHEALEY, for $175.24, pd. by DAVID FIKE of Lex.
Dist...80 A on a branch of Rockey Creek,waters of Saluda River adj. CHRISTENER
HALLMAN, EPHRAIM SHEALEY, URIAH CROUT, DAVID FIKE...1 Aug 1842, payment due...4 Feb 1841
...JESSE SHELEY (LS), Wit: JASPER SAWYER, GEORGE SAWYER. Lexington Dist.: Proven by
GEORGE SAWYER, 8 Sept 1841.

Pp. 378-379: S. C.: 27 Aug 1841...mortgage of 140 A...JESSE WESSINGER stands indebted to
JOHN MEETZE, for $310 on three notes of hand bearing date as above, for
$110 each...for $2, tract of 140 A on Roofs branch, waters of Saluda adj. lands held by
RAMICK ROOF and formerly EDDINGS...JESSE WESSINGER (LS), JOHN MEETZE (LS), Wit: H. J.
CAUGHMAN, C. BOUKNIGHT. Proven by H. J. CAUGHMAN, 8 Sept 1841 before JOHN FOX, Clk. Rec.
8 Sept 1841. Delivered to C. BOUKNIGHT, 4 Oct 1842.

Pp. 379-380: S. C., DAVID RAMICK of Lexington Dist, for $30 pd. by JOHN RAMICK of same...
50 A, part of a large survey originally granted to HENRY P. HAMPTON, conveyed
from JOHN BYNUM to HENRY MILLER and from MILLER to LEONARD BOUGH, thence to DAVID RAMICK,
on 12 Mile Creek, waters of Saluda River adj. JOHN GREGORY, DAVID RAMICK, GEORGE SOUTER...
18 July 1833...DAVID RAMICK (LS), Wit: COLLY SOUTER, JOSEPH SOUTER (X). Proven by COLLY
SOUTER, 6 Sept 1841, before A. H. FORT. Rec. 9 Sept 1841. Delivered to A. H. FORT, Exqr.

Pp. 380-382: S. C., Lexington Dist.: JOHN RAMICK of Lexington Dist., for $35 pd. by SUSAN-
NAH SEASTRUNK...50 A[same land in preceding deed]...27 Apr 1836...JOHN
RAMICK (X) (LS), Wit: M. SEASTRUNK, LUKE SEATRUNK (X). Proven by LUKE SEASTRUNK who
testified to his and MANUEL SEATRUNK's signatures, 6 Sept 1841. MRS. SARAH RAMICK, wife
of JOHN, relinquished dower 7 Sept 1841. Rec. 9 Sept 1841. Delivered to A. H. FORT, 8 May
1844.

Pp. 382-383: S. C., LUKE SEASTRUNK of Lexington Dist., for $20 pd. by SUSANNAH SEATRUNK
of same...I relinquish all my claim in the real estate of my deceased
Father HENRY SEASTRUNK, who departed this life intestate, being possessed of a tract of
land, 50 A on Twelve Mile Creek, waters of Saluda River, adj. land of GEORGE LEAPHART
and others which decends[sic] to myself, Mother and Sisters, heirs and law and tenants
in common which tenancy has not been severed...6 Sept 1841...LUKE SEASTRUNK (X) (LS), Wit:
COLLY SOUTER, WILLIAM FORT. Proven by COLLY SOUTER, before A. H. FORT, 6 Sept 1841.
MRS. MARY SEASTRUNK, wife of LUKE, relinquished dower 6 Sept 1841. Rec. 9 Sept 1841.
Delivered to A. H. FORT, ESQR., 8 May 1844.

Pp. 383-384: S. C.: JACOB HALLMAN "of the South side of Saluda River in Lexington District"
for $107 pd. by THOS K. POINDEXTER of same state and Dist...500 A on waters
of Twelve Mile Creek on Red Bank Creek, part of a tract granted to STEPHEN BONE and JACOB
HALLMAN for 1000 A, 1815...Nov. 1819...JACOB HALLMAN Juner (LS), Wit: JNO. WITHERS, WM.
SEE. Proven by JOHN WITHERS, 8 Dec 1819, before JAMES KENNERLY, J. P. ELIZABETH HALLMAN,
wife of sd. JACOB, relinquished dower 4 Jan 1820, before WEST CAUGHMAN.

Page 385: S. C., BENJAMIN JEFCOAT JR. of Lexington Dist., for $186 pd. by SAMPSON KING
and BARBARA OSWALT of same...248 A on Glaziers branch, waters of N Edsito River
adj. to land of heirs of LEARD, PETER NELSON, FREDERICK LIVINGSTON, DAVID WILLIAMS, BEN-
JAMIN JEFCOAT, and BENJAMIN JEFCOAT SENR...5 Mar 1839...BENJAMIN JEFCOAT JR (LS), Wit:
DAVID KING, ELIJAH JEFCOAT. Proven by DAVID KING, 6 Apr 1841. Rec. 4 Oct 1841.

Page 386: S. C., Lexington Dist.: HENRY McDANIEL of Lex. Dist., for $787 pd. by JAMES
JUMPER of same...212 A on Little Hollow Creek, waters of Saluda, adj. WILLIAM
HONOLD, GEORGE CRAPS, JAMES JUMPER, ISHIAL[?] ANDERSON...9 Mar 1840...HENRY MCDANIEL (+)
(LS), Wit: THOS K. POINDEXTER, JOHIAL ANDERSON. Proven by THOS K. POINDEXTER, 4 Oct 1841.
Rec. 4 Oct 1841.

Pp. 387-388: S. C., BENJAMIN F.TAYLOR, Executor of the Estate of ROBERT STARK, Esq., Decd
of Richland District, for $1000 pd. by JOHN D. A. MURPHY of Orangeburgh Dist.
...3 tracts: 1000 A on Red bank Creek adj. WM WILLIAMS Run of Spring Branch, on lands
granted to MAJ. JOHN HAMPTON & JOHN BYNUM on land of BERLEY GILBERT, vacant land and on

on the run of Big Black Creek, surveyed for R. STARK 10 Oct 1793, also another tract of 780 A in Lexington District bounded by the run of Lightwood Creek, lands of R. STARK, J. THOS FAIRCHILD, and BURGESS, surveyed for R. STARK 19 Aug 1793, and granted 2 June 1817 to sd. STARK, also another tract of 39,380 A on N Edisto River adj. land of JOHN HAMPTON, JOHN BYNUM, J. THOS FAIRCHILD...1 Mar 1834... BEN. F. TAYLOR (LS), Exor of ROBERT STARK, Wit: BENJAMIN HART, THOS. CAMPBELL. Richland Dist.: Proven by THOMAS CAMPBELL, 3 Mar 1834 before BENJ. RAWL, Q. U. Rec. 5 Oct 1841. Delivered to L. BOOZER, Esq., 1 Nov 1841.

Pp. 388-390: WILLIAM L. MILLER, Sheriff of Lex. Dist...by virtue of a writ of fiere facias issued out of the Court of Common Pleas held for Dist..of Lexington tested= 12 Nov 1839 at the suit of JAMES S. GUIGNARD on goods of JOHN G. TAYLOR to levy $63.75 ...375 A adj. land of WM. YALOR, JACOB SWYGERT, A. BERRIS[?], & SMITH, purchased by JAMES S. GUIGNARD of Richland Dist, for $75...WM. L. MILLER (LS), Dated 20 Sept 1841. Wit: JNO. W. BRADLEY, JAS. D. COOGLER, Richland Dist.: Proven by JOHN W. BRADLEY. MRS. ELIZA ANN MARY TAYLOR, wife of JOHN G. TAYLOR, relinquished dower in Richland Dist before A. FITCH, Magistrate. Rec. 6 Oct 1841. Delivered to COL. H. GREGG, 31 May 1842.

Pp. 390-392: S. C., GERHARD MULLER & MARY MULLER (husband and wife) of Lexington Dist., for $4500 pd. by MRS. MARY ANN GEIGER for JACOB W. GEIGER and LAVINIA GEIGER heirs with MARY MULLER of WILLIAM GEIGER decd of Lexington Dist...1/3 part of a tract on Congaree River containing 370 A conveyed to WM. GEIGER JR. by THOMAS JOS. HOWELL, on 30 Sept 1813 for $1100...1/3 of a tract of 218 A represented on the plat by Nos. 1, 2, & 3 executed by JOHN SIGHTLER on 25 & 26 Mar 1829 at the request of LEWIS POU for the heirs of WILLIAM GEIGER ESQR...also 1/3 part of 288 A made up of tracts marker Nos. 1, 2, 3, 4, 5, & 6 on the 6, 7, 8, & 9th days of April 1829 by JOHN SIGHTLER ...also 1/3 part of tract containing 47 A originally granted to GEORGE WISINHUNT now the Estates of GEIGER & KERSHO a plat executed upon a resurvey of WM. BAKERS land by request of his Heirs and JAS. HOP-KINS, JAS. ADAMS, & GEORGE BUTLER, commissioners S. H. BOYKIN, D. S. on 23 Dec 1829, both tracts together 387 8/10 A consisting of partly high lands and swamp lands...25 June 1839 ...GERHARD MULLER (LS), MARY MULLER (LS), Wit: LEW. POU, DAVID BERNHARD, HENRY MULLER. Proven by LEWIS POU 9 Oct 1841. MRS. MARY MULLER relinquished dower18 July 1839. Rec. 9 Oct 1841. Delivered to WM. BAKER by the hand of DR. CAUGHMAN, 1 Jan 1842.

Pp. 392-393: JACOB LITES of Lexington District, for natural love and affection to my son JOSEPH LITES and also for $1...land on Rocky Creek, waters of Saluda, adj. lands of JACOB RALL, WILLIAM GARTMAN, CALEB LITES, the Heirs of WILLIAM HENDRIX decd, and the said JACOB LITES...plat executed by WILLIAM QUATTLEBUM, Deputy Surveyor, 9 & 16 Apr 1836, 124 A...4 Mar 1841...JACOB LITES (L) (LS), Wit: DAVID KYZAR, JOSHUA KYZAR, Proven by JOSHUA KYZAR 9 Oct 1841 before JOHN FOX, Clk. Rec. 9 Oct 1841. Plat included showing aforementioned property, originally surveyed for MICHAEL OSWALT 2 Mar 1773 for 150 A.

Pp. 394-395: S. C., Lexington Dist., 18 Aug 1841, JACOB LITES to GASPER ELLISER...sd. LITES stands indebted to sd. ELLISER for $712...200 A on Saluda River adj. to sd. ELLISER, the widow HENDRIX, the widow CORLEY, HENRY MEETZ...JACOB LITES (L) (LS), Wit: HENRY MEETZE, JONATHAN HARMAN. Proven by HENRY MEETZE, 16 Oct 1841, before JOHN FOX. Rec. 16 Oct 1841. Delivered to GASPER ELISER 6 Dec 1841.

Pp. 395-397: REUBEN HARMAN and SAMUEL LOWMAN of Lexington Dist., for $200 pd. by DAVID WILSON of same...115 A adj. JOHN ROOF SENR., DAVID WILSON, Est. of CAUTY[?] and KENSLER...originally granted to NICHOLAS BONEY 11 Aug 1774...REUBEN HARMAN (LS), SAMUEL LOWMAN (LS), Wit: HENRY A. MEETZE, JOHN WILSON. Proven by JOHN WILSON before L. BOOZER, 20 Sept 1841. SUSAN A. E. LOWMAN, wife of SAMUEL, relinquished dower 20 Sept 1841. LOUISA HARMAN, wife of REUBEN, relinquished dower, 20 Sept 1841. Rec. 16 Oct 1841. Delivered to DAVID WILSON, 20 Dec 1841.

Pp. 397-398: EMANUEL GEIGER of Lexington Dist., for $500 pd. by RIGNAL O. WILLIAMS, 172 A on S side Saluda River on head of Twenty mile branch, adj. lands of JOSEPH CORLEY, SAMUEL P. CAUGHMAN, N. W. by JOHN SCHNIDER, JACOB KAMINER, RIGNAL O. WILLIAMS, HENRY MEETZE....11 Oct 1841...EMANUEL GEIGER (LS), Wit: LEVI WILLIAMS, WILLIAM L. MILLER. Proven by WILLIAM L. MILLER 11 Oct 1841 before JOHN FOX. MRS. POLLY GEIGER, wife of EMANUEL GEIGER, relinquished dower, 21 Oct 1841.

Pp. 399-400: S. C.: JOSEPH J. CORLEY of Lexington Dist., for $450 pd. by HENRY H. SEAY of same...60 A on 18 mile Creek, waters of Saluda River adj. THOS. K. POINDEXTER, GEORGE ROBERTS, JACOB HARNIS, NATHANIEL KLECKLEY...20 Oct 1841...JOSEPH J. CORLEY (LS), Wit: EMANUEL GEIGER, ADAM SMITH. Proven by ADAM SMITH, 20 Oct 1841. MRS. SUSANNAH CORLEY, wife of JOSEPH J. CORLEY, relinquished dower 21 Oct 1841, before JOHN FOX. Rec. 21 Oct 1841. Delivered to HENRY H. SEAY, 22 Oct 1842.

Pp. 400-402: State of S. C.: JACOB W. GEIGER, LEVINIA GEIGER, DR. GERHARD MILLER & wife
MARY GEIGER, HENRY MULLER & wf ELIZABETH GEIGER in Lexington Dist., for
$750 pd. by WILLIAM BAKER of Lexington Dist...150 A granted 27 Jan 1770 to JOHN JACOB
GEIGER...also another tract of 100 A granted 13 Oct 1767 to JACOB GEIGER...___ 1841...
JACOB W. GEIGER (LS), LAVINIA GEIGER (L)S, GERHARD MULLER, MARY MULLER (LS), HENRY MULLER
SR., ANN E. MULLER (LS), Wit: LEW POU, DAVID BERNHARD. Proven by DAVID BERNHARD, 3 Oct
1841. Ann E. & MARY MULLER relinquished dowers 23 Oct 1841, before JOHN FOX. Rec. 23
Oct 1841. Delivered to WM. BAKER by the hand of DR. CAUGHMAN 1 Jan 1842.

Pp. 402-405: 6 May 1835, MARY ARTHUR of Lexington Dist., to J. D. SHARP, C. A. MOODY,
JAMES CAYCE, C. A. GRAESER, DANIEL SHULL, CONRAD SHULL, JOHN SHULL, HENRY
SHULL, and DANIEL MORGAN, Trustees of the Methodist Episcopal Church, for $1...4 acres
on NE side Mill Creek...MARY ARTHUR (LS), Wit: KIZIAH ARTHUR, J. H. MORGAN. Proven by
JOSEPH H. MORGAN, 30 Sept 1841, before EDWARD J. ARTHUR, Magistrate. Rec. 25 Oct 1841.
Delivered to JAMES BELL per order of DANIEL MORGAN 24 Dec 1841.

Pp. 405-407: By virtue of a writ of fiere facias issued out of the Court of Common Pleas
for Lexington Dist., tested 19 Mar 1841 at the suit of HENRY GALLMAN to levy
$739 on the lands and tenaments of G. M. FULMER...271 A adj. lands now held by JOHN H.
FULMER, IVY DANSBY, GEORGE M. SUMMERS & others...purchased by HENRY GALLMAN, for $400...
WM. L. MILLER (LS), S. L. D. Wit: JACOB GAUNTT, REUBEN HARMAN. Proven by REUBEN HARMAN,
29 Oct 1841. Deed made same date. Delivered to COL. WM. COUNTZ, Feb. 8, 1842.

Pp. 407-409: S. C., Lexington Dist.: THOS L. VEALE of Lexington Dist., for love and affection to son in law JACOB K. GAUNTT and my daughter PRISCILLA GAUNTT his wife
...2 3/4 A near Spring Hill on the road from Columbia to Newberry Court House adj. lands
of THOS VEALE, plat executed by WM FORT, D. S., 3 Nov...3 Nov 1840...THOS L. VEALE (LS),
Wit: ELI FRESHLEY, HENRY ELEAZAR. Proven on 5 Nov 1841 by HENRY ELEAZER before JOHN FOX.
Plat Surveyed 8 Oct 1841, included in deed. Rec. 5 Nov 1841. Delivered to DR. J. K.
GAUNTT, Feby 14, 1843.

Pp. 409-410: S. C., Lexington Dist., ELIZABETH M. COLEMAN for$500 pd. by JOHN P. BLEWER...
700 A adj. PETER READHIMER, L. D. JOHNSON, Edisto River...ELIZABETH M.
COLEMAN (LS), Wit: CHARLES GRANDY, A. H. COLEMAN. Proven by CHARLES GRANDY 13 Nov 1841,
before PETER READHIMER, J. P. Deed dated 4 Nov 1841. Rec. 15 Nov 1841. Inclosed in a
letter to MESSRS. COOK & BLEWER of Charleston as per JOHN P. BLEWERS letter filed 9 Feb
1842.

Pp. 410-411: S. C., Lexington Dist., ELIZABETH M. COLEMAN for $1500 pd. by JOHN P. BLEWER
...1/2 of tract of 2240 A with my remaining one half of my Claims in the Saw
Mill on Rocky Cpring Creek, South Edisto River adj. JOHN P. CULLUM JOHN JOHNSON, DAVID
COOK, & L. D. JOHNSON...4 Nov 1841...ELIZABETH M. COLEMAN (LS), Wit: CHARLES GRANDY, A. H.
COLEMAN. Proven by GRANDY, 13 Nov 1841 before PETER READHIMER, J. P. Rec. 15 Nov 184-

Pp. 412-413: S. C., Lexington Dist. Whereas DAVID SHEALEY, one of the Heirs and Distributees of JOHN SHEALEY SENR, decd, filed a petition in the Court of Ordinary
of Lexington Dist., against CHRISTENER SHEALEY, JOHN SHEALEY & others, Heirs of sd. JOHN
SHEALEY, decd, on 27 July 1841 stating that the sd. JOHN SHEALEY SENR died Intestate leaving a tract which has not been partitioned...to be sold on 27Oct 1841...DAVID SHEALEY was
the highest bidder, $1005...220 A on Road from Columbia to Augusta adj. lands of ELIAS
BOUKNIGHT, WILLIAM MABUS, DAVID SHEALEY, DANIEL RAMBO...18 Nov 1841...WM. L. MILLER (LS),
S. L. D. Wit: JOHN HOOK, ELIAS BOUKNIGHT. Proven by JOHN HOOK, 18 NOv 1841. Rec. 18 Nov
1841. Delivered to DAVID SHEALEY, 17 Jan 1842.

Pp. 414-415: S. C., JOHN METZE of Lexington Dist., for $600 pd. by CHRISTIAN B. THUMMELL
of same...2 1/2 A on S side of Augusta Road extending from Road to Branch,
the run of which branch is the Line adj. HENRY HENDRIX, lot in the East, by WEST CAUGHMANs
lot, in the Village of Lexington...26 Mar 1841...JOHN METZE (LS), Wit: WEST CAUGHMAN, C.
BOUKNIGHT. Proven by CALEB BOUKNIGHT, 18 Nov 1841 before JOHN FOX. NANCY MEETZE (X), wife
of JOHN, relinquished dower before LEMUEL BOOZER, 27 Mar 1841. Rec. 18 Nov 1841. Delivered
to C. B. THUMMELL, 12 Mar 1842.

Pp. 415-417: S. C., GEORGE CAUGHMAN of Lexington Dist., for $290 pd. by WILLIAM SEE of
same...106 A on Beach Creek, waters of Saluda River, South Side, adj. JEROME
BONAPARTE, WILLIAM ERVIN SEE, JACOB KYZER, JEFCOAT SEE, HILLIARD SEE, GEORGE CAUGHMAN,
MARGARET WINGARD, part of a tract granted to ANDREW SPENCE, plat made by GEORGE P. DRAFTS,
D. S....12 Oct 1841...GEORGE CAUGHMAN (LS), Wit: ISAIAH CAUGHMAN, H. I. CAUGHMAN. Proven
by H. J. CAUGHMAN, 12 Nov 1841. MRS. NANCY CAUGHMAN, wife of GEORGE, relinquished dower
20 Nov 1841, before JOHN FOX. Plat included dated 27 Augt 1841. Delivered to WM. SEE, 10
Jan 1842. Rec. 20 Nov 1841.

Pp. 417-418: S. C. Lexington Dist.: JOHN FOX, Clerk and Magistrate in and for Dist. afore-
        said, do hereby certify MRS. CATHERINE SEE, wife of WILLIAM SEE, relinquished
dower to GEORGE CAUGHMAN...20 Nov 1841. CATHARINE SEE (+). Rec. 20 Nov 1841. Delivered
to GEO. CAUGHMAN, Feb. 15, 1845.

Pp. 418-420: S. C.: 4 Jan 1841, LAMBERT J. JONES, Esq. of Court of Equity for Newberry
        Dist., to DAVID AMICK ofthe other part...whereas JACOB LONG & others on or
about 11 May 1840 died exhibit their Bill of complaint in the Court of Equity in Newberry
against WILLIAM RABI & wife and others setting forth that FREDERICK JOS. WALLERN died
in the year 1818 possessed in his own right in fee of three tracts of land which yet
remain to be distributed...sell to DAVID AMICK for $150...328 A in Lexington Dist, on
wateree, a branch of Saluda, land adj. GASPER AMIGH, ADAM FULMER, JOHN SHEALEY, JANETT
WIGGERS and others...L. J. JONES (LS), C. E. N. D. Wit: JOHN S. CARWILE, WILLIAM RISH.
Newberry Dist.: Proven by WM. RISH, before P. DICKERT, J. Q. Rec. 6 Dec 1841. Delivered
to DAVID AMICK, Jan 2, 1843.

Pp. 420-422: S. C., Lexington Dist.: Whereas PETER BARLEY, one of the heirs and distribut-
        ees of MICHAEL CHARLES decd, filed a petition in the Court of Ordinary for
Lex. Dist., against JOHN CHARLES, JOHN BERLEY & wife & others, on ____ 1841, stating that
the said MICHAEL CHARLES died intestate, leaving a tract that has not been partitioned...
on 3 Aug 1841, ARTHUR H. FORT, Ordy. ordered that the sd. land be sold on 1st Monday in
____ 1841...purchased by JOHN METZ JR., for $145...250 A in the Fork of Broad and Saluda
adj. lands of COL. SUMMER & others...WM. L. MILLER (LS), S. L. D. Wit: ANDERSON STEADMAN,
JOHN HOOK. Proven by JOHN HOOK, 6 Dec 1841. Rec. 6 Dec 1841. Delivered Jan 27 to JOHN
MEETZE JR., by WM. L. MILLER, Shff.

Pp. 422-423: S. C., Lexington Dist.: PHILLIP GRUBS of Lex. Dist., for $35 pd. by JAMES COOK,
        70 A on waters of N Edisto adj. ZEB GANT, ISRAEL GANT, Estate land of
R. STARK, decd and JOHN M. FELDER....PHILLIP GRUBS (X), Wit: JACOB HOWELL, HIRAM GAUNTT.
Deed dated 13 Feb 1836. Proven by JOHN J. HOWELL, 10 Dec 1841. Rec. 10 Dec 1841. Deliv-
ered to DAVS AUSTIN, March 3, 1845.

Pp. 423-425: S. C.: CHRISTIAN KUNKLE of Lexington Dist., for $600 pd. by HENRY MILLER...
        108 A part of land surveyed for ADAM RICE, and left by will of MAJ. WILLIAM
SUMMER to MICHAEL SUMMER, in Lexington Dist., on a branch of the wateree Creek, waters of
Broad River adj. ANDREW KUNKLE, MICHAEL SUMMER, WM. EPTING, JOHN SULTON...20 Nov 1841...
CHRISTIAN KUNKLE (LS), Wit: ANDREW SHEALEY, P. DICKERT. ELIZA P. KUNKLE (+), WIFE of
CHRISTIAN KUNKLE, relinquished dower 20 Nov 1841, before PETER DICKERT, Magt. for Newberry
Dist. Newberry Dist.: Proven by ANDW. SHEELY, 20 Nov 1841, before P. DICKERT. Plat in-
cluded in deed made 7 Aug 1841, by P. DICKERT, D. S. Rec. 14 Dec 1841. Delivered to
HENRY MILLER 9 Nov 1842.

Pp. 425-426:S.C., Lexington Dist.: JESSE SWIGARD for $400 pd. by JOHN KOON,...101 1/2 A
        part of 200 A surveyed for JOHN RALL 2 Apr 1773 in Lexington Dist., in the
fork of Broad and Saluda, adj. JAMES KENNERLY, the remaining part of the old survey...14
Oct 1830...JESSE SWIGARD (LS), Wit: HENRY KOON, DANIEL DREHR. Proven by HENRY KOON,
1st Aug 1835 before SAMUEL BOUKNIGHT, Q. U. MRS. SALLY SWYGERT, wife of JESSE, relinquished
dower 1 Aug 1835 before SAMUEL BOUKNIGHT, Q. U. Rec. 15 Dec 1841.

Pp. 426-427: S. C., JOHN KOON of Lexington Dist., for $1100 pd. by SAMUEL HUFFMAN of
        same...101 1/2 A, part of 200 A surveyed for JOHN RALL [same land in preced-
ing deed], adj. land held at present by DAVID NUNNAMAKER, HENRY KOON, SAMUEL HUFFMAN...
Plat rec. in Registry of Mesne Conveyance Office for sd. Dist., in Book H, pp. 55, 56,
57...15 Dec 1841...JOHN KOON (+) (LS), Wit: H. J. CAUGHMAN, HENRY A. MEETZE. Proven by
HENRY A. MEETZE, 15 Dec 1841, before JOHN FOX, Clk. Rec. 15 Dec 1841. Delivered to
SAML. HUFFMAN, 18 Mar 1842.

Pp. 428-430: S. C., Lexington Dist.: KIZIAH HAYS for affection to my son JAMES W. T. HAYES
        & NOANA [?] ANN HAYES hiw wife & their child and for $5...I release unto
HENRY FRAZIER in trust, a tract of 135 A on Big & Little Hollow Creeks adj. ABSALOM HEN-
DRIX, DANIEL LEAPHART, other lands of sd. KIZIAH HAYES, lands formerly belonging to JAMES
HAYES, decd, & land of HENRY FRAZIER...KEZIA HAYES (+) (LS), Wit: E. A. AUSTIN, HENRY
EARGLE. S. C. Lexington Dist.: Proven by ELIJAH A. AUSTIN before JOHN FOX, 18 Dec 1841.
Deed dated 27 Nov 1841. Plat included in deed, made 4 Sept 1841. Rec. 18 Dec 1841.
Delivered to HENRY FRAZIER 13 Aug 1842.

Pp. 430-432: S. C.: JOHN CRAPPS of Lexington Dist., for $441 pd by GEORGE CRAPPS of same...
        196 A, a part of three different tracts on a Branch called Kettle Branch,
waters of Congaree River adj. lands of JOHN CRAPPS, Est. of WILLIAM GEIGER, DAVID KAIGLER,
Est. of WILLIAM FITZPATRICK, JOHN CRAPPS...6 Mar 1822...JOHN CRAPS (LS), Wit: D. KAIGLER

B. KAIGLER,"reacknowledge Dec. 16 184_ in presence of GEORGE CRAPS (+), JACOB DRAFTS."
Proven by JACOB DRAFTS & G. CRAPS, 16 Dec 1841, before A. H. FORT, Q. U. MRS. CATHERINE
CRAPS, wife of JOHN, relinquished dower 16 Dec 1841. Rec. 18 Dec 1841. Delivered to
GEORGE CRAPS, 24 Jan 1842. Plat included in deed; GEORGE CRAPS & JOHN J. CRAPS, chain
carriers, "on head of Rooty branch", made 10 Nov 1841, by NATHAN C. D. CULCALSURE, Dept.
Sur. Rec. 18 Dec 1841. Delivered to GEORGE CRAPS, 24 Jan 1842.

Pp. 432-434: S. C., JOHN CRAPS SENR of Lexington Dist., for $50 pd. by GEORGE CRAPS of
          same,...30 A, the west part of a tract granted to sd JOHNCRAPS 3 Sept 1798,
for 67 A, near the State Road on which the sd. GEORGE CRAPS now resides, resurveyed 18
Jan 1837...___ Dec 1841...JOHN CRAPS (LS), Wit: JACOB DRAFTS, GEORGE CRAPS (X). Proven
by both wit, 16 Dec 1841, before A. H. FORT. MRS. CATHARINE CRAPS relinquished dower, 16
Dec 1841. Plat included in deed; chain carriers, JOHN C. GEIGER, GEORGE CRAPS, and
LEWIS POU BLAZER., JOHN SIGHTLER, D. S. Rec. 18 Dec 1841. Delivered to GEORGE CRAPS,
24 Jan 1842. Plat shows adj. lands "land granted to CHRISTOPHER SLAGLE the 13th May 1773,
the widow SLAGLE, land granted 7th Feb. 1791 AND. KAIGLER, Land granted to JACOB SEIBLE,
the 6th December 1790 for 91 acres, The widow GEIGER, DAVID KAIGLER, JOHN C. GEIGER,
HENRY SEIBLES.

Pp. 435-436: S. C., SAMUEL PERCIVAL of Town of Columbia, Richland District, for $5000,
          pd. by DR. WILLIAM F. PERCIVAL of Lexington Dist...one undivided third part
of all my lands in Dist. of Lex, a plantation on the Congaree River & Creek about 2086 A
as conveyed to me by DR. JAMES H. TAYLOR by deed bearing date 17 Jan 1838, Rec. in Lex.
Dist., Book L, pp. 290-291, 27 Oct 1838...22 July 1841...S. PERCIVAL (LS), Wit: THEO. U.
PERCIVAL, E. S. PERCIVAL. Proven by THEO M. PERCIVAL 18 Dec 1841 before A. FITCH, Magistrate. Rec. 21 Dec 1841.

Pp. 436-437: S. C.: ALEXANDER S. CUMMALANDER of lex. Dist., for $260 pd. by GEORGE COMMA-
          LANDER of same...64 A granted 7 Jan 1805 in the Fork of Broad and Saluda Riv-
ers adj. MICHAEL WHEALER, GEORGE HALTIWANGER, MICHAEL FAUR, LAZARUS MILLER, GEORGE PRICE
...4 Jan 1841...ALEXANDER S. COMMALANDER (+), Wit: ROBERT C. BOYD, JOHN LEWIS (X). Proven
by ROBERT C. BOYD 4 Jan 1841, before LEVI METZ, Q. U. MRS. MARY A. COMMELANDER, wife of
ALEXANDER, relinquished dower 5 Jan 1841, before LEVI METZ. Rec. 1 Nov 1841. Delivered to
GEO. COMMALANDER, 30 Sept 1842. "The reason the the date does not correspond with the
date of the preceding record is that the paper was misplaced."

Pp. 438-439: S. C., WILLIAM RAWL of Lexington Dist., for $1050 pd. by SAMUEL RAWL of
          same...224 A on S side Saluda River on branches of Beaver dam Creek, waters
of Saluda River adj. lands of SAMUEL RAWL, WILLIAM GARTMAN, JOSEPH LITES, URIAH HENDRIX,
HENRY HENDRIX, WILLIAM L. MILLER, & JOHN LOWN, being the SE corner of a 680 A grant to
GEORGE GARTMAN 6 Nov 1786...3 Jan 1842...WM. RAWL (LS), Wit: DANIEL LEAPHART, FREDERICK
SEAS. Proven by DANIEL LEAPHART, 3 Jan 1842 before JOHN FOX, Clerk. Rec. 3 Jan 1842.
Delivered to SAML RAWL, 2 Feb 1842.

Pp. 439-440: S. C., Lexington Dist.: JOHN W. HALLMAN, for $150 pd. by JESSE HALLMAN...
          45 A on big and little Horse Creek of Hollow Creek, waters of Saluda adj.
JACOB DRAFTS, JOHN MEETZE, JACOB TAYLOR, JOHN W. HALLMAN...26 Sept 1835...JOHN W. HALLMAN
(LS), Wit: JACOB TAYLOR, WM. QUATTLEBUM. Proven by JACOB TAYLOR, 19 July 1840 before,
GEORGE SAWYER Me. Rec. 3 Jan 1842. Delivered to JESSE HALLMAN, 7 Mar 1842.

Pp. 440-441.: S. C.: ELI SNELGROVE of Green County, Alabama, for $10 pd. by JESSE HALLMAN
          of Lexington Dist., S. C....all interest in three tracts of land, being the
residue of the Real Estate of JOHN SNELGROVE decd,late of sd. dist...26 Feb 1841...ELI
SNELGROVE (LS), Wit: WM. FORT, NOAH HALLMAN. Proven by NOAH HALLMAN, 19 July 1841, before
GEORGE SAWYER, Me. Rec. 3 Jan 1842. Delivered to JESSE HALLMAN 7 Mar 1842.

Pp. 441-442: S. C., Lexington Dist.: ELIJAH GAUNTT to ELI GAUNTT, 18 8/10 A for [Amt. not
          stated]...part of a tract granted to JOSEPH SUMMERS in 1786...5 June 1836...
ELIJAH GAUNTT (LS), Wit: WILLIAM GUNTER, ZILPHA GUNTER. Proven by WILLIAM GUNTER 12 Nov
1836 before JACOB GAUNTT, J. P. Rec. 3 Jan 1842. Delivered to GILPIN GUNTER 7 Feb 1842.

Pp. 442-443: S. C., Lexington Dist.: JOHN GANTT for $100 pd. by ELI GAUNTT...260 A surv.
          for BANKS GUNTER 16 May 1816, granted 14 Dec 1820 adj. JACOB GANTT, REUBEN
STEEDMAN, JOHN W. LEWIS, ELIJAH GANTT, & sd. ELI GANTT...7 Dec 1839...JOHN GANTT, Wit:
BENJAMIN GUNTER, ELIJAH GANTT. Proven by BENJAMIN GUNTER, 12 Feb 1840, before ANDERSON
STEEDMAN. Rec. 3 Jan 1842. Delivered to GILPIN GUNTER, 7 Feb 1842.

Pp. 443-444: S. C., JACOB K. GANTT of Lexington Dist., for $50 pd. by HIMRI GANTT & URIAH
          GANTT of same...203 A originally granted to JACOB GANTT, part of a tract
granted to sd. JACOB GANTT for 1000 A conveyed to ISRAEL GANTT then to J. K. GANTT, JOSEPH

GANTT and myself adj. JOHN A. SALLEY, ZEBULON GANTT, ISRAEL GANTT SR., JACOB GANTT, N Edisto River at mouth of Chalk Hill Creek...2 Nov 1841...JACOB K. GANT (LS), Wit: WM. FORT, EMANUEL GEIGER. Proven by WILLIAM FORT, 3 Jan 1842 before JOHN FOX. Rec. 3 Jan 1842. Delivered to GILPIN GUNTER 7 Feb 1842.

Pp. 444-445: S. C., ISOM HOWARD of Lexington Dist., for $636 pd by JOHN HOWARD...485 A on W side Lightwood Creek, waters of North Edisto River adj. lands of SARAH HOWARD, and land where WILLIAM HALL now lives, WILLIAM HOWARD, ...4 July 1840... ISOM HOWARD (LS), Wit: H. B. KNOX, JOHN KNOX. Proven by HUGH B. KNOX 9 Nov 1840 before NATHANIEL JONES, J. P. Rec. 3 Jan 1842. Delivered to MICHAEL HOWARD, 2 Jan 1852.

Pp. 446-447: S. C.: By virtue of a writ of fiere facias issued out of the Court of Common Pleas for Lex. Dist, tested 17 Apr 1841 at the suit of ZEDEKIAH WATKINS Admr. & NANCY CORDER Admx. to me directed to levy $29 from goods and chattels of ELISHA JONES...374 A adj. lands now held by WM. E. SAWYER, JOHN H. JONES & ELISHA JONES...purchased by ELIAS TAYLOR who ordered me to Execute titles to WM. GASTON for $50...7 Jan 1842...WM. L. MILLER (LS), Wit: ISAIAH CAUGHMAN, ALLEN SEE. Proven by DR. ISAIAH CAUGHMAN, 8 Jan 1842, before JOHN FOX, Clk. Rec. 8 Jan 1842. Delivered to WILLIAM GASTON 22 Dec 1842.

Pp. 447-448: S. C., WILLIAM RUCKER of Lexington Dist, for $350 pd by ANN JEMIMA NEESE[?] of same, planter,...280 A two separate tract, one originally granted to ANDREW BARINER 5 Sept 1771 for 150 A, but by resurvey 202 A vacant on all sides at time of original survey, but now adj. to JOHN CULLER, GEORGE KAIGLER, PETER JUMPER...the other tract granted to CONRAD JUMPER 21 Aug 1798 for 78 A adj. PETER JUMPER, CHARLES BENEKER, ANDREW KAIGLER, HENRY PATRICK, JOHN REPSTONE[?], also 25 A, part of a tract granted to GEORGE PERKET __ Aug 1774 for 200 A on a branch of Sandys new Creek now called Bryer Branch adj. DAVID JUMPERS, now J. & G. KAIGLERs lands...total 305 A...28 Oct 1841... WILLIAM RUCKER (LS), Wit: DAVID BERNHART, JNO. C. GEIGER. Proven by DAVID BERNHARD, 8 Jan 1842. Delivered to J. C. KAIGLER 11 Oct 1845.

Pp. 449-450:S. C.: Lexington Dist.: CHARLES PENCE for $300 pd. by THOS SHULER...240 A part as it was supposed, one half of a tract, granted to PHILLIP PENCE in 1787, conveyed by sd. PHILLIP PENCE to sd. CHARLES PENCE by deed 29 Jan 1794 in the fork of Broad and Saluda adj. THOMAS SHULER, GEORGE LIKES, GEORGE LORICK, ...26 Oct 1827... CHARLES PENCE (+) (LS), Wit: PETER METZ, JOHN A. WINGARD, Proven by JOHN A. WINGARD, 29 Dec 1827 before JACOB NUNAMAKER, J. P. Rec. 17 Jan 1842. Delivered to JOHN S. SHULER, 10 June 1843.

Pp. 450-451: S. C., Lexington Dist.: ELIZABETH ROBERTS for $266 pd. by MOSES S. ROBERTS and ISAIAH ROBERTS...44 A on Hollow Creek, waters of Big Saluda River, part of a tract granted to HENRY WEAVER SEIGNIOR[sic] and sd. ELIZABETH ROBERTS purchased it from CHRISTIAN D. AUSTIN...20 Aug 1841...ELIZABETH ROBERTS (X) (LS), Wit: SIBEY ROBERTS. Proven by C. D. AUSTIN, 4 Nov 1841. Rec. 17 Jan 1842. Delivered to ISAIAH ROBERTS, 18 Mar 1842.

Pp. 451-452: S. C., JAMES RANKIN of Lexington Dist., for $100 pd. by HENRY HALL...100 A, part of land granted to FRANCIS DAVIS, on long branch and the Charleston Road, part of tract conveyed by FRANCIS DAVIS to JESSE ALTMAN, from ALTMAN to HENRY SENTERFEIT, from SENTERFIET to WALTER GANTT, from GANTT, to JAMES RANKIN, adj. ISOM HOWARD, WILLIAM HOWARD, JAMES RANKIN...1 Jan 1842...JAMES P. RANKIN (LS), Wit: EMANUEL QUATTLEBUM, LEWIS JONES JR. Proven by E. QUATTLEBUM, 1 Jan 1842, before ANDERSON STEEDMAN. Rec. 17 Jan 1842. Delivered to ELIJAH HALL, 7 Aug 1843.

Pp. 452-454: S. C., DANIEL S. RUSSELL of Lexington Dist., for $950 pd. by JOHN WHITES of same...47 A near Spring Hill, on the Road from Columbia to Newberry Court House, on a branch of Wateree Creek, waters of Broad River, plat made 4 Jan 1842...20 Jan 1842...D. S. RUSSELL (LS), Wit: JACOB WINGARD, FREDERICK WISE. Proven by JACOB WISE, 20 Jan 1842, before L. BOOZER, Magt. Plat included showing T. S. VEAL, "Church land," Frog Level Road, Charleston Road, H. ELEAZER. [Church land in Spring Hill Baptist Church.] Rec. 20 Jan 1842. Delivered to JOHN WHITES, 29 Jan 1848.

Pp. 454-455: S. C., Lexington Dist.: ADAM BUGG for $610 pd. by JESSE METZ...195 A adj. lands of GEORGE LORICK, CHRISTIAN WEED, JESSE METZ, JOHN NICHOLS, THOMAS SHULER....____ 1839...ADAM BUFF (LS), Wit: JESSE COOGLER, JOHN COOGLER. Proven by JESSE COOGLER, 31 Dec 1839. Rec. 24 Jan 1842. Delivered to JESSE METZ, 31 May 1844.

Pp. 455-456: JAMES WILSON of Lexington Dist., for $119 pd. by WM. HALTIWANGER of same... 60 A in the Dutch Fork on a small branch of the Wateree Creek, originally granted to GEORGE ADDY & by sundry legal transfers became the property of the present grantor...13 Jan 1842...JAS. WILSON (LS), Wit: HENRY W. ELEAZER, JOHN CHAPMAN. Proven by ELEAZER, 24 Jan 1842. Rec. 24 Jan 1842. Delivered to WM. HALTIWANGER, 12 Mar 1842.

Pp. 456-457: S. C., Lexington Dist.: WILLIAM ANDERSON SUMMER for $500 pd. by JOHN G.
KESLER, both of Lex....150 A on head branches of Bear Creek, waters of Saluda River adj. old place belonging to GEORGE H. CHAPMAN, ANDREW KUNKLE, HENRY SHEALY, & SD. JOHN G. KESLER, CONRAD FARR...11 Feb 1841...WM. A. SUMMER (LS), Wit: GEORGE M. FULMER, GEORGE M. SUMMER. Proven by GEORGE M. SUMMER, 10 Mar 1841. Rec. 25 Jan 1842. Delivered to GEORGE CHAPMAN, 7 Mar 1842.

Pp. 457-458: JESSE SHEALEY of Lex. to DAVID TIKES of same, for $162...86 A on branches of
Big Rockey Creek, waters of Saluda...30 Dec 1841...JESSE SHELEY (LS), Wit: SHADRACK VANSANT, JASPER SAWYER. Proven by JASPER SAWYER, 25 Jan 1842 before GEORGE SAWYER, Me. SABRA SHEALEY, wife of JESSE, relinquished dower 25 Jan 1842. Rec. 31 Jan 1842.

Pp. 459-460: S. C....By virtue of a writ of fieri facias issued out of the Court of
Common Pleas for Lex. Dist. tested 16 Apr 1841 at the suit of JAMES S. GUINGARD to levy sum of $643 of lands and tenements of J. J. B. WHITE...15 A on S side Broad River known as the paper mill place, lately occupied by WHITE BRICKELL & WHITE adj. Broad River, Estate of A. B. STARK, JACOB HUFFMAN...sold to sd. JAMES S. GUIGNARD... 20 Sept 1841...WM. L. MILLER (LS), S. L. D. Wit: JNO. W. BRADLEY, JAS. D. COOGLER. Richland Dist.; Proven by JOHN W. BRADLEY 20 Sept 1841 before EDWD. J. ARTHUR, Magistrate Rec. 31 Jan 1842. Delivered to JOHN LORICK, 12 Apr 1842.

Pp. 460-461: S. C., JAMES S. GUIGNARD of Town of Columbia, for $1000 pd. by JACOB HUFFMAN
of Lexington Dist....15 A on Broad River adj. Est. of ALEXANDER B. STACK... 24 Jan 1842...JAMES S. GUIGNARD (LS), Wit: ROBERT MILLER, ROBERT P. MAYRANT. Richland Dist.: Proven by MAYRANT before E. J. ARTHUR, Magistrate., 24 Jan 1842. Rec. 31 Jan 1842. Delivered to JOHN LORICK, 12 Apr 1842.

Pp. 461-463: S. C....By virtue of three writs of fiere facias issued out of the Court of
common Pleas held for Lex. Dist, tested 18 Apr 1840 at the suit of D.J. EWART, & W. R. HARMAN & CO & MEETZE & BOUKNIGHT vs WALTER GAUNTT to levy $75.85... 763 A in Lex. Dist on Chinquepin, waters of North Edisto River adj. JAMES WEST or WINNs land, STEEDMAN & others...3 Feb 1842...WM. L. MILLER (LS), S. L. D. Wit: HENRY A. MEETZE, H. J. CAUGHMAN. Proven by HENRY A. MEETZE, 4 Feb 1842 before JOHN FOX. Rec. 4 Feb 1842. Delivered to DANIEL RAMBO, 2 Mar 1842.

Pp. 463-464: S. C. JEREMIAH HOOK of Lex. Dist., for $700 to me pd. by GASPER ELISER of
Lex. Dist, planter...150 A on Beach Creek, waters of Saluda River originally granted to JAMES SPENCE 13 May 1768, conveyed by his widow ELIZABETH SPENCE to ARCHIBALD GLASGOW 4 Nov 1797, and became part of the real estate of WM. P. RIDDLE decd, & sold by his heirs to HENRY MEETZE, sold by MEETZE to JEREMIAH HOOK adj. lands of GEORGE GARTMAN, ANDREW CAUGHMAN, MICHAEL BEAR, JACOB KYZER...20 Jan 1842...JEREMIAH HOOK (LS), Wit: GEORGE GARTMAN, ANDREW CAUGHMAN, HENRY MEETZE. Proven by ANDREW CAUGHMAN 5 Feb 1842 before JOHN FOX.. MRS. ELIZABETH HOOK, wife of JEREMIAH, relinquished dower 29 Jan 1842. Rec. 5 Feb 1842. Delivered to GASPER ELLISER, 26 Feb 1842.

Pp. 464-466: S. C., Lexington Dist.: GASPER ELLISER for love & affection to my daughter
MARY ANN CALK, wife of JAMES HILLIARD CALK, and for $5 I have sold unto GEORGE GARTMAN in trust, 150 A on Beach Creek, waters of Saluda River [same land in preceding deed]...2 Feb 1842...GASPER ELLISER (LS), Wit: FREDERICK HARMAN, DAVID J. FRIDEL, JOHN RALL. Proven by FREDERICK HARMAN, 5 Feb 1842. Rec. 5 Feb 1842. Delivered to GASPER ELLISER, 26 Feb 1842.

Pp. 466-467: S. C.: H. H. COUNTS of Fairfield Dist., for $1331 pd. by WM CHAPMAN of New-
berry Dist...242 A , part of a tract originally granted to HENRY RUFF and transferred to the present grantor HENRY HARRISON COUNTS by L. W. & T. of sd. HENRY RUFF adj. lands of WM. SWETENBURG, JOHN SUMMER, GEO. CHAPMAN, GEO. ELESOR...25 Jan 1839...H. H. COUNTS (LS), Wit: WM. COUNTS, HENRY GALLMAN. Proven by HENRY GALLMAN, 5 Feb 1842 before GEORGE M. FULMER, Magistrate. MARY ANN COUNTS, wife of H. H., relinquished dower 13 Feb 1839 before JACOB FEASTER, Q. U. Rec. 7 Feb 1842.

Pp. 468-469: S. C., Lexington Dist.: THOMAS DERRICK for $600 pd. by SAMUEL DERRICK...
184 A on Big Rocky Creek, waters of Saluda River, part of a tract originally granted to THOMAS A. GREEN for 379 A 23 Nov 1835...10 May 1841...THOMAS DERRICK (+), Wit: CATHERINE SAWYER, DAVID WINCHELL. Proven by DAVID WINCHELL 10 May 1841 before GEORGE SAWYER Me, Rec. 7 Feb 1842. Delivered to SAML DERRICK 4 Mar 1842.

Pp. 469-470: S. C. Lexington Dist.: ELIJAH STONE of Edgefield Dist., for $32 pd. by JOHN
THRAILKILL of Edgefield Dist...40 A granted to EDWARD MEADOW, conveyed by him
to JAMES JOHNSON 2 Nov 1804, & by sd. JAMES JOHNSON to JOHN STONE 21 Nov 1804, and by sd.
JOHN STONE to ELIJAH STONE 16 Oct 1824...between land whereon JAMES ORTREY now lives, part
of the same tract near JOHN STONE Spring Branch...8 Mar 1836...ELIJAH STONE (X) (LS), Wit:
DANIEL WILLIS, FRANCIS THRAILKILL. Lex. Dist.: Proven by DANIEL WILLIS, before NATHL
JONES, J. P. 8 Mar 1836. ELIZABETH STONE, wife of ELIJAH, relinquished dower 8 Mar "in the
60th year of the Independence of the U. S. of A." Rec. 7 Feb 1842. Delivered to WM. REY-
NOLDS.

Pp. 470-471: S. C., Lexington Dist.: DANIEL GUNTER for the valuable consideration of the
liberty and privilege of drowning or raising waters on the lands of JOHN A. SALLY in the
head of the Mill pond on marrow bond Creek...priviledge of raising a dam and cutting a
canal...20 July 1838. DANIEL GUNTER (LS), Wit: SIDNEY M. DAVIS, WM. B. JONES. Proven by
WM. B. JONES, 1 Aug 1840 before SIDNEY M. DAVIS, Q. U. Delivered to JOSEPH C. FANNING,
30 Dec 1842.

Pp. 471-472: S. C., Lexington Dist.: DANIEL GUNTER for $800 pd. by JOHN A. SALLY...several
tracts of land, one granted to WADSWORTH, 250 A, one granted to BALAAM GUNTER
450 A; one granted to RIVERS GUNTER, 630 A, and one called the DENT tract of 500 A, and
one called the JACKSON tract of 86 A...lands formerly belonging to the estate of BALAAM
GUNTER...1 Aug 1840...DANIEL GUNTER (LS), Wit: SIDNEY M. DAVIS, WM. B. JONES. Proven by
WM. B. JONES 1 Aug 1840 before SIDNEY M. DAVIS. Rec. 7 Feb 1842. Delivered to JOSEPH C.
FANNING, 30 Dec 1842.

Pp. 473-474: S. C.: STEPHEN SENTERFIT of Lexington Dist. for $257 pd. by URIAH CROUT &
JOHN FOX of Lexington Dist...289 A on branches of Marlow and waters of Light-
wood Creek adj. ANDREW SHEALEY SR., THOMAS FOX, DANIEL LOWERMAN, JAMES BODIE, estate of
JOHN W. LEE decd, part of a tract originally granted to FRANCIS DAVIS for 432 A 14 Feb
1810...2 Dec 1841...STEPHEN SENTERFIT (LS), Wit" JACOB VANSANT, ISAIAH VANSANT. Proven by
ISAIAH VANSANT, 4 Feb 1842. Rec. 9 Feb 1842.

Page 474: S. C., JOHN CROUT SR of Lexington Dist., for natural love and affection to son
URIAH CROUT of same...negro woman Matilda about 24 years old...2 Oct 1841...
JOHN CROUT (X) (LS), Wit: HENRY J. DRAFTS, WILLIAM BRYSON. Proven by WM. BRYSON, 22 Oct
1841 before ISAAC VANSANT, Magt. Rec. 9 Feb 1842.

Pp. 475-476: S. C.: JOHN K. JOHNSTON of Lexington Dist., for $250 pd. by A. H. FORT, ESQR.
of same...100 A on which my dwelling house now Stands lying in the fork of
Rocky Creek and a small granch, adj. HENRY JACKSONS land...also one tract of 100 A on
Chinquepin Creek, adj. lands of HANNAH DAILY, HENRY JACKSON & mill tract...also the mill
tract of 2500 A on both sides of Cinquipin Creek adj. THOMAS QUATTLEBUM, JESSE FOX, ISRAEL
GAUNT, DRURY FREEMAN, & others...25 Sept 1841...JNO K. JOHNSTON (LS), Wit:JOHN FOX, JESSE
FOX. Proven by JOHN FOX, 14 Feb 1842 before L. BOOZER, Magt. Rec. 14 Feb 1842.
Delivered to A. H. FORT, ESQR., 30 Mar 1846.

Pp. 476-477: S. C., Lexington Dist.: Whereas CATHARINE ADDY, JACOB ADDY & others the heirs
and distributees of JOHN S. ADDY SENR, decd, filed a petition in the Court of
Ordinary for Lex. Dist., against GEORGE ADDY, 20 Dec 1841...land to be sold by Sheriff...
JOHN FOX became the purchaser of 186 A, adj. THOMAS K. POINDESTER, JOHIAL[?] ANDERSON &
others...21 Feb 1842... WM. L. MILLER (LS), S. L. D. Lex. Dist.:Proven by LEROY HENDRIX
who swore to his and EPHRAIGM CORLEYs signatures, 21 Feb 1842. Rec. 21 Feb 1842.

Page 478: S. C., Lexington Dist.: GEORGE HOLMAN, farmer, for $100 pd. by JOHN HOLMAN,
both of Dist. aforesd....41 A on branches of Big Hollow Creek, waters of Saluda
River adj. WIDOW RISH, GEORGE RISH, CHRISTIAN SWIGARD, WIDOW HOLMAN, ADAM RISH...2 Feb
1814...GEORGE HOLMAN, MARY HOLMAN (X), Wit: ASEL R. ABLE, JOSEPH HOLMAN (/). Proven by
ASEL. R. ABLE, 26 May 1814, before DRURY FORT, J. Q. Rec. 21 Feb 1842.

Pp. 479-480: S. C., Lexington Dist.: Whereas KATHARINE ADDY, JACOB ADDY & others, heirs and
distributees of JOHN S. ADDY, decd, filed a petition in the Court of Ordinary
for Lex. Dist against GEORGE ADDY, on 20 Dec 1841...JOHN S. ADDY SR. died intestate leaving
several parcels of land...41 A sold to URIAH CROUT, the highest bidder, $288, adj. lands
of SAMUEL DERICK, CHRISTIAN GABLE, & others...19 Feb 1842...WILLIAM L. MILLER (SL), S. L. D.
Wit: EPHRAIM CORLEY, LEROY HENDRIX. Proven by LEROY HENDRIX, 21 Feb 1842.

Pp. 480-481: State of Georgia, Macon County: SARAH BERRY of Macon Co., Ga., for $50 pd. by
ANDREW BERRY...398 A in Lex. Dist on or near Black Creek adj. lands now held
by JOHN M. FELDER, ADAM TAYLOR, JOSHUA TAYLOR...25 Jan 1842. SARAH BERRY (X) (LS), Wit:
Wit: ELISHA LEE, DANIEL A. CLARK, SILAS A. STOKES, J. P. Proven by ELISHA LEE, 9 Feb 1842

before JACOB SWYGERT, Magistrate.SARAH BERRY, wife of JOHN BERRY, relinquished dower 21 Jan 1842. Rec. 25 Feb 1842.

Page 482: State of Mississippi, Atally County: ANDREW BERRY of Mississippi and co. aforesaid, for $230 pd by RACHEL BARBARA TAYLOR & LEWANNA TAYLOR of S. C....398 A
being a part of 3 adj. tracts in Lex. Dist, near waters of Black Creek, one of the tracts
containing 860 A granted to MICHAEL SEE, 30 Sept 1807; one tract of 123 A granted to
MICHAEL HYDE, 16 June 1791 adj. MICHAEL SEE, the other 306 A, granted to JOHN BERRY,
24 June 1822...13 Jan 1842...ANDREW BERRY (X) (LS), Wit: ELISHA LEE, JAMES H. TAYLOR.
Lex. Dist.: Proven by ELISHA LEE, 9 Feb 1842 before JACOB SWYGERT. Delivered to JOSHUA
TAYLOR, 11 Apr 1842.

Pp. 483-484: S. C.: 23 Oct 1841, JESSE CORLEY to JOEL CORLEY & DAVID BOOZER...whereas
JESSE CORLEY stands indebted to sd. JOEL CORLEY & DAVID BOOZER, in the
sum of $165.89 and interest on said sum on two notes dated 30 July 1841...mortgage of
50 A adj. lands of THOS RALL, SAMUEL CORLEY, DAVID BOOZER, on twelve mile creek of
Saluda River...JESSE CORLEY (LS), DAVID BOOZER, (LS), JOEL CORLEY (LS), Wit: JOHN C.
LYBRAND, H. J. CAUGHMAN. Proven by H. J. CAUGHMAN, 26 Feb 1842. Rec. 26 Feb 1842.
Delivered to DAVID BOOZER, 14 Feb 1847.

Pp. 484-486: S. C.: 20 Oct 1841, JOHN H. JONES of Lexington Dist, to FOX MILLER & Co.
otherwise called JOHN FOX, WM. L. MILLER, HENRY HENDRIX, & LEROY HENDRIX
& CROUT & FOX, otherwise called U. CROUT & J. FOX, all of Dist. aforesd....mortgage for
two notes one dayed 25 Mar 1840 the other 1 Jan 1840...485 A on Mill Creek, waters of
Chinquepin Creek, whereon I now live, adj. lands of LORENZO D. BORAN, DRURY FREEMAN,
ZEBULON GANTT, RICH & GUNTER, HANNAH DAILY, ELISHA JONES...JOHN K. JONES (LS), Wit:
W. H. FOX, WM. HENDRIX. Proven by W. H. FOX, 8 Feb 1842, before J. H. COUNTS, Magt.
Rec. 28 Feb 1842.

Pp. 486-487: S. C. Lexington Dist.: JOHN G. KESLER for $500 pd. by DAVID McCARTHA of
state of dist. aforesd....150 A on head branches of Bear Creek, waters of
Saluda River adj. GEORGE H. CHAPMAN, ANDREW KUNKLE, HARY[?] SHEALY, and sd. KESLER...19
Mar 1841...JOHN G. KESLER (LS), Wit: GEORGE M. FULMER, GEORGE M. SUMER. Proven by G. M.
FULMER & GEORGE M. SUMMER. HARRIET KESSLER, wife of J. G., relinquished dower 24 Mar
1841. Rec. 28 Feb 1842. Delivered to DAVID McCARTHY, 1 Aug 1842.

Pp. 487-489: S. C., Lexington Dist.: JOHN QUATTLEBUM for $150 pd. by WILLIAM HALLMAN...
209 A on waters of Cinquepin Creek, granted to WILLIAM HOLSTON in 1793,
adj. sd. HOLSTONs line, SENTERFIT, EIFFORD...9 Feb 1837...JOHN QUATTLEBUM (LS), Wit:
MICHL LIVINGSTON, JOSEPH QUATTLEBUM,; Proven by MICHAEL LIVINGSTON, 7 Aug 1837. METER
QUATTLEBUM, wife of JOHN, relinquished dower 29 Mar 1838, except for 1/2 A, of and
burial ground of THOS BURKET, decd including the same...before WILLIAM QUATTLEBUM, Q.
U. Rec. 1 Mard1842. Delivered to WM. HALLMAN, 20 June 1842.

Pp. 489-490: S. C.: GEORGE MABUS of Lexington Dist., for $500 pd. by SAMUEL BOUKNIGHT of
Lexington Dist...257 A on the main road from Columbia to Augusta on waters
of lick creek and lightwood creek adj. D. RAMBO, DRURY FORT, JOHN SHEALY, part of an
original survey laid out of JOSEPH DILL, for 1000 A supposed to be 500 A surveyed & laid
off by THOS CARGILL for JOHN P. BONDS on 14 July 1807...GEORGE MABUS, dated 4 Oct 1841.
Wit: ANDREW SHEALY, JAMES C. BODIE. proven by ANDREW SHEALY, 27 Oct 1841. PRISCILLA
MABUS (X), wife of GEORGE, relinquished dower 27 Oct 1841. Rec. 7 Mar 1842. Delivered
to SAMUEL BOUKNIGHT, 21 June 1842.

Pp. 490-491: S. C.: DAVID SHEALY of Lexington Dist., for $300 pd. by CHRISTENE SHEALY
[CHRISTIAN?]...60 A on the public road from Columbia to Augusta...DAVID
SHEALY (LS), Wit: JOHN K. JOHNSTON, ELIAS BOUKNIGHT. Prove by ELIAS BOUKNIGHT, 10
Mar 1842. Deed dated 11 Nov 1841. Rec.10 Mar 1842. Delivered to ELIAS BOUKNIGHT, 4
May 1842.

Pp. 491-492: S. C.: JOHN FOX of Lexington Dist., for $80 pd by EPHRAIM EDINS of same...
100 A near the head waters of Congaree Creek adj. lands held by sd. EDINS,
MRS. LOUISA EDINS, JOHN MEETZE, CALEB BOUKNIGHT...originally granted to JOHN LEWELLEN for
75 A, the other granted to JONATHAN TAYLOR for 590 A...10 Mar 1842...JOHN FOX (LS), Wit:
W. H. FOX, JOHN HOOK. Proven by W. H. FOX, before L. BOOZER. Rec. 10 Mar 1842. Delivered
to EPH. EDDINS 2 Jan 1842.

Pp. 493-494: S. C., Lexington Dist.: SAMUEL T. LORICK, planter, for $1500 pd. by GEORGE
LORICK of same...200 A granted to JACOB TARRER in 1767, 40 A granted to SAM-
UEL FLEMING in 1802, & part of 150 A granted to SAMUEL FLEMING in 1808, 9 A granted to
DANIEL BOUKNIGHT, all on waters of Saluda adj. DANIEL DREHER, JOHN SHULER, JOHN MATHIAS

JOHN MEETZE...1 Sept 1838...SAMUEL T. LORICK (LS), Wit: JOHN S. SWYGERT, G. WASHINGTON
LORICK. Proven by WASHINGTON LORICK, 19 Feb 1842. M. ANA LORICK, wife of SAMUEL, relin-
quished dower 14 Mar 1842. Sigend MARGARET ANN LORICK. Rec. 14 Mar 1842. Delivered to
SAML LYKES, 11 Apr 1842.

Pp. 494-495: S. C., 15 May 1841, SAMUEL SOX of Lexington Dist. to JACOB H. BOOZER for $325
     ...mortgage of 275 A on six mile Creek adj. SCHULL, KINSLER, MICHAEL WESS-
INGER, being the tract conveyed to SAMUEL SOX on 23 Feb 1833 by JAMES S. GUIGNARD...SAMUEL
SOX (LS), Wit: ROBERT MILLER, JOHN W. BRADLY. Richland Dist.: Proven by JOHN W. BRADLY,
15 May 1841 before JAMES S. GUIGNARD, Clk Court. Rec. 19 Mar 1842.

Pp. 496-498: S. C. Lexington Dist.: LEWIS METZ & wf SARAH, for $206 pd. by JOHN MEETZE of
     same...100 A which was measured off to BRAZER in Lexington Dist., formerly
Orangeburgh Dist., on six mile creek, waters of Congaree Creek, also on the main road
from Augusta to Granby and Columbia, originally granted to MICHAEL LEITNER 300 A, conveyed
by deed of Release 29 Nov 1802 from CHRISTIAN LEITNER, the son & heir of the grantee, to
WM BRAZEL, conveyed from BRAZEL to JOHN HARMAN, 10 Mar 1804, and by JAMES POU, Esqr.
Sheriff pursuant to an order of Court in partition at the suit of THOS RALL & wf against L.
HARMAN & others, 1 May 1815, conveyed from THOMAS RALL 26 May 1817 to JONAS MATHIAS, and
by the heirs of JONAS MATHIAS to sd. LEWIS METZ, by deed 18 July 1835...15 Mar 1842...
LEWIS METZ (LS), SARAH METZ (X) (LS), Wit: REUBEN HARMAN, ADAM BUFF. Proven by ADAM
BUFF, 15 Mar 1842. SARAH METZ relinquished dower 24 Mar 1842, before REUBEN HARMAN, Magt.
Rec. 25 Mar 1842. Delivered to C. BOUKNIGHT 4 Oct 1842.

Pp. 498-499: S. C., Lexington Dist.: WILLIAM BRYSON of Lex. Dist., for $200 pd. by URIAH
     CROUT of same...land on which I now live, 62 A on Hollow Creek, waters of
Saluda River adj. CHRISTIAN GABLE, SAMUEL DERRICK, KATHARINE ADDY, & others...7 Mar 1842
...WILLIAM BRYSON (LS), Wit: JESSE HOOK, R. H. BRYSON. Proven by JESSE HOOK, 9 Mar 1842,
before ISAAC VANSANT, L. D. JEMIMA BRYSON (X), wife of WILLIAM, relinquished dower 9
Mar 1842. Rec. 25 Mar 1842.

Pp. 499-500: S. C., Lexington Dist.: LEWALLEN NEESE to AMOS SPEARS, 47 A for $9.40...
     part of tract granted to JOHN REDMAN, of 1000 A on Bull swamp waters of
North Edisto, the north end of the land tract, divided by survey, containing 301 A,
deeded to sd. LEWALLEN NEESE, and now sold 47 A, plat surveyed for sd. SPEARS, 30 Jan
1841, by JOHN SIGHTLER, surveyor...8 Feb 1841...LEWALLEN NEESE (LS), Wit: HARBERD SPIRES,
HENRY NEESE. Proven by HARBERD SPIRES JNR., 5 Aug 1841, before JOHN WILLIAMS, Magt.
Rec. 26 Mar 1842. Delivered to HERBERD SPIRES 10 Nov 1842.

Pp. 500-501: S. C., Lexington Dist.: LEWALLEN NEESE to HENRY NEESE, 125 A for $50...
     land on Bull Swamp, waters of N Edisto River, part of tract of 1000A...
surveyed made by BENJAMIN BUSBY, Surv....granted to JOHN REDMAN...25 Feb 1841...LEWALLEN
NEESE (LS), Wit: AMOS SPIRES (X) (LS), ABRAHAM NEESE (LS), Proven by AMOS SPIARS, 25 Mar
1842, before ELIJAH JEFCOAT, Magt. Rec. 26 Mar 1842. Delivered to JACOB NEESE JR., 23
Aug 1844.

Pp. 501-505: S. C.: JOEL LOWMAN, MICHAEL LOWMAN, CATHARINE LOWMAN, JESSE LOWMAN, DAVID
     LOWMAN, MARY HOYLER, JOHN SEAS, CHRISRENA SEAS, SAMUEL LOWMAN, JACOB LOWMAN,
JOHN LOWMAN & DANIEL LOWMAN of Lexington Dist, heirs and distributees of GEORGE LOWMAN
of Lex., for $944 pd. by ISAIAH LOWMAN of same...all title and interest in Real Estate
of sd. GEO. LOWMAN, decd...4 separate tracts on N side Saluda, CATHERINE LOWMAN, widow of
GEO....3 Jan 1842...JOEL LOWMAN (LS), JESSE LOWMAN (LS), MICHAEL LOWMAN (X) (LS), DAVID
LOWMAN (LS), MARY HOYLER (+), JOHN SEAS (LS), CHRISTENA B. SEAS (X) (LS), CATHARINE LOWMAN
(+) (LS), SAMUEL LOWMAN (LS),JACOB LOWMAN (LS), JOHANNAS LOWMAN (LS), DANIEL LOWMAN (LS)
Wit: DAVID UNGER, JACOB BICKLEY JUNR. Proven by JACOB BICKLEY 26 Feb 1842 before LEVI
METZ, Magistrate. NANCY LOWMAN, wife of DANIEL, relinquished dower, 3 Mar 1842. SALLY A.
LOWMAN, wife of JACOB, relinquished dower, 4 Mar 1842. CHRISTINA LOWMAN, wife of JOHN,
relinquished dower 5 Mar 1842. CHRISTENA B. SEESE, wife of JOHN, relinquished dower, 5
Mar 1842. JEMIMA LOWMAN, wife of MICHAEL, relinquished dower 5 Mar 1842. ELIZABETH LOW-
MAN, wife of DAVID, relinquished dower 5 Mar 1842. SUSAN E. LOWMAN, wife of SAMUEL, re-
linquished dower 28 Mar 1842. Rec. 28 Mar 1842.

Pp. 506-507: State of Georgia, Jackson Co.: MARY BOYD, GEORGE DRISKELL, NOAH DRISKELL,
GRAY MASON, JAMES BOYD, BERTLEY BOYD, JOHN BOYD, & SARAH BOYD of Jackson Co., for $112
pd. by NATHANIEL W. BUSBY and LEWIS BUSBY of Lex. Dist., S. C....27 A on Hollensheads Creek,
adj. JOHN ROISTER, JOHN ELLISER, Heirs of ADAM SEIGLER, Heirs of JOHN HENRY RUFF, HENRY
METZ, JONES, DANIEL CHAPMAN...19 Feb 1842...JAMES BOYD (LS), For self and others. Wit:
LOVICK G. BUSBY, SUSANNAH BUSBY. Proven by LOVICK G. BUSBY, 27 Feb 1842. Delivered to
NATHL. W. BUSBY, 20 Oct 1845. Rec. 28 Mar 1842.

Pp. 507-510: S. C.: ESAIAH SAYLOR of Lexington Dist., for $8000 pd. by HENRY SEIBLES of
same...845 A on W side Congaree River, part of 4 tracts, to wit, lands
granted to ROBERT WRIGHT, WILLIAM BUSTHE, WILLIAM TUCKER, & WILLIAM TUCKER as the plats
annexed will show made by A. B. STARK, and more recently by JOHN SIGHTLER, also my house
tract of 24 A, part of a grant to WILLIAM TAYLOR on the State Road leading from Columbia
to Charleston...8 Jan 1839...ESAIAS SAYLOR (LS), Wit: LEW POU, JOHN C. GEIGER, Proven by
JOHN C. GEIGER, 4 Apr 1842 before JOHN FOX, Rec. 4 Apr 1842. Delivered to WM. BAKER, 4
July 1842. Plats included in deed showing adj. lands of ROACH, DANIEL HUFEMAN, H. MULLER,
"At the request of Dr. J. T. Roach, ...part of a tract originally granted to WILLIAM
TAYLOR, 6 Oct 1806 for 777 A on Sandy Run Creek,waters of Congaree, 30 Mar 1830., N. C. D.
CULCLASURE, D. S. Rec. 4 Apr 1842. Another large plat showing "land granted to JOHN
BARRISFORD, 14 Feb 1735," "Roads to BELL HALL" "Corner in HAIGS pond" "GEORGE KAIGLER".
" part of 4 tracts, part of one granted to ROBERT WRIGHT JR., 13 July 1737...570 A, part
of a tract granted to WILLIAM TUCKER 4 July 1769....Surveyed 28 & 29 Dec 1838....Chain
carriers, SAMUEL RUCKER, WILLIAM SMITH, JOHN G. WISE, WILLIAM ASSENAR[?], & SAMUEL CORBIN,
& Negroes Barton & Jack blazers., JOHN SIGHTLER, D. S.

Pp. 510-511: ELIZABETH LEWEY of Lexington Dist., for $100 pd. by WM. LANGFORD JR. of
same...34 1/2 A, part of a tract of 74 A by a resurvey made by JOHN W. SEAY,
D. S., 11 Jan 1831 on S side of Big Saluda River on Caney branch adj. sd. LEWEY & ASA
LANGFORD...14 Dec 1841...ELIZABETH LEWEY (X) (LS), Wit: GEORGE A. LEWEY, BUD C. MATHEWS.
Proven by GEORGE A. LEWEY, 4 Apr 1842. Rec. 4 Apr 1842. Delivered to WM. HENDRIX, 1 Dec
1845.

Pp. 511-512: S. C., ASA LANGFORD of Lexington Dist., for $339 pd by WILLIAM LANGFORD of
same...84 3/4 A on S side Saluda River, on both sides Caney Branch...____
1841...ASA LANGFORD (LS), Wit: STANMORE LANGFORD, GEORGE A. LEWEY. Proven by GEORGE A.
LEWEY, 4 Apr 1842. Rec. 4 Apr 1842.

Pp. 513-514: ____ 4 Apr 1842, HENRY H. SEAY to FREDERICK GARMAN and HENRY MEETZE SR.,...
whereas HENRY H. SEAY stands indebted to sd. GARTMAN and MEETZE...mortgage
of 60 A on 18 mile Creek adj. GEORGE ROBERTS, NATHANIEL KLECKLEY, JACOB HARMAN...HENRY
H. SEAY (+) (SEAL), FREDERIC GARTMAN (LS), HENRY MEETZE (LS), Wit: REUBEN HARMAN, FREDERIC
HARMAN. Proven by FREDERICK HARMAN, 5 Apr 1842. Rec. 6 Apr 1842. Delivered 14 May 1842
to F. GARTMAN.

Pp. 514-515: S. C., ISSACHAR H.GANTT of Lexington Dist., for $50 pd. by HEMRI GANTT &
URIAH H. GANTT of same...203 A, part of a tract granted to sd. JACOB GAUNTT,
for 1000 A, and conveyed by JACOB GANTT & ISRAEL GAUNTT SR. to myself, JOSEPH GANTT &
JACOB K. GANTT, adj. land of JOHN A. SALLEY, ZABULON GANTT, ISRAEL GANTT SR., & JACOB
GANT, N Edisto River, and on the mouth of Chalkhill Creek...24 Nov 1841...ISSACHAR H.
GAUNTT (LS), Wit: JOSEPH GANTT, CLEMENT JACKSON. Rec. 4 Apr 1842.

Pp. 516-520: [pp. 516-7 are GENERAL HENRY ARTHURS PLAT]. S. C., SARAH TAYLOR of Town of
Columbia, District of Richland, for $3211...586 A on S side Congaree Creek
adj. to plantation now owned by NANCY CAROLINE and KEZIAH ARTHUR, DR. SAMUEL PERCIVAL...
____ 1842...SARAH TAYLOR (LS), Wit: ALEXR. R. TAYLOR, G. H. HALL. Proven by GEORGE A. HALL
15 Feb 1842, before EDWD. J. ARTHUR, Magistrate.
Know all men by these presents that the President and Directors of the Bank of the
State of South Carolina for $2500...586 A...10 Mar 1835, rec. in Mesne Conveyance Office
for Richland District, Book O, pp. 202-203, 14 Mar 1842., Wit: C. M. FURMAN, C. S. Sims,
F. H. ELMORE (LS), President. Rec. 11 Apr 1842. Delivered to GEN. H. ARTHUR, 11 June
1842.

Pp. 520-522: S. C.: JOSEPH FRESHLEY of Lexington Dist., for $134 pd. by GEORGE WHITES
of same...21 1/2 A on W side Broad River adj. to lands of my own & sd.
WHITES, part of 2 tracts, a small portion of a tract purchased by me from THOS. L. VEALE
and part of a tract purchased by me from THOS. BOYD, Surv. 10 May 1837, by T. FREAM, D. S.,
for 45 9/10 A, plat made by WM. FORT, D. S. 6 Jan 1842...8 Jan 1842...JOSEPH FRESHLEY (LS),
Wit" HENRY ELEAZER, WILLIAM WHITES. Proven by HENRY ELEAZER, 15 Jan 1842 before GEORGE
M. FULMER, Magt. PATSEY FRESHLEY, wife of JOSEPH, relinquished dower, 21 Jan 1842. Rec.
11 Apr 1842. Delivered to GEO. WHITES, 2 Oct 1843.

Pp. 522-523: S. C., HENRY GRUBS, planter, of Lexington Dist., for $200 pd. by JOHN OTT,
planter, of same...300 A granted to HARMAN SIGHTLER 2 Aug 1830, conveyed by
him to DANIEL SENN 22 Jan 1831, $40...on the head Spring of Cedar Creek, waters of N
Edisto River, adj. HAMBLETON SPIRES, and GRUBS which is a part of the same tract granted
to CONRAD NEESE, adj. NICHOLAS COLEMAN, RISTER, granted to EVIN HOWARD, now MICHAEL WISE
...14 Feb 1842...HENRY GRUBS (LS), Wit ARTIMUS GRUBS, JANE BERRY. Proven by ARTIMUS
GRUBS, 14 Feb 1842, before JOHN WILLIAMS, Magt. Rec. 11 Apr 1842. Delivered to JOHN OTT,

Pp. 524-525: S. C. Lexington Dist.: JOHN V. SAWYER of Dist. aforesd., for $1600 pd. by
JOHN P. CULLUM, WILLIS TONEY & SAMUEL WINGARD, all of same...three negroes
[named]...bond entered into by the sd. JOHN V. SAWYER to JAMES TERRY, Comr. in Equity for
Edgefield District, as guardian to STANDMAN B. SAWYER & HEZEKIAH SAWYER, minors...13 Apr
1842...JOHN V. SAWYER (LS), Wit: JNO. C. LYBRAND, JAMES M. JONES. Proven by LYBRAND, 18
Apr 1842, before ISAAC VANSANT, Magt. Rec. 18 Apr 1842. Delivered to SAMUEL WINGARD, 28
Mar 1843.

Pp. 525-526: S. C.: Whereas by virtue of a writ of fiere facias issued out of the Court of
Common Pleas, held for District of Lexington Dist., tested 17 Apr 1841, at
the suit of JAMES WILSON commanding me to levy $28 from goods and chattles of E. S. CUMA-
LANDER...sold for $20, 60 A adj. SIMEON MILLER, CATHARINE WHEELER, & others...6 Dec 1841
...WM. L. MILLER (LS), S. L. D. Wit: JOHN HOOK, J. R. MILLER. Proven by JOSEPH R. MILLER,
13 Apr 1842 before JOHN FOX. Rec. 13 Apr 1842. Delivered to JAMES WILSON 23 June 1842.

Pp. 526-527: S. C., Lexington Dist.: WILLIAM LYBRAND for $200 pd. by LEWIS LYBRAND...66 A
on S side Saluda, on waters of Big Hollow Creek adj. WILLIAM FRAZIER decd.,
Heirs of AQUILLA FRAZIER decd, KATHARINE GARTMAN, DANIEL LEAPHART...1 Jan 1842...WM.
LYBRAND (LS), Wit: SAMUEL LEWIE, AR. HENDRIX. Proven by SAMUEL LEWIE, 26 Feb 1842,
before GEORGE SAWYER, Magistrate. Rec. 14 Apr 1842. Delivered to LEWIS LYBRAND, 3 Oct
1842.

Pp. 527-528: S. C., Lexington Dist.: SIMEON RIDLEHOOVER for $1000 pd. by ADAM RISH SENR...
601 A on Hogpen Branch, waters of North Edisto adj. JOHN DENTS, JAMES CRIM,
REUBEN HALLMAN, JACOB FULMER, A. H. FORT...11 Dec 1839...SIMEON RIDLEHOOVER (LS), Wit:
GEORGE SAWYER, NATHAN WILLIAMSON. Proven by NATHAN WILLIAMSON, 11 Dec 1839 before HENRY
A. SMITH, Q. U. MARY RIDLEHOOVER(+), Wife of SIMEON, relinquished dower 11 Dec 1839. Rec.
19 Apr 1842.

Pp. 529-530: S. C., BENJAMIN C. BUSBY of Lexington Dist., for $532 pd. by JOHN EPTING JR.,
of same...land on W side Columbia Road adj. A. STOUDEMIRE, BENJ. C. BUSBY, WM.
BRIGHT, CRUMPTON, MRS. STOUDEMIRE, plat made by WM. B. ELKIN, 28 Sept 1836...12 Nov 1841
... B. C. BUSBY (LS), Wit: JOHN SUMMER, JAMES A. SUMMER, Proven by JOHN SUMMER, 13 Nov
1841. EVE BUSBY, wife of BENJAMIN C., relinquished dower 13 Nov 1841., before GEORGE W.
FULMER. Rec. 26 Apr 1842. Delivered to JACOB SWYGERT, 7 Sept 1846.

Pp. 530-531: S. C., Lexington Dist., JOHN W. SHEALY of Lex., for $500 pd. by ADAM
SHEALEY JR...100 A on waters of Saluda, Stephens Creek...12 June 1818...JNO W. SHEALY (X)
(LS), Wit: ANDREW SHEALY (X), DRURY FORT. Proven by ANDREW SHEALY in Edgefield Dist., 8
Apr 1819, before A. H. FORT, J. Q. Edgefield Dist.: MARY SHEALEY, wife of JNO. W. SHEALEY,
relinquished dower 24 July 1818 before NATHAN NORRIS, J. Q. Rec. 2 May 1842. Delivered to
LINCOLN MILLER, 12 Sept 1842.

Pp. 531-532: S. C., PETER SCHUMPERT of Lexington Dist., for $300 pd. by ADAM SHELY JR. of
same...110 A, part of 2 tracts, one 100 A, granted to PETER SCHUMPERT, 25 May
1774, and part of 367 A granted to sd. PETER, 6 Aug 1787 adj. lands of sd. ADAM SHELY, on
Stephenings fork, waters of Saluda...26 Jan 1821...PETER SCHUMPERT (LS), Wit: HENRY KOON
(K), SAML CANNON. Proven by HENRY KOON, 26 Jan 1821, before SAML CANNON, Q. U. ELIZABETH
SCHUMPERT, wife of PETER, relinquished dower 30 Jan 1821. Rec. 2 May 1842. Delivered to
SIMEON MILLER, 12 Sept 1842.

Page 533: S. C., Edgefield Dist.: HENRY SAWYER, for $60 pd. by W. C. SAWYER...37 A on long
branch, waters of Chinquepin Creek of North Edisto, part of tract granted to
MARTIN WITT...4 Feb 1841...HENRY SAWYER (LS), Wit: WM. B. NORRIS, ELISHA RAWLS. Proven
by WM. B. NORRIS, 26 Apr 1842, before NATHAN NORRIS, Magt. Rec. 2 May 1842.

Pp. 534-535: S. C., Lexington Dist.: RIVERS GUNTER for $350 pd. by URIAH COLLUM of Edge-
field Dist...130 A, part ofa tract granted to EDWARD JOHNSON, 4 Dec 1785,
260 A on waters of Edisto adj. J. P. BOND, HEZEKIAH PRATER...5 Dec 1840, RIVERS GUNER
(LS), Wit: JAMES T. HANEY, ELIAS GUNTER. Proven by JAMES T. HANEY, 8 Dec 1840, before
NATHAN NORRIS, J. Q. Rec. 2 May 1842. Delivered to EARLEY SAWYER, 31 Oct 1831 [sic].

Pp. 535-536: S. C., Lexington Dist.: Whereas GEORGE H. CHAPMAN & wf, the heirs and distributees of MAJR. WILLIAM SUMMER, decd, filed a Petition against JOHN SHUMPERT
and wife, GEORGE W. LONG for himself, and Guardian for JOHN W. LONG, on 25 Jan 1842, stating
the MAJ. WILLIAM SUMMER, died Intestate, leaving a tract...100 A bought by GEORGE H.
CHAPMAN, for $50...WM. L. MILLER (LS), S. L. D. Wit: HEZEKIAH DREHER, JOHN HOOK. Proven
by JOHN HOOK, 6 May 1842. Delivered to WILLIAM CHAPMAN, 4 Dec 1843.

Page 537: S. C.: GODFREY HARMAN of Lexington Dist., for natural love and affection to my
daughter JULIA ANN MATILDA FRANCKLOW, wife of JOHN J. FRANCKLOW of same...I give
to my son JONATHAN HARMAN, negroes [named] in trust for sd. daughter...7 Apr 1842...GOD-
FREY HARMAN (LS), Wit: H. J. CAUGHMAN, HENRY A. MEETZE, J. N. BOOZER. S. C. Lexington
Dst: Proven by HENRY J. CAUGHMAN, 17 May 1842, before R. HARMAN, Magt.

Page 538: S. C.: Whereas ANNA ARTHUR, widow of FRIDAY ARTHUR, decd, lately instituted a
suit against JAMES S. GUIGNARD for recovery of her dower on 175 A on Congaree
River adj. HARGROVE ARTHUR, COL. JOHN TAYLOR's estate, JAMES S. GUIGNARD, the upper half
of 350 A granted to JOHN STRASS...for $200 pd. by sd. GUIGNARD releases land...ANNA
ARTHUR (LS), Wit: EDWARD J. ARTHUR, WM. F. ARTHUR. Richland Dist.: Proven by EDWARD J.
ARTHUR, 30 Apr 1842. Instrument dated 15 Apr 1842. Rec. 31 May 1842.

Page 539: S. C., Lexington Dist.: JACOB EARHEART for $150 pd. by HENRY J. DRAFTS...105 A
on waters of Saluda, Big Hollow Creek...28 May 1842...JACOB EARHART (LS), Wit:
DANIEL DRAFTS, JOHN P. EARHART. Proven by DANIEL DRAFTS, 30 May 1842 before G. J. HOOK.
Rec. 2 June 1842.

Pp. 540-541: S. C.: JACOB J. BUSBY of Lexington Dist., for $400 pd. by JOHN SUMMER JR.,
of same....87 3/4 A, part of 680 A granted to FREDERICK KICKELIGHTER, adj.
lands held at present by THOMAS L. VEALE, J. SUMMER JUR., on the main Charleston road and
waters of Hog Branch, plat dated 25 Oct 1833...25 Mar 1842...JACOB J. BUSBY (LS), Wit: JA-
COB A. LUCAS, SILAS KNIGHT. Proven by JACOB A. LUCAS, 16 Apr 1842, before GEORGE M. FUL-
MER, Magist. ANN BUSBY, wife of JACOB J. BUSBY, relinquished dower, 16 Apr 1842. Delivered to JACOB J. BUSBY, 5 Dec 1842.

Pp. 541-542: S. C.: JESSE FOX of Lexington Dist for $50 pd. by JOSEPH BURGESS of same...
80 A on N side Chinquepin Creek, waters of N Edisto River...line from the
stake to the FRIDAY Ford, PAGET land, PLATTS land, MIMS LAND, all formerly owned by JOHN
KNOX and JOHN K. JOHNSTON, now owned by A. H. FORT...14 Feb 1842...JESSE FOX (LS), Wit:
THOMAS QUATTLEBUM, SUSANNAH T. FOX. proven by THOMAS QUATTLEBUM, 16 Feb 1842, before
ISAAC VANSANT. Rec. 20 June 1842. Delivered to JOSEPH BURGESS, _____.

Pp. 543-544: S. C.: GEORGE EPTING SENR of Lexington Dist., for $141 pd. by JOHN SHEALEY JUR.,
of same...141 A, part of a 700 A tract originally surveyed for JACOB EPTING
SENR., 8 July 1791 on Drains of Camping Creek, waters of Saluda River adj. lands of THOMAS
LONG, D. LONG, J. WIGGERS, JOHN SHEALEY, & sd. GEORGE EPTING...8 June 1837...GEORGE EPTING
(LS), Wit: ADAM SHEALY, LEVI SHEALY. Newberry Dist.: Proven by ADAM SHEALY, 8 June 1837.
Rec. 4 July 1842. Delivered to JOHN SHEALEY 2 Nov 1842.

Pp. 544-545: GEORGE WINGARD SENR & mother ANNA MARY of Lexington Dist., for $500 pd. by
GEORGE WINGARD JR of same...137 A on S side Saluda adj. WEST CAUGHMAN, JOHN
DREHER...5 July 1842...ANA MARY WINGARD (X) (LS), GEORGE WINGARD SENR (X) (LS), Wit:
JACOB BICKLEY, REUBEN CORLEY SENR. Proven by REUBEN CORLEY SENR., 4 July 1842. Rec. 5
July 1842. Delivered to GEORGE WINGARD JR., 5 Jan 1843.

Pp. 545-548: S. C.: 26 June 1842, HENRY A. MEETZE, Esquire, Commissioner of the Hon. Court
of Equity for Lexington Dist., to NATHAN BUSBY of the other poart....whereas
JACOB J. BUSBY, on or about 10 May 1841, did exhibit his Bill of Complaint in the Court
of Equity at Lexington C. H., against NATHAN BUSBY & others...land to be divided...for
$1270.50 sold by NATHAN BUSBY...181 1/2 A, part of a tract originally belonging to JACOB
BUSBY decd...HENRY A. MEETZE (LS): Wit: J. R. MILLER, JOHN STOUDEMIRE. Plat included in
deed, sworn chain carriers DAVID COUNTS, O H. SWYGERT, BUCK BUSBY & WEATHERSBY, shows
adj. lands of MRS. BRIGHT, BENJ. BUSBY, ADAM STOUDEMYERS, BRIGHT STUCK, MAJ. SWYGERT,
J. J. BUSBY. Deed proven by JOSEPH R. MILLER, 6 July 1842. Rec. 6 July 1842. Plat made
by WM. B. ELKIN, D. S. 23 July 1841.

Pp. 548-549: S. C.: 7 March 1842, THOMAS RALL, the elder, to JOHN SHULER & A. H. FORT, all
of Lexington Dist., for $1000 payable in the Bank of the State of S. C....1000
A adj. THOAMS K. POINDEXTER, & my own land...THOS RALL (LS), Wit: W. H. FOX, JOHNHOOK.
Proven by JOHN HOOK, 15 July 1842. Rec. 15 July 1842. Delivered to WM. FORT, 19 Dec 1842.

Pp. 550-551: S. C., Lexington Dist: 30 Mar 1842, ANTHONY SCHINK to JOHN SHEALY, whereas
sd. SCHINK stands indebted to sd. SHEALY for $250...mortgage of 202 A adj.
lands of heirs of HENRY RUFF, JOHN W. SHEALEY, WILKS F. WATERS, SAMUEL SHEALY, JOSEPH
SHEALY, the sd. JOHN SHEALEY, & MICHAEL DUNCAN, known as the Mountain Mill Tract on waters
of Saluda......MICHAEL A. SCHINK (LS), JOHN SHEELY (LS), Wit: G. M. FULMER, JOHN NESSLY,
Proven by JOHN M. NESSLY, 4 July 1842 before G. M. FULMER. Rec. 25 July 1842. Delivered
to G. M. FULMER, Esqr., 25 July 1842.   Note satisfied 2 Sept 1844, JOHN SHEELY.

Page 552: S. C., Lexington Dist.: Personally appeared MRS. MARY L. STROMAN formerly MRS.
MARY L. AMACKER, and made oath that she saw DR. E. L. AMACKER, receive full
satisfaction in cash for the mortgage 30 Jan 1839...mortgage for Negro woman Frances &
interest in lands of the Estate of JOHN W. HANE decd, by SARAH J. HANE, to EVANS L.
AMACKER., Sworn 13 Augt 1842, before JOHN FOX. Rec. 13 Aug 1842. Mortgage referred to
is recorded in Book K, p. 212 [not now extant--BHH].

Pp. 552-553: S. C.: GEORGE RECKERT of Lexington Dist., for $300 pd. by JULIAN SCHWARTZ of
Newberry Dist....100 A, part of a tract originally granted to GEORGE WIDEMAN
for 200 A on Wateree Creek, waters of Broad River adj. GEO. KOON, S. MARTIN, B. WHEELER
...9 Apr 1842...GEO. RECKERT (R) (LS), Wit: JULIUS HARRIS, P. DICKERT. Proven by J.
HARRIS, before P. DICKERT, Magt for Newberry Dist., 1 July 1842. Rec. 18 July 1842. Delivered to JULIAN SWARTZ [sic] 22 Oct 1844.

Pp. 553-554: S. C., JULIAN SCHWARTS of Newberry Dist., for $300 pd. by JOHN RICKERT of
Lexington Dist...100 A, part of 200 A granted to GEORGE WIDEMAN [same tract
as in preceding deed]...9 July 1842...JULIAN SCHWARTS (X) (LS), Wit: JOHN C. DICKERT, P.
DICKERT. Proven by JOHN C. DICKERT, before P. DICKERT., 9 July 1842. Rec. 18 July 1842.
Delivered to JULIAN SWARTZ, 22 Oct 1844.

Pp. 554-556: S. C.: 14 Mar 1842, JACOB LITES to FREDERICK HARMAN, FREDERICK SEAS, & PHIL-
LIP LITES...whereas LITES stands indebted to HARMAN, SEAS, & LITES...mort-
gage for 200 A on Rocky Creek, waters of Saluda adj. lands of the estate of EMANUEL CORLEY,
Est. of JOHN HENDRIX, HENRY MEETZE, GASPER ELLISER, Saluda River...JACOB LITES (L) (LS),
FREDERIC HARMAN (LS), FREDERIC SEAS (LS), PHILIP LITES (LS), Wit: H. J. CAUGHMAN, REUBEN
HARMAN. Proven by HENRY J. CAUGHMAN, 1 Aug 1842, before R. HARMAN, Magt. Rec. 1 Aug
1842. Delivered to F. HARMAN, 6 Feb 1843.

Pp. 556-558: S. C.: JOHN RAMICK & wf SALLY of Lexington Dist., for $26 pd. by JAMES
DOOLEY & wf RACHEL, formerly RACHEL SEASTRUNK, for her sole use, &c...all
share in real estate of HENRY SEASTRUNK, decd...50 A on Twelve Mile Creek, adj. lands of
GEORGE LEAPHART, JOHN CORLEY, & others, waters of Saluda River...8 June 1839...JOHN
RAMICK (X) (LS), SALLY RAMICK (X) (LS), Wit: EMANUEL SEASTRUNK, LUKE SEASTRUNK. Proven by
EMANUEL SEASTRUNK, 27 July 1839. SALLY RAMICK, wife of JOHN, relinquished dower, 1 June
1839, before A. H. FORT. Rec. 1 Augt 1842. Delivered to JAMES DOOLEY 4 Mar 1844.

Pp. 558-559: By virtue of a writ of fiere facias issued out of the Court of Common Pleas,
held for Lexington Dist., tested 18 Apr 1842 at suit of CHRISTIAN PRICE,
to levy $1069.96 from goods and chattels of GEORGE OSWALT...700 A on Augusta Road, adj.
lands of THOS. K. POINDEXTER & others...sold to JACOB DRAFTS SR., for $250...1 Aug 1842...
WM. L. MILLER (LS), S. L. D. Wit: EPHRAIM CORLEY, JNO. HOOK. Proven by JOHN HOOK, 1 Aug
1842. Rec. 1 Aug 1842.

Pp. 560-562: S. C.: SAMUEL RAWL of Lexington Dist., for $571.43 pd. by WM. L. MILLER...120
A, part of a tract granted to GEORGE GARTMAN, 6 Nov 1786, adj. corner of
SAML. RAWLS & LOWN, adj. lands now held by URIAH HENDRIX, HENRY HENDRIX, WM. L. MILLER,
JOHN LOWN, & sd. RAWL, plat made 25 Feb 1842, by WILLIAM FORT, D. S....25 Feb 1842...SAMUEL
RAWL (LS), Wit: WILLIAM FORT, J. F. FULMER. Proven by WILLIAM FORT, 8 Aug 1842, before
JOHN FOX. MRS. NANCY RAWL, wife of SAMUEL, relinquished dower, 6 Aug 1842. Rec. 8 Aug
1842. Delivered to WM. L. MILLER, 21 Jan 1843.[Plat on page 562.]

Pp. 562-564: S. C., Lexington Dist.: HENRY LYBRAND of Newberry Dist., for $338 pd. by
WILLIAM FULMER of same...169 A on bair [sic] Creek, formerly belonging to
ANNA LYBRAND,adj. WILLIAM BALLENTINE, JACOB HARMAN, MICHAEL SULTON, DANIEL LEAPHART, JAMES
BALLENTINE, THOMAS LONG...23 Dec 1840...HENRY LYBRAND (LS), Wit: SAMPSON C. MERCHANT, ABI-
JAH HENDRIX. S. C. Newberry Dist.: Proven by SAMPSON MERCHANT, 24 Dec 1840, before ML.
BENDENBAUGH , J. P. MRS. ANNA LYBRAND, wife of HENRY, relinquished dower 24 Dec 1840.
Rec. 13 Aug 1842. Delivered to HENRY FRAZIER, 29 Sept 1843.

Pp. 564-566: S. C., 26 Feb 1842, WILLIAM FULMER to DAVID AMICK & HENRY FRAZIER...mortgage
of 169 A, for promissary note [same land in preceding deed], "where I now
reside."...WILLIAM FULMER (X) (LS), Wit: EMANUEL KOON, WM. AMICK. Proven by EMANUEL KOON
before JOHN H. SULTON, Magistrate, 21 Mar 1842. Rec. 13 Aug 1842. Delivered to HENRY
FRAZIER, 29 Sept 1843.

Pp. 566-568: Whereas by a writ of fiere facias issued out of the Court of Common Pleas
for Lex. Dist., tested 7 Apr 1841 at the suit of WILLIS HARTLEY to levy from
the goods & chattels of STEPHEN SENTERFIT, $65.50...sold 1058 A adj. PAUL QUATTLEBUM, JOHN
QUATTLEBUM, HENRY SMITH & WM. C. HART, for $45 pd. by URIAH CROUT & JOHN FOX...29 July
1842. WM. L. MILLER, S. L. D. Wit: JNO. HOOK, L. BOOZER. Proven by HOOK, 26 Aug 1842.

Pp. 568-570: S. C., Lexington Dist.: ANDREW RISH & wf RACHEL for $380 pd. by REUBEN
STEED   STEEDMAN of Dist. aforesd....our Distributive share of Est. of GEORGE STEED-
MAN, decd...ANDREW RISH (X) (LS), RACHEL RISH (X) (LS), Wit: JOSEPH R. MILLER, ISAIAH
CAUGHMAN. Proven by Dr. ISAIAH CAUGHMAN,, 6 Sept 1842. Instrument dated 1 Feb 1841. Rec.
6 Sept 1842. Delivered to ANDERSON STEEDMAN, 19 June 1843. Renunciation of Inheritance
recorded at page____.

Pp. 570-571: S. C., Lexington Dist.: CATHARINE WISE of dist. aforesd., for $260 pd. by
            ESAIAH SAYLOR...66 A, part of grant to JOHN WISE & myself for 253 A, on
waters of Sandy Run adj. JOHN WISE, DOCTER MULLER, JOHN GEIGER...19 July 1842...CATHARINE
WISE (X), Wit: RUFUS D. SENN, DAVID WANNAMAKER SR., Proven by SENN, 7 Sept 1842, before
L. BOOZER, Rec. 7 Sept 1842. Delivered to LEWIS CULLER, 10 Apr 1843.

Pp. 571-573: 31 Aug 1842, HENRY A. MEETZE, Esq., Commr. of Hon. Court of Equity of Lex.
            Dist. to ARTHUR H. FORT...Whereas JOHN K. JOHNSTON on or about 22 June 1841
did exhibit his Bill of complaint in the Court of Equity against JOHN KNOX, stating in
the year 1837 he and sd. KNOX were partners in the Mercantile business, that debt to a
large amount was contracted in Charleston, & both were equally liable, debt due one
JESSE FOX...mortgage made 19 Oct 1839 for certain land, and the debt not being paid, the
mortgage was foreclosed...ARTHUR H. FORT bought for $450, 1400 A called the DAVIS tract,
adj. JESSE FOX, ISRAEL GANTT, HENRY JACKSON, THOS QUATTLEBUM & others on Chinquepin
Creek, main branch of N Edisto River...HENRY A. MEETZE (LS), Wit: JOHN FOX, JOHN HOOK.
Proven by JOHN HOOK, 9 Sept 1842. Rec. 9 Sept 1842. Delivered to A. H. FORT, 30 Mar
1846.

Pp. 573-575: S. C., Lexington Dist.: Whereas GEORGE S. SMOKE et uxor, the Heirs & dis-
            tributees of SAMUEL KAVICK[?], decd filed petition in the Court of Ordinary
against DAVID KAUCH[?], ADAM KAUCK, SOPHIS HARICK[?], and POLLY KARICK on 2 May 1842,
stating that the sd. SAMUEL died intestate, leaving several tracts of land which have
not been partitioned...WM MILLER, Sheriff, sold 25 A to DANIEL HOOK SENR, for $576, on
Saluda River adj. lands formerly WM. SENNS & CHUPPS...10 Sept 1842...WM. L. MILLER (LS),
Wit: ISAIAH CAUGHMAN, JOHN HOOK. Proven by JOHN HOOK, 10 Sept 1842. Rec. 10 Sept 1842.
Delivered to JOSEPH HOOK, 31 Oct 1842.

Pp. 575-577: WILLIAM L. MILLER to DANIEL HOOK SR. [another tract of same estate as
            preceding deed]...50 A, for $556...10 Sept 1842...WM. L. MILLER (LS),
Wit: ISAIAH CAUGHMAN, JNO. HOOK. Proven by HOOK, 10 Sept 1842. Rec. 10 Sept 1842.
Delivered to JOSEPH HOOK, 31 Oct 1842.

Pp. 577-579: WILLIAM L. MILLER to DANIEL HOOK SENR...[another tract of same]...3 A...
            for $6...10 Sept 1842...WM. MILLER (LS), Wit: ISAIAH CAUGHMAN, JOHN HOOK.
Proven by HOOK, 10 Sept 1842. Recording and Delivery same as preceding deeds.

Pp. 579-580: S. C., Lexington Dist.: DAVID CHUPP of Dist. aforesd., for $50 pd. by SAMUEL
            KARICK, of same...75 A on branches of Saluda adj. DAVID SHULL, JOSEPH
CHUPP, NICHOLAS HOOK, JOHN RUFF, part of a tract originally granted to RICHARD HAMPTON,
then conveyed to JACOB CHUPP, and thence directed to me by a Will of JACOB CHUPP SENR,
decd...9 Sept 1833 (LS), Wit: ADAM SHULL, DAVID SENN (X). Proven by DAVID SENN, 21
Sept 1833 before M. HOOK, J. P. Rec. 12 Sept 1842. Delivered to E. D. GILLMORE, 8 Oct
1842.

Pp. 580-582: S. C.: 26 Mar 1842, EPHRAIM CORLEY & A. H. FORT and THOS RALL SENR of the
            other part...Whereas sd. CORLEY & FORT having endorsed a note for $600 which
said note is passed in the bank and money recd by sd. THOMAS RALL SENR,now the sd. THOS
RALL SENR for the premises for the securing them of their liability...mortgage of 1000 A
and mill and fixtures, and negroes [named]...THOS RALL (LS), Wit: GEORGE CAUGHMAN,
GEORGE GARTMAN. Proven by GEORGE CAUGHMAN, 12 Sept 1842. Rec. 12 Sept 1842. Delivered
to SM. FORT, 19 Dec 1842, JOHN FOX, Egr.

Page 583: Plat made at the request of JACOB DRAFTS SR., the same attached to conveyance
            from Sheriff MILLER to sd. DRAFTS, & recorded page 558, plat made by DAVID
KING D. S., 17 Mar 1842. shows land adj. to JACOB RALLS, WM DENT, JOHN MEETZE, HENRY
OSWALT, KEISLER, THOMAS K. POINDEXTER, KELLEY, FREDICKER [KELLY?], FREDERICK LITES, JERE-
MIAH HARMAN.

Pp. 584-585: S. C.: WILLIAM L. MILLER, Sheriff of Lexington Dist., by virtue of a writ of
            fiere facias issued out of the Court of Common Pleas held for Lex. Dist,
tested 18 Apr 1842, at the suit of J. A. CRAWFORD and J. S. SCOTT Assignees to me directed
to levy from goodsa and chattels of MARY KLECKLEY, $95.79...75 A where she now lives...
purchased by DANIEL KLECKLEY, for $75...22 Sept 1842...WM. L. MILLER, S. L. D. Wit:

J. R. MILLER, JNO HOOK. Proven by JOHN HOOK, 22 Sept 1842. Rec. 22 Sept 1842. Delivered to DANIEL KLECKLEY, 4 May 1854.

Pp. 585-586: S. C.: WILLIAM L. MILLER, Sheriff...whereas by virtue of a writ of fiere facias issued out of the Court of Common Pleas, held for Lex. Dist., tested 18 Apr 1842, at suit of J. S. SCOTT against MARY KLECKLEY...interest of MARY KLECKLEY of 50 A adj. SAMUEL T. LORICK, Heirs of DAVID KLECKLEY...purchased by DAVID KLECKLEY for $65...22 Sept 1842...WM. L. MILLER (LS), Wit: J. R. MILLER, JNO HOOK Proven by HOOK 22 Sept 1842. Rec. 22 Sept 1842.

Pp. 587-588: S. C., Lexington Dist.: Whereas GEORGE S. SMOKE et uxor, the Heirs and distributees of SAMUEL KARICK, decd filed a petition in Court of Ordinary against DAVID KARICK, ADAM KARICK, SOPHIA KARICK, and POLLY KARICK, on 2 May 1842, stating that sd. SAMUEL died intestate, having tracts not partitioned...100 A, E. D. GILLMORE became purchaser, for $550...land is adj. to GABRIEL FRIDAY, N. HOOK, & DR. HOOK...1 Oct 1842...WM. L. MILLER (LS), Wit: TYRE SNELGROVE, JOHN HOOK. Proven by HOOK, 1 Oct 1842. Rec. 1 Oct 1842. Delivered to CONRAD SHULL, 31 Oct 1842.

Pp. 589-590: S. C.: BARTHOLOMEW TURNIPSEED and ANN TURNIPSEED of Richland Dist., for $700 pd. by EMANUEL GEIGER of _____, we release to him, a tract formerly conveyed by SAMUEL HUFFMAN, to the late WILLIAM J. GEIGER, on Kennerlys Creek, waters of Big Saluda adj. SAMUEL HUFFMAN, MICHAEL LORICK, Est. of WILLIAM J. GEIGER, 217 1/2 A... 5 Apr 1842...B. TURNIPSEED (LS), ANN TURNIPSEED (X) (LS), Wit: SAMUEL HUFFMAN, ANDERSON D. ABRAHAM. Richland Dist.: Proven by SAMUEL HUFFMAN, 5 Apr 1842. ANN TURNIPSEED, wife of BARTHOLOMEW, relinquished dower 7 July 1842, before HENRY TURNIPSEED, M. R. D. Rec. 3 Oct 1842, JOHN FOX. Delivered to EMANUEL GEIGER, 12 Oct 1842.

Pp. 590-591: S. C.: CHRISTENA WINGARD of Lexington Dist., for $317 pd. by THOMAS A. WINGARD...1/2 of 90 A on 16 mile Branch, waters of Saluda River adj. THOMAS WINGARD, URIAH RAUCH, GEORGE WINGARD SR., JOHN DREHR, & sd. CHRISTENA WINGARD, part of grant to MICHAEL STYLTER[?], 14 Apr 1753, conveyed by JOHN LIPP to sd. CHRISTENA WINGARD ...3 Oct 1842...CHRISTENA WINGARD (X) (LS), Wit: DANIEL WINGARD, HARMAN GEIGER, Proven by DANIEL WINGARD, 4 Oct 1842. Rec. 4 Oct 1842. Delivered to THOS. A. WINGARD, 4 Oct 1842.

Pp. 592-593: S. C.: WILLIAM L. MILLER, Sheriff of Lexington Dist., by virtue of a writ of _____ of fiere facias issued our of the Court of Common Pleas, for Lex. Dist., tested 13 Mar 1841, at the suit of DANIEL WINGARD, to levy of goods, etc. of ISAIAH WINGARD, $1300...90 A, sd. ISAIAH's interest, 1/2 or 45 A...purchased by THOMAS A. WINGARD, for $43...3 Oct 1842... WM. L. MILLER (LS), Wit: EPHRAIM CORLEY, JNO. HOOK. Proven by JOHN HOOK, 4 Oct 1842. MRS. CAROLINE WINGARD, wife of ISAIAH, relinquished dower, 4 Oct 1842. Rec. 4 Oct 1842. Delivered to THOS. A. WINGARD, 10 Oct 1842.

Pp. 594-595: S. C.: 3 Oct 1842, HENRY A. MEETZE, Comr. of Hon Cout of Equity for Lex. Dist., to MOSES MURPHY...whereas L. BOOZER, on or about 9 May 184? did exhibit his bill of Complaint in Court of Equity against CATHARINE TARER & others, stating that ANDREW TARER, late of Sd. Dist., departed this life intestate, in 1841, having a small real estate, one tract of 242 A, that he was legally appointed Admr. of the sd. intestate...land on Twelve mile creek adj. WEST CAUGHMAN, JOHN MEETZE, JOEL CORLEY, & JACOB DRAFTS...HENRY A. MEETZE (LS), Wit: H. J. CAUGHMAN, WM. L. MILLER. Proven by MILLER 5 Oct 1842. Rec. 5 Oct 1842. Delivered to MRS. MURPHY, 19 Nov 1849.

Pp. 596-597: S. C., Lexington Dist.: WHEREAS GEORGE S. SMOKE & wife, Heirs and Dist., of SAMUEL KARICK, decd filed petition against DAVID, ADAM, SOPHIA, & POLLY KARICK in 1842...SAMUEL died intestate, leaving land not partitioned...sold by Sheriff to E. D. GILLMORE, 75 A adj. Heirs of NICHOLAS HOOK, DAVID WILSON & SENN...for $76... 8 Oct 1842...WM. L. MILLER (LS), S. L. D. Wit: DAVID WILSON, JNO HOOK. Proven by JOHN HOOK, 8 Oct 1842. Rec. 8 Oct 1842. Delivered 31 Oct 1842.

Pp. 597-599: S. C.: 6 Oct 1842, JESSE BATES 6f Town of Columbia, and J. C. ERNENPUTSCH of City of New York...the sd. JESSE BATES, in consideration of an agreement entered into with sd. ERNENPUTSCH, by reason of a contract made to sd. Bates...mortgage on a farm of 114 A, on Saluda River, and 18 mile Branch, adj. JOHN EAREHART, MARTIN CAUGHMAN, JOHN ADAM ROBERTS, and land formerly held by KOON, now the property of REIVEs or WINGARD AND GEIGER, sold by JOHN FOX, Sheriff to effect a division amont the heirs of HENRY or ELIZABETH EAREHART, and purchased by sd. JOHN EAREHART, 17 Jan 1832...JESSE BATES, Wit" JESSE COOPER, JOHN PALMER. Richland Dist: Proven by JOHN PALMER, 8 Oct 1842. Rec. 10 Oct 1842, Delivered to COL. H. J. CAUGHMAN, 12 Oct 1842. Letter attached to page 598:"To The Clerk in the office or Records Lexington C. H., S. C., New York, 21 Feby 1843, Dear Sir: I hereby request you to cancel the mortgage which was given to me by MR. JESSE BATES & recorded in your office. Very respectfully your, J. C. ERNENPUTSCH.

Pp. 599-601: S. C.: 7 Oct 1842, HENRY A. MEETZE, Comr. of Hon Cout of Equity for Lex.
Dist., to WILLIAM HALTIWANGER...whereas WILLIAM ABRAMS & wife et al, on or
about 11 Apr 1842, did exhibit their Bill of Complaint, against JOHN MILLER Exor et al,
stating that WILLIAM CHAPMAN, SENR of Newberry Dist., departed this life 1839, leaving
his L. W. & T. unrevokes, that sd. testator left him surviving his wife MARY who has
since intermarried with WILLIAM ABRAMS, and his faive children to wit, ELIZABETH who intermarried with JOHN MILLER, GEORGE H. CHAPMAN...they state that the elevent cluase of
the sd. testators will is I will and direct that my two tracts of land which lie in
Lexington District be equally divided into six lots and I give and bequeath one parcel to
may wife and the other five to my five children...land to be sold at public auction...
sold to HALTIWANGER for $90, 157 A, part of a tract originally surveyed for GEO. RISER,
on Branches of WATEREE Creek, waters of Broad River...HENRY A. MEETZE (LS), Wit: W. H.
FOX, JACOB WINGARD. Proven by JACOB WINGARD, 12 Oct 1842. Rec. 12 Oct 1842.

Page 602: Plat for preceding deed, made 27 Sept 1842, showing adj. land owner, LEWIS
GEORGE, Est. of H. RUFF and SUMMER, JOHN CHAPMAN, GEORGE STOUDEMYER; ABRM.
FULMER, & H. MILLER, Sworn Chain Carriers. Rec. 12 Oct 1842.

Pp. 602-604: S. C.: 4 Oct 1842, HENRY A. MEETZE, Comr. of Equity to GEORGE H. CHAPMAN
[same suit as preceding deed]...for $435.50, 144 A on Crims Creek, waters
of Broad River...HENRY A. MEETZE, Wit: W. H. FOX, SAMUEL BOUKNIGHT. Proven by W. H.
FOX, 12 Oct 1842. Rec. 12 Oct 1842. Delivered to FRANKLIN CHAPMAN, 27 Apr 184?.

Page 605: Plat for preceding deed, made 27 Sept 1842, by P. DICKERT, D. S., showing adj.
land owners WM. SWETENBERG, Est. of H. RUFF, K. SCHMITZ, GEO. ELIOT, M.
SUMMERS, GEO. CHAPMAN. Rec. 12 Oct 1842. Same chain carriers.

Pp. 605-607: S. C.: NATHAN BUSBY of Lex. Dist., for $1270 pd. by JACOB BUNRICK of same...
181 1/2 A on Broad River, being part of a tract originally belonging to JA-
COB BUSBY, decd, assigned by me by Court of Equity...6 June 1842...NATHAN BUSBY (LS),
Wit: J. R. MILLER, JOHN STOUDEMAYER. Proven by JOHN STOUDEMIRE, before GEORGE M. FULMER,
2 Aug 1842. MRS. ELIZABETH BUSBY, wife of NATHAN, relinquished dower 2 Aug 1842. Rec.
12 Oct 1842. Delivered to JACOB BUNDRICK, 4 Oct 1844.

Pp. 607-608: S. C.: 12 Oct 1842, JONATHAN HARMAN to EPHRAIM CORLEY...mortgage for a
debt...lot of 2 A in Lexington village, on Main Street or Augusta Road adj.
MAJ. BOOZERs lot, Back St., GEORGE A. EIGLEBERGERs lot...JONATHAN HARMAN (LS), Wit: ISAI-
AH CAUGHMAN, L. BOOZER. Proven by L. BOOZER, 13 Oct 1842. Rec. 13 Oct 1842. Assigned
to JOHN FOX, see Record Book, pp. 502 & 503.

Page 609: JACOB HYDEs plat, Surveyed 21 Jan 1842, by WM. E. SAWYER, At the request of
JACOB HUDE...211 A exclusive of 26 A which he gave to his son WILLIAM HYDE,
in Lexington and Edgefield Dist., on the Columbia Road on Branches of Clouds Creek,
waters of Saluda River and head waters of Chinquipin Creek, waters of N Edisto River,
shows land adj. ANDREW BATES, JOEL RIDGELS, WILLIAM NORRIS, LEWIS GUNTER. Attached to
the following conveyance.

Pp. 609-610: S. C., Lexington Dist.: WILLIAM NORRIS & NAMO NORRIS, for $100 pd. by JACOB
HITE...20 A, part of tract granted to sd. WILLIAM NORRIS, 19 Sept 1810,
containing 484 A in Edgefield and Lexington Dist...20 June 1842. WILLIAM NORRIS (LS),
NAOMI NORRIS (LS), Wit: A. P. NORRIS, WILLIAM HITE. Proven by WILLIAM HITE, 13 Oct 1842.
Rec. 15 Oct 1842. Delivered to WM. HITE, 9 Dec 1842.

Pp. 611-613: Plat made by JOHN KNOX, Dep. Surv. at the request of WILLIAM HYDE, 28 A
the SE corner of a tract granted to _____ in _____, 21 Aug 1835, shows
adj. lands of JACOB HYDE, LEWIS GUNTER, WADE HOLSTUN.
S. C., JACOB HUDE of Lex. Dist., for $50 paid by WM. HUDE of same...28 A
[land in above plat]...31 Dec 1835...JACOB HYDE (H) (LS), Wit: WILLIS HARTLEY, JOHN HITE.
Proven by JOHN HITE, 7 Jan 1836 before GEORGE SAWYER, Q. U. CATHERINE HITE, wife of JA-
COB, relinquished dower, 7 Jan 1836. Rec. 13 Oct 1842. Delivered to WM. HITE, 9 Dec 1842.

Pp. 613-614: 15 Aug 1842, JACOB HITE, farmer of Lex. Dist., to WILLIAM HITE, son of sd.
JACOB, farmer...for natural love and affection...$1...167 A, part of two
tracts, originally granted to HOWELL JOHNSON, 7 Nov 1791, of 384 A on head branches of
Chinquepin Creek, plat made by WILLIAM QUATTLEBUM for WILLIAM HITE, 2 Jan 1829...the
other tract of 105 A, plat made by WM. SAWYER....JACOB HITE (H) (LS), Wit: JOHN M. NORRIS,
A. P. NORRIS. Proven by JOHN M. NORRIS, 12 Oct 1842. Rec. 13 Oct 1842. Delivered to
WM. HITE, 9 Dec 1842.

Pp. 614-615: 15 Aug 1842, JACOB HITE to JOHN HITE, farmer, son of sd. JACOB...for love &
affection...167 A, part of 2 tracts (1) 48 A granted to HOWELL JOHNSTON
(2) 105 A...[same description as preceding deed, other 1/2 of tract]...JACOB HITE (H)
(LS), Wit: JOHN M. NORRIS, A. P. NORRIS. Proven by JOHN M. NORRIS, 12 Oct 1842. Rec.
13 Oct 1842.

Page 616: GEORGE L. BANKS plat, attached to the following conveyance. 194 A, on Hollow
Creek and Big hole Branch, waters of Saluda, part of tract surveyed for AMOS
BANKS, 25 Nov 1829 adj. GEORGE PRICE, AMOS BANKS', CHRISTIAN GABLE, DANIEL DERRICK. Surv.
1 Dec. 1841, W. E. SAWYER, D. S. Delivered to JAMES FULMER, 6 Mar 1846.

Pp. 616-618: AMOS BANKS, of Edgefield Dist., for love and freidnship to my son GEORGE
LONG BANKS of same...194 Ain Lexington Dist...6 Dec 1841...AMOS BANKS (LS),
Wit: JACOB LONG, MARTIN S. BANKS. EVE MARGARET BANKS, wife of AMOS, relinquished dower
29 Apr 1842, before ISAAC VANSANT, Magt.   Proven by JACOB LONG, 2 Apr 1842. Rec. 18
Oct 1842. Delivered to JAMES FULMER, 6 Mar 1846.

Pp. 618-619: JOHN CORLEY JR. of Lexington Dist., for $450 pd. by JACOB RAUCH of same...
70 A, made up of parts of three separate tracts, one granted to JOHN OSWALT,
another to M. OSWALT and the other to one SPENCE, on Twenty mile branch of Waluda,
adj. lands now owned by URIAH RAUCH, JACOB RAUCH, JACOB KAMINER, and Road from WISES
ferry to Lexington D. H., JOHN MEETZE, part of a tract sold by JOHN A. ADDISON, Comr. on
4 Dec 1837 to sd. JOHN CORLEY JR....29 Oct 1842...JOHN CORLEY JR (LS), Wit: HENRY A.
MEETZE, GEORGE ROBERTS. Proven by H. A. MEETZE, 29 Oct 1842. JEMIMA CORLEY, wife of
JOHN JR., relinquished dower, 29 Oct 1842 before REUBEN HARMAN, Magt. Rec. 29 Oct 1842.
Delivered to JACOB RAUCH, 27 Jan 1844.

Pp. 620-621: DRURY J. HARMAN of Lexington Dist., for $1500 to JONATHAN HARMAN...mortgage
for 8 negroes [named]...29 Oct 1842...D. J. HARMAN (LS), Wit: H. J. CAUGH-
MAN, J. N. BOOZER. Proven by CAUGHMAN, 29 Oct 1842. Rec. 29 Oct 1842. Delivered to
JONATHAN HARMAN, 22 Mar 1845.

Pp. 621-623: 9 Dec 1839, ISAAC WALKER of Richalnd Dist., to Saluda Manufacturing Company
of Lexington Dist (DAVID EWART, president)...Walker stands indebted to
sd. Co. with JAMES T. WADE...mortgage 113 A, part of a tract in Fork of Broad and Saluda,
granted in 1785 to LEONARD MARTIN, on branches of Kennerleys Creek adj. EMANUEL GEIGER,
DOCTOR WALLACE, GEORGE LORICK...I. WALKER (LS), Wit: GEORGE T. SCOTT, WILLIAM KYLE.
Proven by WILLIAM KYLE, 31 Oct 1842, Richland Dist, before JOHN T. SEIBLES, Not. Pu.
Rec. 5 Nov. ¬1842. Delivered to JOHN MEETZE, 6 Dec 1843.

Page 623: S. C. Lexington Dist.: LEWIS GEORGE for natural love to my two children JOEL &
HARRIET GEORGE...sd. JOEL to support me...100 A whereon I now live to JOEL...
all household furniture to HARRIET...5 May 1842...L. GEORGE (LS), Wit: WILLIAM HALTIWAN-
GER, J. SWYGERT. Proven by HALTIWANGER, 9 Nov. 1842. Rec. 9 Nov. 1842.

Page 624: S. C., Newberry Dist.: JOHN KINARD for affection to my nephews, the sons of
JETHRO HARMAN, to BYRTON HARMAN & JOSEPH W. HARMAN, & JOHN W. HARMAN, VANCE
C. H. HARMAN...personal property & cattle...15 Aug 1842...JOHN KINARD (LS), Wit: J. A.
JOHNSON, J. E. HODGES. Proven by J. A. JOHNSON, 5 Nov 1842, before LEVI METZ, Magt.
Rec. 16 Nov 1842.

Pp. 625-626: By virtue of a writ of fiere facias issued out of the Court of Common Pleas...
tested 8 Nov 1841 at the suit of WM. MOBLEY commanding me to levy of lands
of GEORGE S. D. SMITH, $19.94...100 A adj. lands of NATHANIEL JONES, ESQR...purchased by
WILLIAM MOBLEY...7 Mar 1842...WM. L. MILLER, (LS), S. L. D. Wit: HENRY A. MEETZE, JOHN
HOOK, Proven by JOHN HOOK, 29 Nov 1842. Rec. 29 Nov 1842.

Pp. 626-628: S. C.: HENRY LYBRAND of S. C., Lexington Dist., for $310 pd. by THOMAS LONG
of same...155 A, part of a tract granted to ANNA LYBRAND, on Bear Creek,
waters of Saluda adj. lands of WM. BALLANTINE, JOHN LYBRAND, THOS FRICK, JAMES BALLANTINE,
& HENRY LYBRAND...24 Oct 1837...HENRY LYBRAND (LS), Wit: THOMAS FRICK, PETER DICKERT.
S. C., Newberry Dist.: JOHN LYBRAND did in his lifetime joined with his wife ANNA LYBRAND
jointly transfered the above mentioned premises into possession of their two children,
HENRY & ANNA LYBRAND, but by sd. deed bearing date 1828, it appears that the sd. ANNA
LYBRAND SENR., was to be lawfully seized and possessed to the above premises during her
natural life...sd. ANNA LYBRAND, relinquished dower...24 Oct 1837...ANNA LYBRAND (V)
Wit: P. DICKERT. Proven by THOS FRICK, _ Oct 1837. NANCY LYBRAND, wife of HENRY, re-
linquished dower, 24 Oct 1387 before P. DICKERT, J. Q. Rec. 5 Dec 1842. Delivered to
THOS LONG, 27 Oct 1847.

Pp. 628-629: S. C., Lexington Dist.: MARGARET HALLMAN for love and regard to my son in
law ADAM RISH...for $10...gift of notes of hand upon JOHN HALLMAN, for $118,
an acct. upon NANCY DAVIS, for $3, not upon THOS CROUT for $20, also furniture...3 Apr
1842. MARGARET HALLMAN (X). Wit: DAVID TAYLOR, AMANUEL RICE. Proven by DAVID TAYLOR
Sept 1842, before GEORGE SAWYER, Rec. 10 Dec 1842. Delivered to ADAM RISH, 23 Dec 1844.

Pp. 629-630:S. C., Lexington Dist.: DAVID CHUPP of Lex. Dist., for $500 pd. by JOSEPH
HOOK, DANIEL HOOK, & WM HOOK...all that Creek Island, 8 A originally granted
to SAMUEL CHUPP, 27 May 1741, directed unto me by a will of JACOB CHUPP, decd...25 Jan
1841...DAVID CHUPP (LS), Wit: JOHN BUFF, SAMUEL KARICK. Proven by JOHN BUFF JR., 3 Sept
1842, before L. BOOZER. ELIZABETH CHUPP, wife of DAVID, relinquished dower, 21 Sept 1842
before CONRAD SHULL, Magt. Rec. 30 Oct 1842. Delivered to JOBEPH HOOK, 2 Jan 1842.

Pp. 620-632: S. C.: GEORGE LEAPHART of Lexington Dist., for $180 pd. by JOSEPH HOOK of
same...60 A, part of a grant to A. B. STARKS, on branches of Saluda, adj.
SHULL, JOHN BUFF JR., GEORGE LEAPHARD...15 Nov 1839...GEORGE LEAPHART (LS), Wit: JOHN
BUFF JR., WILLIAM HOOK. Proven by JOHN BUFF JR., 3 Sept 1842, before L. BOOZER.
CATHERINE LEAPHART, wife of GEORGE,relinquished dower, 8 July 1841. Rec. 31 Oct 1842.
Delivered to JOSEPH HOOK, 2 Jan 1843.

Pp. 632-633: S. C.: JAMES J. HALL of Lexington Dist., for $140 pd. by BANKS GUNTER of
same...152 A whereon I now live, on Mill Creek, waters of N Edisto River,
originally granted to WILLIAM BURGESS, in 1790 on Lightwood Creek...24 Jan 1842...JAMES
J. HALL (LS), Wit: ADAM GUNTER, JOHN HOOK. Proven by JOHN HOOK, 24 Jan 1842. Rec. 15
Dec 1842. Delivered to JOSIAH GUNTER, 6 Mar 1848. Dower recorded in Book O, pp. 35 &
358.

Pp. 633-635: S. C.:SAMUEL HUFFMAN of Lexington Dist., for $117.50 pd. by EMANUEL GEIGER
of same...11 3.4 A, part of tract of 250 A formerly belonging to SAMUEL
HUFFMAN, on E side Saluda...6 Dec 1842...SAMUEL HUFFMAN (LS), Wit: A. S. CLIFTON, JNO.
MO. MOSELEY. Richland Dist.: Proven by A. S. CLIFTON, 6 Dec 1842, before A. FITCH ,
Magistrate. SALLY HUFFMAN, wife of SAMUEL, relinquished dower, 17 Dec 1842, before LEVI
METZ. Plat included dated 38 Nov 1842, made by GEORGE P. DRAFTS, D. S. Rec. 24 Dec 1842
Delivered to EML. GEIGER, 2 Jan 1843.

Pp. 635-637: S. C.: CATHARINE HOOK, ANNA SWICORD, DAVID HOOK, DANIEL HOOK, JOSEPH HOOK &
WILLIAM HOOK of Lexington Dist., for $1100 pd. by MICHAEL LEAPHART of same...
56 A in Fork of Broad and Saluda and 38 A on Saluda River adj. SIMON YOUNGINER, DAVID
FRIDAY, Est. of MARTIN HOOK, decd...part of tract granted to JOHN JACOB FRIDAY, 150 A,
9 Jan 1755, the other pracel of 18 A on waters of Saluda adj. DAVID FRIDAY, Est. of
MARTIN HOOK JR., decd, conveyed by SAMUEL LEVER to MARTIN HOOK SENR, decd, and devised to
us by his L. W. & T....26 Sept 1842...CATHARINE HOOK (+) (LS), ANNA SWICORD (LS), DAVID
HOOK (X) (LS), DANIEL HOOK SR (LS), JOSEPH HOOK (LS), WILLIAM HOOK (LS), Wit: MARTIN T.
LEAPAHRT, GEORGE LEAPHART. Proven by GEORGE LEAPHART, 12 Oct 1842. MRS. ELIZABETH HOOK,
wife of JOSEPH HOOK, relinquished dower, 27 Oct 1842. MRS. MARY ANN HOOK, wife of DAVID,
relinquished dower, 13 Dec 1842. Rec. 31 Dec 1842. Delivered to MICHAEL LEAPHART , 28
Feb 1843.

Pp. 637-639: S. C.: HENRY MURPH & wf NANCY of Lexington Dist., for $137 pd. by DANIEL
CROMER of same....78 A, part of 670 A granted to WILLIAM KELLY, and con-
veyed by sd. WILLIAM KELLY by a will & testament to sd. NANCY MURPH, on borders of 12
Mile Creek, waters of Saluda River adj. CROMER, MARTIN SOX, MARTIN LYBRAND, ADAM CROMER...
21 Augt 1841._.HENRY MUPH (LS), NANCY MURPH (X) (LS), Wit: ADAM CROMER, WILLIAM SHULL.
Proven by ADAM CROMER, 21 Aug 1842, before CONRAD SHULL. NANCY MURPH, wife of
HENRY, relinquished dower, 28 Aug 1842. Rec. 2 Jan 1843. Delivered to DANIEL CROMER, 10
Jan 1843.

Pp. 639-640: S. C., Lexington Dist.: DANIEL CROMER, JAMES CROMER, NANCY CROMER, MARY CROMER
& POLLY CROMER, for $500 pd. by ADAM CROMER, all of Lex. Dist...188 A on S side Saluda,
on the public road leading from Youngingers Ferry to granby, also on a branch of waters
of Twelve Mile Creek adj. GEORGE LEAPHARD, WILLIAM SHULL, ADAM CROMER, CONRAD SHULL, DAVID
SHULL...the most Eastern part of 2 parcels, one originally [granted] 19 Mar 1773 to
JOHN MELCHIOR ROOF, for 200 A; the orther on 7 May 1787 to JOHN ROOF for 750 A...26 Dec
1842...DANIEL CROMER (LS), JAMES CROMER (LS), NANCY CROMER (X) (LS), MARY CROMER (LS),
POLLY CROMER (LS), Wit: DAVID SHULL, JESSE RUFF. Proven by DAVID SHULL, 27 Dec 1842,
before CONRAD SHULL. Rec. 2 Jan 1843. Delivered to ADAM CROMER 6 Feb 1843.

Pp. 641-642: S. C.: JESSE HOLMAN of Lexington Dist., for $1050 pd. by HENRY J. DRAFTS of
same...two separate tracts totalling 245 A on Horse Creek, waters of Saluda,
part of a tract granted to CHRISTOPHER CAUGHMAN adj. JACOB DRAFTS, JACOB BRICE, J.H.
CAUGHMAN...S. WILEY, JESSE HALLMAN, the other tract of 45 A adj. JACOB DRAFTS, JOHN

HALLMAN...17 Dec 1842...JESSE HOLMAN (LS), Wit: G. J. HOOK, JACOB TAYLOR. HEPZIBAH
HALLMAN, wife of JESSE, relinquished dower, 31 Dec 1842, before GEORGE SAWYER.
Proven by G. J. HOOK, 2 Jan 1843. Rec. 2 Jan 1843. Delivered to H. J. DRAFTS, 26 Jan
1843.

Pp. 642-643: S. C., JACOB DRAFTS SENR. of Lexington Dist., for $500 pd. by JESSE HALLMAN
of same...700 A on road from Columbia to Augusta, on head waters of Flat
Rock adj. THOMAS K. POINDEXTER, FREDERICK KELLY, FREDERICK LITES, DENNIS G. HAYES, JACOB
RALLS, SAMUEL RAWLS, WILLIAM L. MILLER...7 Dec 1842...JACOB DRAFTS (LS), Wit: G. J. HOOK,
JACOB TAYLOR. ELIZABETH DRAFTS, wife of JACOB, relinquished dower 31 lec 1842. Proven
by G. J. HOOK, 2 Jan 1843, before JOHN FOX. Rec. 2 Jan 1843.

Page 644: S. C., Lexington dist.: WILLIAM FORTENER of Edgefield Dist., for $200 pd. by
WILLIAM FORTENER of Lexington Dist...[headed in deed book as WILLIAM FAULKNER]
100 A on a branch of Rocky Creek waters of Saluda River, part of 363 A granted to CHARLES
HARRISON...22 Dec 1835...WILLIAM FORTNER (LS), Wit: JOHN CROUT, THOMAS A. GREEN (X).
Proven by THOMAS GREEN, 28 Mar 1836. Rec. 5 Jan 1843. Delivered to GEO. ROBERTS 3 Apr
1843.

Pp. 645-646: S. C.: By virtue of writs of fiere facias issued out of the Court of Common
Pleas held for Dist. of Lexington tested 26 Mar 1842 at suit of GEORGE
ROBERTS, Trustee for SARAH WINGARD to levy of lands and tenements of JOSEPH J. CORLEY,
$78.59...50 A adj. lands of SAMUEL P. CAUGHMAN, RIGNAL O. WILLIAMS, GEORGE YOUNGINGER...
for $105 pd. by sd. ROBERTS...5 Jan 1843...WM. L. MILLER (LS), Wit: REUBEN CORLEY, NATH-
ANIEL KLECKLY. Proven by NATHANIEL KLECKLEY, 5 Jan 1843. Rec. 5 Jan 1843. Delivered to
GEO. ROBERTS, 24 Mar 1843.

Pp. 646-648: Whereas ANN HOWELL & others, Heirs and distributees of CARSON HOWELL, decd.,
filed a petition in Court of Ordinary for Lex. Dist. against JOHN JOHNSON &
wife on 2 Mar 1842 stating that the sd. CARSON HOWELL, died intestate leaving several
tracts of land which have not been partitioned...360 A, purchased by JOHN GARVIN for
$101 adj. lands of JNO. OTT, JOSIAH HOWELL, & HYDRICK...WM. L. MILLER (LS), Wit:
JNO HOOK, NOAH HOLMAN. Proven by JOHN HOOK, 6 Jan 1843. Rec. 6 Jan 1843. Delivered to
ROBT. GARVIN JR., 8 Apr 1844.

Pp. 648-650: By virtue of two writs of fiere facias issued out of the court of Common
Pleas held for Dist. of Lexington, tested 4 Mar 1841 at the suits of DAVID
HENDRIX to levy from lands of CYRENIUS LOOMIS,$144.40...2 3/4 A on which there is a
Blacksmith shop adj. by MAIN ST or Sugusta Road, EPHRAIM CORLEYs lot, DAVID HENDRIXs lot
...purchased by JOHN HENDRIX...1 Sept 1841...WILLIAM L. MILLER (LS), Wit: JOHN HOOK, S.
R. MILLER. MRS. LEAH LOOMIS, wife of CYRENIUS, relinquished dower, 13 Jan 1843. Proven
by JOHN HOOK, 9 Jan 1843.

Pp. 650-651: S. C.: JOHN HENDRIX of Lexington Dist., for $257.50 pd. by DAVID RAWL of
Lexington Dist...2 3/4 A near or in Lexington Village [same lot as in preced-
ing deed]...10 Jan 1843...JOHN HENDRIX (LS), Wit: HENRY HENDRIX, LEVY HENDRIX. SARAH
HENDRIX, wife of JOHN, relinquished dower 10 Jan 1843. Proven by LEVY [LEROY?] HENDRIX.
Rec. 10 Jan. 1843. Delivered to DAVID RAWL, 17 Feb 1844.

Pp. 651-652: S.C., Lexington Dist.: GEORGE STINGLEY for $1200 pd. by JOHN HILLER...328 A
in fork of Broad and Saluda, on little Johns Creek of Saluda, adj. MICHAEL
BANKS, JOHN HILLER, MALACHI LOWMAN...2 Sept 1842...GEORGE STINGLY (LS), Wit: JACOB WIN-
GARD, FREDERICK WISE. Proven by FREDERICK WISE, 14 Jan 1843. Rec. 16 Jan 1843. Delivered to JOHN HILLER, 6 Mar 1843.

Pp. 652-653: S. C.: HENRY KOON of Lexington Dist., for $400 pd. by JOHN U. COOGLER of
same...137 A on waters of Saluda River, called long branch adj. MICHAEL LOR-
ICK, SAMUEL HUFFMAN, THOMAS SHULAR...25 Feb 1842...HENRY KOON (LS), Wit: JOSEPH COOGLER,
DANIEL YOUNGINER. Proven by JOSEPH COOGLER, 30 Apr 1842. Rec. 16 Jan 1843. Delivered
to JOHN UL COOGLER, 25 SEpt 1843.

Pp. 653-655: By virtue of a writ of fiere facias issued out of the Court of Common Pleas
of Lex. Dist., tested 18 Apr 1842 at the suit of REUBEN GROSS for the use of
R. SONDLY, to levy of lands of GEORGE YOUNGINER $180.52...130 A adj. lands of SAMUEL P.
CAUGHMAN, SAMUEL WINGARD, for $5 pd. by FREDRICK GARTMAN...14 Jan 1843...WILLIAM L. MILLER,
S. L. D. (LS), Wit: JOHN HOOK, F. S. FOX. Proven by JOHN HOOK, 17 Jan 1843. Rec. 17 Jan
1843. Delivered to ADAM YOUNGINER, 15 Feb 1843.

Pp. 655-656:S. C.: FREDERICK GARTMAN of Lexington Dist., for $8 pd. by DANIEL YOUNGER &
ADAM YOUNGINER of same...130 A adj. SAMUEL P. CAUGHMAN, SAMUEL WINGARD & others

...14 Jan 1843...FREDERICK GARTMAN (LS), Wit: WM. L. MILLER, JNO HOOK. Proven by JOHN HOOK, 17 Jan 1843. Rec. 17 Jan 1843. Delivered to ADAM YOUGINER, 15 Feb 1843.

Pp. 656-657: S. C., Lexington Dist: WILLIAM L. MILLER Shff of Lex. Dist...by virtue of writs of fiere facias issued out of the Court of Common Pleas for District of Lexington, tested 8 Nov 1841 at the suit of RICHARD FALLAW to levy of goods, &c. of WM. B. JONES...450 A adj. lands of A. H. FORT, JESSE FOX, & ISRAEL GAUNTT on waters of N Edisto River...sold to WILLIAM T. MALPASS, FOR $16...20 Jan 1843...WM. L. MILLER (LS), Wit: JNO HOOK. C. HARTLEY. Proven by JOHN HOOK, 20 Jan 1843. Rec. 20 Jan 1843.

Pp. 658-659: S. C.: 3 Aug 1842, GEORGE CAUGHMAN of Lexington Dist., to FREDERICK & JACOB DRAFTS SR of same...whereas sd. CAUGHMAN is endebted to them.-.mortgage of 120 A on waters of Saluda River, adj. ANDREW CAUGHMAN, MICHAEL WESSINGER, JOHN H. FRANCK-LOW, JOSHUA KYZER, JACOB KIZER...GEORGE CAUGHMAN (LS), JACOB DRAFTS (LS), FREDERICK HARMAN (LS), Wit: G. J. HOOK, DANIEL LEAPHART. Proven by LEAPHART, 20 Jan 1842. Rec. 20 Jan 1843. Delivered to FREDK HARMAN, 21 July 1846.

Pp. 659-660: S. C.: DANIEL KLECKLY of Lexington Dist., for $214 pd. by WILLIAM SLOAN of same...125 A on Saluda River adj. SAMUEL T. LORICK, DANIEL KLECKLY, and the heirs of DAVID KLECKLY, sold by the Sheriff of Lex., 5 Sept 1842 in two separate tracts, as the right titile & interest of MRS. MARY KLECKLY, in the lands of DAVID KLECKLY decd at the suit of J. A. CRAFORD, J. A. SCOTT, against sd. MARY KLECKLY...1 Jan 1843...DANIEL KLECKLY (LS), Wit: HENRY A. MEETZE, JNO. HOOK. Proven by H. A. MEETZE, 30 Jan 1843. Rec. 30 Jan 1843. Delivered to WILLIAM SLOAN, 4 May 1854.

Pp. 661-662: S. C.: 1 Jan 1843, DANIEL KLECKLY to WILLIAM SLOAN...sd. SLOAN stands indebted to sd. KLECKLY...mortgage of 125 A on Saluda River adj. SAMUEL T. LORICK, DANIEL KLECKLY and heirs of DAVID KLECKLY, sold by Sherriff of Lex. Dist., on 5 Sept 1842 at the suit of J. A. CRAWFORD, & J. A. SCOTT...WILLIAM SLOAN (X) (LS), DANIEL KLECKLEY (LS), Wit: HENRY A. MEETZE, JNO. HOOK. Proven by HENRY A. MEETZE, 30 Jan 1843, Rec. 30 Jan 1843. Delivered to DANL. KLECKLEY, 1 Dec 1845. Recd. satisfaction in full 4 May 1854. DANIEL KLECKLEY, Wit: SAMUEL T. LORICK, JAMES E. LEE.

Pp. 662-663: S. C.: WILLIAM HURNOLD of Lexington Dist., to JAMES JUMPER for $400...154 A adj. JAMES JUMPER, GEORGE PRICE, HENRY KRAPS, SARAH JONES...3 Feb 1843... WILLIAM HURNOLD (X), Wit: HENRY A. MEETZE, F. S. FOX. Proven by MEETZE, 3 Feb 1843. Rec. 3 Feb 1843.

Pp. 663-668: An agreement between THOS K. POINDEXTER &JOHN FOX, MARIA W. POINDEXTER, MARY ANN POINDEXTER, & MARTHA JANE POINDEXTER. Lexington Dist.: 16 Feb 1842 whereas THOS K. POINDEXTER stands indebted to H. & L. HENDRIX for $99.50, to CHRISTIAN PRICE, for $238, to JOHN BLACK for $235, to JOHN FROST, for $___, to JOHN LORICK, Admr. about $18, to FOX MILLER, & Co. for $884 & $682, to sd. JOHN FOX, for $161, to WM. HONOLD for $30 or $45, to MEETZE & BOUKNIGHT for $40, amount not ascertained to MRS. ELIZA A. WILLIAMSON, as their guardian[??]...whereas sd. THOMAS K. POINDEXTER is desiours of making suitable provisions and advancements ot his son in law sd. JOHN FOX, and his daughters, sd. MARIA W., MARY ANN, MARTHA JANE POINDEXTER......tracts of land (1) land whereon I now live, on the road from Columbia to Edgefield Court House, adj. lands of GEORGE KREPS, JOHN KEASLER, GEORGE OSWALT, Heirs of JOHN S. ADDY, decd, & JOHIAL ANDERSON, 664A composed of three tracts a tract granted to GEORGE WEAVER, for 271 A purchased by sd. THOMAS K. POINDEXTER from JAMES KENNERLY, a tract of 124 A and 3/4 part of a tract granted to JOHN OSWALT for 300 A, 7 Oct 1793, and 140 A granted to sd. POINDESTER, on 1 Jan 1842 (2) plantation, known as my Plantation on 18 Mile Creek, and Twenty Mile Creek, on the Wise Ferry Road, adj. lands of E. J. SCOTT, HENRY MEETZE, DENNIS GIBSON, JACOB HARMAN, HENRY H. SEE, NATHANIEL KLECKLEY, SAMUEL WINGARD, DANIEL & ADAM YOUNGINER, Heirs of JOHN HENDRIX, decd and JOHN SNIDER, made of sundry smaller tracts purchased by sd. THOMAS K. POINDEXTER and MARY KENNERLY from diferent individuals (3) all that plantation on head of Long Branbh, purchased by sd. POINDEXTER from JOHN D. A. MURPHY, 156 A part of a tract granted to JOHN SWINT for 250 A 4 May 1775, adj. GEORGE CAUGHMAN (4) plantation on Boggy Branch, waters of 12 Mile Creek adj. land held by GEORGE WINGARD, THOMAS RALL & others, 290 A, part of 580 A granted to MARY KENNERLY, 6 May 1811 (5) plantation on Red Bank Creek, waters of Congaree Riverr, 505 A, granted to JAMES EDWARDS, 6 Jan 1817 adj. lands of JOSEPH LYBRAND, GREEN & ANDERSON & others (6) plantation on Two Notch Road on waters of Twelve Mile Creek and Red Bank Creeks, 500 A part of a grant to STEPHEN BONE and JACOB HALLMAN for 1000 A (7) plantation of 76 A on Red Bank Creek conveyed to sd. POINDEXTER, to STEPHEN DICKENSON, 29 July 1833...also various cattle and swine, etc....THOS K. POINDEXTER (LS), JOHN FOX (LS), MARIA W. POINDEXTER (LS), MARY ANN POINDESTER (LS), MARTHA JANE POINDEXTER (LS), Wit: JAMES JUMPER, JOSEPH R. JONES. Proven by JAMES JUMPER, 29 Dec 1842. Rec. 3 Feb 1842.

Pp. 668-669: S. C., Lexington Dist.: WILLIAM LUCAS SENR., for $60 pd. by M. W. LUCAS, all
                of Lex. Dist....330 A, part of grant to GEORGE STEEDMAN SR., 4 June 1813,
adj. JOHN LUCAS, JAMES LUCAS, DANIEL J. LUCAS, DANIEL LUCAS, JAMES DUNBAR, on waters old
Road that leads from the up Country to Charleston...7 Oct 1842...WM. LUCAS SR. (LS), Wit:
PERNETHY TAYLOR (X), JAMES J. CLARK. Proven by TAYLOR, 27 Oct 1842. Rec. 6 Feb 1843.
Delivered to JOHN C. LUCAS, 8 July 1843.

Page 670: S. C., Lexington Dist.: GEORGE STINGILEY for $600 pd. by JACOB WINGARD, 108 A
                in fork of Broad and Saluda, adj. JACOB WINGARD, FREDERICK WYSE, GODFRY DERICK
...3 Dec 1842 GEORGE STINGILY (LS), Wit: JOHN HILLER, FREDERIC WISE. Proven by WISE, 6
Feb 1843. Rec. 6 Feb 1843. Dld. to JACOB WINGARD, 24 Feb 1844.

Pp. 671-672: S. C. Lexington Dist.: DANIEL LOWMAN for $400 pd. by JACOB WINGARD...31 A,
                part of a grant to GEORGE KATE on Saluda River, adj. JACOB STINGLEY,
FREDERIC WYSE, GEORGE STINGLEY...7 Feb 1840 DANIEL LOWMAN (LS), Wit: JOHANNES LOWMAN, FRED-
ERIC BICKLY. Proven by BICKLEY, 7 Sept 1840 before J. H. COUNTS. NANCY LOWMAN, wife of
DANIEL, relinquished dower, 3 Aug 1840. Rec. 6 Feb 1843. Delivered to JACOB WINGARD, 24
Feb 1844.

Pp. 672-673: S. C., Lexington Dist., GEORGE STINGILY for $200 pd. by JACOB WINGARD...68
                A in fork of Broad and Saluda adj. CAPT. COUNTS, LOWMAN, DERRICK...3 Dec
1842...GEORGE STINGILY (LS), Wit: JOHN HILLER, FREDERIC WISE. Proven by WISE, 6 Feb 1843.
Rec. 6 Feb 1843. Delivered to JACOB WINGARD, 24 Feb 1844.

Pp. 673-674: JACOB UNGHER & SALLY, WILLIAM HALTAWANGER & KEZIA, JACOB WINGARD & CHRISTENA,
                & JOHN HILLER and MARTHA, all of Lexington Dist., bound unto each other,
for $1500, 12 Mar 1842...agreement, whereas HENRY LYBRAND decd of Lexington Dist., did in
his L. W. & T. bequeath to MARY BARBARA his wife, two Negroes, with other property, which
with their increase, at her death to be divided among his four daughters, SALLY, KEZIA,
CHRISTIANA, & MARTHA, now the sd. heirs all being of age and of sound and discretionary
minds....now wives of above...JACOB UNGER & wife to take the negroes and divide...[all
above named persons signed (LS).] Wit: FREDERIC WISE, MICHAEL HILLER (H). Proven by
WISE, 6 Feb 1843. Rec. 6 Feb 1843. Delivered to JACOB WINGARD, 24 Feb 1844.

Pp. 674-676: S. C.: By virtue of writs of fiere facias issued out of the Court of Common
                Pleas held for Dist. of Lexington Tested 13 Apr 1840, at the suit of R.
HARMAN, & S. LOWMAN to levy $78.39 of goods &c. of CORNELIUS CLARK...513 A adj. JONATHAN
TAYLOR, DANIEL SMITH, JOHN DERRICK...purchased by HARMAN LOWMAN for $231, and had titled
made to JACOB H. PEARSON...20 Jan 1843...WILLIAM L. MILLER (LS), Wit: JOHN LORICK, F. S.
FOX. Proven by F. S. FOX, 8 Feb 1843. Rec. 8 Feb 1843.

Pp. 676-678: S. C., Lexington Dist.: Whereas SUSANNAH FALKNER, one of the Heirs and dis-
                tributees of WILLIAM FALKNER decd, filed a petition in the Court of Ordinary
of Lex. Dist., against CAROLINE FALKNER, WILLIAM W. FALKNER, and LAWRENCE FALKNER on 6
Oct 1842, stating that sd. WILLIAM FALKNER died intestate, leaving a tract which has not
been partitioned...100 A sold to GEORGE ROBERTS, for $401...land on Rocky Creek, waters of
Saluda, adj. JOHN FORTNER SR., BENJ. SNELGROVE, & DERRICK...15 Feb 1843...WM. L. MILLER
(LS), Wit: F.S. FOX, JNO. HOOK, Proven by F. S. FOX, 15 Feb 1843. Rec. 15 Feb 1843.
Delivered to GEORGE ROBERTS, 3 Apr 1845.

Pp. 678-679: S. C.: JACOB BERNHARD, whereas my Father CHRISTOPHER BERNHARD late of Lex.
                Dist., by his L. W. & T. devised his whole estate to his wife, my mother,
during her life, and his real estate of 100 A in fork of Broad and Saluda River adj. JOHN
SHULER, THOMAS SHULER, and Est. of DANIEL DREHER, to his four sons...I relinquish to my
mother MARGARET BERNHARD, widow now residing in sd. dist., my distributive share...22 Dec
1842...JACOB BERNHARD (LS), Wit: JAMES D. STINGILY, FREDERICK WISE. Proven by STINGILY,
20 Feb 1843. Delivered to JOHN SHULER, 26 Aug 1844.

Pp. 679-680: S. C.: MARGARET BERNHARD (widow) of Lex. Dist., for $500 pd. by JOHN SHULER
                of same...100 A in fork of Broad and Saluda [same land in preceding deed]...
20 Feb 1843..MARGARET BERNHARD (+) (LS), Wit: A. H. FORT, JNO. HOOK. Proven by JOHN HOOK
20 Feb 1843. Rec. 20 Feb 1843. Delivered to JOHN SHULER, 26 Aug 1844.

Pp. 680-682: S. C., Richland Dist.: MICHAEL CORLEY of Richland Dist., for $650 pd. by JNO.
                YOUNGINGER of Lexington Dist...115 A on S side Saluda adj. JNO DREHER, FREDER-
CIK GABLE, SANDERS SWIGERT, originally granted to MICHAEL GARTMAN...7 Feb 1843...MICHAEL
CORLEY (LS), Wit: E. D. GILLMORE, BENJAMIN EDWARDS. Proven by E. D. GILLMORE & BENJ.
EDWARDS, 7 Feb 1843, before CONRAD SHULL. Richland Dist.: MARY CORLEY, wife of MICHAEL,
relinquished dower, 7 Feb 1843 before HENRY TURNIPSEED. Rec. 6 Mar 1843. Delivered to
E. C. GILLMORE, 3 Apr 1843.

Pp. 682-683: S. C. Lexington Dist.:   RIVERS GUNTER JR., for $150 pd. by THOMAS RAWLS
          of Lex. Dist...162 A granted to EDWARD WATTS, 7 June 1786 another granted to
WILLIAM AULTMAN SENR, antoher granted to JAMES DUNBAR SENR...mortgage...1 Mar 1843...
RIVERS GUNTER JUR., Test ELDRIDGE GUNTER. Proven by ELDRIDGE GUNTER, 6 Mar 1843, before
JOHN J. ABLE, ESQR., Rec. 6 Mar 1843. Delivered to THOS RAWLS, 29 Jan 1844. Satisfied
Jan. 29, 1844, THOMAS J. RAWLS .

Page 683: S. C., Lexington Dist.: ISAAC VANSANT, one of the Magistrates of the Dist. afore-
          said, certify that RACHEL RISH, wife of ANDREW RISH, relinquished inheritance
from estate of GEORGE STEEDMAN, to REUBEN STEEDMAN...13 Feb 1843. RACHEL RISH (+),
Wit: ISAAC VANSANT. Rec. 6 Mar 1843. JOHN FOX, Regr.

                            END OF DEED BOOK M.

Page 1: TUNIS CONYELL, JOHN BYRUM & ELISHA DANIEL of Lexington and Richland District bound
to BENJAMIN HAILE, Comr. of Equity in sum of $5000...26 Aug 1809...petition of 28
June last appointed TUNIS CONYEL, Guardian of JESSE CONYEL, a minor under 21 years of age.
Before WM TAYLOR.

Page 2: DAVID KAIGLER, JOHN WOLF and JOHN CRAPPS, bound to JAMES DELLET, Comr. of Equity
in sum of $12,000...29 Feb 1815..petition 27 February inst...DAVID KAIGLER, Guar-
dain of ANN HARRIET [two people?] and LAURENS [?] KAIGLER, offspring of MICHAEL KAIGLER,
decd, under under 21 years of age. Before CALEB CLARKE.

Page 3: MARGARET KAIGLER (X), ROBERT SEAWRIGHT, & WILLIAM H. LEE, bound to JAMES DELLET,
Comr. of Equity, in sum of $800...29 Feb 1815...petition of 27 Feb inst...MARGARET
KAIGLER, guardian of ANN KAIGLER, offspring of JOHN KAIGLER, decd, a minor under 21 years
of age. Before CALEB CLARKE.

Page 4: MARGARET KAIGLER (X), ANDREW KAIGLER, ROBERT SEAWRIGHT, & WILLIAM H. LEE, bound
to JAMES DELLET, in sum of $300...29 Feb inst, [1815]...petition of 27 Feb inst....
MARGARET KAIGLER & ANDREW KAIGLER, guardians of JOHN JAMES, THOMAS REUBEN, and WILLIAM
KAIGLER, offspring of WM KAIGLER, decd, minors under 21 years of age. Before CALEB
CLARKE.

Page 5: JOHN NICHOLS (X), GEORGE LORICK (X) bound to JAMES DELLET for $800...26 June
1815...petition 26 June...JOHN NICHOLS, guardian of TOBIAS GEIGER, a minor under
21 years of age...Before JOHN LINCH[LINCK?].

Page 6: JOHN HENDRIX & HENRY HENDRIX & THOMAS K. POINDEXTER bound to JAMES DELLET, in
sum of $500...1 April 1816...petition of 26 Feb last...JOHN HENDRIX, guardian of
WILLIAM HENDRIX and ELIZABETH HENDRIX, minors under 21 years of age...Before DANL HARRISON.

Page 7: MICHAEL WINGARD & JACOB BICKLEY, bound to JAMES DELLET in sum of $900...11 Oct
petition of same day...MICHAEL WINGARD, guardian of JACOB WINGARD, MICHAEL WINGARD,
and JULIA ANNA WINGARD, minors under 21 years of age...Before ROBERT STARKE, JR.

Page 8: JOHN T. SEIBLES and SIMPSON WILSON bound to JAMES DELLET in sum of $8000...25 Jan
1817...Petition of February term last...JOHN T. SEIBLES, guardian of JAMES SEIBLES,
a minor under 21 years of age...Before RICHARD A. GANTT, "As to MR. SEIBLES."

Page 9: ABRAHAM GEIGER and SAMUEL GREEN to JAMES DELLET in sum of $600...21 Mar 1818...
petition of 23 February last...ABRAHAM GEIGER, guardian of MARY BELL, a minor
under 21 years of age. Before JOHN G. BROWN, SAMUEL M. GREEN.

Page 10: JACOB BATES & ELISHA HAMMOND bound to JAMES DELLET in sum of $1000...23 June 1818
...petition of 23 June 1818...JACOB BATES, guardian of JACOB KELLY, a minor under
21 years of age. Before JOHN D. BROWN.

Page 11: JACOB BATES & ELISHA HAMMOND bound to JAMES DELLET in sum of $1000...23 June 1818
...petition of 23 June 1818...JACOB BATES, guardian of GEORGE KELLY, a minor
under 21 years of age. Before JOHN D. BROWN.

Page 12: JAMES LANGFORD, ASA LANGFORD, & SAMUEL SIMONS bound to JAMES DELLET in sum of
$1200...21 June 1818...petition of 24 June 1818...JAMES LANGFORD, guardian of
JULIA KELLY, a minor under 21 years of age. Before WM BRANTHWAITE[?].

Page 13: GEORGE LEAPHART & WEST CAUGHMAN of Lexington District bound to THOMAS T. WILLISON
in sum of $3000...22 Feb 1819...petition of 22 Feb...GEORGE LEAPHART, guardian of
ANDREW RUFF and JOHN RUFF, minors under 21 years of age...Before ANDREW P. BUTLER.

Page 14: JOHN DREHR & JOHN BRYER bound to THOMAS T. WILLISON, for $1000...23 Feb 1819...
petition of 22 Feb...JOHN DREHR, guardian of ANN KEIGLER, a minor under 21 years
of age. Before AMOS BANKS.

Page 15: MARY KOON (X), JAMES KENNERLY & SAMUEL KOON of Lexington District, bound to
THOMAS T. WILLISON, for $4000...28 Sept 1819...petition of 28 June...MARY KOON,
guardian of MARY ANN, SARAH, JOHN HENRY, MARGARET and JOHN KOON, minors under 21 years of
age. Before C. CLIFTON.

Page 16: ANDREW TARRAR (A) & JACOB DRAFTS of Lexington District to THOMAS T. WILLISON
in sum of $10,000...17 July 1819...petition of 20 June...ANDREW TARRAR, guardian
of JOHN DRAFTS & REUBEN DRAFTS, minors under 21 years of age. Before JOHN RABB.

Page 17: THOMAS K. POINDEXTER, JAMES KENNERLY bound to THOMAS T. WILLISON, in sum of
$2000...2 July 1819...petition same day...THOMAS POINDEXTER, guardian of
BENJAMIN, MARY and ROBERT POINDEXTER, minors under 21 years of age. [No wit.]

Page 18: THOMAS SHULER and JOHN WITHERS of Lexington District bound to THOMAS T. WILLI-
SON in sum of 2000...17 July 1820...petition 17 July...THOMAS SHULER, guardian
of JOEL, HARRIET, FANNY, JOHN & DAVID HAMITER, minors under 21 years of age. Before
WM. HILLIARD.

Page 19: DANIEL KAIGLER, ELIZABETH KAIGLER (X), & PETER INABINET to JAMES DELLET in sum
of $4000...27 Feb 1815...petition of 27 Feb...DANIEL KAIGLER and ELIZABETH
KAIGLER, guardians of DRUSILLA & HENRY KAIGLER, offspring of MICHAEL KAIGLER, decd, minors
under 21 years of age. Before CALEB CLARKE.

Page 20: JACOB SWYGERT & SOLOMON SLIGH of Lexington District bound to THOMAS T. WILLISON
in sum of $5000...17 July 1820...petition of 17 July...JACOB SWYGERT, guardian
of JOHN A., JOHN G., and ELIZABETH HOUSEAL,minors under 21 years of age. Before R. STARK.

Page 21: GEORGE EIGLEBURGER, JOHN EIGLEBURGER, & ADAM MAYER bound to THOMAS T. WILLISON
in sum of $25,000...26 Feb 1822...25 Feb 1822, petition...GEORGE EIGLEBURGER,
guardian of GEORGE A., MARY ELIZABETH and JOHN ADAM EIGLEBURGER, minors under 21 years
of age... Before WM. BAUSKETT.

Page 22: JOHN SEE & CHRISTIAN RALL of Lexington District bound to THOMAS T. WILLISON in
sum of $10,000...25 Feb 1822...petition 22 Feb....JOHN SEA, guardian of HARMAN
SEA, a minor under 21 years of age...Before ROBT WESTUS[?], Jr.

[All of the preceding bonds are headed Columbia District; the next two only are headed
Richland District; and the remaining bonds in the volume are headed Lexington District.

Page 23: ELIZABETH BUTLER, ELIAS HAUGABOOK & DANIEL HAUGABOOK of Lexington District
bound to THOMAS T. WILLISON in sum of $10,000...25 June 1822...petition same
day...ELIZABETH BUTLER, guardian of ELIZABETH, JOHN ADAM and MARY BUTLER, minors under
21 years of age. Before W. PANOLT[?].

Page 24: A. H. FORT & MICAJAH MATI[?] bound to THOMAS T. WILLISON in sum of $1200...24
June 1823...petition same day...A. H. FORT, guardian of STEPHEN, GABRIEL & JOHN
CENTERFEIT[?], minors under the age of 21 years. Before HENRY ARTHUR.

Page 25: MARY ARTHUR and JOHN J. KEISLER of Lexington District bound to JOHN A. ADDISON
for $5000...26 June 1830...petition 15 Feb...MARY A. ARTHUR, gdn of MARY ANN
ARTHUR & SARAH ARTHUR, minors under 21 years of age. Before H. J. CAUGHMAN.

Page 26: THOS K. POINDEXTER, GEORGE OSWALT, and JACOB LEAPHART bound to JOHN A. ADDISON
for $3000...16 Mar 1832...THOMAS K. POINDEXTER, trustee of ELIZA ANN WILLIAMSON,
wife of JAMES E. WILLIAMSON. Before JOHN A. ROBERTS.

Page 27: MARY Y. ARTHUR, THOMAS H. SUMMERS, and HENRY ARTHUR bound to JOHN A. ADDISON for
$1800...4 June 1832...petition 13 Feb 1832...MARY Y. ARTHUR, gdn of JOSEPH
ARTHUR, a minor under 21 years of age. Before JOHN SHULER.

Page 28: MARY Y. ARTHUR, THOMAS H. SUMMERS, and HENRY ARTHUR bound to JOHN A. ADDISON for
$1800...4 June 1832...petition 13 Feb 1832...MARY Y. ARTHUR, gdn of SARAH
ARTHUR, a minor under 21 years of age. Before JOHN SHULER.

Page 29: MARY Y. ARTHUR, THOMAS H. SUMMERS, and HENRY ARTHUR bound to JOHN A. ADDISON for
$1800...4 June 1832...petition 13 Feb 1832...MARY Y. ARTHUR, gdn of WILLIAM E.
ARTHUR, a minor under 21 years of age. Before JOHN SHULER.

Page 30: MARY Y. ARTHUR, THOMAS H. SUMMERS, and HENRY ARTHUR bound to JOHN A. ADDISON for
$1800...4 June 1832...petition 13 Feb 1832...MARY Y. ARTHUR gdn of THOMAS S.
ARTHUR, a minor under 21 years of age. Before JOHN SHULER.

Page 31: MARY Y. ARTHUR, THOMAS H. SUMMERS, and HENRY ARTHUR bound to JOHN A. ADDISON for
$1800...4 June 1832...petition 13 Feb 1832...MARY Y. ARTHUR gdn of MARY C.
ARTHUR, a minor under 21 years of age. Before JOHN SHULER.

Page 32: ELEANOR LEE and DANIEL QUATTLEBUM of Lexington District and AMOS BANKS and JACOB
LONG SENR of Edgefield District bound to JOHN A. ADDISON for $1200...[nd]...
petition Feb. term 1833, ELEANOR LEE, gdn of ANDREW LEE, a minor under 21. Before JAS.

E. LEE

Page 33: ELEANOR LEE & DANIEL QUATTLEBUM and AMOS BANKS & JACOB LONG SENR bound to JOHN
A. ADDISON for $1200...[nd]...petition Feb. term 1833...ELEANOR LEE, gdn of
THOMAS C. LEE, a minor under 21...Before JAS. E. LEE.

Page 34: ELEANOR LEE & DANIEL QUATTLEBUM and AMOS BANKS and JACOB LONG SENR bound to
JOHN A. ADDISON for $1200...[nd]...petition Feb. term 1833...ELEANOR LEE gdn of
PATRICK H. LEE, a minor under 21. Before JAS. E. LEE.

Page 35: ELEANOR LEE & DANIEL QUATTLEBUM and AMOS BANKS and JACOB LONG SENR bound to
JOHN A. ADDISON for $1200...[nd]..petition Feb. term 1833...ELEANOR LEE gdn of
BENJAMIN F. LEE, a minor under 21. Before JAS. E. LEE.

Page 36: ELEANOR LEE & DANIEL QUATTLEBUM and AMOS BANKS and JACOB LONG SENR bound to
JOHN A. ADDISON for$1200...[nd]...petition Feb. term 1833...ELEANOR LEE gdn of
WILLIAM H. LEE, a minor under 21. Before JAS. E. LEE.

Page 37: ELEANOR LEE & DANIEL QUATTLEBUM and AMOS BANKS and JACOB LONG SENR bound to
JOHN A. ADDISON for $1200...[nd]...petition Feb. term 1833...ELEANOR LEE gdn of
ELIZABETH LEE, a minor under 21. Before JAS. E. LEE.

Page 38: LEMUEL BOOZER, EDWIN J. SCOTT, and JOHN MEETZE of Lexington District bound to
JOHN A. ADDISON for $2000...__ Mar 1833...petition 18 Feb 1833...LEMUEL BOOZER,
gdn of JACOB BOOZER, a minor under 21. Before JOHN R. DREHER.

Page 39: HENRY L. CORBEN, SAMUEL P. CORBEN and JNO P. CORBEN of Lexington District bound
to JOHN A. ADDISON for $3500 16 May 1833...petition 18 Feb...HENRY L. CORBEN,
gdn of NAPOLEON B. CORBEN, a minor under 21...Before N. C. D. CULCLASURE.

Page 40: HANNAH CORBEN & N. C. D. CULCLASURE, DAVID MARMADUKE and DANIEL CULCLASURE of
Lexington District, bound to JOHN A. ADDISON...18 Dec 1833...petition 18 Feb
1833...HANNAH CORBEN, gdn of JEROME B. CORBEN, a minor under 21. Before D. KAIGLER,
JOHN CRAPS.

Page 41: HANNAH CORBEN, N. C. D. CULCLASURE, DAVID CULCLASURE, and DAVID MARMADUKE
bound to JOHN A. ADDISON for $3500 10 Dec 1833...petition 18 Feb 1833...HANNAH
CORBEN, gdn of ELIZABETH ANN CORBEN, a minor under 21. Before D. KAIGLER, JOHN CRAPS.

Page 42: WILLIAM COUNTS, JOSEPH W. WYSE and GEORGE M. FULMER of Lexington District bound
to JOHN A. ADDISON for $1500...3 Mar 1834...petition 17 Feb...WILLIAM COUNTS,
gdn. of MARTHA ELIZABETH and MARY M. COUNTS, minors under 21. Before NICHOLAS SUMMER.

Page 43: JOHN W. HOLLMAN, JACOB GANTT, and GEORGE HOLLMAN of Lexington District bound to
JOHN A. ADDISON for $3042...3 Mar 1834...petition 17 Feb 1834...JOHN W. HOOL-
MAN, gdn. of MALISSIA ABLE, minor under 21. Before JOHN S. ONEIL.

Page 44: JOHN W. HOLLMAN, JACOB GANTT, and GEORGE HOLLMAN bound to JOHN A. ADDISON for
$3042...3 Mar 1834...petition 17 Feb 1834...JOHN W. HOOLMAN, gdn. of PEARCE
ABLE, a minor under 21. Before JOHN S. ONEIL.

Page 45: JOHN W. HOLLMAN, JACOB GANTT and GEORGE HOLLMAN bound to JOHN A. ADDISON for
$3042...3 Mar 1834...petition 17 Feb 1834...JOHN W. HOOLMAN, gdn. of KAIN [HAIN?]
ABLE, a minor under 21. Before JOHN S. ONEIL.

Page 46: JOHN W. HOLLMAN, JACOB GANTT and GEORGE HOLLMAN bound to JOHN A. ADDISON for
$3042... 3 Mar 1834...petition 17 Feb 1834...JOHN W. HOOLMAN, gdn. of SEARCY
ABLE, a minor under 21. Before JOHN S. ONEIL.

Page 47: A. H. FORT, THOMAS K. POINDEXTER, and HENRY J. DRAFTS of Lexington District
bound to JOHN A. ADDISON for $400...____ 1836...petition 2 Feb 1836...A. H.
FORT, gdn of NANCY E. HOLMAN, a minor under 21. Before BENJAMIN POINDEXTER.

Page 48: A. H. FORT, THOMAS K. POINDEXTER, HENRY J. DRAFTS bound to JOHN A. ADDISON, for
$400...A. H. FORT, gdn. of ELIZEBETH HOLEMAN, a minor under 21. Before BRNJA-
MIN POINDEXTER.

Page 49: JACOB HARMAN, JACOB HENDRIX, REUBEN HARMAN, & EDWIN J. SCOTT of Lexington Dist.,
bound to J. A. ADDISON, for $2000...__ Feb 1836...petition 2 Feb 1836...JACOB
HARMAN, gdn. of DANIEL EARHART [part stating "Minor..." stricken]. Before DAVID C. ANDER
SON.

Page 50: SAMUEL BOUKNIGHT, JOHN BOUKNIGHT SENR, and JOHN U. COOGLER of Lexington Dist.,
        bound to JOHN A. ADDISON, for $6933.33...2 Feb 1836...petition 1 Feb 1836...
SAMUEL BOUKNIGHT, gdn of J. R. W. KENNERLY, minor under 21. Before LEMUEL BOOZER.

Page 51: WILLIAM H. HOLEMAN, MARY HOLEMAN (X), WILLIAM LYBRAND, and FREDERICK SEAS of
        Lexington Dist., bound to JOHN A. ADDISON for $4000...1 Aug 1836...petition
2 Feb 1836...WILLIAM W. HOLEMAN, gdn. of DAVID HOLEMAN, a minor under 21. Before WEST
CAUGHMAN, JOHN FOX "as to F. SEAS."

Page 52: THOMAS K POINDEXTER, JOHN FOX and WM. L. MILLER of Lexington Dist., bound to
        JOHN A. ADDISON, for $4000...25 Apr 1837...THOMAS K. POINDEXTER, trustee of
ELIZA ANN WILLIAMSON, wife of JAMES E. WILLIAMSON, Before ISAIAH CAUGHMAN.

Page 53: WEST CAUGHMAN, JOHN MEETZE, and EDWIN J. SCOTT of Lexington District bound to
        JOHN A. ADDISON, for $1600...8 Jan 1838...petition __Nov 1837...WEST CAUGHMAN,
gdn. of RUBEN & EMANUEL CORLEY, minors under 21. Before JOHN H. SOUTER.

Page 54: WEST CAUGHMAN, JOHN METTZE, and EDWIN J. SCOTT bound to JOHN A. ADDISON, for
        $1600...WEST CAUGHMAN, gdn. of WESTLY CORLEY and LEONORA CORLEY, minors under
21. Before JOHN H. SOUTER.

Page 55: REUBEN HARMAN bound to JOHN A. ADDISON for $1000...____ 1839...petition 21 Oct
        ...REUBEN HARMAN, gdn of JOHN WOLF AIRHART, a minor under 21...Signed: REUBEN
HARMAN, JONATHAN HARMAN, SAMUEL LOWMAN, Before N. HARMAN.

Page 56: REUBEN HARMAN bound to J. A. ADDISON for $1000...1839...petition 21 Oct...REUBEN
        HARMAN, gdn. of EVE B. S. C. EARHART, a minor under 21...Sigend: REUBEN HARMAN,
JONATHAN HARMAN, SAMUEL LOWMAN, before N. HARMAN.

Page 57: JAMES JUMPER, DANIEL LEAPHART, & WILLIAM GEIGER of Lexington bound to JOHN A.
        ADDISON for $800...20 July 1839...petition 19 July 1839...JAMES JUMPER, gdn. of
REBECCA A. LEAPHART, a minor under 21. Signed: JAMES JUMPER, DANIEL LEAPHART, W. H.
GEIGER, Before EPHRAIM CORLEY.

Page 58: JAMES JUMPER, DANIEL LEAPHART, & WM GEIGER bound to JOHN A. ADDISON for $800...
        20 July 1839...petition 19 July 1839 ...JAMES JUMPER, gdn. of JOSEPH E. LEAPHART,
a minor under 21.

Page 59: JAMES JUMPER, DANIEL LEAPHART, & WM GEIGER, bound to JOHN A. ADDISON for $800...
        20 July 1839...petition 19 July 1839...JAMES JUMPER, gdn. of EDWARD F. LEAPHART,
a minor under 21.

Page 60: JAMES JUMPER, DANIEL LEAPHART, & WM GEIGER, bound to JOHN A. ADDISON for $800...
        20 July 1839...petition 19 July 1839...JAMES JUMPER, gdn. of MARTHA E. LEAPHART,
a minor under 21.

Page 61: JAMES JUMPER, DANIEL LEAPHART, & WM. GEIGER bound to JOHN A. ADDISON for $800...
        20 July 1839...petition 19 July 1839...JAMES JUMPER, gdn. of MARIAH W. LEAPHART,
a minor under 21.

Page 62: JAMES JUMPER, DANIEL LEAPHART, & WM. GEIGER bound to JOHN A. ADDISON for $800...
        20 July 1839..petition 19 July 1839...JAMES JUMPER, gdn. of ROBERT H. LEAPHART,
a minor under 21.

Page 63: JAMES JUMPER, DANIEL LEAPHART, & WM. GEIGER bound to JOHN A. ADDISON for $800...
        20 July 1839...petition 19 July 1839...JAMES JUMPER, gdn. of ELIZA H. LEAPHART,
a minor under 21.

Page 64: SAMUEL LYKES, JACOB BOOKMAN, & THOMAS BOOKMAN bound to JOHN A. ADDISON for $1600
        ...1 Aug 1839...petition 18 July 1839...SAMUEL LYKES, gdn. of ANN E. BOUKNIGHT,
a minor under 21...before HENRY SMITH.

Page 65: SAMUEL LYKES, JACOB BOOKMAN, & THOMAS BOOKMAN bound to JOHN A. ADDISON for $1600
        ...1 Aug 1839...petition 18 July 1839...SAMUEL LYKES, gdn. of CAROLINE T. BOUK-
NIGHT, a minor under 21.

Page 66: SAMUEL LYKES, JACOB BOOKMAN, & THOMAS BOOKMAN bound to JOHN A. ADDISON for $1600
        ...1 Aug 1839...petition 18 July 1839...SAMUEL LYKES, gdn. of HARRIET L. BOUK-
NIGHT, a minor under 21.

Page 67: SAMUEL LYKES, JACOB BOOKMAN & THOMAS BOOKMAN bound to JOHN A. ADDISON for $1600
...1 Aug 1839...petition18 July 1839...SAMUEL LYKES, gdn. of [no name given]....

Page 68: SAMUEL LYKES, JACOB BOOKMAN & THOMAS BOOKMAN bound to JOHN A. ADDISON for $1600
...1 Aug 1839...petition 18 July 1839...SAMUEL LYKES, gdn. of MARY M. BOUKNIGHT,
a minor under 21.

Page 69: JOSEPH H. MORGAN, JAMES CAYCE (+), & ROBERT W. GIBBS bound to JOHN A. ADDISON
for $5000...16 Sept 1840...JOSEPH H. MORGAN, trustee of MARY MORGAN. Before
C. S. MORGAN & DANIEL MORGAN.

Page 70: WILLIAM HOWARD, SARAH HOWARD & JACOB GAUNTT bound to JOHN A. ADDISON for $1277...
12 Nov 1840...petition 16 June 1840...WILLIAM HOWARD, gdn. of MICHAEL HOWARD,
a minor under 21...Before JOHN HOOK.

Page 71: JESSE COOGLER, JOHN M. COOGLER, & WILLIAM L. MILLER bound to JOHN A. ADDISON
for $300...2 Aug 1841...petition 21 June 1841...JESSE COOGLER, gdn. of ANDREW
T. HALTIWANGER, a minor under 21...also singed SAMUEL HUFFMAN (LS), Before FRANKLIN
CORLEY.

Page 72: JACOB EARGLE, HENRY ELEAZER, & JOHN SUMMERS JR., bound to BENJAMIN T. SAXON, for
$1500 ...14 Dec 1841...petition 28 June 184_...JACOB EARGLE, gdn of JACOB SUMMERS,
a minor...Before HENRY A. MEETZE.

Page 73: JESSE METZ, JOHN SHULER, & SAMUEL HUFFMAN bound to HENRY A. MEETZE for $1000...
28 Feb 1842...petition 25 Jan...JESSE METZ, gdn of JANE C. MATHIAS, a minor
under 21...before JOHN FOX.

Page 74: JESSE METZ, JOHN SHULER, & SAMUEL HUFFMAN bound to HENRY A. MEETZE for $1000...
28 Feb 1842...petition 25 Jan...JESSE METZ, gdn. of JOHN MATHIAS, a minor under
21...before JOHN FOX.

Page 75: JESSE METZ, JOHN SHULER, & SAMUEL HUFFMAN bound to HENRY A. MEETZE for $1000...
28 Feb 1842...petition 25 Jan...JESSE METZ, gdn. of ELIZA MATHIAS, a minor under
21...before JOHN FOX.

Page 76: JESSE METZ, JOHN SHULER, & SAMUEL HUFFMAN bound to HENRY MEETZE, for $1000...
28 Feb 1842...petition 25 Jan ...JESSE METZ, gdn. of SARAH BELINDA MATHIAS, a
minor under 21...before JOHN FOX.

Page 77: JESSE METZ, JOHN SHULER, & SAMUEL HUFFMAN bound to HENRY A. MEETZE, for $1000...
28 Feb 1842...petition 25 Jan ...JESSE METZ, gdn. of MARY LOUISA MATHIAS, a
minor under 21...before JOHN FOX.

Page 78: JESSE METZ, JOHN SHULER, & SAMUEL HUFFMAN bound to HENRY A. MEETZE, for $1000...
28 Feb 1842...petition 25 Jan...JESSE METZ, gdn. of ELLEN MATHIAS, a minor under
21...before JOHN FOX.

Page 79: JOSIAH CORLEY of Barnwell Dist., & JOSHUA CORLEY of Orangeburgh Dist., bound to
HENRY A. MEETZE...3 Oct 1842...JOSIAH CORLEY, gdn. of MARGARET ANN CORLEY, a
minor under 21...before JESSE HOOK.

Page 80: JOSIAH CORLEY of Barnwell Dist., & JOSHUA CORLEY of Orengeburgh Dist., bound to
HENRY A. MEETZE...3 Oct 1842...JOSIAH CORLEY, gdn. of THOMAS FUMIAR[?] CORLEY,
a minor under 21...before JESSE HOOK.

Page 81: JACOB K. GANTT, WARREN WILLIAMSON, DANIEL B. CHAPMAN, CHRISTIAN LITES (X), &
THOS. L. VEAL bound to HENRY A. MEETZE for $300...4 May 1843...petition 12 Apr
1843...JACOB K. GANTT, gdn. of JOHN M. RUSSELL, a minor under 21...before H. J. CAUGHMAN.

Page 82. JACOB K. GANTT, WARREN WILLIAMSON, DANIEL B. CHAPMAN, CHRISTIAN LITES (X), &
THOS. L. VEAL bound to HENRY A. MEETZE, for $300...4 May 1843...petition 12 Apr
1843...JACOB K. GANTT, gdn. of HENRY W. RUSSEL, a minor under 21,..before H. J. CAUGHMAN.

Page 83: [Repeat of preceding bond].

Page 84: JACOB K. GANTT, WARREN WILLIAMSON, DANIEL B. CHAPMAN, CHRISTIAN LITES (X), &
THOS. L. VEAL, bound to HENRY A. MEETZE, for $300...4 May 1843...petition 12 Apr
1843...JACOB K. GANTT, gdn. of SORSEY[?] RUSSELL, a minor under 21...before H. J. CAUGHMAN.

Page 85: JACOB K. GANTT, WARREN WILLIAMSON, DANIEL B. CHAPAMAN, CHRISTIAN LITES (X), &
     THOS. L. VEAL bound to HENRY A. MEETZE, for $300...4 May 1843...petition 12 Apr
1843...JACOB K. GANTT, gdn. of THOMAS D. RUSSELL, a minor under 21...before H. J. CAUGHMAN.

Page 86: EDWIN F. ARTHUR & JOSEPH A. BLACK of Richland Dist. bound to HENRY A. MEETZE...
     24 June 1843...petition of 3 Jan ____...EDWIN F. ARTHUR, gdn. of SUSANNAH[?] &
ADALINE GRADDICK, minors under 21...before JOHN W. BRADLEY.

Page 87: JOHN LORICK, EMANUEL GEIGER, & JACOB WINGARD bound to HENRY A. MEETZE for $800
     ...7 Aug 1843...petition 19 June 1843...JOHN LORICK, gdn. of ELIZABETH RAWL, a
minor under 21...before JOHN J. SEAY.

Page 88: JOHN LORICK, EMANUEL GEIGER, & JACOB WINGARD bound to HENRY A. MEETZE for $800
     ...7 Aug 1843...petition 19 June 1843...JOHN LORICK, gdn. of ELIZABETH RAWL, a
minor under 21...before JOHN J. SEAY.

Page 89: SAMUEL BOUKNIGHT, DANIEL DERRICK & ELIAS BOUKNIGHT bound to HENRY A. MEETZE for
     $1000...5 Nov 1844...petition 17 June 1844...SAMUEL BOUKNIGHT, gdn. of ANN E.
BANKS, a minor under 21....before H. J. CAUGHMAN.

Page 90: SAMUEL BOUKNIGHT, DANIEL DERRICK & ELIAS BOUKNIGHT bound to HENRY A. MEETZE for
     $1000...5 Nov 1844...petition 17 June 1844...SAMUEL BOUKNIGHT, gdn. of ANN E.
BANKS, a minor under 21...before H. J. CAUGHMAN.

Page 91: REUBEN HARMAN, JONATHAN HARMAN, & JACOB HARMAN bound to HENRY A. MEETZE for
     $1000...22 Mar 1845...petition 21 Oct 1837...REUBEN HARMAN, gdn. of EVE B. C.
EARHART, a minor under 21...before H. J. CAUGHMAN.

Page 92: JACOB BICKLEY & MICHAEL WINGARD bound to HENRY A. MEETZE for $1400...6 Oct 1845
     ...petition 23 June 1845...JACOB BICKLEY, gdn. of CHARLOTTE CAROLINE BICKLEY,
a minor under 21...before SAMUEL BOUKNIGHT.

Page 93: JACOB BICKLEY & MICHAEL WINGARD bound to HENRY A. MEETZE for $1400...6 Oct 1845
     ...petition 23 June 1845...JACOB BICKLEY, gdn. of JAMES MORGAN BICKLEY, a minor
under 21...before SAMUEL BOUKNIGHT.

Page 94: JACOB BICKLEY & MICHAEL WINGARD bound to HENRY A. MEETZE for $1400...6 Oct 1845
     ...petition 23 June 1845...JACOB BICKLEY, gdn. of MARGARET J.[?] BICKLEY, a minor
under 21...before SAMUEL BOUKNIGHT.

Page 95: JOHN SIGLER & JAMES SIGLER of Edgefield and Barnwell Dists. bound to HENRY A.
     MEETZE for $2000...21 Dec 1845...petition 3 Nov...JOHN SIGLER, gdn. of THOMAS
ANN WELLS, a minor under 21...before C. BOUKNIGHT.

Page 96: JOHN FOX, ANDERSON STEEDMAN, SAMUEL RAWLS, & DANIEL DRAFTS JR bound to HENRY A.
     MEETZE for $3000...3 Jan 1848...petition June term 1847...JOHN FOX, gdn. of JOHN
FOX MILLER, a minor under 21...before JOHN CORLEY.

Page 97: ELIZABETH HENDRIX (X), LEWIS RIDDLE bound to HENRY A. MEETZE for $700...7 May
     1848...petition 29 June 1847...ELIZABETH HENDRIX, gdn. of SOLOMON HENDRIX, a
minor under 21...before JOSEPH E. HENDRIX.

Page 98: ELIZABETH HENDRIX (X), LEWIS RIDDLE bound to HENRY A. MEETZE for $700...7 May
     1848...petition 29 June 1847...ELIZABETH HENDRIX, gdn. of HENRY E. HENDRIX, a
minor under 21...before JOSEPH E. HENDRIX.

Page 99: JOHN HILLER, JOHN H. COUNTS, & JOHN B. HYLER bound to HENRY A. MEETZE for $1600
     ...15 Sept 1848...petition 27 Sept 1848...JOHN HILER, gdn. of HENRY E. UNGER, a
minor under 21...before JOHN H. SUTTON.

Page 100: JOHN HILLER, JOHN H. COUNTS, & JOHN B. HYLER bound to HENRY A. MEETZE for $1600
     ...15 Sept 1848...petition 27 Sept 1848...JOHN HILER, gdn. of SARAH E. UNGER, a
minor under 21...before JOHN H. SUTTON.

Page 101: JOHN HILLER, JOHN H. COUNTS, & JOHN B. HYLER bound to HENRY A. MEETZE for $1600
     ...15 Sept 1848...petition 27 Sept 1848...JOHN HILER, gdn. of MARTHA UNGER, a
minor under 21...before JOHN H. SUTTON.

Page 102: JOHN HILLER, JOHN H. COUNTS, & JOHN B. HYLER bound to HENRY A. MEETZE, for
$1600...15 Sept 1848...petition 27 Sept 1848...JOHN HILER, gdn. of PATRICK D.
UNGER, a minor under 21...before JOHN H. SUTTON.

Page 103: JOHN HILLER, JOHN H. COUNTS, & JOHN B. HYLER bound to HENRY A. MEETZE, for
$1600...15 Sept 1848...petition 27 Sept 1848...JOHN HILER, gdn. of ANN UNGER,
a minor under 21...before JOHN H. SUTTON.

Page 104: JOHN HILLER, JOHN H. COUNTS, & JOHN B. HYLER, bound to HENRY A. MEETZE, for
$1600...15 Sept 1848...petition 27 Sept 1848...JOHN HILER, gdn. of JOHN J.
UNGER, a minor under 21...before JOHN H. SUTTON.

Page 105: SAMUEL T. LORICK, GEORGE LORICK, & JOHN S. SWYGERT bound to HENRY A. MEETZE, for
$8000...11 Dec 1848...petition June term 1848...SAMUEL T. LORICK, gdn. of
WILLIAM GEIGER LORICK, a minor under 21. No wit.

Page 106: SAMUEL T. LORICK, GEORGE LORICK, & JOHN S. SWYGERT bound to HENRY A. MEETZE,
for $8000...11 Dec 1848...petition June term 1848...SAMUEL T. LORICK, gdn. of
CAMELL[?] PRESTON LORICK a minor under 21. No wit.

Page 107: SAMUEL T. LORICK, GEORGE LORICK, & JOHN S. SWYGERT bound to HENRY A. MEETZE,
for $8000...11 Dec 1848...petition June term 1848...SAMUEL T. LORICK, gdn. of
JAMES HAMILTON LORICK, a minor under 21. No wit.

Page 108: JOHN H. COUNTS, JOSEPH P. SUMMER & MRS. REBECCA COUNTS bound to HENRY A. MEETZE,
for $5000...8 Oct 1849...petition 25 June 1849...JOHN H. COUNTS, gdn. of
CHARLTON B. COUNTS, a minor under 21...Before W. M. SUMMER.

Page 109: JOHN H. COUNTS, JOSEPH P. SUMMER, & MRS. REBECCA COUNTS bound to HENRY A.
MEETZE for $5000...8 Oct 1849...petition 25 June 1849...JOHN H. COUNTS, gdn. of
MARTHA M. E. COUNTS, a minor under 21...Before W. M. SUMMER.

Page 110: JOHN H. COUNTS, JOSEPH P. SUMMER, & MRS. REBECCA COUNTS bound to HENRY A.
MEETZE for $7000...8 Oct 1849...petition 25 June 1849...JOHN H. COUNTS, gdn. of
MARY C. COUNTS, a minor under 21...Before W. M. SUMMER.

Page 111: JOHN H. COUNTS, JOSEPH P. SUMMER, & MRS. REBECCA COUNTS bound to HENRY A.
MEETZE for $7000...8 Oct 1849...petition 25 June 1849...JOHN H. COUNTS, gdn. of
WM. J.[F?] COUNTS, a minor under 21...Before W. M. SUMMER.

Page 112: JAMES JUMPER, WILLIAM GEIGER JR., & WILLIAM H. GEIGER bound to HENRY A. MEETZE
for $800...3 Dec 1849...petition 19 July 1839...JAMES JUMPER, gdn. of MARTHA E.
LEAPHART, a minor under 21...before JOHN KLECKLY, WILLIAM P. SEE.

Page 113: JAMES JUMPER, WILLIAM GEIGER, JR., & WILLIAM H. GEIGER, bound to HENRY A. MEETZE
for $800...3 Dec 1849...petition 19 July 1839...JAMES JUMPER, gdn. of MARIAH
W. LEAPHART, a minor under 21...before JOHN KLECKLY, WILLIAM P. SEE.

Page 114: JAMES JUMPER, WILLIAM GEIGER, JR., & WILLIAM H. GEIGER, bound to HENRY A. MEETZE
for $800...3 Dec 1849..petition 19 July 1839...JAMES JUMPER, gdn. of REBECCA
A. LEAPHART, a minor under 21...before JOHN KLECKLY, WILLIAM P. SEE.

Page 115: JAMES JUMPER, WILLIAM GEIGER, JR., & WILLIAM H. GEIGER, bound to HENRY A. MEETZE
for$800...3 Dec 1849,..petition 19 July 1839...JAMES JUMPER, gdn. of EDWIN F.
LEAPHART, a minor under 21...before JOHN KLECKLY, WILLIAM P. SEE.

Page 116: JAMES JUMPER, WILLIAM GEIGER, JR., & WILLIAM H. GEIGER bound to HENRY A. MEETZE
for $800...3 Dec 1849...petition 19 July 1839...JAMES JUMPER, gdn. of JOSEPH
E. LEAPHART, a minor under 21...before JOHN KLECKLY, WILLIAM P. SEE.

Page 117: DR. PATRICK TODD, HENRY FRAZURE, & JAMES LANGFORD bound to HENRY A. MEETZE for
$300...8 Oct 1850...petition July term 1850...DR. PATRICK TODD, gdn. of ISABEL
R. HOFF, a minor under 21...before WILLIAM LANGFORD.

Page 118: DR. PATRICK TODD, HENRY FRAZURE, & JAMES LANGFORD bound to HENRY A. MEETZE for
$300...8 Oct 1850...petition July term 1850...DR. PATRICK TODD, gdn. of WALTER
M. HOOF, a minor under 21...before WILLIAM LANGFORD.

Page 119: ISIAH LOWMAN, JESSE SWYGERT, & JOHN KLECKLY to HENRY A. MEETZE for $675...11
Nov 1850...petition 22 Oct 1850...ISIAH LOWMAN, gdn. of PATRICK G. LOWMAN, a
minor under 21...before JACOB BICKLEY, JOHN FOX.

Page 120: GEORGE MABUS, JAMES BODIE & LEWIS GUNTER (X), bound to HENRY A. MEETZE for
$136...15 Jan 1851...petition 3 Dec 1850...GEORGE MABUS, gdn. of JOSHUA MABUS,
a minor under 21...before JOHN KLECKLY.

Page 121: GEORGE MABUS, JAMES BODIE & LEWIS GUNTER (X), bound to HENRY A. MEETZE for
$136...15 Jan 1851...petition 3 Dec 1850...GEORGE MABUS, gdn. of JACOB MABUS,
a minor under 21...before JOHN KLECKLY.

Page 122: GEORGE MABUS, JAMES BODIE & LEWIS GUNTER (X), bound to HENRY A. MEETZE for
$136...15 Jan 1851..petition 3 Dec 1850...GEORGE MABUS, gdn. of PAUL MABUS,
a minor under 21...before JOHN KLECKLY.

Page 123: GEORGE MABUS, JAMES BODIE & LEWIS GUNTER (X), bound to HENRY A. MEETZE for
$136...15 Jan 1851...petition 3 Dec 1850...GEORGE MABUS, gdn. of JAMES MABUS,
a minor under 21...before JOHN KLECKLY.

Page 124: JOHN W. LEE & DAVID C. SHEALY bound to HENRY A. MEETZE, for $1100...14 July
1851...petition 26 June 1851...JOHN W. LEE, gdn. of BENJAMIN F. BANKS,...before
ELIAS BOUKNIGHT.

Page 125: URBAN E. JEFCOAT, JOSHUA A. JEFCOAT, & WILEY J. JEFCOAT bound to HENRY A. MEETZE
for $800...13 Jan 1852...petition June term 1851...URBAN E. JEFCOAT, gdn. of
MARY TINDAL...before ISAAC VANSANT.

Page 126: URBAN E. JEFCOAT, JOSHUA A. JEFCOAT, & WILEY J. JEFCOAT bound to HENRY A. MEETZE
for $800...13 Jan 1852...petition June term 1851...URBAN E. JEFCOAT, gdn. of
CAROLINE JEFCOAT, a minor under 21...before ISAAC VANSANT.

Page 127: URBAN E. JEFCOAT, JOSHUA A. JEFCOAT, & WILEY J. JEFCOAT bound to HENRY A. MEETZE
for $800...13 Jan 1842...petition June term 1851...URBAN E. JEFCOAT, gdn. of
VANDY V. R. JEFCOAT, a minor under 21...before ISAAC VANSANT.

Page 128: JAMES E. DRAFTS, GEORGE P. DRAFTS, & JOHN WINGARD bound to HENRY A. MEETZE for
$480...4 Aug 1852...petition 8 Apr 1851...JAMES E. DRAFTS, gdn. of CALVIN
DRAFTS, a minor under 21...before ISAAC VANSANT.

Page 129: ARTHUR H. FORT, ISAAC VANSANT & JAMES E. LEE bound to HENRY A. MEETZE for $1950
...23 Nov 1852...petition June term 1852...ARTHUR H. FORT, Trustee of MRS.
MARY ANN JONES...before HENRY A. FORT.

Page 130: JOSEPH LEAPHART, JOHN LEAPHART, & JAMES BARR bound to HENRY A. MEETZE, for
$9000...5 Jan 1853...petition 27 Nov 1852...JOSEPH LEAPHART, gdn. of CHARLTON
B. LEAPHART, a minor under 21...before ISAAC VANSANT.

Page 131: JOHN FOX, ANDERSON STEEDMAN, & REUBEN STEEDMAN bound to HENRY A. MEETZE, for
$1000...5 Feb 1853...petition June term 1852...JOHN FOX, gdn. of MARY M.
HENDRIX, a minor under 21...before JAS. E. LEE.

Page 132: JOHN FOX, ANDERSON STEEDMAN, & REUBEN STEEDMAN bound to HENRY A. MEETZE, for
$1000...5 Feb 1853...petition June term 1852...JOHN FOX, gdn. of JAMES E.
HENDRIX, a minor under 21...before JAS. E. LEE.

Page 133: HENRY MEETZE, JOHN H. MEETZE, & ISAAC VANSANT bound to HENRY A. MEETZE, for
$1200...5 July 1853...petition 27 June 1853...HENRY MEETZE, trustee of MRS.
MILLY GROSS...before E. S. HAYES.

Page 134: HENRY FRAZURE, WILLIAM HENDRIX, & J. A. LAMANICK bound to HENRY A. MEETZE,
for $300...6 July 1853...petition 27 June 1853...HENRY FRAZURE, trustee of
MRS. NORMA ANN HAYES...before WM. FRAZURE.

Page 135: JOHN H. COUNTS, JOHN J. DREHER, & JOHN LONG bound to HENRY A. MEETZE, for $900
...7 Nov 1853...23 June 1851, petition...JOHN H. COUNTS, gdn. of JANE CATHERINE
MATHIAS, a minor...before JAMES E. LEE.

Page 136: GEORGE EPTING, JOHN MINNICK, & JOHN H. COUNTS, bound to HENRY A. MEETZE, for
$900...7 Nov 1853...petition 27 June 1853...GEO. EPTING, gdn. of FRANCIS JANE
CHAPMAN, a minor under 21...before E. S. HAYES.

Page 137: GEORGE EPTING, JOHN MINNICK, & JOHN H. COUNTS, bound to HENRY A. MEETZE, for
$900...7 Nov 1853...petition 27 June 1853...GEO. EPTING, gdn. of POLLY D.
CHAPMAN, a minor under 21...before E. S. HAYES.

Page 138: GEORGE EPTING, JOHN MINNICK & JOHN H. COUNTS, bound to HENRY A. MEETZE, for
$900...7 Nov 1853...petition 27 June 1853...GEO. EPTING, gdn. of MARY K.
CHAPMAN, a minor under 21...before E. S. HAYES.

Page 139: ABRAM CHAPMAN, JOHN A. BLACK, & WM CHAPMAN of Edgefield District bound to
HENRY A. MEETZE for $900...5 Dec 1853...petition 27 June 1853...ABRAM CHAPMAN,
gdn. of JOHN S. CHAPMAN, a minor under 21...before GEORGE EPTING.

Page 140: ABRAM CHAPMAN, JOHN A. BLACK, & WM. CHAPMAN of Edgefield District bound to
HENRY A. MEETZE for $900...5 Dec 1853...petition 27 June 1853...ABRAM CHAPMAN,
gdn. of DAVID N. CHAPMAN, a minor under 21...before GEORGE EPTING.

Page 141: ISAAC VANSANT, SAMUEL LEWIE & GEORGE GARTMAN bound to HENRY A. MEETZE for $2000
...4 July 1854...21 June 1854...ISAAC VANSANT, gdn. of WILLIAM CAPERS LEAPHART,
a minor under 21...before JAS. E. LEE.

Page 142: ISAAC VANSANT, SAMUEL LEWIE & GEORGE GARTMAN bound to HENRY A. MEETZE for $2000
...4 July 1854...21 June 1854...ISAAC VANSANT, gdn. of MARTHA ANN VANSANT,
a minor under 21...before JAS. E. LEE.

Page 143: F. SIMS LEWIE, SAMUEL LEWIE, & ISAAC VANSANT, bound to HENRY A. MEETZE for
$2000..7 Aug 1854...petition 27 June...F. S. LEWIE, gdn. of JOSEPH LEAPHART, a
minor under 21...before JAS. E. LEE.

Page 144: F. SIMS LEWIE, SAMUEL LEWIE, & ISAAC VANSANT, bound to HENRY A. MEETZE for
$2000...7 Aug 1854...petition 27 June... F. S. LEWIE, gdr. of HENRY LEAPHART,
a minor under 21...before JAS. E. LEE.

Page 145: F. SIMS LEWIE, SAMUEL LEWIE, & ISAAC VANSANT, bound to HENRY A. MEETZE for
$2000...7 Aug 1854...petition 27 June...F. S. LEWIE, gdn. of WADE LEAPHART, a
minor under 21...before JAS. E. LEE.

Page 146: JOSEPH SIGHTLER, JOHN H. THREWITS, & EDWARD W. GEIGER, bound to HENRY A.
MEETZE, for $6000...7 Aug 1854...petition 27 June 1854...JOSEPH SIGHTLER, gdn.
of HENRY HARMAN GEIGER, a minor under 21...before J. K. GAUNTT.

Page 147: F. SIMS LEWIE, ISAAC VANSANT, & BENNET A. M. LEAPHART, bound to HENRY A.
MEETZE, for $28,000...23 Apr 1855...petition 17 Apr 1855...F. SIMS LEWIE,
trustee ot MRS. MARGARET DREHER, wife of REV. GODFREY DREHER...before JAS. E. LEE.

Page 148: JOHN J. CHANEY, JAMES O. B. CHANEY, & ISAAC VANSANT, bound to HENRY A. MEETZE
for $1400...10 Spet 1855...petition 17 Aug 1855...JOHN J. CHANEY, gdn. of ALLEN
MARTIN, a minor under 21...before JAS. E. LEE.

Page 149: DANIEL D. D. MITCHELL, WM. C. MITCHELL, & JOHN W. LEE bound to HENRY A. MEETZE
for $3000...19 Feb 1856...petition 3 Dec 1855...D. D. MITCHELL, gdn. of
HENRIETTA MITCHELL, a minor under 21...before JAS. E. LEE.

Page 150: DANIEL D. D. MITCHELL, WM. C. MITCHELL, & JOHN W. LEE bound to HENRY A. MEETZE
for $3000...19 Feb 1856...petition 3 Dec 1855...D. D. MITCHELL, gdn. of
JOSEPH L. MITCHELL, a minor under 21...before JAS. E. LEE.

Page 151: JACOB N. HUFFMAN, JOHN LORICK & JAMES E. HUFFMAN bound to HENRY A. MEETZE for
$8000...3 Apr 1856...petition 20 Aug 1856...JACOB HUFFMAN, gdn. of JOSEPH
HUFFMAN, a minor under 21...beofre JAS. E. LEE.

Page 152: DANIEL JEFCOAT, JACOB REDMAN, & WILLIAM KNOTTS of Lexington and Orangeburg
Districts, bound to HENRY A. MEETZE for $1600...21 July 1856...petition 23
June 1856...DANIEL JEFCOAT, gdn. of MARTHA JEFCOAT, a minor under 21...before JACOB F.
WITT.

Page 153: DANIEL JEFCOAT, JACOB REDMAN, & WILLIAM KNOTTS of Lexington and Orangeburg
Districts, bound to HENRY A. MEETZE, for $1000...21 July 1856...petition 25
June 1856...DANIEL JEFCOAT, gdn. of MARY BELTON JEFCOAT, a minor under 21...before
JACOB F. WITT.

Page 154: LEMUEL BOOZER, JOHN FOX, & HENRY J. DRAFTS bound to HENRY A. MEETZE for $1200
...25 Apr 1857...petition 23 June 1856...LEMUEL BOOZER, gdn. of JOSEPHINE M. E.
BOOZER, a minor under 21...before JAS. E. LEE.

Page 155: LEMUEL BOOZER, JOHN FOX, & HENRY J. DRAFTS bound to HENRY A. MEETZE for $1200
...25 Apr 1857...petition 23 June 1856...LEMUEL BOOZER, gdn. of ALBERT MARABEAU
BOOZER, a minor under 21...before JAS. E. LEE.

Page 156: LEMUEL BOOZER, JOHN FOX, & HENRY J. DRAFTS bound to HENRY A. MEETZE for $1200
...25 Apr 1857...petition 23 June 1856...LEMUEL BOOZER, gdn. of PAULINE
LAVINIA BOOZER, a minor under 21...before JAS. E. LEE.

Page 157: LEMUEL BOOZER, JOHN FOX, & HENRY J. DRAFTS bound to HENRY A. MEETZE for $1200
...25 Apr 1857...petition 23 June 1856...LEMUEL BOOZER, gdn. of BAYLIS EARLE
BOOZER, a minor under 21...before JAS. E. LEE.

Page 158: LEMUEL BOOZER, JOHN FOX & HENRY J. DRAFTS bound to HENRY A. MEETZE for $1200...
25 Apr 1857...petition 23 June 1856...LEMUEL BOOZER, gdn. of LEMUEL HOUSTON
BOOZER, a minor under 21...before JAS. E. LEE.

Page 159: LEMUEL BOOZER, JOHN FOX & HENRY J. DRAFTS bound to HENRY A. MEETZE for $1200...
25 Apr 1857...petition 23 June 1856...LEMUEL BOOZER, gdn. of MARIA ANTOINETTE
BOOZER, a minor under 21...before JAS. E. LEE.

Page 160: JOSEPH FRESHLEY, GEORGE W. FRESHLEY, & JAMES P. FRESHLEY bound to HENRY A.
MEETZE, for $24,600...10 Nov 1857...petition 21 Aug 1857...JOSEPH FRESHLEY,
gdn. of LEONORAH FRESHLEY, a minor under 21...before LEVI METZ.

Page 161: ISAIAH WARNER, NOAH D. MEETZE, & NATHAN W. HYLER bound to HENRY A. MEETZE for
$1200...21 Nov 1857...petition 14 Sept 1857...ISAIAH WARNER, gdn. of SUSANNAH
METTS, a minor under 21...Before S. P. WINGARD.

Page 162: SAMUEL SHEALY, WILLIAM MONTS, & WILLIAM W. SHEALY bound to HENRY A. MEETZE for
$4000...11 Jan 1858...petition June term 1857...SAMUEL SHEALY, Trustee of
ELIZABETH DUNCAN, a married woman...before H. B. ADDISON.

Page 163: JOHN W. BALLENTINE, EMANUEL DERRICK, & JOHN S. DERRICK bound to HENRY A. MEETZE
for $ 1800...19 June 1858...petition 20 May 1858...JOHN W. BALLENTINE, gdn. of
GEORGE W. BALLENTINE...before C. CAUGHMAN.

Page 164: JOHN W. BALLENTINE, EMANUEL DERRICK, & JOHN S. DERRICK bound to HENRY A. MEETZE
for $1800...19 June 1858...petition 20 May 1858...JOHN W. BALLENTINE, gdn. of
MISSOURIA BALLENTINE, a minor under 21...before C. CAUGHMAN.

Page 165: EMANUEL DERRICK, JOHN S. DERRICK & JOHN W. BALLENTINE bound to HENRY A. MEETZE
for $2100...19 June 1858...petition 12 June 1858...EMANUEL DERRICK, gdn. of
EUGENIA C. BALLENTINE, a minor under 21...before C. CAUGHMAN.

Page 166: EMANUEL DERRICK, JOHN S. DERRICK & JOHN W. BALLENTINE bound to HENRY A. MEETZE
for $2100...19 June 1858...petition 12 June 1858...EMANUEL DERRICK, gdn. of
LAURA M. BALLENTINE, a minor under 21...before C. CAUGHMAN.

Page 167: ANDERSON STEEDMAN, REUBEN STEEDMAN, & JOHN FOX bound to HENRY A. MEETZE for
$900...28 June 1858...petition 25 June 1858...ANDERSON STEEDMAN, gdn. of MILTON
ABLE, a minor under 21...before JAS. E. LEE.

Page 168: ANDERSON STEEDMAN, REUBEN STEEDMAN, & JOHN FOX bound to HENRY A. MEETZE for
$900...28 June 1858...petition 25 June 1858...ANDERSON STEEDMAN, gdn. of ELIZA-
BETH ABLE, a minor under 21...before JAS. E. LEE.

Page 169: ANDERSON STEEDMAN, REUBEN STEEDMAN, & JOHN FOX bound to HENRY A. MEETZE for
$900...28 June 1858...petition 25 June 1858...ANDERSON STEEDMAN, gdn. of MILLICE
ABLE, a minor under 21...before JAS. E. LEE.

Page 170: ANDERSON STEEDMAN, REUBEN STEEDMAN, & JOHN FOX bound to HENRY A. MEETZE for
$900...28 June 1858...petition 25 June 1858...ANDERSON STEEDMAN, gdn. of NAOMI
ABLE, a minor under 21...before JAS. E. LEE.

Page 171: ANDERSON STEEDMAN, REUBEN STEEDMAN, & JOHN FOX bound to HENRY A. MEETZE for
$900...28 June 1858...petition 25 June 1858...ANDERSON STEEDMAN, gdn. of
NEWTON ABLE, a minor under 21...before JAS. E. LEE.

Page 172: NATHANIEL HARMAN, GEORGE GARTMAN, ANDREW CAUGHMAN, ROBERT P. GARTMAN, & JOSEPH
COUNTS bound to HENRY A. MEETZE for $7500...2 Aug 1858...petition 28 June 1858

...NATHANIEL HARMAN, gdn. of MERADI FRANCKLOW, a minor under 21...before S. P. WINGARD.

Page 173: JOHN FOX, L. BOOZER, & ANDERSON STEEDMAN bound to HENRY A. MEETZE, for $9000
...29 Oct 1858...petition 4 Oct 1858...JOHN FOX, gdn. of EUDICIA J. HENDRIX,
a minor under 21...before W. E. SAWER.

Page 174: JOHN FOX, L. BOOZER, & ANDERSON STEEDMAN bound to HENRY A. MEETZE, for $9000...
29 Oct 1858...petition 4 Oct 1858...JOHN FOX, gdn. of BENNEDICT L. HENDRIX,
a minor under 21...before W. E. SAWER.

Page 175: JOHN H. COUNTS, B. B. WISE, & JOHN HILLER bound to HENRY A. MEETZE for $6000...
7 Feb 1859...28 Sept 1858...JOHN H. COUNTS, gdn. of FRANKLIN M. HENDRIX, a
minor under 21...before J. A. HENDRIX.

Page 176: JOHN H. COUNTS, B. B. WISE, & JOHN HILLER bound to HENRY A. MEETZE for $6000...
7 Feb 1859...petition 28 sept 1858...JOHN H. COUNTS, gdn. of CLAUDIA D. HENDRIX,
a minor under 21...before J. A. HENDRIX.

Page 177: JOHN H. COUNTS, B. B. WISE, & JOHN HILLER bound to HENRY A. MEETZE for $6000...
7 Feb 1859...petition 28 Sept 1858...JOHN H. COUNTS, gdn. of ADELAIDE E. E.
HENDRIX, a minor under 21...before J. A. HENDRIX.

Page 178: JOHN S. DERRICK, JOHN A. HILLER, JOHN H. COUNTS & EMANUEL DERRICK bound to
HENRY A. MEETZE for $3300...3 Jan 1860...petition 15 Nov 1859...JOHN S. DERRICK,
gdn. of CATHARINE LOUISA DERRICK a minor under 21...before J. W. HENDRIX.

Page 179: JOHN S. DERRICK, JOHN A. HILLER, JOHN H. COUNTS, & EMANUEL DERRICK bound to
HENRY A. MEETZE for $3300...3 Jan 1860...petition 15 Nov 1859...JOHN S. DERRICK,
gdn. of MARY ANN ELIZABETH DERRICK, a minor under 21...before J. W. HENDRIX.

Page 180: JOHN S. DERRICK, JOHN A. HILLER, JOHN H. COUNTS, & EMANUEL DERRICK bound to
HENRY A. MEETZE for $3300...3 Jan 1860...petition 15 Nov 1859...JOHN S. DERRICK,
gdn. of BENJAMIN JACKSON DERRICK, a minor under 21...before J. W. HENDRIX.

Page 181: JOHN S. DERRICK, JOHN A. HILLER, JOHN H. COUNTS, & EMANUEL DERRICK bound to
HENRY A. MEETZE for $3300...3 Jan 1860...petition 15 Nov 1859...JOHN S. DERRICK,
gdn. of JAMES WILLIAM DERRICK, a minor under 21...before J. W. HENDRIX.

Page 182: JOHN S. DERRICK, JOHN A. HILLER, JOHN H. COUNTS, & EMANUEL DERRICK bound to
HENRY A. MEETZE for $3300...3 Jan 1860...petition 15 Nov 1859...JOHN S. DERRICK,
gdn. of MARTHA ANN ELIZABETH DERRICK, a minor under 21...before J. W. HENDRIX.

Page 183: JOHN S. DERRICK, JOHN A.HILLER, JOHN H. COUNTS, & EMANUEL DERRICK bound to
HENRY A. MEETZE for $3300...3 Jan 1860...petition 15 Nov 1859...JOHN S. DERRICK,
gdn. of WILLIAM ANDREW DERRICK, a minor under 21....before J. W. HENDRIX.

Page 184: JACOB GEIGER, ABRAM W. GEIGER & JOHN C. GEIGER bound to HENRY A. MEETZE for
$1800...JACOB GEIGER, gdn. of ANNA E. GEIGER, a minor under 21...before JAS. E.
LEE.

Page 185: JOHN A. HILLER, B. R. WYSE, JOHN H. COUNTS, & JOHN S. DERRICK bound to HENRY
A. MEETZE for $2500...3 Jan 1860...petition 12 Nov...JOHN A. HILLER, gdn. of
PAUL WASHINGTON DERRICK, a minor under 21...before J. W. HENDRIX.

Page 186: JOHN A. HILLER, B. R. WYSE, JOHN H. COUNTS & JOHN S. DERRICK bound to HENRY A.
MEETZE for $2500...3 Jan 1860...petition 12 Nov...JOHN A. HILLER, gdn. of
MARY CUMMINGS DERRICK, a minor under 21...before J. W. HENDRIX.

Page 187: JOHN A. HILLER, B. R. WYSE, JOHN H. COUNTS, & JOHN S. DERRICK bound to HENRY A.
MEETZE for $2500...3 Jan 1860...petition 12 Nov...JOHN A. HILLER, gdn. of
NOAH SAMUEL DERRICK, a minor under 21...before J. W. HENDRIX.

Page 188: JACOB GEIGER, ABRAM W. GEIGER, & JOHN C. GEIGER, bound to HENRY A. MEETZE for
$18,000...9 Jan 1860...petition 16 May 1859...JACOB GEIGER, gdn. of MARY C.
GEIGER, a minor under 21...before JAS. E. LEE.

Page 189: JOHN H. COUNTS, JOHN A. HILLER, B. R. WYSE, & JOHN S. DERRICK bound to HENRY
A. MEETZE for $10,000...3 Jan 1860...petition 2 Dec 1859...JOHN H. COUNTS, gdn.
of EDWIN SCOTT HENDRIX, a minor under 21...[no wit.]

Page 190: JACOB GEIGER, ABRAM W. GEIGER, & JOHN C. GEIGER bound to HENRY A. MEETZE for
$27,000...9 Jan 1860...petition 16 May 1859...JACOB GEIGER, gdn. of WILLIAM M.
GEIGER, a minor under 21...before JAS. E. LEE.

Page 191: OLIVER P. FULMER, JACOB J. DERRICK, & LEVI DERRICK bound to HENRY A. MEETZE
for $6300...16 Jan 1860...petition 12 Nov 1859...OLIVER P. FULMER, gdn. of
MARY E. DERRICK, a minor under 21...before S. P. WINGARD.

Page 192: OLIVER P. FULMER, JACOB J. DERRICK, & LEVI DERRICK bound to HENRY A. MEETZE
for $6300...16 Jan 1860...petition 12 Nov 1859...OLIVER P. FULMER, gdn. of
MARY E. DERRICK a minor under 21...before S. P. WINGARD.

Page 193: JOHN F. FULMER, JOHN FULMER SENR (X), & JACOB MAYER bound to HENRY A. MEETZE
for $3000...17 Jan 1860...petition 16 Jan 1860...JOHN FULMER, Gdn. of MARY ANN
ELIZABETH FULMER, a minor under 21...before H. J. CAUGHMAN.

Page 194: JOHN F. FULMER, JOHN FULMER SENR (X), & JACOB MAYER bound to HENRY A. MEETZE
for $3000...17 Jan 1860...Petition 16 Jan 1860...JOHN FULMER, gdn. of SEDETIA
A. R. FULMER.

Page 195: GERHARD MULLER bound to HENRY A. MEETZE for $7000...25 Jan 1860...petition 25
June 1859...GERHARD MULLER, gdn. of HENRY CHRISTOPHER MULLER, a minor under 21
...before J. CAUGHMAN.

Page 196: URIAH JEFCOAT, D. J. JEFCOAT, & JOHN A. KNIGHT bound to HENRY A. MEETZE for
$3000...28 Mar 1860...petition 28 Mar 1860...URIAH JEFCOAT, gdn. of LAVINIA
JEFCOAT, a minor under 21...before J. K. GAUNTT.

Page 197: URIAH JEFCOAT, D. J. JEFCOAT & JOHN A. KNIGHT bound to HENRY A. MEETZE for
$3000...28 Mar 1860...petition 28 Mar 1860...URIAH JEFCOAT, gdn. of MURREL
JEFCOAT, a minor under 21...before J. K. GAUNTT.

Page 198: ADAM EFIRD, JOHN FOX, & JAMES E. LEE bound to HENRY A. MEETZE for $6000...
26 May 1860...12 Apr 1859...ADAM EFIRD, gdn. of CAROLINE AUGUSTA MENOAH
FRANCKLOW, a minor under 21...before N. HARMAN.

Page 199: ADAM EFIRD, JOHN FOX & JAMES E. LEE bound to HENRY A. MEETZE for $6000...
26 May 1860...12 Apr 1859...ADAM EFIRD, gdn. of SALLIE RACHAEL FRANCKLOW, a
minor under 21...before N. HARMAN.

Page 200: ADAM EFIRD, JOHN FOX & JAMES E. LEE bound to HENRY A. MEETZE for $6000...26
May 1860...petition 12 Apr 1859...ADAM EFIRD, gdn. of MARIA LOUISA E. FRANCKLOW,
a minor under 21...before N. HARMAN.

Page 201: DANIEL QUATTLEBAUM, REUBEN STEEDMAN, & JAMES E. LEE bound to HENRY A. MEETZE
for _____ 3 July 1860...petition 25 June 1860...DANIEL QUATTLEBAUM, gdn. of
JAMES CHAPPLE HARTLY, a minor under 21...before C. CAUGHMAN.

Page 202: DANIEL QUATTLEBAUM, REUBEN STEEDMAN, & JAMES E. LEE bound to HENRY A. MEETZE
for _____ 3 July 1860...petition 25 June 1860...DANIEL QUATTLEBAUM, gdn. of
JOSEPH L. HARTLY, a minor under 21...before C. CAUGHMAN.

Page 203: DANIEL QUATTLEBAUM, REUBEN STEEDMAN, & JAMES E. LEE bound to HENRY A. MEETZE
for ___ 3 July 1860...petition 25 June 1860...DANIEL QUATTLEBAUM, gdn. of
ELIZABETH R. HARTLEY, a minor under 21...before C. CAUGHMAN.

Page 204: DANIEL QUATTLEBAUM, REUBEN STEEDMAN, & JAMES E. LEE bound to HENRY A. MEETZE
for _____ 3 July 1860...petition 25 June 1860...DANIEL QUATTLEBAUM, gdn. of
JOHN J. HARTLY, a minor under 21...before C. CAUGHMAN.

Page 205: DR. JOHN W. GEIGER, WILLIAM GEIGER SENR, & SOCRATES M. SIGHTLER bound to HENRY
A. MEETZE, for $6000...10 Oct 1860...petition 10 Oct 1860...DR. JOHN W. GEIGER
gdn. of JEMIMA REID, a minor under 21...before W. H. FOX.

Page 206: DR. JOHN W. GEIGER, WILLIAM GEIGER SENR, & SOCRATES M. SIGHTLER bound to HENRY
A. MEETZE, for $6000...10 Oct 1860...petition 10 Oct 1860...DR. JOHN W. GEIGER,
gdn. of ELIZABETH REID, a minor under 21...before W. H. FOX.

Page 207: DR. JOHN W. GEIGER, WILLIAM GEIGER SENR., & SOCRATES M. SIGHTLER bound to HENRY
A. MEETZE, for $6000...10 Oct 1860...petition 10 Oct 1860...DR. JOHN W. GEIGER,
gdn. of L. REED, a minor under 21...before W. H. FOX.

Page 208: SIMEON CORLEY, L. BOOZER & JOHN H. COUNTS, bound to HENRY A. MEETZE for $2500
...6 Aug 1861...petition June 1860...SIMEON CORLEY, trustee of MRS. CHARLOTTE
HARMAN, a married woman...before J. G. WOLFE.

Page 209: CAREY P. SNELGROVE, JOHN H. COUNTS, & EVE M. SNELGROVE (X), bound to HENRY A.
MEETZE for $1600...25 Dec 1863...petition 22 Dec 1863...CAREY P. SNELGROVE,
trusee of ELIZABETH HENDRIX...before ISAIAH VANSANT.

Page 210: JOHN H. COUNTS, J. R. SHULER, & S. P. WINGARD bound to HENRY A. MEETZE for
$500...19 Mar 1864...petition 19 Mar 1864...JNO. H. COUNTS, gdn. of JACOB
LEONARD SPICE, a minor under 21...no wit.

Page 211: JOHN H. COUNTS, J. R. SHULER, & S. P. WINGARD bound to HENRY A. MEETZE for
$800...19 Mar 1864...petition 19 Mar 1864...JNO. H. COUNTS, gdn. of JAMES
AUSTIN WESSINGER, a minor under 21...no wit.

Page 212: JOHN H. COUNTS, J. R. SHULER, & S. P. WINGARD bound to HENRY A. MEETZE for
$500...19 Mar 1864...petition 19 Mar 1864...JNO. H. COUNTS, gdn. of WEST
ROBERT SPICE, a minor under 21...no wit.

Page 213: JOHN H. COUNTS, J. R. SHULER, & S. P. WINGARD bound to HENRY A. MEETZE for
$800...19 Mar 1864...petition 19 Mar 1864...JNO. H. COUNTS, gdn. of WILSON
URIAH WESSINGER, a minor under 21...no wit.

Page 214: JOHN H. COUNTS, J. R. SHULER, & S. P. WINGARD bound to HENRY A. MEETZE for
$800...19 Mar 1864...petition 19 Mar 1864...JNO. H. COUNTS, gdn. of PATRICK
RUFUS WESSINGER, a minor under 21...no wit.

Page 215: JOHN H. COUNTS, J. R. SHULER, & S. P. WINGARD bound to HENRY A. MEETZE for
$800...19 Mar 1864...petition 19 Mar 1864...JNO. H. COUNTS,gdn. of DAVID
CALVIN WESSINGER, a minor under 21...no wit.

Page 216: JOHN H. COUNTS, J. R. SHULER, & S. P. WINGARD bound to HENRY A. MEETZE for
$800...19 Mar 1864...petition 19 Mar 1864...JNO. H. COUNTS, gdn. of AMANDA
LUGINIA WESSINGER, a minor under 21...no wit.

Page 217: JOHN H. COUNTS, J. R. SHULER, & S. P. WINGARD bound to HENRY A. MEETZE for
$500...19 Mar 1864...petition 19 Mar 1864...JNO. H. COUNTS, gdn. of JAMES
LEVI SLICE, a minor under 21...no wit.

Page 218: JOHN H. COUNTS, J. R. SHULER, & S. P. WINGARD bound to HENRY A. MEETZE for
$800...19 Mar 1864...petition 19 Mar 1864...JNO. H. COUNTS, gdn. of GEORGE
WASHINGTON WESSINGER, a minor under 21...no wit.

Page 219: JOHN H. COUNTS, J. R. SHULER, & S. P. WINGARD bound to HENRY A. MEETZE for
$500...19 Mar 1864...petition 19 Mar 1864...JNO. H. COUNTS, gdn. of MARY
CAROLINE SLICE, a minor under 21...no wit.

Page 220: JOHN H. COUNTS, J. R. SHULER, & S. P. WINGARD bound to HENRY A. MEETZE for
$800...19 Mar 1864...petition 19 Mar 1864...JNO. H. COUNTS, gdn. of LAURA ANN
WESSINGER, a minor under 21...no wit.

Page 221: JOHN H. COUNTS, J. R. SHULER, & S. P. WINGARD bound to HENRY A. MEETZE for
$800...19 Mar 1864...petition 19 Mar 1864...JNO. H. COUNTS, gdn. of SILAS
WALLER WESSINGER, a minor under 21...no wit.

Page 222: JOHN H. COUNTS, J. R. SHULER, & S. P. WINGARD bound to HENRY A. MEETZE for
$800...19 Mar 1864...petition 19 Mar 1864...JNO. H. COUNTS, gdn. of CATHARINE
ELIZABETH WESSINGER, a minor under 21...no wit.

Page 223: JOHN H. COUNTS, J. R. SHULER, & S. P. WINGARD bound to HENRY A. MEETZE for
$800...19 Mar 1864...petition 19 Mar 1864...JNO. H. COUNTS, gdn. of ELVIRA
JOANNA WESSINGER, a minor under 21...no wit.

Page 224: JOHN H. COUNTS, J. R. SHULER, & S. P. WINGARD bound to HENRY A. MEETZE for
$800...19 Mar 1864...petition 19 Mar 1864...JNO. H. COUNTS, gdn. of JOHN JACOB
WESSINGER, a minor under 21...no wit.

Page 225: JOHN H. COUNTS, J. R. SHULER, & S. P. WINGARD bound to HENRY A. MEETZE for
$800...19 Mar 1864...petitoin 19 Mar 1864...JNO. H. COUNTS, gdn. of IVY VASLINE
WESSINGER, a minor under 21...no wit.

Page 226: JOHN H. COUNTS, J. R. SHULER, & S. P. WINGARD bound to HENRY A. MEETZE for
$500...19 Mar 1864...petition 19 Mar 1864...JOHN H. COUNTS, gdn. of JOHN SILAS
SLICE, a minor under 21...no wit.

Page 227: JOHN H. COUNTS, J. R. SHULER & S. P. WINGARD bound to HENRY A. MEETZE for
$500...19 Mar 1864...petition 19 Mar 1864...JOHN H. COUNTS, gdn. of MARY ANN
MAHALA SLICE, a minor under 21...no wit.

Page 228: GEORGE S. SWYGERT, J. A. SWYGERT, & H. A. SWYGERT bound to HENRY A. MEETZE for
$500...19 Jan 1866...petition 17 Jan 1866...GEORGE S. SWYGERT, gdn. of PAUL
S. SWYGERT, a minor under 21...before J. S. WEED.

Page 229: LEWIS W. RAST, JOHN INABNET & JAMES INABNET bound to HENRY A. MEETZE for $8000
...6 Apr 1866...petition 6 Apr 1866...LEWIS W. RAST, gdn. of MISS C. F.
STIVENDER, a minor under 21...before R. D. P. RUCKER.

Page 230:JAMES B. SHEALY, H. J. EARGLE, JOHN A. SHEALY, JOHN E. FULMER, GEORGE HILLER, &
A. A. GUISE bound to HENRY A. MEETZE for $6000...17 Ag 1866...petition 17 Ag
1866...JAMES B. SHEALY, gdn. of AMANDA E. SWYGERT, a minor under 21...before JOHN B.
HILLER.

Page 231: REDDICK M. SENN, DAVID SHULL, & JACOB SENN bound to HENRY A. MEETZE for $1800
...15 Nov 1866...petition 20 Apr 1866...REDDICK M. SENN, gdn. of SARAH CHAR-
LOTTE EMILY HOOK, a minor under 21...before N. F. CORLEY.

Page 232: REDDICK M. SENN, DAVID SHULL, & JACOB SENN bound to HENRY A. MEETZE for $1800
...15 Nov 1866...petition 20 Apr 1866...REDDICK M. SENN, gdn. of MARGARET EVE
HOOK, a minor under 21...before N. F. CORLEY.

Page 233: REDDICK M. SENN, DAVID SHULL, & JACOB SENN bound to HENRY A. MEETZE for $1800
...15 Nov 1866...petition 20 Apr 1866...REDDICK M. SENN, gdn. of JANE KIZIAH
HOOK, A Minor under 211..before N. F. CORLEY.

Page 234: REDDICK M. SENN, DAVID SHULL, & JACOB SENN bound to HENRY A. MEETZE for $1800
...15 Nov 1866...petition 20 Apr 1866...REDDICK M. SENN, gdn. of NANCY CAROLINE
HOOK a minor under 21...before N. F. CORLEY.

Page 235: JASPER N. EPTING, WILLIAM MONTS & ANNA E. DERRICK bound to HENRY A. MEETZE for
_____ 19 Nov 1866...petition 10 Nov 1866...JASPER N. EPTING, gdn. of MARY
CUMMINGS DERRICK, a minor under 21.

Page 236: JASPER N. EPTING, WILLIAM MONTS & ANNA E. DERRICK bound to HENRY A. MEETZE for
_____ 19 Nov 1866...petition 10 Nov 1866...JASPER N. EPTING, gdn. of WILLIAM
ANDREW DERRICK a minor under 21.

Page 237: JASPER N. EPTING, WILLIAM MONTS & ANNA E. DERRICK bound to HENRY A. MEETZE for
_____ 19 Nov 1866...petition 10 Nov 1866...JASPER N. EPTING, gdn. of MARTHA ANN
DERRICK, a minor under 21.

Page 238: JASPER N. EPTING, WILLIAM MONTS, & ANNE E. DERRICK bound to HENRY A. MEETZE for
_____19 Nov 1866...petition 10 Nov 1866...JASPER N. EPTING, gdn. of NOAH S.
DERRICK a minor under 21.

Page 239: BENJAMIN JEFCOAT, URIAH JEFCOAT, & ANDERSON B. CHANEY bound to HENRY A. MEETZE
for $16,000...3 Dec 1866...petition 23 June 1863...BENJAMIN JEFCOAT, committer
of MRS. MARY ROBINSON, a Lunatic...before J. N. ROOF.

Page 240: GEO. W. ASBELL, WILLIAM POWELL, & JOHN W. NOBLE bound to HENRY A. MEETZE for
$6000...13 Feb 1867...petition 13 Feb 1867...GEO. W. ASBELL, gdn. of THOMAS S.
WILLIAMS, a minor under 21...before J. F. KIRKLAND.

Page 241: SAMUEL M. ROOF, WILLIAM SHULL, & JULIA ANN CROMER, bound to HENRY A. MEETZE for
$600...19 Apr 1867...petition 19 Apr 1867...SAMUEL M. ROOF, gdn. of ANN REBECCA
CROMER, a minor under 21...before S. P. WINGARD.

Page 242: SAMUEL M. ROOF, WILLIAM SHULL, & JULIA ANN CROMER bound to HENRY A. MEETZE for
$600...19 Apr 1867...petition 19 Apr 1867...SAMUEL M. ROOF, gdn. of JAMES
ALBERT CROMER, a minor under 21.

Page 243: SAMUEL M. ROOF, WILLIAM SHULL, & JULIA ANN CROMER bound to HENRY A. MEETZE for $600...19 Apr 1867...petition 19 Apr 1867...SAMUEL M. ROOF, gdn. of ELLEN CATHERINE CROMER, a minor under 21...before S. P. WINGARD.

Page 244: SAMUEL M. ROOF, WILLIAM SHULL, & JULIA ANN CROMER, bound to HENRY A. MEETZE for $600...19 Apr 1867...petition 19 Apr 1867...SAMUEL M. ROOF, gdn. of MARGARET EMILY CROMER, a minor under 21...before S. P. WINGARD.

Page 245: SAMUEL M. ROOF, WILLIAM SHULL, & JULIA ANN CROMER, bound to HENRY A. MEETZE for $600...19 Apr 1867...petition 19 Apr 1867....SAMUEL M. ROOF, gdn. of JOHN ADAM CROMER, A minor under 21...before S. P. WINGARD.

Page 246: SAMUEL M. ROOF, WILLIAM SHULL, & JULIA ANN CROMER, bound to HENRY A. MEETZE for $600...19 Apr 1867...petition 19 Apr 1867...SAMUEL M. ROOF, gdn. of ALICE CROMER, a minor under 21...before S. P. WINGARD.

Page 247: JOHN A. HILLER, B. R. WYSE, JOHN H. COUNTS, & JOHN S. DERRICK bound to HENRY A. MEETZE for $2500...3 Jan 1860...12 Nov 1859, petition...JOHN H. COUNTS, gdn. of MARTHA ANN ELIZABETH DERRICK, a minor under 21...before J. W. HENDRIX.

END

Pp. 1-2: L. W. & T. of BAMUEL GAMBLE of Fairfield,Co., Blacksmith, being weak of body...
     18 Sept 1791...my dearly beloved wife MARGARET GAMBLE, her living on the planta-
tion during her life and the disposal of all things not mentioned in this my will and at
her decease to be divided among my children ...to my son JAMES GAMBLE, the sum of s 10
sterling...to son HUGH GAMBLE, plantation whereon I formerly lived, 300 A...to son SAMUEL,
plantation whereon I now live, 100 A & all Blacksmith tools...to my daughter AGNES, wife
of JAMES McMULLEN, a two year old heifer...to daughter SARAH GAMBLE, two cows and calves...
...to my grandson SAML McMULLEN, my bay Colt...wife, sole Extx...SAMUEL GAMBLE (X) (LS),
Wit: ROBERT REID, JOHN ROBINSON,DA. HAMILTON. Proven 16 June 1792. Rec. 12 July 1792.

Pp. 2-4: Will of HENRY FUNDERBURGH of Fairfield Co., sick & weak of Body...to grandson
     HENRY FUNDERBURGH, 50 A, part of 100 A granted to MICHAEL HOOPER 25 Apr 1768 &
conveyed from HOOPER by L & R ፧ 29 & 30 Apr 1770 & land granted to HENRY FUNDERBURGH 4 &
5 June 1786 by GOV. MOULTRIE...to beloved wife MARY, 27 A granted to HENRY FUNDERBURGH
5 June 1786 & negroes [named]...DANIEL MABRY & THOMAS MOBLEY, Exrs...3 Jan 1792...HENRY
FUNDERBURGH (X) (LS), Wit: JOHN BROWN, CALLIN MOBLEY (C), JACOB MEADORS (X). Proven 16
June 1792.

Pp. 4-5: Will of JAMES COLHOUN of Fairfield Co....to nephew JAMES COLHOUN, my plantation,
     Bible, & clothes...to nephew WILLIAM COLHOUN, grey mare & gun...to nephes ALEX-
ANDER COLHOUN, filley...to neice DICEY[?] COLHOUN...heirs of my Brother ALEXANDER, sisters
ELIZABETH and LIDDEY, sisters JANE, NANCY & MARY...brother WILLIAM COLHOUN, Exr...13 Mar
1792...JAMES COLHOUN (LS), Wit: JOHN CAMERON, ROBT GIBSON, WILLIAM CRAIG. Rec. 24 July
1792. Proved 16 June 1792.

Page 6: JOHN MILES died Intestate...admn. granted to FREDERICK ARMINGER...to return inven-
     tory on 2nd Monday in September...18 June 1792.

Pp. 6-7: THOMAS FRANKLIN died Intestate...admn. granted to FREDERICK ARMINGER...to return
     inventory on 2nd Monday in September...18 June 1792.

Page 7: JOHN LEE died intestate...admn. granted to ALEXANDER GORDON...return inventory by
     12 Jan next...13 Sept 1792. Same letters granted to ALEXANDER GORDON on estate
of REBECCA LEE.

Page 8: THOMAS MEEK died intestate...admn. granted to MARY MEEK, JAMES MEEK and JOHN
     McCRORAY[?]...to return inventory by 12 Jan next...13 Sept 1792.

Pp. 8-9: WILLIAM BOILSTONE died Intestate...admn. granted to JOHANNA and GEORGE BOILSTONE
     ...to return inventory by 12 Jan next...13 Sept 1792.

Page 9: Appraisement of Estate of AMOS DAVIS, decd...Ƀ 296. 7. 10. Appraised by THOMAS
     CROSBY, NATHN. HARBIN, WM. HARBIN, JAMES THOMAS. Rec. 25 Sept 1792.

     Appraisement of estate of HENRY FUNDERBURGH...Ƀ 273. 2. 0. Appraised by ADAM
EFFOURT[?], ISAIAH MOBLEY, WILLIAM MOBLEY (X). Dated 3 Sept 1792. Rec. 25 Sept 1792.

Pp. 10-11: Estate of AMOS DAVIS in Account with EDWARD and SARAH TILMAN.
     Cash paid to THOMAS PARROT, MOSES ARNOLD, NATHANIEL STARLIN, to estate of
JOHN DAVIS, decd, BENJAMIN LINDSAY, AMBROSE NIX, NATHAN JAGGERS, JOSEPH FROST, JESSE
BRIANT, "Elijah's Bond," JESSE O'SWAMP[?], ZACHARIAH ROBERT, KIRKLAND & Co., to estate of
JOHN DAVIS Pr JAS DAVIS Bond dated 17 Dec 1787. Paid: GEORGE BOLE as pr note. Rec.
25 Sept 1792. Cash recd from THOMAS HUMPHREYS, FRIZZLE McTYRE, WILLIAM JOHNSTON, JAMES
DAVIS BOND. Amt. of sales Ƀ 199 15 1.

Page 11: Inventory of estate of ISAAC LOWE, late of Fairfield Co., Decd. Sept 8, 1792.
     Ƀ 49 11 10. JOHN L. BRADFORD, JAMES RABB [ROBB?], CHARLES BRADFORD, Appraisers.
Rec. 25 Sept 1792.

Page 12: JAMES BRIANT and WILLIAM BRIANT, orphans, appeared on 11 Sept inst. and chose
     BENJAMIN McKINNEY as their Guardian 14 Sept 1792.

Page 13: Inventory of GEORGE SCOT, decd [no appraisal] 7 Oct 1792, HUGH MONTGOMERY, CHARLES
     MONTGOMERY, Exors.

     BENJAMIN McKINNY died intestate....admn. granted to JANE McKINNEY, REUBEN HARRI-
SON and JOHN BOYKIN...return inventory before 2nd Monday in April next...21 Jan 1793.

Pp. 13-14: JOHN STEWART, planter, died intestate...admn. granted to MARY STEWART, and
     GEORGE BEAZELEY...return inventory by 2nd Mon. in April next...21 Jan 1793.

Page 14: SAMUEL LOCKRIDGE, planter, died intestate...admn. granted to ELIZABETH LOCKRIDGE
and JAMES BICKET...inventory to be returned by 2nd Monday in April next...21
Jan 1793.

Page 15: Guardianship of orphan MARY LOVE granted to GARDNER FORD...21 Jan 1793. Bond
Ƚ 200

Page 16: OBED KIRKLAND orphan on 20th inst. chose WILLIAM KIRKLAND as guardian...21 Jan
1793.

Pp. 16-17: 18 Jan 1793, L. W. & T. of FRANCIS KIRKLAND was proved...admn. granted to
AMBROSE KIRKLAND and MARY KIRKLAND...2nd Mon in Apr 1793, inventory to be
returned.   21 Jan 1793.

Pp. 17-18: Will of FRANCIS KIRKLAND...wife MARY, land where I now live to the west of
Little River...sons WILLIAM & JOHN & FRANCIS KIRKLAND...children: WILLIAM,
JOHN, FRANCIS, SARAH, ELIZABETH, MARY, ABIGAIL, & CONSTANCE...RICHARD WINN & JOHN WINN,
Exrs....12 Oct 1790....FRANCIS KIRKLAND (   ) Wit: THOMPSON WHITEHOUSE, C. D. BRADFORD.
Proven by BRADFORD 1793. Executors refused to qualify.

Page 18: DAVID MOTTE died intestate...admn. granted to AGNES MOTTE...inventory to be returned by 12 Jan next...11 Oct 1785[?]...WM. BOYD, ROBT BOYD, security Ƚ 100.

Page 19: In Appraisement of the Estate of WILLIAM BOILSTON taken 22 Sept 1792....includes
Negroes [named]   Ƚ 242 6 0.   GARDNER FORD, THOMAS MUSE[?], THOS STARKE,
Appraisers.
          [nd], Appraisement of JOHN MILES Estate   Ƚ 6 19 10
          Inventory of Estate of REBECCA LEE, ALEXANDER GORDON, Admn.
          Negro girl Seel, Ƚ 45. HENRY MOORE, JAMES TURNER, HUGH McKEOWN, Appraisers.
Rec. 2 Feb 1793. Dated 27 Sept 1792. Bond Ƚ 500, WM MARSHAL, Secy.
          Inventory of the Estate of JOHN LEE, ALEXANDER GORDON, Admr.
includes Negro Sam   Ƚ 79 14 4. Appraised 27 Sept 1792, HENRY MOORE, JAMES TURNER, HUGH
McKEOWN. Rec. 2 Feb 1793.

Page 20: Inventory of JAMES COLHOUNs Estate.
          includes 100 A of land   Ƚ 174 13 6. Dec. 22, 1792. SAML HINNAN, ROBERT GIB-
BON, JOHN CAMERON. Rec. 2 Feb 1793.
          Appraisement of Estate of DAVID MOTTE   Ƚ 11 13 16 & Ƚ 10 10 0. JAMES BROWN,
JAMES MANN, ROBERT BOYD, Appraisers.
          On 12 Feb 1793, L. W. & T. of JOHN McCLURKIN was proved...ANDREW WALKER & WILL-
IAM McQUISTON, Exrs...14 Jan 1793.

Page 21: Will of JOHN McCLURKIN of Fairfield Co...to wife MARGARET all her apparell,
          spinning wheel, & saddle & 1/3 of estate...to sons ANDREW & JAMES the remainder
to be divided at a convenient age...remainder to be sold for schooling of sons...brother
SAMUEL, sister ELEANOR's daughter MARY, sister JANE's son JOHN, sister GENNET[?]'s daughter CATHERINE...father in law ANDREW WALKER & WM McQUISTON, Exrs...22 Sept 1792...JOHN
McCLURKIN (LS), Wit: STAFFORD CURRY, MATHEW McCLURKIN, JOHN BOYLS Rec. 21 Feb 1793.

Page 22: Inventory & appraisement of estate of JOHN STEWART. Ƚ 44 11 2 and Ƚ 51 2 11.
          DAN HUFFMAN, ALEXR DICKEY, HEN: McBRIDE, Appraisers. 2 Feb 1793.
Account of sale, the remainder taken by the widow. Buyers: JOS: CAMERON, CHRISR. HUFF-
MAN, JOHN CAMERON, ANDREW CAMERON, HENRY McBRIDE. Ƚ 25 19 7. Rec. 23 Feb 1793.

          Memorandum of Sale of Goods of Estate of JOHN MILES sold at the house of LUKE
RAWLS Jan: 29 1793. Admr: FREDERICK WESSINGER[??]. Buyers: LUKE RAWLS, ELISHA HAYGOOD.
Ƚ 0 92
          Inventory of personal property of Estate of JOHN McCLURKIN. Exrs: WILLIAM
McQUISTON, ANDREW WALKER. Appraised by MATHEW McCLURKIN, ROBT KILPATRICK, WM LOWRIE,
12 Dec 1792. Ƚ 45 4 0. Rec. 11 Apr 1793.

Page 23: Memorandum on estate of BENJAMIN McKINNY decd taken 11 Feb 1793. THOMAS STILL,
          NICHOLAS PEAY, DARLING JONES, Appraisers. Ƚ 228. 1. 4 Rec. 11 Apr 1793.

          ADAM ARKIN [ACKIN?], planter, died intestate...admn. granted to JENNET KENNEDY
...inventory to be returned by 12 June next. 9 Apr 1793. Rec. 11 Apr 1793.
          THOMAS DUKES, plnater, died intestate...admn. granted to MARY DUKES...inventory
to be returned by 12 June next...10 Apr 1793.

116

Page 24: 8 Apr 1793, L. W. & T. of CHARLES AIKEN was proven...admn. granted to RICHARD
GLADNEY & ADAM EGGAR, the surviving Exrs...inventory to be returned by 2nd
Monday in June...9 Apr 1793.

Pp. 24-5: L. W. & T. of CHARLES AIKEN of Fairfield County...3 Aug 1792...to wife MARTHA
2 beds, etc., & 1/3 of other property...to daughter JENNET, wife of HUGH HAR-
BISON, one guinea...to grandson CHARLES HARBINSON, ₤ 6 if he comes into this country, if
not to be divided between my brother ADAM AIKEN and my daughter SARAH...to my brother
ADAM AIKEN, 4 guineas to be paid in property...to my daughter SARAH, wife of HUGH McKEL-
VEY, 2/3 of property after the above mentioned legacies., viz., those left to my daughter
JENNET and grandson CHARLES & my wife...friends RICHARD GLADNEY, SAMUEL LOUGHRIDGE [?],
of Fairfield County and ADAM EGGAR of Rockey Creek, Exrs....CHARLES AIKEN ( ) Wit: Dd.
HAMILTON, WM. McCORMICK, JOHN DODS. Rec. 12 Apr 1793.

Page 25: To WILLIAM KENNEDY...whereas JOSEPH KENNEDY late of Fairfield County died Intestate...admn. granted to WM. KENNEDY...return inventory by 12 June next...13 Apr
1793.

Page 26: On 18 June 1793, L. W. & T. of JOSEPH DODS was proved, admn. granted to ROBERT
GRYSON, JOSEPH McCASH, Exrs...return inventory by 2nd Monday in Sept...19 June
1793.
L. W. & T. of JOSEPH DODS of Fairfield County & Camden Dist...to brother SAML.
DODS, the crop for this year...my mother to get ₤ 5 sterling...allow little JOSEPH ₤5
"for to school him"...my suit of clothes to SAMUEL DODS...to JAMES HENAN[?], my big Coat
...rest of clothes to be divided between JOHN and JAMES, only my little coat to NEEL
SOUTHERLAND...ROBERT BRISON & JOSEPH McCASH, Exrs...rest of money divided among my brothers and sisters...10 May 1793...JOSEPH DODS (J) (LS), Wit: JOHN CUBIT, SAMUEL DODS,
JOHN DODS, Rec. 22 June 1792.

Page 27: 12 June 1793, L. W. & T. of WILLIAM FRAZER proved...admn. granted to WM. FRAZER,
Junr., the surviving executor...inventory to be returned by 2nd Monday in Sept.
next...19 June 1793....

Pp. 27-28: L. W. & T. of WILLIAM FRAZER of Fairfield County...to sons JOHN WILLIAM, JOHN,
SAMUEL & EZEKIEL, all my lands...to be drawn by lot...JACOB GIBSON SR. &
WILLIAM FRAZIER JUNR, Exrs...21 Feb 1793. WILLIAM FRAZER (LS), Wit: HARRIS FREEMAN, LUCY
CURRY (X), BENJN. SCOTT, DANIEL FRAZER. Rec. 22 June 1793.

Page 28: JAMES WINN, Gentleman, died Intestate...admn. granted to MINOR WINN...inventory
to be returned by 2nd Monday in September next...18 June 1793.

Pp. 28-29: JAMES SCOT, late of Fairfield County, miller, died intestate...admn. granted
to Nancy SCOTT and EDWARD GOYEN...inventory to be returned by 2nd Monday in
September next...18 June 1793.

Page 29: Estate of DANIEL DANSBY in acct. with MARTHA DANSBY, Admx. Paid: ZACH ESTES,
JNO STEPHESON, J. A. SUMMERS, J. OYSTER, JNO PARKS, WM. HOLLEY SENR., J. PEARSON,
ESQ., J. SWETENBURGH, WM. HENRY, JOS. SHIRER, MR. WITTLEHOVER, JACOB COUNTS, BENJ. BOYD,
ISAAC HOPKINS, RICHD HOPKINS, CHARLES MILLS, DANIEL WOOTAN, BURR HARRISON, PHILLIP PEAR-
SON, THOS THORNLEY, JANIE SMITH, SHAD: JACOBS, S. BUSBY, MARTIN WAGNER, THOMAS MEANS, WM.
NELSON, JAMES DAVIS, RANSOM STROUD, ADAM FREW [??], FRIZZLE M cTYRE, J. BRADFORD, THOS
PARROT SENR., J. PEARSON, THOS WILLINGHAM. Total payments ₤ 47. 10. 32. Rec. 24 June 1792.

Pp. 29-30: Inventory and appraisement of Goods and Chatels of THOMAS MEEK, decd. Total
amt. ₤ 94.10.11. Taken 19 SEpt 1792 by JAS CHESTNUT, ANDREW GRAHAM, JNO. McWILLIAMS.
Rec. 25 July 1793.

Page 30: Appraisement of ADAM AIKEN, decd. ₤4. 16. 7. EDWARD MARTIN, WILLIAM AIKEN,
DAVID MARTIN, Appraisers. Rec. 26 July 1793.

Pp. 30-31: To JOHN GRAY, Esq....on 18 June Instant, it was represented to us that JOHN
SMITH was an orphan and desirous that you be appointed his guardian...so ordered
until he becomes 21...24 June 1793.

Page 31: On 9 Sept 1793, L. W. & T. of PHILLIP SHAVER was proved...admn. granted to MARIA
MARGARET SHAVER, the Sole Extx. inventory to be returned by 12 January next...
9 Sept 1793.

Pp. 31-32: L. W. & T. of PHILLIP SHAVER of Little River in Camden District...to wife MARIA
MARGARET SHAVER, use of plantation where I now live, 250 A in 3 different tracts

; river plantation of 450 A in 3 different tracts...5 negroes [named]...upper part of Broad River plantation of 225 A, to daughter MARIA MARGARET POLICK; also to her 100 A called PHILLIPS tract, also negro Ben...1/2 of Broad River plantation to daughter MARY SCOT, also 150 A where I now live, & 100 A called Cateys, negro Jack...200 A on Flat lick to wife...wife, MARIA MARGARET, Extx....18 July 1793...PHILIP SHAVER (X) (LS), Wit: MARGARET POOLE (X), PHIL. PEARSON, GEORGE LEIGNER (GL). Proven in Ct. 9 Sept by GEORGE LEIGNER. Rec. 12 Sept 1793.

Page 33: HENRY McNIEL, late of Fairfield County, died intestate...admn. granted to ARCHIBALD McNIEL & ROBERT REED... inventory to be returned by 12 January next...9 Sept 1793. Rec. 12 Sept 1793.

Page 34: JOHN SWINNEY, late of Fairfield, diest intestate...JOHN WILSON made admn...inventory to be returned by 12 January next...9 Sept 1793...Rec. 12 Sept 1793.
WILLIAM GLADDEN, late of Fairfield, died intestate...admn. granted to ELIZABETH GLADDEN and JAMES LUCAS...inventory to be returned by 12 January next...9 Sept 1793...Rec. 12 Sept 1793.

Pp. 35-36: An account of the sale of Goods and Chattels of THOS MEEK, decd, Buyers: JONAS McCULLOUGH, JOHN McCULLOUGH, MARY MEEK, WILLIAM McQUISTON, ELIZ. McCULLOUGH, JAMES GRAHAM, JAMES HARBISON, MAT. McCLURKEN, EDWD. McDONALD, JAMES ELIOT, PAUL GUTHRIE, JAMES SLOAN, BENJ. HARRIS, WILLIAM ESSLER, THOMAS LOGAN, HUGH PARKS, JOHN McWILLIAMS, WILLM. McCULLOGH, THOS EWART, JAMES MEEK, ANDREW WALKER, DAVID WIER, JAS. CHESNUT, JOHN McDILL, THOS ESLER, JOHN McCRARY, ROBT JAMESON, ROBT MILLER, ROBT STRONG, FRANCIS KING, THOS McKEE, WILLM McCAW, THOS McDILL, THOS HARBISON, SAML McCOWN. Total ₤ 85.16.12...Rec. 16 SEpt 1793. JAS CHESNUT, AND: GRAHAM.

Page 37: Fairfield Co., 25 Mile Creek, July 6, 1793. Inventory of THOMAS DUKES, late of Fairfield, Decd. Total ₤ 144. 17. 4. Appraisers: SAMUEL PERRY, DANL STARKINS, LEWIS PERRY. Sale of Goods: Buyers: 17 Aug 1793, MARY DUKE, JOHN WILSON, Esq. Rec. 16 Sept 1793.

Page 38: to MR. ROBERT RABB...on 10 Sept, JAMES POWELL, an orphan, appeared and chose ROBT. RABB as his guardian...17 Sept 1793.

Pp. 38-39: A catalogue of property of the estate of DANIEL DOUGHARTY, 9 Sept 1791. Buyers: RICHARD STROTHER, NATHAN NORWOOD, BARBARY DOUGHARTY, ANN SIMS, GEORGE OWENS, JOB OWINS, GEORGE DOUGHARTY, NIMROD MOORIS, JAMES DOUGHARTY, JAMES DOUGHARTY, JR., JAMES DAVIS, JAMES BUCHANAN, DAVID WHITMAN, WILLIAM GABRUTH[?], PHILLIP HOLCOMB, JAMES MOOTY, JOSHUA DURHAM, JOHN McCAMIE, JOHNSON McCAMIE, THOMAS DAWKINS, GEORGE FRU, JOHN MATHEWS, JAMES MORGAN, ADAM WICKER, JOHN WICKER, JOHN MATHEWS. Rdc. 21 Sept 1793.

Page 40: Fairfield County--12 Oct 1793. Memorandum of sale of Negro Quan, property of JOHN SWINNEY, decd ₤ 32. 10. 0. 100 A on bear Creek, Appraisers: JAMES HOY (₤) ROBERT CRAIG, QUINTIN CRAIG. Creid off to JOHN WILSON, Esqr., for ₤ 11. Rec. 25 Oct 1793.
   On 15 Jan 1794, L. W. & T. of EPHRAIM PETTYPOOL was proved...admn. granted to URSULA & ABRAHAM PETTYPOOL, Exrs. named in the will...inv. to be returned by 2nd Monday in April. 16 Jan 1794.

Pp. 40-41: Will of EPHRAIM PETTIPOOL, being weak in body..to wife URSULA, all estate real & personal...all my lands whereon I now live, 300 A to my two youngest sons EPHRAIM & THOMAS PETTIPOOL, after wife's decease or widowhood...EPHRAIM not to have control until THOMAS is 21... to son WILLIAM, negro George, to have possession as soon as I recover from JAMES HART...to son ABRAHAM, 2 negroes [named]...my four youngest daughters TABITHA, FRANCES, NANCY URSILLA...wife and son ABRAHAM, Exrs...2 Feb 1793...EPHRAIM PETTIPOOL (LS),Wit: JOHN YARBROUGH, WILLIAM GRAHAM (X), CHARLES GRAHAM (X).

Page 42: JAMES BURKE, late of Fairfield, died Intestate...admn. granted to THOMAS HARDEN ...inventory to be returned by 2nd Mon. in Apr next...15 Jan 1794.

Pp. 42-43: on 13 Jan 1794, L. W. & T. of PETER CASSITY was proved...admn. granted to JOHN BOYKIN, JAMES CASITY, WILLIAM WATSON, Exrs...23 Jan 1794.
Will of PETER CASSITY of Fairfield Co...wife KATHARINE, to have negroes [named]...to brother ROBERT CASITY, suit of Clothes I was married in...to wife, all earthen & stoneware I have a suit for in Charleston by the hand of ISHAM MOORE, also writing desk and painted chest...friends JOHN BOYKIN, JAMES CASITY, WILLIAM WATSON, Exrs...18 Nov 1793... PETER CASSITY (LS), Wit: JOHN GOODRUM (G), REBEKAH WATSON, JAMES ALEXANDER WATSON. Codicil 18 Nov 1793, JAMES CASSITY's oldest son JOHN may have legacy expected to him... Recorded 25 Jan 1794.

Page 44: On 14 Jan 1794, L. W. & T. of NATHAN SANDERS was proven...admn. granted to BART-
LET HENSON & JOHN ELLISON, Exrs. named in the will...ret inv. 2nd Mon. in Apr
next...23 Jan 1794.

Pp. 44-45: L. W. & T. of NATHAN SANDERS of Fairfield County...to wife MARY SANDERS, all
lands, negro Saml, cattle &c....son BARTLET, may have land at her death...
eldest daughter [not named], to have negro...second daughter [not named], and 3rd and
last daughter [not named]...friends BARTLET HENSON, JOHN ELLISON, Exrs. 2 Dec 1793...
NATHAN SANDERS (LS), Wit: JAMES ALEX: WATSON, BENJAMIN HENSON, GEORGE COONE (X).

Page 45: 14 Jan 1794, L. W. & T. of MATHEW HAYS was proven...admn. granted to JAMES Mc-
CREIGHT, DAVID HAMILTON & NANCY HAYS, Exrs. anmed in sd. will...inventory to
be returned by 2nd Mon in April...23 Jan 1794.

Pp. 45-46: L. W. & T. of MATHEW HAYS of Jacksons Creek, Parish of ST. Mark, Fairfield Co.
...9 Mar 1788...to my [son] JOHN HAYS, 70 A whereon we now live, also 79 A
on the Watteree [sic] and plantation tools when he comes to age...to daughter MOLLY HAYS,
50 A of land at Hennings[?] old plan, 100 A at Watteree...to my daughter ESEBEL HAYS, land
at Hummy's[?] old plan...to wife, 50 A...friend JAMES McCREIGHT, DANIEL HAMILTON & wife
NANCY HAYS, all of Jacksons Creek, Exrs...MATHEW HAYS (LS), Wit: DAVID McCREIGHT, MARY
OWENS (☙), JOHN McCREIGHT (Ϡ).

Page 47: 14 Jan 1794, L. W. & T. of WILLIAM PHILLIPS...admn. granted to EDWARD MARTIN &
JAMES NEELY, Exrs... inventory to be returned by 2nd Monday in April...23 Jan
1794.

Pp. 47-48: L. W. & T. of WILLIAM PHILLIPS of Fairfield County...6 Nov 1793...to my mother
JANE PHILLIPS, Ł 20...to nephew JOHN PHILLIPS, 200 A of my plantation where I
now live, that he pay to his brother WILLIAM PHILLIPS, Ł15 & to my sister MARY CAMPBELL,
Ł 15 in 7 years from my decease...to nephew THOMAS PHILLIPS, 50 A & he is to pay to his
sister JANE & BETSY PHILLIPS, Ł 7 each...to my nephew JOHN SLOANE, JR., 100 A, part of
the plantation where I now live adj. THOMAS GLADNEY& including a spring...to pay to my
sister ELIZABETH's children Ł 10 & Ł 5 to my sister MARY CAMPBELL...remainder to be divided between sisters MARY, JANE & ELIZABETH...except Ł 5 to nephew JAMES PHILLIPS...EDWARD
MARTIN & JAMES NEELY, Exrs...WILLIAM PHILLIPS (LS), Wit: DAVID MCCREIGHT, JOHN McVEA, Dd.
HAMILTON. Rec. 3 Jan 1794.

Pp. 48-49: HUGH MORRISON, late of Fairfield County, died intestate...admn granted to JOHN
TURNER, HENRY MOORE & ABRAHAM MILLER...inv. to be returned by 2nd Monday in
April....23 Jan 1794.

Page 49: JOHN ROBINSON of Fairfield County, planter, died intestate...admn. granted to
HANNAH & THOMAS ROBINSON...inventory 2nd Monday in April next...23 Jan 1794.

Page 50: SAMUEL HOLLIS, late of Fairfield County, planter, died intestate, admn. granted
to ELIZABETH & BERRY HOLLIS...inventory to be returned by 2nd Mon. in April next
...23 Jan 1794.

Page 50: Acct. of sale of ADAM AIKEN's estate. Buyers ROBT MARTIN, ROBT ROSS, THOMAS
GLADNEY, EDWD. MARTIN, JANNET KENNEDY, ARTHUR McNEIL, JOHN TINKLER, JAMES AIKEN,
THOMAS REID, EDWARD MARTIN....SIMON CAMERON.

Page 51: Appraisal of estate of SAMUEL LOCKRIDGE, decd, Jan. 14, 1794. Appraisers: ROBT
BARKLEY, JAMES McMASTER, PETER ACKESON.

Pp. 51-52: Sale of WILLIAM FRAZER decd. Buyers: SAML RICHARDSON, BARTHOLOMEW TURNIPSEED,
FRANCIS SUMMERS, WILLIAM FRAZER, JOHN FRAZER, JOHN CHAPPEL, JACOB BONEY,
WILLIAM FREEMAN, ISAAC FRAZER, RACHEL FRAZER, JACOB GIBSON, JACOB NATES, JACOB TURNIPSEED,
JAMES ELLETT, STEPHEN GIBSON, THEOPHILUS WILSON, THOMAS RICHARDSON.

Page 53: Inventory of Estate of WILLIAM GLADDEN, decd. 28 Sept 1793. Ł 106.2.10. WILLIAM
WATSON, JOHN GOODRUM (G), JOHN HOLLIS, Appr. Rec. 5 Mar 1794.
Sale, 7 Feb 1794. Buyers: ELIZABETH GLADDEN, JAMES LUCAS, JAS. ALEXR. WATSON, CHARLES
LEWIS, JESSE HEVIS[?], QUINTIN CRAIG, Crier.

Page 54: Inventory of goods of PHILLIP SHAVER, deed. Ł 185.7.6. Certified 11 Jan 1794.
PHILLIP RAIFORD, BARHW. TURNIPSEED (BT). GEORGE LIGHTNER (Ͻ∂). Rec. 7 Mar 1794.

Page 55: Estate of WM. BOYD decd. Cr.--Notes & bonds on ALEXR. CAMERON, JAMES MANN,
      JOHN BUCHANAN, Est. of WM. DURPHEY, DAVID EVANS, J. MILBEY, JAS. BROWN Camden,
ALEXR. JOHNSTON. MARTYN ALKIN.
      Estate of WM. BOYD decd Dr. Accounts: NANCY BOYD, JOHN BELL, ROBERT CRAIG, WM.
BOYD, HUGH McDONALD, JAMES BROWN, JAMES BOWLES, MAJOR WINN, DAVID EVANS, ALEXR. JOHNSTON,
JOHN BELL.

Pp. 55-56: Inventory and appraisal of SAML NEAL decd, taken 6 Aug 1791. Ł 172 3 0.
      JOHN WATSON, MOSES COCKRELL, JOHN McCLURKIN, appraisers. Rec. 21 Mar 1794.

Page 56: Sale of est. of SAML. NEAL decd, 4 Oct 1791. Buyers: JOHN CAMERON, THOS BROWN,
      GEORGE KENNEDY, ANDREW WALKER, JAMES TURNER, WILLIAM BONNER, WILLIAM LESLIE,
STAFFORD CURRY, ROBERT KIRKPATRICK, ANDREW McQUISTON, MICHAEL WOOLFE, CHARLES RUDY,
MAURICE WEAVER, WILLIAM JOYNER, SAML FEARIS, JANE PIDIAN. Ł 29 15 0.
JOHN TURNER, ABRAHAM MILLER, STAFFORD CURREY. Rec. 22 Mar 1794.

Page 57: Inventory and appraisal of NATHAN SANDERS decd Ł 103 4. 0. March 19, 1794.
      CLEMENTS ARLEDGE, JOSEPH ARLEDGE, ROBERT HENSON, Appraisers. Rec. 5 Apr 1794.

      [N.D.] Inventory and appraisal of HUGH MORRISON Ł 22 15 2. HUGH McKEOWN,
JAMES TURNER, ALEXR. ROBINSON, Appr. Rec. 17 Apr 1794.

      Inventory and appraisal of JAMES BURK taken 14 Apr 1794. Ł15 3 8. THOS GOODRUM
(R), JESSE GLADDEN (A), THOMAS GOODRUM (cA). Rec. 17 Apr 1794.

Page 58: Appraisement of Est. of WILLIAM FRAZER, decd, Ł 48. 5. 4. JACOB GIBSON, PHILIP
      GENT[?], JOHN ROBERSON, Appraisers. 15 Dec 1793. Rec. 18 Apr 1794.
Appraisement of Est. of JAMES SCOT, decd. Ł 19 __. 10. 22 Jan 1794. THOMAS DAWKINS,
ADAM BYERLY, JOHN ELLET, Appraisers. Rec. 18 Apr 1794.
      On 16 July 1794, L. W. & T. of JACOB GIBSON was proved...JACOB GIBSON, Exr.
20 July 1794.

Pp. 59-60: L. W. & T. of JACOB GIBSON of Camden Dist., State of S. C....for the interests
      of my present wife SARAH GIBSON, requires a large consideration...I shall allow
her to give to her children, the value of the stock that she first brought to me...My
sons ABLE & JAMES...to my two sons JACOB and JOSEPH GIBSON, 200 A...my next two sons DAVID
and STEPHEN GIBSON...who of the Brothers will take BENJAMIN and look after him shall have
what they can make of my lands and my fathers in Virginia...to daughter JUDITH GIBSON,
negro (named)...& featherbed on her marriage...to my daughters LUCY and PRISCILLIA...my
dear beloved friends and Brothers THOMAS HALSAL and JOHN KINNERLY and son JACOB, Exrs...
8 Dec 1784...JA GIBSON SENR (LS), Wit: THOMAS BAMARE, JESSE BARMAR, ELIZABETH KENNERLY.

Page 60: Amt. of sale of perishable items of Est. of JOHN ROBERSON, Ł 28. 6. 4 1/2.
Sold 22 July 1794. THOS ROBERSON, Admr.
      Inventory of goods and chattels of JOHN ROBERSON, Ł 537. 16. 2. Appraised 29
Mar 1794, by ROBERT RABB, PHILLIP RAIFORD, WM. McMORRIS. Rec. 31 July 1794.

Page 61: On 24 July 1794, L. W. & T. of WILLIAM WHITTED was proved...NAZARUS, JOHN, GIDEON
      WHITTED, Exrs.
L. W. & T. of WILLIAM WHITTED of Fairfield Co....to wife ELIZABETH WHITTED, negro Bob,
cattle...son HIRAM WHITTED, 2 negroes [named], when he arrives at age 21 or marries...
100 A where I now live and remainder of estate to be sold at the discretion of friends
NAZARUS, JOHN & GEIDEON WHITTED whom I appoint my Exrs. 10 Mar 1794...WM. WHITTED (LS),
Wit: JOHN CONNERY, JOHN LAND, ELISHA OWENS Rec. 2 aug 1794.

Page 62: April 10, 1794, Inventory & appraisement of est. of PETER CROSSITY, decd...
      Ł 138. 18. 4. JESSE GLADDEN, JOSEPH HELLAMS, JOHN GOODRUM, Appraisers. Rec. 2
Aug 1794.
      Inventory and appraisement of EPHRAIM PETTIPOOLs Est....2 Negroes [named]...
Ł 287. 13. 8. THOMAS STARKS, REUBEN HARRISON, BURREL BURGE, Appraisers.

Pp. 62-63: L. W. & T. of GEORGE LEWEY, proved 17 July 1794.
      L. W. & T. of GEORGE LEWEY of Fairfield Co....being very sick and weak in
body....to wife [not named]...to son GEORGE FREDERICK LEWEY, 100 A on Little River and on
back of the tract I now live on...to son HENRY LEWEY, 100 A in Lexington Co., on a branch
of Broad River, called Hollingsheads creek, originally granted to JOHN EATER[?]...to my
youngest son MICHEL LEWEY, 150 A adj. Broad and Little River...MARY LEWEY & GEORGE FREDER-
ICK LEWEY, Exrs...4 Nov 1791...Wit: WM. FRAZER, DANIEL FRZER, PAUL NEATTS[?].

Pp. 63-64: L. W. & T. of MOSES HOLLIS proved 17 July 1794.

L. W. & T. of MOSES HOLLIS of Fairfield Co...9 Apr 1793...wife ROSANNA HOLLIS, furniture, negro [named]...son MOSES...to JOHN, negro [named]...to son ELIJAH, negro [named]...to daughter NANCY GLADDEN, featherbed...to granddaughter CATHERINE PATTERSON, cattle... remainder to be divided among my children...ZACHARIAH CANTEY and sons JOHN & ELIJAH, Exrs...MOSES HOLLIS (LS), Wit: THOMAS GOODRUM, EDMOND TIDWELL (X), BERREY HOLLIS. Rec. 4 Aug 1794.

Pp. 64-65: L. W. & T. of ANNE McFADEN, proved 17 July 1794.
     L. W. & T. of ANNE McFADDEN of Fairfield Co...to HANNAH LONG, heifer...to ANNE GRAHAM, s5...to RACHEL AYRES, heifer...to ELISHA McFADDEN, one colt...to daughter MARY McFADDEN, one new Bible & other items [named]...to JESSE McFADEN & REBECCAH McFADDEN, remainder of my property, three youngest children to go to one house...cattle at JOHN LONGS ...JAMES BLARE on Fishing Creek...RICHARD CAMPBELL, JOHN LONG JUNR, Exrs...31 May 1794... ANN McFADEN (/) (LS), Wit: RACHEL CAMPBELL (X), JOHN SMITH (X), MARY TUDOR (X). Rec. 4 Aug 1794.

Page 65: ROBERT ECKLES, late of Fairfield Co., planter, died intestate...admn. granted to
     ROBERT WINFIELD ECKLES & CHARNEL DURHAM...inv. to be returned by 16 Oct next...
17 July 1794.
     ABRAHAM PETTIPOOL, planter, died intestate...admn. granted to WILLIAM PETTIPOOL...
inventory ret. by 16 Oct next...17 July 1794.

Pp. 66-67: L. W. & T. of DAVID McCREIGHT of Jacksons Creek, Camden District, planter...
     15 Sept 1779...to wife MARY McCREIGHT, cattle, etc., the field the house stands in to be kept in repair by my son JAMES...to son JOHN, my great coat...to son MATHEW McCREIGHT, one blue coat...to son DAVID, one Blue coat and Jacket, whip & razor, etc...to son JAMES, plantation, 150 A...grandchild, DAVID, son of DAVY, and grandson WILLIAM, son of WILLIAM...grandson ROBERT, son of WILLIAM, leather breeches & other clothes...to grandson JOHN, son of WILLIAM, saddle, musket...granddaughter AGNES, daughter of WILLIAM and his daughter MARY, one heifer...ROBERT REED, "overseer" of my will...sons DAVID & JAMES, Exrs...DAVID McCREIGHT (O) (SEAL), Wit: WILLIAM HAMILTON ( ), ROBERT GRAY, DA. HAMILTON. Proved 18 July 1794.

Pp. 67-69: Bill of sale of personal estate of PHILLIP SHAVER, SENR., decd. Feb 6, 1794.
     Buyers: M. MARGT. SHAVER, LEVI RAALS, BENJAMIN SCOTT, SAML CROSLIN, ANTHONY PULLICK, SAML MOYL, STEPHEN HAIRES, WM. CRAIG, ROBIN ROTH, THOMAS JONES, JAS: TAYLOR, ROB. RABB, GEORGE ZAGHNER, JOHN AMMONS, JOHN ORSS, JOHN CROSLIN, JOHN FRAZER, SAM RICHARDSON, GEORGE SMITH, J. CHAPPEL, JOS: MILLS, EISOM SMITH. Total Ł 210. 14. 8.

Page 69: Debts, Notes &c. of estate of PHILLIP SHAVER, decd Ł 106. 11.
     Estate...names mentioned in bonds, debts, etc. GEO: LIGHNER, MR. KUBLER, MAYER & SUMMERS Store, WM. BALLENTINE, JACOB NERLES, BERNARD THRAMS, BART. TURNIPSEED, Blacksmith. Ł 44. 19. 8.

Page 70: Rec. of MARY MARGARET SHAVER, Extx. of Est. of PHILLIP SHAVER, share of estate
     4 Mar 1794. ANTHONY PULLIG, MARGARET PULLICK (X). Wit: BENJAMIN SCOTT, FRED.
JOS. WALLERN. GEO. LIGHTNER (L). Rec. 8 Sept 1794.

Page 70: INV. & Appraisaiment of MATHEW HAYS, decd., 1 Nov 1793. Ł 64. 14. 2 1/2.
     Appraised by SAMUEL GLADDIN, DAVID McCREIGHT, ROBERT McCREIGHT. Rec. 10 Sept
1794.

Page 71: [Estate of PHILLIP SHAVER]. Pd. M. M. SHAVERS share, MRS. B. SCOTT, MRS. A.
     PULLICK.
Recd. of MARY MARGARET SHAVER, share of est. 4 Mar 1794. BENJAMIN SCOTT. Wit: FRED: JO:
WALLERN, GEORGE LIGHTNER (L). Rec. 8 Sept 1794.

     Appraisement of estate of FRANCIS KIRKLAND, late of Fairfield, decd. Ł 57 16.
Cert. 29 May 1793. RICHD DUGGAN, JOHN JOHNSTON, CHARLES BEADFORD, Appraisers.

Page 72: Sale of Estate of FRANCIS KIRKLAND, 22 June 1794. Buyers: MARY KIRKLAND, AM-
     BROSE, ELIZABETH KIRKLAND, RICHARD DUGGINS, JONATHAN HARRISON, CHRISR ADDISON,
CHARLES BRADFORD. Rec. 28 Sept 1794. Ł.34. 14. 6.

Page 72: On 16 Oct 1794, L. W. & T. of SAMUEL WAUGH was proved...admn. granted to JOHN
     WAUGH, JAMES McNEAL, Exrs...inve. to be ret. by 16 Jan next...16 Oct 1794.

Page 73: L. W. & T. of SAMUEL WAUGH, 8 Apr 1794...son JOHN WAUGH, 150 A upon Wateree
     Creek, Fairfield County...granddaughter MARGARET WAUGH...son in law JAMES Mc-
NEEL, Ł 1 d9....grandson SAMUEL McNEEL...son in law JOHN RICHMOND,Ł1 d9...grandsons ANDREW

and JAMES RICHMOND...son in law THOMAS WALKER, if he comes out in the expiration of three years....grandson JOHN WRIGHT...granddaughter JANE WAUGH...to ROBERT LATHAN [no relation stated]...son JOHN, son in law JAMES McNEEL, Exrs...SAMUEL WAUGH (X) (LS), Wit: ROBERT ADAMS, JOHN MARTIN (X), ROBERT LATHAN. Rec. 21 Oct 1794.

Pp. 73-74: 16 Oct 1794, L. W. & T. of ROBERT McBRIDE was proved...JAMES PAUL, Exr... inventory to be returned by 16 Jan next. Rec. 16 Oct 1794.

Pp. 74-75: L. W. & T. of ROBERT McBRIDE of Fairfield County, being sick & weak in body... wife CATHERINE McBRIDE, cattle, household...to son HENRY McBRIDE, $1 in trade ...to son JOHN MCBRIDE, $1 in trade...to daughter AGNES McBRIDE, clothes, cattle... to daughter SARAH McBRIDE, cattle...to HENRY McBRIDE, my son HENRY's son, black mare... to MARY McBRIDE, daughter of my son JOHN McBRIDE...son in law JAMES PAUL, Exr...ROBERT McBRIDE (☾) (LS), Wit: STAFFORD CURRY, JOHN EFFELHELM, JOHN CATHCART.

Page 75: JOHN OWENS, late of Fairfield, planter, died Intestate...JAMES OWENS & WILLIAM OWENS, admrs...inventory to be returned by 16 Jan next...16 Oct 1794.
    Before JAMES CRAIG appeared JOHN ANDREWS and made oath that he was present with the late JOHN OWENS/who died at his own House on the 19th instant/ and was desired by the sd. OWENS to take Notice that he desired his Estate after his decease to be divided between his Brother JAMES OWENS, and his brother JOSEPHs son WILLIAM...Sworn 22 Aug 1794.
    Personally appeared MRS. PHEBE ANDREWS who made oath that her husband, JOHN ANDREWS [similar statement to above]...22 Aug 1794...Rec. 31 Oct 1794.

Page 76: 16 Oct 1794, Whereas the Executors named in the will of FREDERICK BRIGGS refused to qualify...ELIZABETH BRIGGS & WILLIAM WATSON, are admrs. with the will annexed See Will Rec. Book 1, pp. 101-102.
    WILLIAM TIDWELL, late of Fairfield County, died intestate...SIMEON TIDWELL, admr...inventory returned by 16 January next...16 Oct 1794.

Pp. 76-77: HANNAH McGRIFFIN, late of Fairfield County, spinster, died intestate...admn. granted to THOMAS LEWERS...inventory to be returned by 16 Jan next...16 Oct 1794.

Page 77: WILLIAM EDERINGTON, late of Fairfield County, planter, died intestate...admn. granted to JEMIMA EDERINGTON...inventory to be returned by 16 January next... 16 Oct 1794.
    ROBERT DUNLAP, late of Fairfield County, died intestate...admn. granted to SAMUEL MAHOOD.   ...inventory to be returned by 16 Jan next...16 Oct 1794.

Page 78: DAVID THOMPSON, late of Fairfield County, died intestate...admn. granted to SAMUEL GLADNEY & WILLIAM AIKEN...inventory to be returned by 16 Jan next...16 Oct 1794.
    Appraisement of Estate of ROBERT EIKLES, decd. ₺ 140. 0. 6. THOS STARKS, EDWD MAYNARD, ABNER SMITH, Appraisers. Rec. 4 Nov 1794.
    Appraisement of ABRAHAM PETTIPOOLS Estate. ₺ 31. 14. JAMES HUNT, ROBT WINFIELD ECKLES, ABNER SMITH, Appraisers. Rec. 5 Nov 1794.

Page 79: Appraisement of property of WILLIAM EDERINGTON, decd, taken 1 Oct 1794, by FRANCIS EDERINGTON, ROBERT MAYFIELD, & SAMUEL FANT (X). ₺719.11. 6. Rec. 5 Nov 1794.
    Appraisement o f Estate of ANN McFADDEN, decd, ₺ 70. 6. 7. JOHN SMITH (X), JAMES SEAL, & DENNIS BURNIS, Appraisers. Rec. 6 Nov 1794.

Page 80: Inventory and appraisement of personal Estate of GEORGE LEWEY, decd, taken 25 Aug 1794, ₺ 124. 9. 7. PHILLIP BUIFS[?], JACOB NEATS, GEORGE LIGHTNER (X), Appraisers. Rec. 7 Nov 1794.

Pp. 80-81: Amt. of sale of GEORGE LEWEY's Effects. Buyers: GEORGE F. LEWEY, MARY LEWEY, DANIEL ROUF, JACOB FRAZER, ROBERT RABB, PETER CURRIE, WILLIAM CRAIG, JACOB BRUEBAKER, WILLIAM FRAZER, JACOB BRIGHT, JOHN LIGHTNER, BART. TURNIPSEED, JOHN TERRY, ANTHONY POLLIG, WILLIAM DOUBER, MARGT. SHAVER, HARRIS FREEMAN, ADAM HAMETER, JACOB NERTS, JOHN CHAPPEL, O. SUMMERLIN, JNO. TROXCHORD [?], HENRY LEWEY, GEO: LEIGHTNER, JACOB ELEA- ZAR, HENRY COATS. Sold 26 Aug 1794. Rec. 8 Nov 1794.

Page 82: Appraisement-of WILLIAM TIDWELLs Estate. ₺ 145. 9. 8. SIMON TIDWELL, Admr. 4 Nov 1794. JOHN KING, MOSES KING, JESSE GINN, Appraisers. Rec. 7 Apr 1795.

Pp. 82-83: Sale of Estate of WILLIAM TIDWELL. Buyers: JOHN TURNER ESQ., EDMOND TIDWELL, JOHN KING SENR, HENRY RUGELEY, SIMON TIDWELL, JOHN KING JUNR., CHARLES PICKETT ESQ., WILLIAM ENGLAND, ROBERT SMITH, RICHARD LAND, SAMUEL OATS, CORDEL HOGAN, BENJAMIN

HENSON, THOMAS GOODRUM, FALBY TIDWELL, JAMES LAND, CHARLES JOHNSTON, MOSES KING, LEONARD HORNSBY, WILLIAM WATTS, JOHN MORRIS, JAMES STONE, BIRD OWEN, JOHN BARR, GEORGE TIDWELL. Rec. 7 Apr 1795.

Pp. 83-84: Acct of sale of ANN McFADDEN, decd. Buyers: JOHN LONG, MOSES AYERS, JOHN SMITH, SAMUEL OATS, GARDNER FORD, RICHARD CAMPBLE, WILLIAM McDANIEL, JOHN MARTIN, WILLIAM MARTIN, EDWARD BRYANT, JOSEPH MARTIN, THOMAS TRAPP, THOMAS STARKE, JOHN DASER, ALEXANDER IRWIN, RHUBEN HARRISON, DENNIS BURNS, DENNIS BURNS SEN., RICHARD CAMPBELL, Admr. Rec. 8 Apr 1795.

Pp. 84-86: Inventory of ROBERT DUNLAP, decd by order of SAMUEL MAHOOD, Admr. ROBERT KIRKPATRICK, JOHN McCULLOH, & JAMES SWAN, Appraisers. Rec. 8 Apr 1795. Ł 81. 0. 10.
Sale, 10 Nov 1794. Buyers: JAMES YONGUE, JOHN HERMAN, JOHN McCULLAH, ALEXR ROBINSON, STAFFORD CURRY, WILLIAM FUERYS, JAMES SWANN, GUIN THOMPSON, MARY PATTEN, ADAM BLAIR, ROBERT GIBSON, JOHN CAMMERON, ROBERT ARURDOCK, ISAAC BEAN, THOMAS EDWARDS, MARGRET ROSS, JAMES TURNER, JOHN BOYLES, JOHN CATCHSON, ANDREW CAMMERON, WILLIAM JOINER, JOHN GLEN, FRANCES McDONALD, ANDREW WALKER, JAMES McQUISTON, JOSEPH CAMMERON, ANDREW GRAHAM, ROBERT KIRKPATRICK, JOSEPH LEWERY, HUGH McCORMICK. Rec. 9 Apr 1795.

Page 87: Inventory of Public Sale of WILLIAM EDERINGTON, decd Buyers: JAMIMA EDERINGTON, THOMAS MAY, WILLIAM EDERINGTON, GEORGE EDERINGTON, HENRY EDERINGTON, FANNY EDERINGTON, JOHN EDERINGTON, JAMES TALENT, DANIEL MABRY. Rec. 9 Apr 1795. Ł 717. 14. 7.
Return of the apraisment of Richard GLADNEYs Estate. 29 Nov 1793, RT. ELLISON, E. MARTIN, ALEXR ROSEBOROUGH. Rec. 9 Apr 1795. Ł 359. 2. 6.

Page 88: Acct. of Property of WM WHITTED. by appraisers, JESSE GLADDEN, THOMAS GOODRUM, JOHN BYRNS. Taken 5 Aug 1794. Ł 28. 9. 8. Rec. 9 Apr 1795.
Sale,Buyers: NAZE WHITTED, GIDEON WHITTED, KENAY STRANGE, THOMAS GOODRUM, JOHN GOODRUM, JOHN TURNER ESQ., ROBERT SMITH, JOHN WHITTED, THOMAS LAND, JAMES WIER, MUSCO BOULER, ALLEN GOODRUM. Rec. 9 Apr 1795.
Acct. of sale of Est. of ABRAHAM PETTIPOOL, sold Aug 1794. Buyers: WILLIAM PETTIPOOL, THOMAS STARK. Rec. 10 Apr 1795.

Page 89: BENJAMIN MAY, Admr. of BRIANT RILEYs Estate. Names mentioned: THOS & ROLT RICHARDSON, SAMUEL ALSTON, MRS. RILEY attendance & Buring [sic], JAMES CRAIG, ROBERT RICHARDSON, SARAH RILEY. Rec. 10 Apr 1795.

Page 90: Appraisement of SAMUEL WAUGHS Estate &C. Ł 14. 10. 10. JAMES JOHNSTON, ROBERT LEATHEN, JAMES MARTIN. Rec. 10 Apr 1795.
Sale, buyers: ROBERT LEATHEN, HUGH WHITE, DAVID WIER, MATHEW RICHMOND, ESQUIRE TURNER, JAMES JOHNSTON, JOHN FLAK, WILLIAM ENGLAND, JAMES McMULLEN, WILLIAM FERIS, ROBERT BLACK, JOHN WAUGH. Rec. 10 Apr 1795.

Page 91: Apprasement of JOHN WRIGHTS Estate, 3 Jan 1795. JAMES JOHNSTON, ROBERT LEATHEN, JAMES MARTIN, Appraisers. Rec. 10 Apr 1795.
L. W. & T. of THOMAS MICKLE proven 16 Apr 1795...JONATHAN BELTON, DARLING JONES, & CANNON CASON, Exrs. Inventory to be returned by 16 July next. 17 Apr 1795.

Page 92: L. W. & T. of THOMAS MICKLE...to my eldest daughter BETSEY, her bed & furniture, exclusive of her equal share...mortgage & ready money to be placed in the hands of JONATHAN BELTON to collect...the small children and those not able to get their schooling...each child shall have an equal share on arriving at 21...JONATHAN BELTON, DARLING JONES, & CANNON CASON, Exrs...27 Jan 1795...THOMAS MICKLE (SEAL), Wit: POLLY HUNT, JAMES HUNT, AUSTIN F. PEAY. Proved by AUSTIN F. PEAY 15 Feb 1795. Rec. 17 Apr 1795.

Page 93: On 16 Apr 1795, L. W. & T. of MOSES KNIGHTON was proved...admn granted to PETER KNIGHTON & MOSES KNIGHTON, two of the executors named...inventory to be returned by 16 July next...17 Apr 1795.
L. W. & T. of MOSES KNIGHTON of Fairfield County...all estate real & personal to wife SUSANNAH KNIGHTON, for the term of eight years...to son PETER, negro Milly...to son MOSES, negro JENNY...to son JAMES, negro Linda...other negroes [named] to PETER, MOSES, JAMES, MARGARET & MARY...griend NICHOLAS PEAY & sons MOSES & PETER, Exrs...MOSES KNIGHTON (SEAL), Wit: WILLIAM LENOX, JAMES PATTERSON, THOMAS HUSE (+), Rec. 17 Apr 1795.

Pp. 94-5: L. W. & T. of WILLIAM COLHOUN proven 16 Apr 1795...admn. granted to CATHERINE COLHOUN, Extx...inventory to be returned by 16 July next...17 Apr 1795.
L. W. & T. of WILLIAM COLHOUN of Fairfield County, sick & weak in body...to wife CATHERINE household goods, cattle, full authority of my plantation...to son JAMES, Ł 15 sterl & shot gun...to sons WILLIAM & ALEXANDER, all my plantation & tools...to daughter NANCY, Ł 20

sterl....my wife now being pregnant, if it is Gods will it should come to life, if a
daughter, ₺ 20 sterl., if a son ₺ 30 with horse & saddle...if any of the children die,
that part to be divided among the others...wife CATHERINE, Extx...2 Aug 1794...WILLIAM
COLHOUN, Wit: STAFFORD CURRY, ALEXANDER DICKEY, GAVIN CURRY. Rec. 18 Apr 1795.

Page 95: 16 Apr 1795, L. W. & T. of JAMES HARDAGE proved...admn. granted to MATHEW Mc-
          CREIGHT & WILLIAM BRIANT, Exrs...inventory to be returned by 16 July next...
17 Apr 1795.

Page 96: L. W. & T. of JAMES HARDAGE of Fairfield County...to MATHEW McCREIGHT and WILLIAM
          BRIANT, all my estate...19 Aug 1793...JAMES HARDAGE, Wit: QUINTIN HAY, WILLIS
CASON, JAMES PORTER.

Pp. 96-97: EZEKIEL FRAZER appeared on 16 Apr 1795, and chose WILLIAM FRAZER as his
          guardian...return to be made at court to be held at Winnsborough 16 July next,
& annual return until orphan arrives at 21...16 Apr 1795. Rec. 21 Apr 1795.

Page 97: VICTOR NEALY, late of Fairfield County, planter, died intestate...admn. granted
          to PATTY NEALY, JOHN NEALY, & SAMUEL CLAMPET...inventory to be returned by
16 July next...Rec. 17 Apr 1795.

Page 98: THOMAS GRUBBS, late of Fairfield County, planter, died intestate...admn. granted
          to THOMAS JOHNSTONE...inventory returned by 16 July next...17 Apr 1795.

Pp. 98-99: A Memorandum of Goods and Chattels of Estate of CHARLES AIKEN, decd, appraised
          by SAMUEL LOUGHRIDGE, ADAM EAGER. ₺ 36. 4. 6. Debts: ADAM AIKEN. Rec. 22 Apr
1795.

Page 99: Acct. of sale of Estate of JOSEPH DODDS, 10 July 1794...Buyers: JOSEPH McCASH,
          JAMES KENNING, SAMUEL McMULLIN, NEAL SUTHERLAND, SIMON CAMERON, ROBERT BRICEN,
WIDOW DODDS, SAMUEL DODDS, SAMUEL CLARKE, JAMES DODDS, ALEXR. ROSEBOROUGH. Rec. 23 Apr
1795. by us. JOSEPH McCOSH, ROBERT BRYSON.

Pp. 100-101: Fairfield County, Inventory and appraisement of Estate of THOMAS MICKLE,
          May 27, 1795. ₺ 551. 14. 4. THOS STARKE, HENRY RUGELEY, JOHN KING. Rec. 6
July 1795.

Page 101: CHRISTIAN MORGAN, late of Fairfield County, planter, died intestate...admn
          granted to CHRISPIN MORGAN...inventory to be returned by 16 Jan next...16
July 1795.

Page 102: On 16 October 1795, L. W. & T. of JOHN McMULLIN was proved...admn. granted to
          MARY MCMULLIN, EXTX...JOHN McKEWN JUNR, JOHN HARVEY, EXRS...16 Oct 1795.

Pp. 102-103: 25 Aug 1795, L. W. & T. of JOHN McMULLIN of Fairfield County...wife MARY,
          Extx, with JOHN McKEWN JUNR & JOHN HARVEY...50 A to wf MARY...child my wife
is suppoed to be with, shall have sd. land if child should reach maturity...furniture &
clothing to JOHN HARVEY JUNR...JOHN McMULLIN (₤) (SEAL), Wit: JOHN McEWEN, JNO HARVEY,
THOMAS CALDWELL (X).

Page 104: HENRY HAILS, planter, died intestate...admn. granted to SARAH HAILS ..inventory
          to be returned by 16 Jan next...16 Oct 1795.
ROBERT WALKER, planter, died intestate...admn. granted to HENRY WALKER...inventory to be
returned by 16 Jan next...16 Oct 1795.

Page 105: Inventory and appraisement of estate of MOSES KNIGHTON decd...included negroes
          [named]...₺ 640. 16. 2. 7 July 1796. NICHOLAS PEAY, CHARLES LEWIS, JOHN KING,
Rec. 4 Feb 1796.
          Appraisers bill of the property of WILLIAM PHILLIPS, decd. ₺ 45. 11. 0. ROBERT
MARTIN SENR (R), ROBERT PHILLIPS SNR (P), HUGH GAMBLE SENR (W). Rec. 4 Feb 1796.

Pp. 106-107: Sale of personal estate of JOHN ROBERTSON decd. Buyers: THOMAS ROBERTSON,
          MRS. ROBERTSON, WILLIAM ROBERTSON JUNR (by guardian), JOHN MICKLE, BARTLEE
SMITH, JAMES KINCAID, THOMAS BELL, WILLIAM McMORRIES JUNR., WILLIAM McMORRIES SENR, JAMES
NEILEY, ALEXR KINCAID, WILLIAM HATCHER, JOHN MAY, WIDOW WOODARD, THROP. PARROT, DAVID
McGRAW, WILLIAM ROBERTSON SENR., WILLIAM HARDAGE, JACOB GIBSON, JOHN BELL, JOHN WALLACE.
Total ₺ 676.14.5. THOMAS ROBERTSON, admr., HANNAH ROBERTSON, Admx. Rec. 4 Feb 1796.

Page 107: Appraisement of some perishable articles of Estate of JOHN ROBINSON decd, ₺ 33
15. 6. ROBERT RABB, WILLIAM McMORRIES.

Pp. 107-108: Estate of CHARLES AIKEN, decd, appraised by Exrs. SAMUEL LOUDRIGE, ADAM
EAGER, & RICHARD GLADNEY. Rec. 5 Feb 1796.

Page 108: Bill of Property of Estate of WILLIAM COLHOUN, appraised 11 May 1795. Ŀ 44. 16.3
JOHN CORKE, ALEXR DICKEY, JAMES HINDMAN. Rec. 5 Feb 1796.
Sold 16 Dec 1795. Buyers: SUSANNAH NOLAN, GEORGE BEESLEY, JAMES ROGERS, ANDREW CAMERON,
JAMES SWAN, GEHON CURRY, JOHN GILBREATH, JOSH. CAMERON, JAS. HINDMAN, JOHN TODD, ALEXR.
ROBERTSON, ROBERT CASHEY. Signed, CATHARINE COLHOUN. Rec. 5 Feb 1796.

Page 109: Memorandum of Appraisement of Estate of SAMUEL HOLLIS, decd, Ŀ 22. 6. 10.
CHARLES LEWIS, JOHN HOLLIS. Rec. 5 Feb 1796.
June 6. 1795. Appraisement of the Estate of THOMAS GRUBBS, decd. Ŀ 1052. JOHN McKEWEN JR.,
ALEXR McKEWEN, ANDR. McDOWEL, Rec. 5 Feb 1796.
Return of Estate of WILLIAM MORGAN SENR, decd by CRISPIN MORGAN, admr. Ŀ 34. 16.
3. Aug 18, 1794. WM. NELSON, GEO. PRAT, WM. POWELL. Rec. 5 Feb 1796.

Page 110: Nov. 27, 1795. The property of MARY McMULLIN Widow sold at publick Vandue.
Buyers: JOHN HARVEY, JOHN McKEWEN,SENR, RICHARD GUIRVIN, JAMES WILSON,EDWARD
GRIFFIN, JAMES GAMBLE, HENRY CREW, WILLIAM CALDWELL, JOHN SIMPSON, WILLIAM MARTIN, MRS.
McMULLIN, JOHN MOON, JOHN DARANNON, THOMAS CALDWELL, JAMES RUTLAND.

Page 111: Appraisement of Estate of JOHN McMULLIN, decd. Ŀ 43. 4. 6. 7 Nov 1795. THOMAS
JOHNSTON, ANDR. McDOWELL, ALEXR. McKEWN, Rec. 6 Feb 1796.

Pp. 111-112: 1791-1795, Cash pd. to Sundries for the Estate of JOHN MILLING. Pd: JOHN
BUCHANAN, ROBERT ELLISON, MORRIS WEAVER, COL. WINN, JAMES BROWN, COL. BRIS-
BANE, HUGH McKEWN, JOHN DRAYTON, MRS. BLAKE, SHERIFF HAMPTON, McCORKLE, SAMUEL MATHIS,
Expenditures at Richland Court vs. GOODWIN, WIDOW MILLING, McMINNES.
Cash recd on the action of JAMES OWENS from JERREY COCKRILL, MARTIN ATKIN, WILLIAM
BRUMMIT, JOHN BELL, JOHN GOODWIN. Rec. 6 Feb 1796.

Pp. 112-116: Sale of public Auction 20 & 21 May 1795, Estate of THOMAS MICKLE, decd.
Buyers: ROBERT MICKLE, DARLING JONES, JOHN BOYKIN, JAMES HUNT, JONATHAN
BELTON, RUEBEN HARRISON, MOSLEY COLLINS, JOHN MICKLE, JAMES BISHOP, NICHOLAS PEAY,
ELIZABETH MICKLE, JOSEPH MICKLE, BURWELL BURGE, RICHARD CLAYBROOKS, THOMAS STARKE, JOHN
COATS, HENRY RUGELEY, CHARLES PICKET, JAMES LEWIS, JOSIAH KNIGHTON, ALEXANDER IRVIN,
CHARLES LEWIS, ALEXR CROMPTON, THOMAS STONE SENR., MATHEW McKNIGHT, GARDNER FORD, HENRY
PETTIPOOL, WILLIAM WELLS, REUBEN STARK JUNR., JAMES WIER, THOMAS MUSE, THOMAS HUGHES,
JONATHAN BARNS, JESSE HAVIS, DENNIS BURNS, NATHANIEL FORD, SAMUEL OATES, SAMUEL SMITH,
ANTHONY SEAL, JOHN ELLISON, WILLIAM KIRKLAND, MICAJAH PICKETT JUNR., JOHN MORRIS, MADDEN
LEGGE, THOMAS MICKLE, WILLIAM BERRY, JOHN BARR, JOHN MARTIN, BARTLET SMITH, JESSE FULGHUM.
16 Jan 1796. Rec. 8 Feb 1796.

Page 116: On 20 Jan 1796, L. W. & T. of ROBERT COLEMAN proved...admn. granted to WILLIAM
CHAPMAN, ISAIAH MOBLEY, Exrs. named in sd. will.

Pp. 117-118: L. W. & T. of ROBERT COLEMAN of Fairfield county, being very weak of Body...
to wife SUSANNAH COLEMAN, cattle etc. "to be taken out of the Stock I had
by my wife in marriage," 1/3 part of 100 A...to children: THOMAS COLEMAN, SARAH CHAPMAN,
MARY PARKER, CLORY MOBLEY, FANNY MOBLEY, NANCY MOBLEY & SUSANNAH PRICHET, one shilling
sterling to each...to my children STEPHEN COLEMAN, MORNING COLEMAN, & TABITHA COLEMAN,
all personal estate except what I have given away above...WILLIAM CHAPMAN & ISAIAH MOBLEY,
Exrs...31 Mar 1795...ROBERT COLEMAN (R) (SEAL), Wit : ANDERSON THOMAS, THOMAS COLEMAN.

Page 118: WILLIAM HILL, late of Fairfield County, planter, died intestate...ABEL HILL,
ASAPH HILL, & THOMAS MOBERLY, Exrs...inventory to be returned by 2nd Monday in
April next...__ Jan 1796.

Page 119: JOHN HARRISON of Fairfield County, planter, died intestate...admn. granted to
MINOR WINN...inventory returned by 16 Apr next...23 Jan 1796.
Inventory of Estate of ROBERT WALKER, Decd. Ŀ 27. 7. 7. 6 Jan 1796, by WM. KIRKLAND, JAS.
HART, ROBERT NEIL (O).

Page 120: On 16 April 1796, L. W. & T. of ALEXANDER ROBERTSON was proved...DAVID HAMILTON,
SIMON CAMERON, Exrs...inventory returned by 16 Jan next...16 Apr 1796.

Pp. 120-122: L. W. & T. of ALEXANDER ROBERTSON of Fairfield county...to wife MARGARET
ROBERTSON, all plantation & negroes for raising & education the children...
each child gets a part, the girls when she married, the boys when they reach 21...to son
JOHN ROBERTSON, 100 A purchased of ANDREW CAMERON & negroes [named]...JOHN is to give his

two youngest brothers Ł 15 shen he comes of age...to son ALEXANDER ROBERTSON, 100 A out of that tract formerly McCLELANDS, to pay Ł 15 to his two youngest brothers JOSEPH & SIMON...to son JOSEPH ROBERTSON, plantation where I now live...youngest son SIMON, remainder of tract formerly McCLELANDS...to daughter JANE MORE, 100 A of tract formerly McCLELANDS...to daughter JULIANA CALDWELL, negro girl Suckey...to daughter ELIZABETH ROBERTSON, negro girl Cuba...to youngest daughter MARGARET AGNES ROBERTSON, negro Prince ...SIMON CAMERON, JAMES CAMERON, & DAVID HAMILTON, Exrs...25 Jan 1796...ALEXANDER ROBERTSON (X), Wit: HENRY MOORE, ADAM ROBERTSON (R), HENRY AKESON (O).

Page 123: On 16 Apr 1796, L. W. & T. of ESTHER COOK was proved...SAMUEL YONGUE, Exrs... inventory of estate to be returned by 16 July next...16 Apr 1796.

Page 124: L. W. & T. of ESTHER COOK of Fairfield County, being weak of body...31 Dec 1795 ...to my neice SARAH MILLING, negro Lucy, 1/2 dozen silver Table Spoons, 1/2 dozen silver tea spoons, 1 silver soup Ladle, one silver scissors[sic], 1/2 dozen damask Napkins, 1 table cloth, and all the china...to my neice MARY QUARRELL, one feather bed and patch quilt, & trunk...to my sister SUSANNA QUARREL, the full amount of a note due BY HUGH MILLING, Esq., for a negro firl...sisters JANE MILLING & SUSANNA QUARRELL...suit of clothes for DAVID MILLING my nephew...to MRS. MARGARET McCREIGHT, my hat...all other clothes to my sister JANE MILLING & her two daughters SARAH & MARY ANN MILLING...to ESHOR DUNLAP of Kershwa County, one mare colt...to my sister LETTICE HUTCHINSON, s10...to my sister MARTHA MILLER, s10...SAMUEL YONGUE, Exr...ESTHER COOK (⊠). Wit: JAMES PHILLIPS, ROBERT PHILLIPS, ROBERT MILLING.

Page 125: JOHN MARPLE, late of said county of Fairfield, died intestate...admn. granted to ROBERT RABB...inventory to be returned by 16 July next...16 Apr 1795. Appraisement of Estate of WILLIAM HILL, decd, [no total]...11 Feb 1796. DANIEL MABRY, ISHAM MOBLEY, MICAJAH MOBLY. Rec. 22 Apr 1796.

Pp. 126-127: Sale of Estate of WILLIAM HILL, decd Buyers: RICHARD HILL, ABEL HILL, ASAPH HILL, THOMAS MOBLEY, THOMAS BURNS, EDWARD MEADOR, WILLM McQUISTON, DANIEL MABRY, ALEXR GALLOWAY, YOUNG ALLEN, THOMAS MEADOR, STEVENS DUMAS, JOHN HILL, SAMUEL MOBLEY, JOSEPH McDANIEL, ADAM POOL JUNR, JOHN FOOTE, DANIEL MAJOR, JACOB HOSH, WILLIAM MOBLEY, JOHN LOVEJOY, EDWD MOBLEY, JOHN SMITH, WM CHAPMAN, TAPLEY WATSON, THOMAS SHELTON, MICAJAH MOBLEY, BENJA. BARKE. Ł 112.9.11. Notes due on COL. JOHN WINN, GEORGE DYR. Rec. 22 Apr 1796.

Pp. 127-128: Appraise [sic] of goods and chattles of ROBERT COLEMAN, decd. WILEY COLEMAN, WILLIAM MOBLEY, D. COLEMAN, Appraisers. Sale, Ł 27.1.5. Signed WILLIAM CHAPMAN, ISAIAH MOBLEY. Rec. 23 Apr 1796.

Pp. 128-129: L. W. & T. of MARGARET ROBINSON of Sawneys Creek, Craven County, Camden District, being weak in body...100 Ain possession of Robert Robinson, my dear Father, to him and his wife SUSAN ROBINSON, my dear mother, during their lives and then to my Brother JAMES ROBINSON, provided that he live along with and take care of my said father and mother...father & CHARLES SEAR, Exr...16 June 1776...MARGARET ROBINSON (M). Wit: JOHN GOODWIN, WILLIAM JOYNER (J), SALLY JOYNER (⚹). Proved by ROBERT ROBINSON, 13 Sept 1778 before WM. SIMMONS, J. P. Proven by WILLIAM JOYNER, 12 Nov 1778 before WM. SIMMONS. Rec. 28 July 1796.

Page 130: JAMES GIBSON appeared on the 16th inst., with advice and consent of his mother, SARAH GIBSON, relict of JACOB GIBSON, chose WILLIAM McMORRIES as his guardian... return to be made annually, until sd. JAMES attains the age of 21...17 Oct 1796.

Pp. 130-131: L. W. & T. of AVES WILLINGHAM of Fairfield County, very sick & weak in body ...to my Nees[sic] AVES ELLIS, all my body Apparel, Bed and cloaths...to JOURDAN GINN, my Exrs., the remainder of my Estate...15 Sept 1796...AVES WILLINGHAM (X-her mark). Wit: JAS. BROWN, WM. BROWN, MARGARET McKINSTRY. Proved by WILLIAM BROWN, 8 Oct 1796, before SAMUEL ALSTON, J. P. Rec. 20 Oct 1796.

Page 132: On 17 Oct 1796, L. W. & T. of AVES WILLINGHAM was proved and admn. granted to JOURDAN GINN, Exr...17 Oct 1796...Rec. 20 Oct 1796.

Pp. 132-133: ALEXANDER YOUNG, late of Fairfield County, Weaver, died intestate...admn. granted to JESSE HAVIS & JOHN HARVEY...inventory returned by 16 Jan next... 17 Oct 1796...Rec. 25 Oct 1796.

Page 133: DAVID MILLER, late of said County, died intestate...admn. granted to ROBERT RABB & ROBERT MILLER, inventory to be returned by 16 Jan next...17 Oct 1796. Rec. 25 Oct 1796.

Pp. 134-135: L. W. & T. of MARCELLUS LITTLEJOHN of Campden [sic] District, being weak in
body...to wife SARAH LITTLEJOHN, negro Poll, & remainder of estate, real &
personal...at her decease to grandchildren, SARAH HARRISON, MARY TYLER, half of estate...
to grandchildren THOMAS ROBERTSON, WILLIAM ROBERTSON, MARY ROBERTSON, ANN ROBERTSON,
ELIZABETH ROBERTSON, MARTHA ROBERTSON, & SAMUEL ROBERTSON...wife SARAH, THOMAS ROBERTSON,
JONATHAN HARRISON, Exrs...30 June 1795...MARCELLUS LITTLEJOHN (LS), Wit: WM McMORRIES
JUNR., JOHN BELL. Rec. 17 Oct 1796.

Page 135: Inventory of Estate of AVIS WILLINGHAM, decd, 8 Nov 1796. Returned by JOURDAN
GINN. Rec. 10 Nov 1796.

Page 136: A Direct Account of the sale of the property of ROBERT WALKER Ꝑ 22. 1. 5. the
whole of which was purchased by me. HENRY WALKER, Admr. Rec. 20 Oct 1796.
The Estate of ROBERT WALKER, Decd: to HENRY WALKER (1792-1795), Acct "To cash for going
to No. Carolina, to MR. JONES for publishing Citation, to DAVID EVANS. Rec. 20 Oct 1796.

Page 137: Estate of WM. SCOTT. To JAMES ROBERS, 17 Oct 1796, signed JOHN TURNER, J. F. C.,
HENRY MOORE.
        WILLIAM MACKEY, late of Fairfield county, Taylor, died Intestate...admn. granted
to MARIAME MACKEY...inventory to be returned by 16 Apr next...16 Jan 1797. Rec. 24 Jan
1797.

Page 138: On 16 Jan 1797, L. W. & T. of DENNIS BURNS was proven...JAMES LAUGHLON &
        WILLIAM BERRY, Exrs...inventory to be returned by 16 April next...16 Jan
1797. Rec. 27 Jan 1797.

Pp. 138-139: L. W. & T. of DENNIS BURNS SENIOR of South Carolina, Fairfield County...
        to wife MARY, the part of my land on the West side Morrisons Creek, 2 cows
& calves, ...land at her decease to son JAMES...& moveable furniture to my daughter
SARAH...to son JAMES, land on E side of the creek...to daughter DOLLEY, 3 cows and calves
...to son JOHN, s 20...to son DENNIS, s 20...25 Apr 1796...JAMES LAUGHLON, WILLIAM BERRY,
Exrs...DENNIS BURNS (Ø) (SEAL), Wit: JOHN LONG SENR., JOSEPH MICKEL, THOMAS MORE[?].
Rec. 27 Jan 1797.

Page 139: JOHN McBRIDE, late of Fairfield County, died intestate...admn. granted to
        HENRY McBRIDE, JAMES ROGERS...Inventory returned by 16 Apr next...16 Jan 1797.
Rec. 27 Jan 1797.

Page 140: On 16 Jan 1797, L. W. & T. of JACOB BONEY, proved...admn. granted to SARAH
        BONEY & JACOB BONEY...inventory to be returned by 16 Apr next...16 Jan 1797.

Pp. 140-141: L. W. & T of JACOB BONEY, 2 Feb 1795...all estate of wife SARAH and son
        JACOB, to make an equal division to every one of my children when they
become 21...SARAH & JACOB BONEY, Exrs...JACOB BONEY (♋)Wit: JOSEPH WOODWARD, JOHN
CHAPPLE, PETER CUGLAR (X). Rec. 7 Feb 1797.

Page 141: To MRS. SUSANNAH KNOX, widow of DOCTOR JAMES KNOX; ROBERT KNOX, MATILDA KNOX,
        ELIOIZA KNOX, children of sd. SUSANNAH, have chosen you their guardian...annual
return to be made until they reach 21...17 Jan 1797. Rec. 19 Feb 1797.
        The Estate of WILLIAM SCOT decd to JOHN SCOT "To Boarding a child of sixteen
months old for the year 1787 to the present date." 17 Jan 1797. JOHN SCOT (8). Rec. 20
Feb 1797.

Page 142: Appraisement of Estate of JACOB GIBSON decd. Ꝑ 96.6. 12. 14 Jan 1797. WILLIAM
        CRAIG (·), DAVID LONG (D). Rec. 20 Feb 1797.
Appraisement of Estate of ALEXANDER YOUNG Ꝑ 37.12.4. 3 Nov 1796. JOHN McEWEN JUNR., ALEXR
McEWEN, DANL GOWEN (G). Rec. 20 Feb 1797.

Page 143: Sale of Estate of ALEXANDER YOUNG, 15 Nov 1796, Buyers: JOSEPH WILEY, JAMES WASON,
        DAVID WEAR, WILLIAM ENGLAND, JOHN HERVEY, HUGH WHITE, JESSE HAVIS, WILLIAM
MARTIN, MARY McMULLEN, JOHN MARTIN, JOHN McEWEN, DAVID GOWEN, JAMES RUTLAND, ALEXR McHENRY,
SAMUEL CROWDER, GUERARD DUNTZE, JAMES McCREIGHT. Ꝑ 36. 8. 6. Rec. 21 Feb 1797.

Pp. 143-144: L. W. & T. of WILLIAM WRIGHT, being weak of body...to my daughter LEATICIA
        HUTCHISON, all personal Estate...granddaughter POLLY HUTCHISON...to my
daughters JENNY, SUSANNA, & MARTHA one shilling...daughter LEATICIA, Exr...27 Aug 1796.
WILLIAM WRIGHT (LS), Wit: JAMES PHILLIPS, SUSANNAH GRAY, JAMES HUTCHISON. Rec. 21 Feb
1797. Prov. 11 Jan 1797 before EDWARD MARTIN J. P.

Page 144: On 17 Apr 1797, L. W. & T. of HENRY REUGLEY was proved...admn. granted to
ELIZABETH RUGELEY & ZACHARIAH CANTEY...18 Apr 1797. Rec. 18 Apr 1797.

Pp. 144-146: L. W. & T. of HENRY RUGELEY of Fairfield County...to wife ELIZABETH, negroes
[named] & plantation I now live on bought of THOMAS GRIGS YARBROUGH, on
Taylors Creek, 137 1/2 A...to son ROWLAND RUGELEY, plantation on Wateree River, 250 A
adj. JONATHAN BELTON, & 100 A on Taylors Creek adj. land I live on...to sons HENRY &
JOHN, 3 plantations I purchased on Wateree River, each each to the other...650 A...to
daughter MARY ANN CAROLINE RUGELEY, negro [named] & plantation at my wife's decease...
until eldest son ROWLAND attains the age of 21...brother MATHEW RUGELEY, Esq. of Potton,
Bedfordshire, Kingsdom of Great Britain, ZACHARIAH CANTEY Merchant in Camden, NICHOLAS
PEAY, planter on Wateree, & wf Exrs...16 June 1796. HENRY RUFELEY (LS), Wit: ISAAC AR-
LEDGE, THOS GRIGGS YARBOROUGH (X), THOS STAKE JUNIOR. Rec. 18 Apr 1797.

Page 146: On 17 Apr 1797, L. W. & T. of MOSELY COLLINS was proved...admm granted to
MICHAEL COLLINS, Exrs...inventory to be returned by 16 July next...20 Apr 1797.
Rec. 20 Apr 1797.
L. W. & T. of MOSELEY COLLINS, of Fairfield County, haberdasher...to my brother
MICHAEL COLLINS, My Sorrel mare...estate to be divided among my sisters and brothers
SALLY KIRVY, RUBY[?] DRAKE, ANN COLLINS, MICHAEL COLLINS, & ELIZBAETH COLLINS...10 Jan
1797. MOSELY COLLINS (LS), Wit: JAS.BOONY, JOSIAH BONEY, JAS. PERRY. Rec. 20 Apr 1797.

Page 147: DOCTOR DANIEL COCHRAN, late of Fairfield County, died intestate...admn. granted
to PHOEBE COCKRAN & JOHN GREY...inventory to be returned by 16 July next...
17 Apr 1797. Rec. 18 Apr 1797.
JAMES WARD, late of Fairfield County, died intestate...admn. granted to MARY
WARD...inventory to be returned by 16 July next...17 Apr 1797. Rec. 20 Apr 1797.

Page 148: JACOB LOVE, late of Fairfield County, died intestate...admn. granted to NICHOLAS
PEAY...inventory to be returned by 16 July next...17 Apr 1797. Rec. 21 Apr 1797.
THOMAS EDERINGTON of Fairfield County, died intestate...admn. granted to JOHN MEANS...
inventory to be returned by 16 July next...17 Apr 1797. Rec. 21 Apr 1797.

Page 149: JOSEPH FROST, late of Fairfield County, died intestate...admn. granted to JOHN
LAROWE...inventory to be returned by 16 July next...17 Apr 1797...Rec. 21 Apr
1797.
To EDWARD MARTIN...ESTHER WILSON hath chosen you her guardian...17 Apr 1797.
Rec. 21 Apr 1797.

Page 150: On 17 Apr 1797, L. W. & T. of DAVID EVANS, Esq. was proved...15 Apr 1797.
L. W. & T. of DAVID EVANS of Fairfield County...to wife MARY, all estate real
& personal...at her decease, to son JOSEPH, negro [named]...to son DAVID REED EVANS,
negro [named] and house & lot in Winnsborough, furniture of the common Parlour...wf
MARY , Extx....11 Dec 1796...D. EVANS (LS), Wit: GERARD DUNTZE, JOHN BUCHANAN, JAMES
AUSTIN. Rec. 22 Apr 1797.

Pp. 150-151: L. W. & T. of JAMES PORTER of Jacksons Creek, Parish of St. Mark, Craven
County 5 Apr 1775...to son JAMES PORTER, 100 A...to son JOHN 100 A...to wf
MARGARET...she is to live with my son...daughter JENET ROBISON...to MARY PORTER, 50 A "
if she comes over her[e]"...wife Extx...JAMES PORTER (R) (SEAL), Wit: WILLIAM WILSON,
JAMES McCREIGHT, DAVID McCREIGHT. Rec. 27 Apr 1797. Proved April Ct. 1797 by JAMES Mc-
CREIGHT. JAMES McCREIGHT JUNR swore in Exr.

Pp. 151-152: L. W. & T. of JOHN McCULLOCH of Fairfield County, being sick & weak of body...
wife JEAN McCULLOCH should have full power & authority over all my estate...
sons WILLM & JNO. , should have the plantation if they marry & pay to my youngest son
SAMUEL, 1/3 value of the plantation...daughters MARTHA and ISBLE...wife JEAN & brother
SAML McCULLOCH, & friend JOHN WILSONS, Exrs...13 Sept 1796...JNO. McCULLOCH (I) (LS), Wit:
STAFFORD CURRY, JOSEPH CURRY. Proved by STAFFORD CURRY, 17 Apr 1797. Rec. 27 Apr 1797.

Page 152: Appraisement of property of HENRY McNEIL, decd...Ł 14. 6.1. EDWARD MARTIN,
WILLIAM BRICE, ROBERT MARTIN. Rec. 27 Apr 1797.
March 6, 1797, Inventory and appraisement of Estate of DENNIS BURNS, decd. Ł 119.3.0.
WILLIAM McDANIEL (X), THOMAS MUSE, JAMES LEWIS.

Pp. 152-153: Sale of Estate of JACOB GIBSON, decd. Buyers: LUCEY GIBSON, PRICILA GIBSON,
JACOB GIBSON, JOHN WILLINGHAM, HENRY JONES, JOSEPH McMORRIS, WM McMORRIS, BARW. TURNIPSEED,
ABEL GIBSON, WM. HOMES, DUDLY CURRY, OWEN ANDREWS, ALEXR McMORRIS, JOHN MATHEWS, WM.
BURNS, DAVID GIBSON, SAML RICHESON, Negroe John, JOSEPH GIBSON, JAMES RABB, SILVESTER
LAY, SILAS McGRAW, JOHN BRENT, BARY. W. POPE, JOSEPH PERRY, HUGH HARTIN, WM. YARBOROUGH,

WM. FREEMAN, STEPHEN GIBSON, DAVID McGRAW. Returned by JACOB GIBSON, Exrs. Rec. 27 Apr 1797.

Page 153: Account of sales of Estate of MAJOR YARBOROUGH, July 24, 1788. Buyers: MRS. RACHEL YARBOROUGH, MINOR WINN. M. WINN, Admr. Rec. 28 Apr 1797.

Pp. 153-154: BURREL BURGE of Fairfield County, died intestate...admn. granted to WILLIAM NETTLES JUNIOR...inventory to be returned by 16 Oct next...17 July 1797.

Page 154: HENRY LEWEY & CATHERINE LEWEY have chosen BARTHOLOMEW TURNIPSEED as their guardian...18 July 1797.

Pp. 154-155: Inventory and appraisement of Estate of COL. HENRY RUGELEY, 24 Apr 1797.
negroes [named] [no total], JOHN ELLISON, THOS STONE (T), JOHN KING (   ). Rec. 23 July 1797.

Page 156: Appraisement bill of JOSEPH FROST, decd. Ʌ 13. 0. 6. ELIJAH MAJOR, WILLIAM EDERINGTON, JAMES NEWTON, Rec. 23 July 1797.
Inventory and appraisement of Estate of WILLIAM MACKEY, decd, 2 Feb 1797. Ʌ 20. 4. 6. Accounts: MR. BENJN. HART, REUBEN STARK, JOHN STARK, BETSY NETTLES, JOHN BOYKIN, DANIEL GOWEN, JOHN MOON, SAMUEL P. JOHNSON, Estate of BENJAMIN McKENNY. Rec. 23 July 1797.
Appraisement of MOSELEY COLLINS Estate, 2 May 1797. Ʌ 129. 10. 11. REUBEN HARRISON, JOHN MICKLE, JOHN BOYKIN. Rec. 23 July 1797.

Page 157: Sale of Estate of MOSELEY COLLINS, decd. Buyers: MICHAEL COLLINS, ZACH. NETTLES, JONATHAN BARNS, JAMES POOVEY, ZADOCK, RICHARD BURGE, REUBEN HARRISON, DARLING JONES, JOHN MICKLE, THOMAS MUSE, JOHN SMITH, JOHN McDUGLE, ANN GRAVES, JOSEPH MICKLE, THOMAS HANKS, GEORGE PERRY, JEREMIAH BURGE, WILLIAM CLANTON, EDWARD RUTLEDGE, JAMES MORRIS, AUSTIN PEAY, ISAAC RUNNELS, ALEXANDER IRVIN, ENOCH SEAL, JOHN BRADLY, Ʌ 105. 7. 9. 19 May 1797, Rec. 24 July 1797.
Appraisement of Estate of JAMES WARD, decd. Ʌ 56. 10. JOSHUA DERHAM, JOHN OGLEVIE, JAS. MOTZE (B). Rec. 24 July 1797.

Page 158: Sale of estate of JAMES WARD, Decd, 18 May 1797. Buyers: JOHN MATHEWS, JAMES DAVIS, CHARS. MONTGOMERY, NATHAN COOK, JOHN SPILLAR, PHILLIP MATHEWS, MARY WARD, SAMUEL PARKE, EDWD WILLINGHAM, JOSHUA DURHAM, ALMON YARBOROUGH, PHILN HOLCOM, JOHN BARKER, JAMES BAIRD, THOMAS NETTERVILLE, JAMES MOOTEY, JOHN BRENT, PHILLIP PEARSON, ABEL GIBSON, THOS PARROT JUNR, DAVID JAMES JUNR, WILLIAM SIMMONS, MINOR WINN, ELISHA MORRIS, JOHN PEARSON, JAMES McMORRIS, JOSEPH McMORRIS, Rec. 24 July 1797, Ʌ 62. 19. 8.
Appraisement of Estate of Alexander TURNER, decd, appraised by JAMES MEEK, JAMES PADIEN, and JAMES BROWN. Ʌ 258.14. 3. Including The 1st and 2nd volumes of Shaws Law & Simmons. 5 Books of Divinity.

Pp. 159-160: Sale of Estate of ALEX TURNER, Decd. Buyers: JAMES McCLURKIN, MR. MOORE, WILLIAM DUNN, RICHARD EVINS, ROBERT JAMISON, THOMAS McCLURKIN, JOHN BURNS, JOHN BELL, RISE HUGHES, WILLIAM DICKSON, WIDOW TURNER, JAMES STEVENSON, WILLIAM WILLIAMS, ANDREW WALKER, HUGH GASTON, JOHN TURNER, JOHN MORTON, JAMES YOUNG, GEORGE LOTT, WILLIAM LUCKEY, JAMES TURNER, ROBERT STRONG, ROBERT LUCKEY, ALEXANDER CHESNUT, JOSEPH DALE, WILLIAM ARCHER, JOHN WALKER, RICHARD EVANS, SAMUEL WALKER, ROBERT KIRKPATRICK, SAMUEL COLWELL, JOHN McQUARTERS, JACOB HUFFMAN, JAMES NORTON, THOMAS DYE, ANDREW HEMPHILL, JAMES BROWN, WILLIAM ANDERSON, ADMONT STRANGE, JOHN GASTON, JOHN GAFFNEY, ANDREW GRAHAM, BENJN. DOVE, JOHN LOOL. Widow TURNERs Acct. , MR. MILLIGANS Acct. Rec. 24 July 1793.

Pp. 160-161: Estate of ALEXANDER TURNER, Decd, Accts. [1783-1793]. Names mentioned: DOCTOR DOCKORN, JOHN SEALY, EDWARD MOOREHEAD, JOHN LEE, JOHN WALKER, THOMAS ROBISON, WILLIAM GORDON, DAVID GRAHAM, SAMUEL ARMSTRONG, HUGH McDONALD, ROBERT MARTIN, THOMAS H. McCAULE, SAMUEL NISBIT, PETER WILEY, JOHN GREY, GEORGE KENEDY, MARGARET TURNER, JOHN STENSON, SAML ADAMS, RICHARD GLADNEY, for schooling children; McCLERKIN, SAML COLWELL, JOHN McCULLIN, JOHN BELE, STEPHEN TERRY, DANIEL MAZEECK, JAMES ALEXANDER, ROBERT MARSHALL, WM. GRISOM; WILLIAM TURNER, in part his share as an heir. Ʌ 224.19.7. Rec. 24 July 1797.

Page 161: JAMES GIBSON, orphan has chosen WILLIAM McMORRIS SENIOR as his guardian...18 Oct 1797. Rec. 18 Oct 1797.
ALEXANDER WATSON of Fairfield County, died intestate...admn. granted to ANN WATSON and WILLIAM LEWIS...inventory to be returned by 16 Jan next...17 Oct 1797...Rec. 18 Oct 1797.

Page 162: ELIJAH BEAM of Fairfield County, died intestate...admn. granted to ANN BEAM... inventory to be returned by 16 Jan next...16 Oct 1797...Rec. 18 Oct 1797.
To CAPTAIN HENRY MOORE...MARY WILSON, orphan, chose you as her guardian...16 Oct 1797... annual returns to be made until she is 21...18 Oct 1797, Rec. 18 Oct 1797

Pp. 162-163: To RICHARD BURGE...NANCY BURGE, orphan has chosen you as her guardian...
17 Oct 1797. Rec. 18 Oct 1797.

Page 163: Inventory & appraisement of Estate of JOHN MARPLE, 16 Sept 1797. negroes [named]
₤ 155.0.0. WM. McMORRIS, JOHN BELL, ROBERT MILLER, Rec. 19 Oct 1797.
Appraisement of estate of BURREL BURGE, ₤ 292. 4. 6. JOHN BOYKIN, ALEXR IRVIN, ZACH
NETTLES., Rec. 19 Oct 1797.

Page 164: Appraisement Bill of Effects of DANIEL DOCKRAN, decd, by WM. McMORRIS, THOS.
LEWERS, & THOS SAINT., 7 Aug 1797. ₤ 112. 8.10. Rec. 19 Oct 1797.

Pp. 164-165: Sale of Estate of D. DOCKRAN, decd., 14 Aug 1797. Buyers: PHEBE DOCHRAN,
JAMES McGILL, ROBERT MILLER, WILLIAM RABB JUNR., WILLIAM McMORRIS SENR.,
ARCHD. PAUL, THOMAS LEWERS, JAMES RABB JUNR, WILLM RABB SENR., ALEXR. CALHOUN, JOHN
DERRY[?], JOHN McCOY, WILLM ELLISON, JAMES GREY, EDWARD MARTIN, ALEXANDER KINCAID, JAS.
PHILLIPS SENR., JOHN PAUL, SAML McGILL, ANDR. McGILL, DAVID JAMES, WILLM JOHNSTON, JAMES
NEALY., ₤ 140.4.10. Rec. 19 Oct 1797.

Page 165: Sale of Estate of JOSEPH FROST, 14 Oct 1797. ₤13. 6. 0. [No buyers given].
JOHN LAROWE, Rec. 19 Oct 1797.
Appraisement of Goods and Chattles of JACOB BONEY, decd by HARRIS FREEMAN, JOHN CHAPPLE,
& WM KENEDY. 13 Feb 1797, ₤ 1776. 6. Rec. 19 Oct 1797.

Pp. 165-166: 16 Jun 1797, L. W. & T. of DAVID WEAR SENR of Fairfield County, being very
sick and weak in body...son GEORGE WEAR of Chester County with DAVID WEAR
& ANDREW McDOWELL, Exrs...to son DAVID WEAR JR., copper still with grey mare & sorrel
mare...big coat to youn DAVID WIER, son of JAMES WIER...$1 to GEORGE WIER...$1 to THOMAS
GILLESPIE...$6 to GEORGE WIERs son DAVID...$6 to THOMAS GILLASPYS son DAVID...to sonJAMES
my streat[sic] coat & my smallest Bible...DAVID WIER (LS), Wit: JNO McEWEN JUNR., HUGH
SMITH, Rec. 20 Oct 1797.

Pp. 166-167: L. W. & T. of JAMES JOHNSTON, 1797...to wife MARY, 1/2 of plantation of 165
A...other half to sons MATHEW & DAVID JOHNSTON & JOHN JOHNSTON...negroes
[named]...daughters SARAH JOHNSTON, JEAN (JEAN) JOHNSTON, & ELLENOR JOHNSTON...WILLIAM,
JOHN & SAMUEL JOHNSTON, Exrs...13 Mar 1797. JAMES JOHNSTON (LS), Wit: Wit: SAML JOHNSTON,
CHARLES McCREA, ROBERT LEATHEN, Proven 17 Oct 1797, Rec. 20 Oct 1797.

Page 167: THOMAS PARROT SENR, died intestate...admn. granted to THOMAS PARROT JUNR...inv.
to be returned by 16 Apr next...19 Jan 1798. Rec. 20 Jan 1798.

Pp. 167-168: MARY MARTIN died intestate...admn. granted to WILLIAM MARTIN...inventory to
be returned by 16 Apr next...25 Jan 1798. Rec. 25 Jan 1798.

Page 168: To WILLIAM McMORRIS SENR & ALEXANDER KINCAIN...PATRICK McCONNEL & CATHARINE
McCONNEL, late CATHARINE CALHOUN, relinquish right to admn. on estate of JAMES
CALHOUN & JAMES CALHOUN, in your favor...18 Jan 1798...Rec. 20 Jan 1798.
Appraisement of estate of JOHN McBRIDE, by DAVID CAMICK, ARCHIBALD PAUL, &
ANDREW CAMERON. ₤ 26. 5. 0. Rec. 23 Jan 1798.

Page 169: Memorandum of Appraisement of Estate of ELIJAH BEAM, ₤ 69. 3. 1 1/2. JOHN HILL
(₤), JOHN FEASTER, JESSE BEAM. Rec. 23 Jan 1798.
Oct. 31, 1797, Appraisement of Estate of JAMES ALEXANDER WATSON, ₤ 458, 14. 10 1/2. Rec.
25 Jan 1798. N. PEAY, J. GLADDEN.
Return of property of MARY WILSON by her guardian HENRY MOORE. Notes on H.
HUNTER, JAMES CRAIGE, SAML & JOHN ROBINSON, JOHN BELL, JAMES HENERY. THOMAS GLADNEY,
Jan. 18, 1798. Rec. 25 Jan 1798.
Bill of payment of Debts of Estate of JOSEPH FROST. Notes due MARTHA BOLE,
JOHN MEANS, JACOB MINKS, JAMES RUSSEY; JOHN LAROWE, Admr. Rec. 25 Jan 1798.

Page 170: On 16 April 1798, L. W. & T. of JAMES PAUL was proved. Rec. 17 Apr 1798.
Will of JAMES PAUL of Fairfield County, being at this time weak in body...two
sons JAMES & ARCHIBALD PAUL, when they come of age...land between Fishing Creek and
Catawba River, to be sold, when the oldest of my sons comes of age, and if possible to
buy a plantation joining the one I live on Jacksons Creek...wife [not named]...friend
EDWARD MARTIN, ESQR. and MOSES PAUL, Exrs...4 Mar 1798...JAMES PAUL (LS), Wit: JAMES
CRAIG, JAMES CAMPBELL, JOHN PAUL. Rec. 17 Apr 1798.

Pp. 170-171: DANIEL McCOYE of Fairfield County, died intestate...admn. granted to ELIZABETH
McCOYE & GEORGE BEASELY...inventory to be returned by 16 July next...16
Apr 1798...Rec. 17 Apr 1798.

Page 171: JAMES FEARIS of Fairfield County, died intestate, admn. granted to JAMES BECKET
& DAVID MARTIN...inventory returned by 16 July next...17 Apr 1798. Rec. 18 Apr
1798.
  FIELD FARRAR, late of Fairfield County, died intestate...admn. granted to THOMAS
MEANS...inventory to be returned by 16 July nest...16 Apr 1798. Rec. 18 Apr 1798.
  Estate of SAMUEL WILSON to THOMAS GLADNEY, admn. "funeral expenses for MR.
WILSON & wife"...Paid for education of 3 children...to cash pd. GAWIN THOMPSON for Boarding
a male boy of 4 years. Rec. 19 Apr 1798.

Page 172: 7 Dec 1795, Memorandum of appraisement of Estate of SAMUEL HOLLIS, decd.
  Ŀ 22. 6. 10. Rec. 19 Apr 1798.
Memorandum of sale of above estate. Buyers: ELIZABETH HOLLIS. BERRY HOLLIS WILLIAM HOLLIS,
MOSES HOLLIS, MOSES KNIGHTON, JOHN STARKS. Ŀ 17. 8. 6. by BERRY HOLLIS, Admn. Rec. 19 Apr
1798.
  Estate of SAMUEL HOLLIS Dr. to BERRY HOLLIS, Admn. Suit with estate of HENRY
RUGELEY & attending on sd. business in Camden. Rec. 19 Apr 1798.
  Augt 28, 1797, Recd. of THOMAS GLADNEY, Admr. of Est. of SAMUEL WILSON, Decd.
in full of MARY WILSON's part of sd. estate. Recd pr me as her chosen gdn. HENRY MOORE.
Test. D. HAMILTON, Rec. 19 Apr 1798.
  Augt 28, 1797, Recd. of THOMAS GLADNEY, in full of ESTHER WILSON, her part of
estate of SAML WILSON, as her chosen gdn. EDWARD MARTIN. Rec. 19 Apr 1798.

Page 173: Inventory of Goods and Chattles of Estate of THOMAS PARROT decd, app. 5 Feb 1798.
PHLP PEARSON, WM. CATO, Appraisers. Rec. 20 Apr 1798.

Pp. 173-174: Acct. Sale of Estate of THOMAS PARROT, 7 Feb 1798. Buyers: THOMAS PARROT,
  MARY WATSON, ALEXANDER McMORRIS, WILLIAM CATO, MRS. J. WHITE, JAMES DAVIS,
THOMAS NELSON, JAMES BAIRD, JAMES McGILL, JOSEPH JAMES, MR. WOOD, JOHN RHODAS, JOHN
EDERINGTON, WINNIFRED PARROT, MRS. MONTGOMERY. MRS WATSON, SAMUEL MAYFIELD, WILLIAM Mc-
GRAW, THOMAS NELSON JUNR., SAMUEL DAWSON, CHARLES BRADFORD, ADAM HAWTHORN, PHILLIP MAT-
THEWS, WALTER POOLE, GEORGE EDERINGTON, JOHN BARKER, WILLIAM EDERINGTON, PHILLIP PEARSON,
AMBROSE KIRKLAND, JACOB HENRY, GEORGE REDDISH. Cert. 16 Apr 1798. Rec. 20 Apr 1798.

Pp. 174-175: Inventory of Goods and Chattles of MARY MARTIN, decd. Ŀ 40. 15. 4. 1[?] March
1798. Rec. 20 Apr 1798.

Page 175: S. C. Fairfield Co.: I, ANN PARROT, wife of THOMAS PARROT SENR decd, do relin-
  quish all my Right of Dower both real & personal to THOMAS PARROT JUNR. 21 Dec
1797. ANN PARROT, (X). Wit: RICHD WINN, WM. CATO. Sworn 18 Jan 1798. Rec. 20 Apr 1798.
  To the Court of Fairfield. We having muttually[sic] agreed to relinquish all
right of admn. of the Estates of JAMES & WILLIAM CALHOUN & recommend WM. McMORRIS &
ALEXANDER KINCAID as proper persons to admn. on sd. estate. 7 Jan 1798. HUGH MILLING, J. P.
PATRICK McCONNELL, CATHARINE McDONNEL (X). Rec. 20 Apr 1798.
  CHARLES PALMER of Fairfield County, died intestate...admn. granted to JAMES
KINCAID...inventory to be returned by 16 Oct next...20 July 1798.

Page 176: JOHN MARPLE, late of Fairfield county, died intestate...admn. granted to NORTH-
  RUP MARPLE...inventory to be returned by the 16 Oct next...20 July 1798.
On 20 July 1798, L. W. & T. of HUGH GAMBLE was proved...admn. granted to AGNES GAMBLE,
JOHN BELL, & NATHAN MAJORS...20 July 1798.

Pp. 176-177: L. W. & T. of HUGH GAMBLE of Fairfield County, 16 May 1798...wife AGNES, her
  own Bed and Bed Cloaths...to wife AGNES, 1/3 of all monies from sale...the
other 2/3 to daughter NANCY, excepting two guineas to little BETSEY...my daughter NANCY
to be schooled, if daughter NANCY dies, then estate to be divided among my 5 sisters in
Ireland MARGARET, MARY, SARAH, JEAN,NANCY...wife, JOHN BELL SENIOR of Mill Creek & NATHAN-
IEL MAJOR, Exrs...HUGH GAMBLE (H) Test: ROBERT BELL, WILLM BELL, JOHN BELL. Rec. 20 July
1798.

Page 177: On 17 July 1798, L. W. & T. of JAMES ANDREWS was proved...admn. granted to
  MATHEW ANDREWS & EDWARD ANDREWS, Exrs....23 July 1798.

Pp. 177-178: L. W. & T. of JAMES ANDREWS of Fairfield County...wife PRISILAH ANDREWS may
  be maintained out of my estate should she be the longest liver...to son
MATHEW ANDREWS, the plantation whereon I now live, 300 A, formerly granted to ISAAC POR-
CHER, & from him to JOSEPH KIRKLAND & then to myself...to daughter PATIENCE WALLACE, 1
shilling sterling...to son ENOCH ANDREWS, 1 shilling sterling...to son JAMES ANDREWS, 1
shilling sterling...to son EDWARD ANDREWS, 1 shilling sterling...to son DAVID ANDREWS,
1 shilling sterling...to son WILLIAM ANDREWS, 1 shilling sterling...to son OWEN ANDREWS,
1 shilling sterling...to daughter MARY McGRAW, 1 shilling sterling...sons EDWARD & MATHEW

Exrs...JAMES ANDREWS (⧻⧓) (LS), Wit: EDWARD ANDREWS, W. HARDAGE.

Pp. 178-179: On 16 July 1798, L. W. & T. of JOSEPH CAMERON was proved...admn. granted to
ANDREW CAMERON & JOHN McEWEN...23 July 1798.

Pp. 179-180: L. W. & T. of JOSEPH CAMERON of S. C., Fairfield Co...being very sick & weak
of body...to be buried in the family burying place on Jacksons Creek...to
wife JEAN CAMERON, negro Abigil & decent and genteel support from my son ANDREW and from
my son in law and daughter JNO & MARGARET McEWEN...to daughter ROSANNA McCORMICK, during
her separation from her husband WILLIAM McCORMICK...increase of negro divided among JOHN
& JOSEPH CAMERON, & JOHN & MARGARET McEWEN...to wife, a tract called EWINGS, also 67 A adj.
same...son JOSEPH CAMERON...to grandson JOSEPH CAMERON, son of JOHN CAMERON...to son JO-
SEPH, 200 A in Chester County, called COOPERS place...to son in law WILLIAM McCORMICK,
s7 sterling & no more...to JOHN & MARGARET McEWEN, 1/2 of 200 A & 1/2 of 638 A...son
ANDREW, son in law JOHN McEWEN & HENRY MOORE, Exrs...7 May 1798...JOSEPH CAMERON (LS),
Wit: ANDREW McDOWELL, MARY McDOWELL (O), ANN McDOWELL (1).

Page 181: WILLIAM RABB, SENIOR, late of Fairfield County, died intestate...admn. granted
to JOHN RABB & WILLIAM RABB...inventory to be returned by 16 Oct next...23 July
1798. Rec. 23 July 1798.
ALBERT BEAM, of Fairfield Co., died intestate...admn. granted to SARAH BEAM...
inventory to be returned by 16 Oct next...23 July 1798. Rec. 23 July 1798.

Page 182: WILLIAM BALL, late of Fairfield Co., died intestate...admn. granted to JOHN KING
SENIOR...inventory to be returned by 16 oct next...11 Sept 1798...Rec. 11
Sept 1798.
On 17 July 1798, L. W. & T. of THOMAS BELL was proved...admn. granted to JAMES
CRAIGE & WILLIAM BELL, 23 July 1798.

Page 183: L. W. & T. of THOMAS BELL, weak of Body...to sister JENNY CRAIG, the whole of
goods I bought when last in town, to her son JAMES CRAIG, the whole of what money is collected for me by ANDREW PATTERSON, ESQ. of Richland...brother WILLIAM BELL, sister MARGARET BELL, to them at the death of my Mother...note on JAMES SMTIH...to brother
JOHN BELL...to sister JEAN McEWEN...Brothers JAMES CRAIG & WILLIAM BELL, Exrs...11 June
1798...THOS BELL (SEAL), Wit: ROBT BRADFORD (X), JANE McCUNE (X). Rec. 23 July 7198.

Pp. 183-185: L. W. & T. of JOHN CORK of Fairfield Co., being sick & weak of Body...to
wife ELIZABETH CORK... to son in law & daughter ROBERT & MARK CASKEY [CALKEY?]
7 shillings sterling...to daughter MARGRET, ₺ 20...to daughter ISBELL, ₺ 20...to youngest
daughter ELIZABETH, ₺ 20...to son JOHN & JAMES, tract on little River adj. JAMES BANKHEAD,
150 A...to son WILLIAM CORK, plantation on which I now live, his mother to rule over him
until he becomes of age...son JAMES, Exr....9 Feb 1798...JNO CORK (G) (LS), Wit: STAFFD.
CURRY, JAMES HINDMAN, WILLIAM JENSON.

Page 185: To THOMAS MEADORS...SAMUEL HILL & ELIJAH HILL have chosen you their gdn...22
July 1798. Rec. 24 July 1798.

Page 186: HENRY FURDERBURGH [sic] an orphan, hath chosen RICHARD HILL as gdn...22 July
1798. Rec. 24 July 1798.

Pp. 186-187: To ABEL HILL...ELIZABETH HILL, JOHN HILL & MARY HILL, orphans, have chosen
you their gdn...22 July 1798...Rec. 24 July 1798.

Page 187: Sale of personal estate of HENRY RUGELY, decd, sold at his plantation, 20 Apr
1798. Payable 1 Jan 1799. Buyers: THOMAS STARK SENR, REUBEN STARK, THOMAS
MEREDITH, ZACHARIAH CANTEY, SAMUEL McKINNEY, JOHN MOSELEY, ABNOR SMITH, SAML STARK, MOSES
ALDRIGE, MRS. STARK, AUSTIN PEAY, THOMAS STARKE. Rec. 24 July 1798. ZACHARIAH CANTEY, Admr.

Page 188: Appraisement of Estate of DANIEL McCOY, 22 May 1798. ₺ 5. 8. 3. GAVIN CURRY, AN-
DREW CAMERON, & ADAM BEASELY, Appraisers. Rec. 24 July 1798.
Sale of estate of ELIJAH BEAM, ANN BEAM, Admr. Buyers: JOHN BEAM, EDWARD MEADOR, WILLM
SMITH, ASAPH HILL, THOMAS MEANS, JESSE BEAM, JOB MEADOR, RICHARD HILL, WILLM MOBLEY, MOSES
LACKLEY, JOHN McCRORY, JACOB JEASTER[?], THOMAS COLEMAN, JOHN McCAWN[?], JOHN FOOTE,
JACOB HOETH, WILLM CHAPMAN, DANIEL BEAM.

Page 189: HUGH GAMBLE of Fairfiled Co., died intestate...admn. granted to PRUDENCE GAMBLE...
inventory to be returned by 16 Jan next...17 Oct 1798. Rec. 18 Oct 1798.
JAMES AIKEN SENR., died intestate...admn. granted to HUGH AIKEN & JAMES AIKEN JUNR...
inventory to be returned by 16 Jan next. 18 Oct 1798. Rec. 19 Oct 1798.

Page 190: THOMAS LESHLEY, of Fairfield Co., died intestate...admn. granted to ANN LESHLEY
...inventory to be returned by 16 Jan next...18 Oct 1798. Rec. 19 Oct 1798.
On 17 Oct 1798, L. W. & T. of   MOSES COCKREL was proved...admn. granted to JEREMIAH
COCKREL & NATHANIEL COCKREL, Exrs...19 Oct 1798.

Page 191: L. W. & T. of MOSES COCKRAL of Fairfield County, being weak of body...to wife
JANE, chief part of plantation I now live on adj. LAVENDER, HUGH YOUNG...to son
JEREMIAH COCKRAL, tract he now lives on & negro...to son NATHANIEL COCKRAL, 250 A adj.
land he lives on...to daughter MARY NOLAND, land adj. JOHN RICHMOND & SAMUEL ARMSTRONG...
to daughter SARAH MARTIN...to daughter LEAH NEEL; sons JEREMIAH & NATHANIEL, Exrs...30
Jan 1788...MOSES COCKRAL (LS), Wit: BURR HARRISON, JOHN BOYD. Rec. 19 Oct 1798.

Page 192: On 17 Oct 1798, L. W. & T. of RICHARD BURGE was proved...FRANCIS BURG, Extx...
18 Oct 1798.
L. W. & T. of RICHARD BURGE SENR of S. C....wife FRANCIS BURGE, whole estate...19 Oct 1797.
RICHD BURGE. Wit: JOHN MUKLE, JOSEPH MUCKLE.

Page 193: Appraisement of Estate of CHARLES PALMER. Accts of PHIL HOLCOM, JOHN OGILVIE.
Ь 44. 18. 5. JAMES McMORRIS, ALEXR KINCAID, WM. McMORRIS. Rec. 19 Oct 1798.
Appraisement of JOHN MARPLE...negroes [named]...7 Sept 1798. JOSEPH McMORRIS, ALEXR
KINCAID, THOS PARRISH, Appraisers. Rec. 19 Oct 1798.
Appraisement of property of HUGH GAMBLE JUNR, 20 Oct 1798. Ь 43. 6. 5.   JOHN
D. TINKER, SIMEON CAMERON, WM AKIN, Appraisers. Rec. 22 Oct 1798.

Page 194: Appraisement of Personal estate of ALBERT BEAM, 2 Oct 1798. ASAPH HILL, RICHARD
HILL, MICAJAH MOBLEY, Ь 88. 10. 4. Rec. 22 Oct 1798.
Memorandum of personal estate of HUGH GAMBLE. 11 Aug 1798. AGNES GAMBLE, JOHN BELL, NATHAN
MAJORS.

Page 195: Apprasiement of estate of JOSEPH CAMERON, decd. 13 Augt 1798. Ь 283. 1. 4.
DAVID WEAR, ALEXR McEWEN, JOHN HARVEY, JAMES BARBER. Rec. 22 Oct 1798.

Page 196: Inventory of personal estate of ESTHER WILSON, an orphan, taken by EDWARD
MARTIN, gdn. 23 Oct 1797. Note on JOHN WINN & HUGH MILLIN, JAMES McCREIGHT &
JOHN PORTER, On Estate of DANIEL MILLER. Ь 28. 15. 0.
Sale of Estate of BURRELL BURGE. Ь 312. 18.10. Rec. 22 Oct 1798. WM. NETTLES,
JUNR., Admr.

Pp. 196-197: Sale of Estate of HUGH GAMBLE SENR. Buyers: ARTHUR McNEEL, JOHN ROBERTSON,
WILLM BRICE, JOHN BELL, JOHN SLOAN, JOHN BRAHAM, DAVID PATTON, JOHN PORTER,
JAMES McMULLEN, JAMES ROBISON, ELIAS HENDRICKS, JOHN CRAIG, JOHN GAFFNEY, ROBERT MARTIN,
ADAM ROBISON, WILLM JOHNSTON, NATHAN MAJORS, JAMES GAMBLE, AGNES GAMBLE, JAMES CRAGE,
JOHN CAMPBELL, HENRY ECKISON, ROBERT BOYD, JOHN HARRIS, WILLM BLAIR, DAVID MARTIN, JOSEPH
MILES, ROBERT BELL, THOMAS BLAIR, ROBERT PHILLIPS, JAMES ANDREWS, ROBERT GARDNER, SAML
GLADNEY, JAMES HOGE, SAML CLERK, THOMAS GLADNEY, SAML GAMBLE, JOHN PHILLIPS, HUGH BARTLEY,
THOMAS PORTER. Ь 69. 9. 6. AGNES GAMBLE, JOHN BELL, NATHAN MAJORS, EXrs. Cert. 14 Aug
1798. Rec. 22 Oct 1798.

Pp. 197-198: Bill of sale of JAMES PAUL, decd. Buyers: WIDOW PAUL, JOHN ROBISON, JAMES
ROBISON, ROBT. PHILLIPS, NATHL MAJORS, JOHN BRICE, JOHN THOMPSON, THOS
BLAIR, WILLIAM ROBISON, JOHN BELL, ARTHUR McNEIL, JAMES HOYE, JAMES GARDENER, WM BLAIR,
ROBERT BRISON, DAVID BOYDE, EDWARD MARTIN, ALEXANDER DUPAS [?], ARCHD McNEIL, JOHN CLAN,
MOSES PAUL, JOHN MAJORS, JAMES ANDREWS, JOHN McNEIL, SAMUEL MONTGOMERY, HUGH GAMBLE, SAML
GAMBLE, JANE McNEIL, ADAM ROBISON, MICHAEL ANDREWS, JOHN GAFFNEY, MORRIS WEAVER, JOHN
PORTER, JOHN HARRISON, WILLM AYRES, ROBERT MARTIN JUNR, ROBERT MARTIN. Cert. 17 Apr 1798.
EDWARD MARTIN, MOSES PAUL, Exrs. Rec. 22 Oct 1798.

Page 199: Bill of sale of property of JOHN MARPLE. Biyers: JOHN BARKER, 16 Nov 1797,
ROBERT RABB, Admr. Rec. 22 Oct 1798.
ROBERT HANCOCK of Fairfield, died intestate, admn. granted to LUCY HANCOCK...inventory to
be returned by 16 Apr next...17 Jan 1799. Rec. 18 Jan 1799.

Pp. 199-201: L. W. & T. of RICHARD NEILEY...24 July 1793...to wife ANN, 50 A whereon I now
live...to son VICTOR NEILEY...daughters MARY & JANE, each 1 shilling...to son
JOHN NEILEY, tract where he lives, 48 A...& set of Smiths tools now in possession of SAML
CLAMPET..to son RICHARD NEILEY, 50 A, 1/2 of tract I live on when he becomes 21...to daughters ANN, ABIGAIL, SUSANNAH & SARAH, each one cow & calf...to sons CLEMENT & ALEXANDER,
tract adj. JOHN BRENT, SAML CLAMPET, BARTHOW. JONES, & land I now live on...wife ANN &
son VICTOR, Exrs...RICHARD NEELEY (LS), Wit: THOMAS SMITH (T), JOHN BRENT (Ŧ), J. PEARSON.
Proven 17 Jan 1799...ANN NEILEY, the surviving Exr...rec. 19 Jan 1799.

Page 201: On 18 Jan 1799, L. W. & T. of PETER LEMLEY was proved...MILLEY LEMLEY & GEORGE
LEMLEY, Exrs...inventory to be returned by 16 Apr next...18 Jan 1799.

Pp. 201-202: L. W. & T. of PETER LEMLEY of Fairfield Co., planter...to daughter RUTH LEM-
LEY, one cow & calf when she is married...to son GEORGE, 1/2 of my land where
I now live adj. SHADRICK WOOLEY...to wife MILLEY...son AROMANOSES, EPHRAIM, ₺ 5 sterling
...household furniture to three youngest children [not named]...wife MILLEY & son GEORGE,
Exrs...3 Jan 1799...PETER LEMLEY (X) (SEAL), Wit: SHADRACK WOOLEY, BARET WHEAT, ELI WHEAT.

Page 202: On 19 Jan 1799, L. W. & T. of SARAH BENNET was proved...admn. granted to WILLIAM
KIRKLAND, with the will annexed....19 Jan 1799.

Page 203: S. C., Camden District, L. W. & T. of SARAH BENNET of Fairfield County...to son
WILLIAM KIRKLAND, negroes [named] & property...23 Augt 1794...SARAH BENNET (Լ)
Wit: ZACHARIAH KIRKLAND, JESSE KIRKLAND, Rec. 19 Jan 1799.
Part of Estate of CHARLESPALMER, decd, appraised 22 Dec 1798. WM. McMORRIS,
ALEXR. KINCAID, JESS MCMORRIS.

[The pagination in this volume ends with page 203; however, pagination will continue for
the convenience of the reader.]

Page 204: Inventory of Estate of JOHN MARPLE, decd 15 Nov 1798. Buyers: NORTHRUP MARPLE.
₺ 80. 11. 1. 2 negroes [named]. Rec. 19 Jan 1799, NORTHRUP MARPLE.
Bill of sale of estate of HUGH GAMBLE, decd. Buyers: PRUDENCE GAMBLE, SAML
GAMBLE, QUINTEN CRAIGE, WM. BEARD, JAS GAMBLE. HUGH CARSON, JOS. ROGERS. 19 Jan 1799.
Signed: PRUDENCE GAMBLE (Ŧ)
Bill of sale of estate of DANIEL McCOY. Buyers: ANDREW CAMERON, STAFFORD CURRY,
GEORGE NITON[?], ADAM BEASLY, GEORGE BEASLY, ARTHUR McNEIL, JAS ROSEBOROUGH, JEREMIAH
WALKER, ZEPH CAMERON, ARTHUR McNEIL, 3d Augt 1798. ELIZABETH McCOY. Rec. 21 Jan 1799.
Inventory of Estate of SARAH BENNET, Rec. 21 Jan 1799. WM KIRKLAND, Admr.

Page 205: Bill of sale of estate of CHARLES PALMER. Buyers: HENRY OWENS, JOHN NORWOOD,
JOHN McCRELLUS, JAMES OWENS, WM RABB, DAVID EDERINGTON, JOHN PAUL, SAML OWENS,
ALEXR KINCAID, JOHN BRADFORD, BARTLY SMITH; JOS. KINCAID, Adm.
Bill of sale of estate of ALBERT BEAM. Buyers: JOHN FOOT, WM BEAM, SARAH BEAM,
JOHN BEAM, WILEY COLEMAN, ROBT WATSON, DANL MABY [MABRY?], D. COLEMAN, WM. SMITH, THOS
MEADOR, RICHD HILL, JACOB HOTCH[?], JOHN COLEMAN, SAML HILL, HUGH BANKS, LEVY MOBERLY,
WM. ALSUP, CHAVIS LEA, EPHM. MABRY, DAVID SHELTON. SARAH BEAM, Admx. Rec. 18 Nov 1798.
Rec. 21 Jan 1799.
Inventory of Estate of JAS. FEARIS. RT. MARTIN, WM McCROY, D. MARTIN, Appraisers.
5 Dec 1797. Rec. 21 Jan 1799.

Page 206: Bill Sale Estate JOSEPH CAMERON. Buyers: JOHN McEWEN SENR, JOSEPH CAMERON,
MATHEW RICHMOND, JEAN CAMERON, ANDREW CAMERON, ROBT WILSON, JESSE HAIRS, THOS.
HUGHES, JOHN PHILLIPS, WM. EWEN, JOHN McEWEN JUNR., JAMES CAMERON, JAS. WILSON, JOS. WILSON,
DANL GOWENS, SINA[?] TIDWELL, ANDREW McDOWELL, WM ENGLAND, GARVIS GIBSON, JOHN HOLLIS,
JOS BARBER, JEAN CAMERON, JOHN JOHNSTON, JACOB GIBSON, JOS McMULLEN, JOS AIKENS, HENRY
PAGE, ISAAC GIBSON, ALEXR McHENEY, ROBT SMITH, RICHARD GARVIN, HUMPHREY GIBSON, D. CAMBLE,
WIDOW CAMERON, ROSEY[?] CAMERON, RICHD GARVIN; JOHN McEWEN, ANDW CAMERON, Exrs. 16 Jan
1799. Rec. 21 Jan 1799.

Page 207: JOHN BOYKIN, of Fairfield Co., d intestate...admn. granted to FANNY BOYKIN...
16 Apr 1799. Rec. 16 Apr 1799.
On 16 Apr 1799, L. W. & T. of GEORGE MARTIN was proved...admn. granted to SOLOMON MARTIN,
& JOSHUA MARTIN, Exrs...16 Apr 1799.

Pp. 207-208: JESSE GODBOLT of Fairfield Co., died intestate...admn. granted to ELIZABETH
GODBOLT...16 Apr 1799.
THOMAS GRAFFIN of Fairfield Co., died intestate...admn. granted to MARY GRAFFIN...16 Apr
1799.

Pp. 208-209: L. W. & T. of GEORGE MARTIN of Fairfield County, being very sick...Eldest
son SOLOMON MARTIN & nephew JOSHUA MARTIN, Exrs...to son OWEN MARTIN, one
saddle & cow & calf...to son SAMUEL MARTIN, bay horse & saddle...to daughter MARY MARTIN,
mare, saddle, etc....to son GEORGE MARTIN...to son DAVID MARTIN...to son HIRAM MARTIN...
land and other property to 3 youngest sons GEORGE, DAVID & HIRAM...22 Feb 1799...GEORGE
MARTIN (SEAL), Wit: DAVID JAMES, DAVID BOSHART. Rec. 16 Apr 1799.

Page 209: Inventory of Estate of ROBERT HANCOCK...Note on WM FINCH, THOS NEILLVILER[?],
WM. HARPER, MARY SMITH; 14 & 15 Mar 1799 by A. LYLES, WM. WOODWARD, PHIL PEAR-
SON, PHIL RAYFORD.

Pp. 209-210: on 16 July 1799, L. W. & T. of ALEXANDER McDOWELL was proved...admn. granted
to JAMES McDOWELL & ALEXANDER McKAIN, Exrs...16 July 1799. Rec. 16 July 1799.

Page 210: L. W. & T. of ALEXANDER McDOWELL...to wife JANE, 5 A fenced in & the house where
I now live & also negro Hannah...to sons ALEXANDER & SMITH now living with me,
when they become 21...daughter JANE[?] ARNET, $1...wife JANE, JAMES McDOWELL, & ALEXANDER
McKAIN, Exrs...2 July 1793...ALEXR McDOWELL (X) (LS), Wit: D. R. EVANS, HUGH CARSON, D.
EVANS. Rec. 16 July 1799.
MICHAEL KING, died in the State of North Carolina & an authentic copy of his
will was recorded in the Secretaries office of that State...admn. granted to JOHN KING...
16 July 1799.

Page 211: On 16 July 1799, L. W. & T. of ROBERT BROWN was proved...admn. granted to WILL-
IAM KIRKLAND...16 July 1799. Rec. 16 July 1799.
L. W. & T. of ROBERT BROWN of Kershaw Co....to sister MARY BROWN, my mare...to AGNES
[no relation given], 1/2 money due me from my father's estate, then AGNES is to pay the
same to MOSES HOLLIS, & his children MOUNCER HOLLIS & MARY HOLLIS...to JOHN BROWN &
WASHINGTON BROWN, the other 1/2 of sd. money...WILLIAM KIRKLAND, Exrs...23 Jan 1797...
ROBERT BROWN. Wit: MOSES HOLLIS (X), Rec. 16 July 1799.
On 17 July 1799, L. W. & T. of JOHN ANDREWS was proved...admn. granted to PHEBE
ANDREWS, & JOHN BELL, Exrs...inventory 16 Oct 1799. Rec. 17 July 1799.

Page 212: L. W. & T. of JOHN ANDREWS of Fairfield County, being very sick...to my six
children, RACHEL MICAJAH, LUCRITIA, ELOISA, WARREN, MARTHA...wife PHEBE...
friend JOHN BELL & wf PHEBE, Exrs...19 Mar 1799. JOHN ANDREWS (SEAL), Wit: DAVID McGRAW,
JOHN WALLACE.

Pp. 212-213: On 18 July 1799, L. W. & T. of WILLIAM HOLMES was proved...Exrs. anmed JAMES
ROGERS & CHARLES MONTGOMERY having declined...admn. with will annexed granted
to MARY HOLMES, widow of sd. decd....
L. W. & T. of WILLIAM HOLMES of Fairfield County...wife MARY HOLMES...child-
ren ANN, JANE, MARY, FANNY [HARRY?], WILLIAM & JOSEPH...4 Oct 1798. WILLIAM HOLMES (SEAL)
Wit: JAMES DAVISON, WM. DAVISON. Rec. 18 July 1799.

Page 213: JOHN ROBERTSON & ALEXANDER ROBERTSON, orphans chose HUGH McEWEN as their gdn....
16 July 1799. Rec. 18 July 1799.
MARGARET ANGES ROBERTSON, orphan, chose SIMEON CAMERON as her gdn...18 July 1799.

Page 214: JAMES BISHOP of Fairfield county, died intestate...admn. granted to SARAH BISHOP
& JOSIAH KNIGHTON...19 July 1799.
Appraisement of Estate of JOHN BOYKIN...1 July 1799, DARLING JONES, ZACH NETTLES. Rec.
19 July 1799.
Appraisement of Estate of GEORGE MARTIN, 6 July 1799 by WALTER POOLE, WM. LILES,
& CRISPIN MORGAN. Rec. 19 July 1799.

Pp. 214-215: Appraisement of Estate of JESSE GODBOLT...28 May 1799. G. FORD, WM. GASSA-
WAY, JOHN SMITH. Rec. 19 July 1799.

Page 215: Appraisement of Estate of THOMAS LESHLEY...29 Oct 1798. by WM McCRORY, SAML
WELDON, & JAS. HENERY[?]. Rec. 19 July 1799.
On 18 July 1799, L. W. & T. of ELIZABETH AUSTEN was proved...admn. granted to ROBERT RABB
& DAVIS AUSTEN.
L. W. & T. of ELIZABETH AUSTEN of Jacksons Creek...all left me by the will of
DRURY AUSTEN, to my & his children RESIA[?] RAUSEN, WILLIAM, MARY DAVIS, NANCY & ELIZA-
BETH...friends JON. PHILLIPS & ALEXR ROBISON...3 July 1788...ELIZA AUSTIN (O). Wit:
ALEXR MACKA, JON SLOAN (X), HELLENOR MAYNES[?] (X). Rec. 18 July 1799.
Appraisement of Estate of THOMAS GRAFFIN, decd. 10 June 1799, by JESSE GLADDIN,
MOSES HOLLIS & EDMUND TIDWELL. Rec. 19 July 1799.

Page 216: Inventory of Estate of PETER LEMLY...16 July 1799 by MILLEY LEMLEY (X), Extx.
Rec. 19 July 1799.
Bill of Appraisement of Estate of WM. RABB by WM McMORRIS SENR, WM McMORRIS JUNR., JOS
McMORRIS. Rec. 19 Apr 1799.
Sale of Estate of WM. RABB. Buyers: JOHN RABB, WM. RABB, JAMES RABB, JACOB
THORPE, NICHOLAS RINGER, ROBT RABB, CHAS BRADFORD', JOS HUTCHISON, JAS McGILL, ALEXR RABB,
GEORGE REEDISH, ELIZABETH RABB. ₺ 598.10. 10 1/2. JOHN RABB, WM. RABB. Rec. 19 July 1799.

Page 217: ALEXR IRVIN of Fairfield County, died intestate...admn. granted to POLLY IRVIN...
16 Oct 1799.
ELIZABETH ROBERTSON & MARTHA ROBERTSON, orphans, have chosen WILLIAM ROBERTSON

as their gdn....16 Oct 1799. REc. 16 Oct 1799.
     Appraisement of Estate of JAMES BISHOP, decd...by THOS KNIGHTON`, MUSER BOULARE, MOSES
KNIGHTON.
     Inventory of ELIZABETH AUSTEN, decd ₺ 89.2.8. Rec. 16 Oct 1799.
Inventory of JOHN ANDREWS. 15 Oct 1799. Rec. 16 Oct 1799.

Page 218: Appraisement of Estate of ALEXANDER IRVIN by GARDNER FORD, THOS MUSE, ZACH^H.
          NETTLES, Rec. 20 Oct 1799.
Inventory of ALEXANDER McDOWELL, by JEAN McDOWELL, JAS. McDOWEL, ALEXR McKAIN. Rec. Oct
20, 1799.
          Bill of Saleof Estate of JOHN GRAFFIN, decd. Buyers: ANDREW CROSET, WIDOW
GRAFTON, by MARY GRAFFIN, admx. Rec. 20 Oct 1799.

Pp. 218-219: Bill of Sale of JAMES AIKEN, decd. Buyers: SAML McMULLEN, THOMAS PORTER,
             MARGARET MARTIN, HUGH AIKEN, WIDOW AIKEN, ALEXR SMITH, EDWARD MARTIN, EPHM.
LILES, MORRIS WEAVER, MARGARET MARTIN, JOHN BRICE, JAMES AIKEN, JOHN PHILLIPS, CREATON
BUCHANNON, ALEXR DUGLAS, SAML McGILL, EDWARD WATTS, JOHN PHILLIPS, JAMES SMITH. DAVID
AIKEN, JOHN LEWELLEN, MAJOR DILLARD, THOS NELSON, WM. HAMILTON. Cert. by HUGH ACKIN,
JAMES AIKEN. Rec. 20 Oct 1799.

Page 219: Bill sale JOHN ANDREWS. Buyers: JAS MON, PHEBE ANDREWS, JOHN BELL, TIMOTHY
          McGRAW, JAS MCGRAW, HENRY HAYWOOD, JOHN STONTON, WM. STROTHER, JACOB GIBSON,
MATHEW ANDREWS, ROBT RABB, JOHN BELL ESQR., Cert. by JOHN BELL, PHEBE ANDREWS. Rec.
11 Apr 1800.

Pp. 219-220: Bill Sale JESSE GODBOLT, decd. Buyers: ELIZABETH GODBOLT, BRADLY LEWIS, THOS
             MUSE, JOSHUA GREGHAM[?], WM LEGRAVES, JAMES CAMBELE, JAMES BEVINS, Cert.
by ELIZABETH GODBOLT, Admx. 8 Oct 1799. Rec. 11 Apr 1800.

Page 220: Conclusive Inventory of SARAH BENNET, decd. ₺ 17.17. WM. KIRKLAND, Admr. Rec.
          20 July 1800.

Pp. 220-221: Bill of Sale of Estate of ALEXR ROBINSON, not disposed of by his will....
             Buyers: ANDREW CAMERON, JAMES TURNER, HUGH McKEOWN, CHRISTOPHER HUFFMAN,
JOHN McCRORY, JAMES SANDERS, JOHN ROBISON SENR[?], JAMES CAMERON, WIDOW HERMAN, JOHN TODD,
SAML CLARKE, JOHN STERLING, HENRY MOORE, SAML McKEOWN, THOS KILPATRICK, WM. DIAL, SAML
BANKS, JAS. KENEDY, ADAM ROBISON, ANDREW WALKER, ROBERT NIEL, ALEXR DICKEY, MRS. PATTON,
AGNESS ROBISON, ADAM BLAIR, GEORGE HALLSAL, ANDW MONTGOMERY, THOS POLLEY, HENRY McBRICE,
JOSEPH CAMERON. ₺ 76. 7. 3. by SIMEON CAMERON, D. HAMILTON, Exrs. Rec. 20 July 1800.

                    END OF FAIRFIELD WILL BOOK 2.

INDEX